CRIMINAL BEHAVIOR: A PSYCHOSOCIAL APPROACH

CURT R. BARTOL
Castleton State College
Department of Psychology

PRENTICE-HALL, INC.
Englewood Cliffs, New Jersey 07632

Library of Congress Cataloging in Publication Data

Bartol, Curt R
  Criminal behavior.

  (Prentice-Hall series in criminal justice)
  Bibliography: p.
  Includes index.
  1. Criminal psychology.   2. Crime and criminals.
  3. Criminal behavior, Prediction of.   4. Crime and
  criminals—United States.   I. Title.
  HV6080.B37   364.3   79-18292
  ISBN   0-13-193169-5

Editorial/production supervision and interior design
by Natalie Krivanek
Cover design by Saiki/Sprung Design
Manufacturing buyer: John Hall

Prentice-Hall Series in Criminal Justice
James D. Stinchcomb, Editor

© 1980 by Prentice-Hall, Inc., Englewood Cliffs, N.J. 07632

Printed in the United States of America

10   9   8   7   6   5

Prentice-Hall International, Inc., London
Prentice-Hall of Australia Pty. Limited, Sydney
Prentice-Hall of Canada, Ltd., Toronto
Prentice-Hall of India Private Limited, New Delhi
Prentice-Hall of Japan, Inc., Tokyo
Prentice-Hall of Southeast Asia Pte. Ltd., Singapore
Whitehall Books Limited, Wellington, New Zealand

to Anne

my colleague in all things that matter

CONTENTS

v

PREFACE

The idea for this book developed during several years of experience as a college professor and police academy instructor, consultation with an assortment of police and correctional agencies, prison research, and discussions with persons involved in the criminal justice system. From these contacts I have come to appreciate the desperate need for integrating contemporary psychology into an understanding of criminal behavior. Surprisingly, most criminologists still regard psychology as principally psychodynamic and Freudian. Understandably, many of them have become disenchanted with this classical psychological thinking and have discarded the field altogether, not realizing that there is available within psychology a large body of contemporary knowledge on the development of criminal behavior. I think that this book can communicate a substantial amount of empirical information to law enforcement personnel, social workers, psychology students, criminal justice students, and law and sociology students at the undergraduate, graduate, and professional levels.

Traditionally, psychology has been divided into three major forces or schools of thought: behaviorism, humanism, and psychodynamic (or psychoanalytic) theory. Some psychologists believe that a well-balanced presentation of their field should include all three positions. However, almost all authors of textbooks, despite frequent claims to the contrary, have a certain bias and training which color their writing. If my own orientation had to be placed into one of these three schools it would be in behaviorism, although I resist being considered a strict behaviorist.

I favor behaviorism because I firmly believe in the clarity of its concepts and terms and in its empirical examination of these concepts in order to understand human behavior.

On the other hand, and in spite of the conceptual neatness portrayed by textbooks when discussing these schools of thought, I have known few colleagues who consider themselves strict behaviorists, humanists, or neo-Freudians. Most will admit to being slanted toward a certain orientation, but they will maintain that they are eclectic and open to all points of view. Moreover, it is difficult to determine where the three schools of thought begin and where they leave off. They overlap extensively in referring to similar aspects of human behavior. All three schools encompass a wide variety of theoretical orientations and practical applications. With the possible exception of the radical Skinnerian behaviorists, few contemporary behaviorists see human beings as lifeless, passive, and mechanical creatures, as Shaffer (1978) has accused.

The basic premise of this book is that human beings react to a situation according to their individual perceptions and interpretations of that particular situation, and that those perceptions and interpretations are strongly influenced by previous experience and knowledge. It is unlikely that any major school of thought would dispute this contention.

Since psychology is the *science* of behavior, this book's content is largely dictated by available research and psychological theory. In this sense, it will feature the psychological viewpoint which has been most active in formulating and testing theory relating to criminal behavior. Until recently, most of this work was conducted by psychologists and psychiatrists with a psychodynamic leaning and, therefore, there is much discussion of psychodynamic research. Some readers, I fear, will quickly associate the psychodynamic material with psychiatry and claim I have given undue attention to psychiatry at the expense of psychology. But the extensive psychodynamic literature on crime cannot be ignored and should remain an integral part of any discussion of criminal behavior. In fact, it may be argued in some ways that psychodynamic-Freudian psychology seeded present day psychology. Also, I have borrowed freely from the valuable research findings of sociologists and sociological criminologists throughout the book. These research findings provide a good informational platform from which to discuss psychological perspectives of criminality. I am convinced that the more interdisciplinary we are, the more meaningful and productive will be our understanding of criminal behavior.

In recent years psychologists with behavioristic or humanistic orientations have become more actively involved in corrections and in examining criminal behavior. Leonard Krasner (1978) recently observed that in the near future behaviorism and humanism will make good bed partners and that their efforts will be combined for a better understanding of human behavior. For example, take the issue of free will. Humanists have advocated the incorporation of free will into discussions of the human being for many years, while those with empirical-behavioristic leanings have avoided it because of its evasive, unmeasurable qualities. However, in an outstanding monograph, James A. Easterbrook (1978) has defined free will in a way which brings the humanistic-behavioristic dialogue much closer together. He conceives of human behavior as a result of both cognitive free will and environmental stimuli, and attempts to define free will in a manner which should be acceptable to both the strict behaviorists and the "defenders of freedom."

It is also my belief that the cognitive aspects of the person will be a meeting ground for psychologists who subscribe to most schools of thought. I have tried to emphasize cognition throughout the book as a means of understanding criminal behavior, insofar as the empirical evidence will allow. The issues of control, self-esteem, moral development, and cognitive interpretations, as they relate to criminal behavior, are presented throughout and add "humanism" to behavior, while at the same time being definable and measurable.

I have tried to keep the writing level comprehensible to readers who have not had much contact with academic psychology. However, the reader should also realize that criminal behavior, like human behavior in general, is an extremely complex and poorly understood phenomenon. Psychology is a science which tries to understand, explain, and predict human behavior. Direct and simple answers are rarely available. Only through the careful and competent execution of research will we be able to understand, control, and prevent crime. Consequently, research findings are stressed throughout the book, and numerous references are found within the materials presented.

The book's organization runs from broad, theoretical positions on crime to specific, observable criminal offenses. Biological positions are presented in the early chapters, while environmental and learning viewpoints come later. The major theme is the hypothesis that each person engaged in criminal behavior is a unique individual trying to adapt the best way he or she knows how to in a particular set of circumstances.

The major goal is that people interested in criminal behavior will, as a result of reading this book, avoid oversimplified, prejudicial, dogmatic answers to the complex issues involved in crime. If, after studying the book with an open mind, the reader puts it down seeking additional information, and if the reader has developed an avid interest in discovering more precise answers, then the book will have fulfilled its purpose.

Many individuals have helped with this book, but a few deserve special mention. I especially want to express deep gratitude to my wife, Anne, who helped substantially and competently in all phases of this project. I am convinced this book could not have been completed without her continued encouragement and her professional skills and expertise. Special thanks are also due Mike Drazic and Mary Costello, formerly of the Castleton State College library staff, who supported and assisted me in my overwhelming need for research materials, in spite of the great burden my requests placed on a small college library. I also appreciate the guidance and criticism offered by the many reviewers of the manuscript. Professor Robert Patterson was especially helpful during the early phases of the project.

Finally, the Prentice-Hall staff was patient and encouraging throughout the course of the project. Terry Heagney worked competently with me during the initial phase of the work. Steve Cline offered commitment and freedom in the writing of the book, a combination which proved effective in motivating me to complete it. Natalie Krivanek somehow managed to orchestrate the final production phases smoothly and with finesse. To them and to the many anonymous staff members at Prentice-Hall I express my appreciation.

CREDITS

Photographs 4-2 (p. 107) and 8-1 (p. 235), Courtesy of Professor Philip G. Zimbardo, Department of Psychology, Stanford University.

Photograph 7-2 (p. 199), Reprinted with the permission of Harper & Row, Inc. From: *MARK, VH & ERVIN, FR: VIOLENCE AND THE BRAIN*, Harper and Row, Hagerstown, Md., 1970.

Photographs 11-1 (p. 301), 11-2 (p. 303), 11-3 (p. 320), and 11-4 (p. 323), Courtesy of United States Department of Justice, Federal Bureau of Investigation, Washington, D.C.

Four excerpts, used as epigrams (pp. 1, 85, 242, and 297), from Halleck, Seymour L., M.D., *PSYCHIATRY AND THE DILEMMAS OF CRIME*, Copyright © 1967 by Harper & Row, Publishers, Inc. Reprinted by permission of the publisher.

INTRODUCTION

ONE

Crime is an adaptation to life stress. It is best understood in terms of the manner in which the individual experiences the biological, psychological and socially determined situations of his existence.

(Halleck, 1967, p. 63)

Crime intrigues people. Sometimes it attracts, sometimes it repels, occasionally it does both at once. It can amuse us, as we hear about capers and practical jokes that do not harm anyone. It can frighten, if we interpret what happened to one victim as possibly happening to us. Crime can also anger, as when a community's beloved police officer is brutally killed. Some crimes can sexually excite, such as the rape of a "willing" victim portrayed by an actress on the movie or television screen. Crime, particularly violent crime, has interested people for thousands of years. Murder has always drawn the most attention; consider the rampant excitement and fear in a small town or neighborhood when news of a local murder hits the street.

While interest in crime has always been high, understanding why it occurs and what to do about it has always been a problem. Public officials, politicians, "experts," and streetcorner philosophers continue to offer simple and ineffective solutions for obliterating crime: better police patrols, closed-circuit TV, better street lighting, stiffer penalties for criminals, judo classes, quick imprisonment, or capital punishment. Academe invariably contributes its share of pedantic and abstract expositions which often have little practical relevance. As in most areas concerned with human behavior, there is no shortage of experts, but there are few effective solutions.

Our inability to prevent or reduce crime stems partly from our lack of understanding of criminal behavior, a complex phenomenon. Because of this complexity, explanations of crime will require complicated, involved answers. Psychological research has indicated that people have a limited tolerance for complexity and ambiguity. Most people, it seems, like simple, straightforward, easily understandable answers, no matter how complex the issue. Parents become impatient when psychologists answer questions about child rearing by saying, "it depends"—on the situation, on parents' reaction to it, on any number of variables. The preference for simplicity helps to explain the popularity of the fast, do-it-yourself, 100 easy ways to a better life books at our disposal. Most people want simple answers to all problems.

This book will present criminal behavior as a vastly complex, poorly understood phenomenon. The reader looking for a simple solution will either have to re-orient his or her thinking or set the book aside. There is no one earth-shattering, all-encompassing psychological explanation for crime. In fact, it is unlikely that any one discipline can formulate basic "truths" about crime without help from other disciplines and areas of research. In this book we will explore what psychological research has to offer toward the understanding of crime; to date the psychological perspective has been neither fairly represented nor accurately integrated in the criminological literature.

SOCIOLOGICAL VS. PSYCHOLOGICAL VIEWPOINTS

Criminology, the study of crime, can be psychological, sociological, anthropological, psychiatric, or even economic in emphasis. Unfortunately, much interdisciplinary disinterest (and some animosity) exists among proponents of each of the areas. Authors of sociology textbooks on crime typically acknowledge, in a cursory manner, the existence of psychology as a discipline, indicate that psychologists as a group see criminals as "sick," and blast away at a few out-dated theories of personality; they then continue on the sociological path to discuss the causes and prevention of crime. In addition, far too often sociologically oriented texts confuse psychology with psychiatry and mistakenly accept psychiatric concepts as established *psychological* principles about crime.

Psychology textbooks on crime (of which there are too few) can be equally unkind to sociological points of view. Cortes and Gatti (1972, p. 166), for example, commenting about the sociologist Edwin Sutherland's differential association theory of criminality, wrote ". . . it is our intention to prove that differential association as a theory of delinquent and criminal behavior is inadequate, incomplete, vague, superficial, useless, tautological, invalid, that it goes against the established facts, and finally, that it was rejected by its author long ago." Although Cortes and Gatti offer some good arguments against some aspects of Sutherland's theory (which will be discussed in detail later in the book), their reasoning fails to annihilate it. The point here, however, is to underscore the strong, sometimes angry, reaction of psychologists to sociological theories of criminality.

Dozens of examples of such interdisciplinary criticism can be found. This text seeks to integrate some of the information and research findings from sociological, psychological, and psychiatric criminology without stimulating more ill feeling among these fields. Through scholarly disagreement and argument supported by empirical findings and well-anchored theory, we should gain a better understanding and subsequent control over the long-standing and escalating problem of crime. Criminology should be an interdisciplinary science, with theory and research on crime from all disciplinary fronts dropped into the brew.

To review in detail, and objectively, the universe of theories and the relevant research on criminality is beyond the scope of this book. So great an endeavor would require a collection of scholars representing all theoretical perspectives. Instead, this book attempts to fill a void in criminology by presenting a psychological perspective. Contemporary, relevant psychological research and theory have not been well integrated into mainstream criminology, possibly because until recently few psychologists have been actively interested in studying crime. Hence, the content will be heavily in favor of psychological principles and concepts, with some sociological and psychiatric perspectives introduced when they pertain to the topic being discussed. This should not suggest that psychology has all of the answers to the problem of crime. As mentioned above, no one discipline has all the answers, and without some integration of the research data it will be a long time before we can even approach the goal of satisfactorily explaining criminal behavior.

PSYCHOLOGICAL CRIMINOLOGY

Ideally, *sociological criminology* concentrates on the effects of social variables on groups. Thus, we might find sociologists studying the characteristics of groups, such as age, race, sex, interpersonal relationships, and social class, as they relate to the tendency to engage in criminal action. With these data, we learn whether Blacks are more likely than other races to be arrested and convicted for criminal offenses. We can answer questions pertaining to what types of crime women are most likely to commit. Sociological criminologists also examine the social conditions that are most conducive to criminal activity—in other words, the time, place, and circumstances surrounding the criminal event, or even the kinds of weapons used in violent crimes.

Psychological criminology, on the other hand, searches for the factors that play significant roles in determining *individual* behavior. It is the science of determining how criminal behavior is acquired, evoked, maintained, and modified. More precisely, psychological criminology recognizes that criminal behaviors are acquired by daily living, in accordance with the principles of learning, and are stored and organized in a unique fashion in the individual's brain. The process of storing and organizing the mental representations of daily experiences in the brain is known as *cognition.* Basically, criminal behaviors depend upon how the individual perceives and interprets a situation, and what he or she expects to gain by certain behavior. Thus, this analysis requires examining both the individual's personality and situation. Personality in this context refers to the individual's own experiential history, interacting with his or her cognitive and physiological-genetic equipment. Each of these personality factors—learning, cognition, and genetic-physiology—will be examined in detail in later sections of the book.

The point here is that people do not "have" personality traits (characteristics which are consistent, persistent, and stable across situations) which drive them to behave in certain ways regardless of the situation or circumstances. Rather, people have acquired certain responses for certain circumstances; whether they employ these acquired responses depends upon how they assess the situation, what they expect to gain, and what has happened to them in previous events.

In the past, psychologists have assumed that the best way to understand human behavior was to search for stable, highly consistent personality dispositions or traits that exert widely generalized effects on behavior (Mischel, 1973). Similarly, criminal psychologists have assumed they must search for the personality traits or variables which underlie criminal behavior. Very little attention was given to the person's situation at any particular point in time. Presumably, once the variables were identified, it would be possible to determine and predict which personality was most likely to engage in criminal behavior. As we shall learn, the search for the personality of the murderer, the rapist, the "psychopathic killer" has not been fruitful.

A wide variety of people engage in different kinds of criminal activity for different reasons; also, many investigators have been excessively one-sided in their search for clues. Sociologists have often looked for strictly social-situational clues, assuming that situational factors exert overwhelmingly powerful influences on the individual. More often than not, sociological criminologists have treated the individual as if he or she were "empty headed" and invariably swayed one way or the other by persons and events. Psychologists, on the other hand, have generally searched for evasive personality variables to over-ride the situational variables. Both sides, working independently, have provided partial information about criminal activity, but neither seems to have been successful in offering a cogent, empirically verifiable theory of criminality.

Which is more important in criminal activity, the person or the situation? The answer does not crucially concern us here. Why? Because it depends on the person and the situation. In some cases, personality is the major determinant of whether or not a person engages in criminal action, while in other cases the situation might exert the more powerful influence. We should shift our focus from examining the situation-free person or the situation-bound person and analyze instead the specific interactions between the situation and the person's cognitions and behavior patterns. A viable psychological study of criminal behavior demands attention to personality factors and how they interact with situational variables.

PSYCHOLOGICAL VS. PSYCHIATRIC VIEWPOINTS

Psychiatry and psychology are often confused by the lay person and even by professionals in other disciplines. Psychiatric concepts and theories are frequently interpreted as accepted tenets in the field of psychology. Although there are numerous exceptions, the two professions see things quite differently. Psychiatry remains predominantly steeped in the psychoanalytic or psychodynamic tradition. This appears to be especially true of psychiatric criminology, sometimes called forensic psychiatry (e.g., Sadoff, 1975; MacDonald, 1976). The orthodox psychoanalytic position assumes that we must delve into the deeper abysses of the human personality and find the unconscious determinants of human behavior, including criminal behavior. For example, the prominent criminal psychiatrist David Abrahamsen (1952, p. 21) comments, ". . . the criminal very rarely knows completely the reasons for his conduct." Only through analyses designed to uncover deeper motivations will we become aware of the causes of criminal behavior.

Although psychodynamic theories acknowledge that behavior varies across situations, they also conclude that there are enduring and generalized underlying dynamic or motivational dispositions that account for the diversity. "Surface" behaviors indirectly signal more dynamic, underlying attributes. Defenses distort and disguise the "true" meaning of external or observed behaviors. The trained clinician, therefore, must interpret the external behaviors. So, while psychologists have looked for consistencies in external behaviors commonly known as traits, psychodynamic theorists have searched for consistencies in generalized dispositions which are basically internal.

Reviews of the relevant research have consistently shown that psychodynamically oriented clinicians have not been able to predict behavior better than behaviorally oriented clinicians (Mischel, 1968, 1973). Overall, the psychodynamic position has a poor record in producing hard data, partly because the psychodynamic concepts are not easily submitted to empirical examination. They are ambiguous concepts which presumably reside in the intangible, unidentifiable recesses of the human mind. The vagaries of the id, the ego, the superego, unconscious urges and impulses, symbolism, and psychosexual development as explanations of crime are well known to most criminologists, but they are not accepted by a majority of psychologists. Despite their questionable usefulness, psychodynamic theories have dominated the field of psychiatric criminology and, to a large extent, what is thought to be the "psychological" perspective of criminology.

A reason for this has to do with the way psychiatrists and psychologists approach their respective professions. Psychiatry has been developed on the basis of clinical experience and observation, while psychology is based primarily on research and experimentation. Because of this research bent, psychologists have tried to avoid becoming entangled with intangibles and have concentrated on overt, observable behavior. Behaviorists argue that what is most amenable to scientific investigation is what we can observe. Also, due to the necessary requirements that relevant variables be controlled and that research be quantified, psychology has conducted much of its investigation on animals in the laboratory. Many useful principles of learning have been discovered by carefully designed experiments on rats pushing levers, pigeons picking buttons, and the like. However, psychologists are also becoming keenly aware that research findings on animals are not always generalizable to humans. Because of this, there has been a notable shift in emphasis from behavior to the cognitive and intellectual attributes of humans (Mischel, 1973). Animals do not perceive and organize experiences as humans do; nor have they the cognitive equipment humans have. Psychiatrists, meanwhile, have seldom submitted themselves to the rigors of the scientific laboratory. Although they have gained valuable time as a result, their theories have remained unscrutinized and extremely difficult to verify.

The psychiatric and psychoanalytic perspective has long dominated the individual perspective in criminology. Recently, criminologists and the legal profession have become increasingly disenchanted with psychiatric and/or psychoanalytic interpretations of criminality (see Bazelon, 1974). Part of the weakness of the psychoanalytic process in legal determinations is the heavy reliance on post hoc explanations of unconscious motivations for the criminal act, explanations typically cloaked in terminology which is difficult for both the layperson and the professional to understand. The concepts used are often abstract and refer to intangible "dynamic forces" and require equally abstract, complex, and vague interpretations. For example, psychoanalytically oriented psychiatrists generally attempt to discover unconscious reasons for murder sometime after the event has occurred. This author is familiar with several court cases in which testifying psychiatrists concluded that defendants killed male victims because of unconscious incestuous attractions to their mothers. That is, the accused person allegedly killed because of an unresolved Oedipal conflict, and thus the sexual battle waged with his father for his mother still lingers in his psyche. At the time of the murder, according to the psychiatrist, the id breaks through the defenses of the ego, resulting in an intensified conflict with a victim (symbolic father) who was pursuing his symbolic mother.

Although psychoanalytic theory has been most enthusiastically adopted by psychiatry, it has also played an important role in the history and development of psychology. In fact, it is generally considered one of the big three forces or schools of thought in psychology, alongside behaviorism and humanism. Psychoanalysis has had an especially powerful influence on clinical psychology, and many psychologists still accept and use its concepts and tenets.

Experimental psychologists have been drawn primarily to behaviorism, with its heavy emphasis on the experimental method and its empirical approach toward the understanding of human behavior. Because the science of behaviorism, like any other science, requires precision, quantification, and clearly defined, observable variables and events, behaviorists have been accused by some psychologists of removing the human aspect from the study of human beings.

Humanism in Psychology

The humanistic psychologist sees the psychoanalytic and behavioristic viewpoints as limiting the person to being a creature of instincts and stimulus-response learning paradigms. The humanist argues that there is more to human behavior. In understanding it, we must consider the many features unique to the human being, such as free will, personal initiative, self-actualization, self-awareness, and independent judgment. Most humanists believe crime is basically a result of some interference or constraint which restricts the individual's psychological growth and personal fulfillment. Typically, the culprit is seen as society, not the individual. Society and its social agents have in some way limited normal personal growth and the discovery of self. Therefore, humanistic treatment is based on helping the individual reassert a sense of self.

In many ways the humanistic perspective of crime is probably correct. Many criminals, probably most, lack the skills necessary to master their environment and achieve personal competence. This point will be referred to a number of times in subsequent discussions. However, this heavy reliance on free will and human qualities as the basic explanation for human behavior and criminality, excluding the principles of learning, reinforcement, and conditioning, is too narrow an approach and perspective. The complexity of criminal behavior requires that we utilize numerous perspectives. Also, one of the major drawbacks to humanism is the vague, ephemeral quality of the concepts and terms it uses. Because the principles of humanism cannot be subjected to empirical investigation, they lead to speculation, conjecture, and philosophical debate rather than a scientific understanding of human behavior.

A DEFINITION OF CRIMINAL BEHAVIOR

In a book of this nature, a very difficult question must be answered: "How do we go about defining criminal behavior?" Should we restrict our study and definition to individuals who have been arrested and convicted? Or should we include individuals who indulge in deviant and antisocial behaviors which often fall outside the legal definitions of crime? And perhaps the material should include those individuals who are hypothesized to be "psychologically predisposed" to be criminal. A review of criminology textbooks and articles shows that there is no universally accepted belief as to what group or groups should be the targets in the study of criminal behavior.

Probably the best place to begin is by defining crime: "an intentional act in violation of the criminal law (statutory and case law) committed without defense or excuse, and penalized by the state as a felony or misdemeanor" (Tappan, 1947, p. 100). Criminal behavior, therefore, is behavior which violates a criminal code. Obviously, this legal definition encompasses a great variety of acts which may range from homicide to a traffic violation.

Some researchers have found the variety of criminal behavior so unwieldy that they have proposed typologies for studying it (e.g., Clinard & Quinney, 1967). A *typology* is a system used to classify individuals or events into types or categories. Using typology helps us reduce criminal phenomena to manageable units, which simplifies the formation of research ideas. Presumably, by splitting up crime in this way, we can develop a general theory. Clinard and Quinney (1973) suggest eight types: violent personal crime, occasional property crime, political crime, organized crime, conventional crime, occupational crime, corporate crime, and public order crime. To some extent, this book has been organized on a typological basis—for the above reasons and because of the conceptual neatness this achieves. We shall consider crime under the major headings of criminal homicide and violence, sex offenses, female crime, drug-related offenses, special crimes, and property crimes. Yet, keep in mind that criminals often cannot be classified in distinct categories; for example, individuals who have murdered may also be drug addicts who have engaged in property crimes.

The incidence of crime is usually measured in one of three ways:

1. Official police reports concerning the number of detections or arrests made. These tabulations are usually sent to the FBI for a national statistical report on crime and published in the *Uniform Crime Reports*.

2. Self-report studies, which involve asking members of a sample population what offenses they have committed, and how often. Many researchers believe this method provides a more accurate estimate of the actual offenses committed in society than do official police statistics.

3. National victimization studies, which have become popular in recent years. Victimization surveys sample a large population of households asking individuals to report how often they have been victims of specified crimes.

Offical crime statistics such as those found in the FBI *Uniform Crime Reports* are notoriously low in their accounts of most offenses. The total criminal offenses committed, known as the *dark figure*, will probably never be known, but estimates from a victimization survey conducted by the U.S. Census Bureau suggests that out of every 100 offenses committed, 72 are never recorded in the official statistics (Skogan, 1977). However, Skogan also reports that a majority of the unreported violations appear to be minor property offenses rather than more serious crimes.

If we abide strictly by the legal definition of crime and base our discussion only on those people who have committed crimes, do we discuss those who have been arrested, convicted, and incarcerated, or do we include those who have broken the criminal law but have escaped conviction? And do we also include individuals who violate the law but escape detection? In an astonishing self-report survey (Wallerstein & Wyle, 1947), 1,698 persons were asked to indicate on a list of 49 criminal offenses which, if any, they had committed. The list included felonies and misdemeanors but excluded traffic violations. Ninety-one percent of the nearly 1,700 respondents admitted they had committed one or more offenses for which they might have received jail or prison sentences. This study suggests that most people have broken the criminal law at some point in their lives.

Some argue (e.g., Sellin, 1970; Tappan, 1947) that one who engages in undetected "criminal" activity is not a criminal in the strictest or operational sense, because a criminal is by definition one who has been detected, arrested, and convicted. However, we also encounter thorny problems when we limit ourselves to studying persons legally defined as criminals. Legal classifications are determined by what society, at some point in time, considers "socially harmful" or, in some cases, "morally wrong." Therefore, because each society has a different and changing set of values, what may be judged to be a criminal act in one society may not meet the criteria in another, or even in the same society at a later time. Many states in the U.S. differ significantly in their criminal codes. Laws relating to homosexuality, abortion, chemical possession, and pornography are prime examples of areas which generate moral controversy and ever-changing statutes.

In addition, members of every society (and consequently every society's judicial system) perceive and process violators of the criminal code with some discrimination, so that the offender's background, social status, personality, motivation, sex, age, race, and legal counsel, as well as the circumstances surrounding the offense, all may affect the legal process and the legal definition of crime. It is highly likely that individuals who have been arrested, convicted, and incarcerated represent a distinctly different sample of people from those who participate in illegal activity but avoid detection, conviction, or incarceration.

For example, it has been demonstrated that the characteristics of the victim influence how much if any punishment is assigned to the accused by the judicial process. Landy and Aronson (1969) report evidence that if the victim is a respectable citizen (i.e., successful and altruistic), the offender will receive a stiffer sentence than if the case involves an "unrespectable" victim (i.e., despicable and dishonest). Jones and Aronson (1973) found that defendants who raped a married woman or virgin were considerably more likely to receive longer sentences than defendants who tried or succeeded in raping a divorced woman. It has also been found that the more serious a traffic accident the greater the tendency for people to believe that the principals involved were at fault and negligent (Walster, 1966). All the above studies support Lerner's hypothesis (1965, 1970) that people need to believe they live in a just world in which the undeserving are appropriately deprived or punished. This "just-world hypothesis" predicts, for example, that some victims of rape, assault, or even homicide are assumed by many people to have gotten what they deserved or asked for. The implications of this hypothesis in relation to juries' determination of guilt, and therefore to the determination of who are "criminals," are obvious.

Consequently, if we adopt a legal definition of criminal behavior and discuss legally determined criminals in this book, we will be neglecting a considerable segment of the population that actually breaks the law. However, because the orientation of this book is empirical and research based, the kinds and amounts of available research on crime dictate a large portion of the material covered. Since almost all the available "hard data" on crime are based on arrested or convicted persons, the book's content will, by necessity, focus on this legally defined population.

However, we will not be restricted to research findings. It is important that we try to pull meaning out of the research by making observations and interpretations, with the ultimate goal of integration. That is, we shall attempt to interpret the available research from a psychological perspective in order to provide some explanation, theory, and suggestions for the treatment and prevention of criminal behavior. In so doing, we will make assumptions about who is most likely to be involved in certain types of criminal behavior. So we will be studying not only the legal criminal, but the potential criminal as well.

Remember that to provide a comprehensive psychological analysis of criminal behavior, we must carefully examine the relevant variables involved in both the personality of the offender (and of the victim) and the situation surrounding the criminal action. The word "personality" includes a number of major variables: cognition, genetic and physiological factors, and interaction with living experiences. Since personality is assumed in this text to constitute a major component in the criminal behavior equation, it is important to understand what is meant by the term and what some of the restrictions are on its use.

PERSONALITY AND LAWFUL BEHAVIOR

"Personality" has many meanings, and it is likely that one person's definition will differ from someone else's in many respects. When people have been asked to jot down what the word "personality" means to them, they inevitably produce an array of definitions, and there are considerable differences in the degree of confidence each person has in his or her own definition. Yet the word "personality" has attained popular use, with everyone having a vague notion of what it means. This state of affairs is similar to the problems psychologists themselves encounter in arriving at a precise meaning of personality for scientific or clinical usage. Although there are groups of psychologists who can agree to a broad definition, there is at present no universally accepted definition of the term. It might be easier at this point to define what the scientific study of personality tries to do. This will give a better grasp of the assumptions involved in the study of personality and sidestep some of the unwieldy definitions that come from varied sources.

In general, the scientific study of personality deals with measurable individual differences which occur with some regularity from situation to situation. Thus, when we study personality we are concerned not only with how people differ, but also with the amount of consistency one person demonstrates under different conditions. For example, if we were interested in discovering how individuals respond to frustration, we would design a situation which offers an appropriate "frustrating" set of circumstances. After exposing experimental subjects to identically frustrating conditions, we find that some responded angrily, others withdrew, and others took an approach somewhere in between. It would be foolhardy for us, however, to designate those who responded angrily to the situation "aggressive personalities" and those who did not "unaggressive personalities" just on the basis of one situation. We should test these and other subjects, both under similar and different conditions which are also assumed to promote frustration. If we discover that certain individuals consistently respond to frustration with aggression and others consistently withdraw, we might have justification for hypothesizing the existence of aggressive, nonaggressive, and somewhere-in-between personalities, *when frustrated.*

Thus, the two key concepts in personality research are *behavior* or *response consistency* and *individual differences.* Behavior consistency is especially important, because it is crucial in determining the probability that a person will engage in criminal activity at some time in the future. If we learn that a certain behavioral pattern (or personality) is consistent under a certain type of situation, then we have the power of *prediction.* If we can predict behavior, we might be tempted to go one step further and conclude that behavior is "lawful." (The term lawful as used here refers to the scientific connotation and is defined below; it should not be confused with judicial lawfulness.) In fact, the scientific study of behavior generally does assume that behavior is lawful and follows lawful principles like other natural phenomena. Psychologists, however, differ widely in the extent to which they accept the lawfulness of behavior. Rychlak (1968, p. 97) posits that most psychologists, especially experimentalists, would accept the statement, "All behavior is not lawful, but much—maybe most of it—is."

In oversimplified form, a law may be expressed as, "If A, then B." That is, if all the relevant variables in a situation, A, are understood, we should be able to predict behavior, B, all the time. Realistically, probably no science understands completely all the relevant variables in a particular situation. In chemistry, for example, if we understand the specific effects of temperature on a specified mixture of chemicals (A), then we can predict the reaction (B) with considerable consistency, but not absolutely perfectly. The science of psychology assumes that if we can identify, measure, and understand many of the complex combinations of relevant variables operating in situation A, we can increase the accuracy of predicting a person's behavior in a future situation A. It should be noted that situation A includes both past and present events. Psychologists concerned with personality are primarily interested in how past events interact with present events (the present environment). Past events may include, among other things, physiological and biochemical changes, genetic predispositions, and past learning experiences.

What does all this have to do with crime? Theoretically, if behavior is lawful, we should be able to predict with a high degree of accuracy the probability that an individual will become engaged in criminal activity, provided we understand how personality interacts with a particular situation. As already described, personality in this sense includes the physiological, genetic, and learning history of a particular individual. But let's be realistic. Human behavior is the result of nearly unlimited combinations of poorly understood variables, making the chances of total predictability very remote in view of our present knowledge. However, the more we understand about the relevant variables, the more accurate our predictions will be and the more effective our chances for changing the behavior in the future. The scientific study of personality can provide us with information on a portion of situation A, thereby improving our understanding of criminal behavior B.

The theory of lawful behavior precludes—or, if you prefer, weakens—the notion of free will, and this assumption is one of the most difficult for many people to accept. On the other hand, if there are no lawful relationships in human behavior and predictions cannot be made, we must be content with describing behaviors only after they happen (post hoc explanations). If this is the case, we will never be able to understand personality and human behavior, but will only involve ourselves in philosophical debates. Prediction is the hallmark of understanding. This very important issue in human behavior will be discussed in detail in the chapter on abnormal behavior and insanity, especially as it relates to legal determinations of intentions and free will. For the time being, it is sufficient to realize that one of the most important assumptions in the scientific study of personality is that behavior is lawful, even though we are a long way from establishing behavioral laws.

Criminal Personalities

The research literature increasingly agrees that a majority of the criminal population may be roughly categorized into three very broad personality clusters: 1. the undersocialized delinquent or psychopathic offender, 2. the socialized or subcultural delinquent or offender, and 3. the highly frustrated or emotionally disturbed delinquent or offender. Although there is at least one chapter devoted to each of these behavioral patterns in the book, it might be helpful at this point to present a thumbnail sketch of each.

Most serious criminal offenses appear to be committed by a very small percentage of the entire population in any given society. Estimates are that only about 1 percent of the male population can be characterized as extremely "recidivistic" (i.e., repeatedly committing crimes), and that this small fraction accounts for *more than half* of the criminal offenses committed (Mednick, 1977). Both Mednick and Hans Eysenck (1977) hypothesize that most of these extreme recidivists were poorly socialized and have inadequate social learning abilities, because of deviant physiological mechanisms; that is, they cannot learn social rules and appropriate social behavior because of faulty biological functioning of their nervous systems. They are referred to as the undersocialized or psychopathic offenders and will be discussed in Chapter 3.

The socialized or subcultural delinquent or adult offender readily acquires criminal behaviors from significant models in the environment. This offender has the capacity to learn appropriate behavior, and probably has done so, but he or she has also learned criminal behavior, and that has been more rewarding. The reward for this socialized criminal may be personal power, status, or economic gain. In addition, the socialized or subcultural criminal may emerge from any socioeconomic class and may participate in crimes ranging from white collar to auto theft, from burglary to murder. This group will be discussed in Chapter 4.

It is important to note here that criminal behavior is largely the result of some combination of three types of learning: 1. social learning, 2. instrumental learning or operant conditioning, and 3. classical or Pavlovian conditioning. Each of these three learning processes plays a significant role in every criminal or antisocial action, though one type of learning may play a more predominant role in any given crime. In addition, the three types of learning often overlap considerably; we are delineating them primarily to add conceptual neatness to the discussion. Through each of these three types of learning processes, we can analyze both the personality of the offender and the situational variables which evoke, maintain, or modify the offender's behavior. The book's organization is built upon the foundation of learning, which requires the examination of experiences and the physiological and cognitive competencies of the individual.

The third offender category includes anxious, tense, discouraged people who resort to criminal or antisocial behavior to gain control or to change their unpleasant predicament. The sudden murderer or the vindictive arsonist might be examples. It is important to realize that this group does not simply include the "insane" or "crazy" person. In fact, as we shall learn in Chapter 6, the so-called "mentally ill' are no more likely to commit a criminal offense than the normal population. Most members of the third group engage in antisocial or criminal activity to alter their condition, which is fraught with daily living disappointments and faulty social skills. The frustrated individual may experience continual blows to self-esteem and, in a desperate attempt to change the course of events, may suddenly and vehemently use a crowbar to re-establish his or her worth.

Regardless of the personality pattern of an individual, the perspective in this book is that antisocial or criminal behavior, while deviant in most of society's eyes, is *subjectively adaptive*. The offender expects his or her behavior to gain something or change some event. The expected gain may be psychological, such as increased feelings of control and significance, or social, such as increased status among peers and friends. The offender's expectancy may also be material, including money or tangible possessions. In fact, the expectancy may be any or all three of these gains. These expectancies are adaptive in that the offender feels these goals will improve his or her condition, even if only to the extent of increasing self-satisfaction.

RESEARCH TERMS AND METHODS

Since this book relies heavily on research literature for discussions of crime, the reader must become acquainted with some of the research terminology and methodolgy. Although most of the research terms and methods are buried in different chapters of the book, the following points are so common and essential they must be stressed early and distinctly.

Most of the research studies mentioned are "correlational." A *correlation* is a statistical term for a relationship between two variables. A *variable* essentially is anything which can be measured. A correlation tells us two important things about a relationship: 1. the magnitude of the relationship and 2. the direction of that relationship. The more closely related two variables are, the greater the magnitude of the relationship. This magnitude is expressed statistically in numbers. For example, the relationship between juvenile delinquency and IQ might be expressed as .60, while the relationship between juvenile delinquency and social class might be expressed as .30. Thus, the relationship between delinquency and IQ is greater than the one between delinquency and social class, indicating that IQ is a better predictor of delinquency than social class. The numbers are obtained through mathematical calculations set up by a formula which compares the two variables. Due to the nature of the statistical formula for the correlation, the magnitude will never be larger than 1.00. We will come back to this point in a moment.

The correlation also tells us something about the direction of the relationship. *Direction* informs us what one variable does if the other variable has changed. If the number of guns sold in any given year is reduced, does the rate of crime involving guns increase, decrease, or stay the same? Direction is expressed either by a positive (+) sign or a negative (−) sign. If one variable changes and the other variable changes in the same direction, we have a positive relationship. For example, if gun sales decreased and the crime rate also decreased, we would have a positive relationship. However, if gun sales increased and crime decreased, this would be a negative relationship. In a negative relationship, as one variable changes, the other variable changes in the opposite direction. When both change in the same direction, whether there is an increase or a decrase, the relationship is positive.

Thus, one relationship might be expressed as − .60 and another one as − .30. The first tells us that the variables are more closely related than the variables in the second relationship (.60 is closer to 1.00 than .30). In both cases, the negative sign tells us that as one variable increases the other decreases. If the sign were positive, we would know that the variables both increased or both decreased.

There is one crucial point that must be understood about a correlation. It can help us predict something about one variable if we know the nature of the other one, but it cannot tell us what is causing what. Simply because a low IQ may be related to a high incidence of delinquency, we cannot conclude that low IQ causes delinquency, or that delinquency causes low IQ. A correlation cannot provide a cause, although it may *suggest* one.

A bulk of the research in criminology is correlational. That is, researchers isolate two variables and measure and analyze them to determine whether there is a significant relationship. Significance implies that the relationship could not have occurred by chance or by some quirk in the selection of the variables. Far too often, however, investigators have concluded that a significant relationship indicates that one variable is causing the other. In fact, the reader should realize early that, when it comes to studying human behavior, determining what is causing what is not only one of the most challenging tasks, but also extremely elusive.

KEY CONCEPTS FOR REVIEW

Sociological criminology
Psychological criminology
Psychiatric criminology
Psychoanalysis
Behaviorism
Humanism
Criminal behavior
Scientifically lawful behavior
The undersocialized or psychopathic offender
The socialized or subcultural offender
The emotionally disturbed offender
Correlation

SUGGESTED READINGS

Bourne, L.E., and Ekstrand, B.R. Psychology: Its principles and meanings, 2nd ed. New York: Holt, Rinehart & Winston, 1976.
A comprehensive and balanced overview of psychology.

Brodsky, S.L. Psychologists in the criminal justice system. Urbana, Ill: Univ. of Illinois Press, 1973.
An introductory overview of the role of psychologists in the criminal justice system.

Feldman, M.P. Criminal behavior: A psychological analysis. London: John Wiley, 1977.
An upper-level review of behavioristic contributions to the explanation of criminal behavior written primarily for researchers.

Wright, B., and Fox, V. Criminal justice and the social sciences. Philadelphia: W.B. Saunders, 1978.
A clean, readable overview of the contributions of the various disciplines within the social sciences to the criminal justice system.

PSYCHOBIOLOGICAL
FACTORS

TWO

Social, educational, and political thinking is currently being carried along on a wave of environmentalism which, while paying lip-service to the fact that one reason why people differ is because they vary in genetic make-up, in reality ignores it.

Claridge, 1973, p. 158

Lay persons as well as criminal justice professionals are often heard to say, "Yes, genetics may play a role in criminality, but it is certainly an insignificant one. There is little doubt that environment is the principal determinant and cause of criminal behavior." Poverty, dilapidated housing, high unemployment, poor education, overpopulation, and subcultural social learning are claimed to be the major culprits producing and intensifying crime. Very often people scoff at heredity-based physiological components and deliberately reject their role as causal agents in criminality.

Why so? Perhaps because accepting heredity as a factor in criminal behavior implies that criminal acts are unavoidable, inevitable consequences of the "bad seed," "bad blood," or "mark of Cain," so that little can be done to prevent the ill-fated person from becoming a criminal. A classic example of this viewpoint is reflected in Cesare Lombroso's

(1911) doctrine that criminals (at least some of them) are born that way.

Many social and most behavioral scientists today recognize that most behavioral traits result from an *interaction* of heredity and environmental factors (Krech, Crutchfield, & Livson, 1974). We no longer ask whether behavior is a result of hereditary factors or environmental factors. We commonly agree that both are involved in a complex way. However, psychologists often concentrate on one or the other to study their effects. Biopsychologists, who will be highlighted in this chapter, try to determine which genetic and physiological variables play a part in criminal behavior, how important they are, and what can be done to modify them. Psychologists who subscribe to biopsychological determinants of criminality do not believe that genetic or physiological components are the sole causal agents in the formation of criminal behavior. They believe that understanding the social environment is as important as understanding the biological one, but they focus their attention on the biological elements.

How far have biopsychologists come? What conclusions have they been able to make about the relationship between genetic-physiological variables and criminal behavior? These are questions we will answer after we take a brief look at the history of biopsychological research in criminality.

THE BORN CRIMINAL

A pioneer researcher on the relationship between crime, genetics and personality was Cesare Lombroso (1836–1909), an Italian physician and self-coined "criminal anthropologist." Lombroso was greatly influenced by the views expounded by Charles Darwin in *The Descent of Man*, especially by the notion that some men are genetically closer to their primitive ancestry than others (Savitz, 1972). Lombroso's original and basic premise, published in *L'Uomo Delinquente (Criminal Man)* in 1876, was that some individuals are born with strong, innate predispositions to behave antisocially. The criminal, Lombroso believed, represented a separate species which had not yet evolved sufficiently toward the more "advanced" *homo sapiens*, but was genetically somewhere between modern humans and their primitive origins in physical and psychological makeup. He referred to this evolutionarily retarded species as *homo delinquens*, and saw those individuals as mutations or natural accidents living among civilized humans (Savitz, 1972). Collecting extensive data on the physical measurements of Italian prisoners as compared to Italian military personnel (noncriminals), Lombroso concluded that the criminal was distinguished by certain physical anomalies: an asymmetrical skull, flattened nose, large ears, fat lips, enormous jaws, high cheekbones, and mongolian eye characteristics (1972). Homo delinquens, also derisively called "born criminal," had a strong affinity for tattoos and "cruel games" and orgies, and had a peculiar primitive slang, all believed to be behavioral throwbacks to savage, undeveloped human or subhuman species. Moreover, the born criminal's art works were often faithful reproductions of the first, crude artistic attempts of primitive races. Thus, this primitive creature, who instinctively demonstrated behaviors which were once adaptive to the wilds in the millennia past, could not adjust socially and morally to the demands of modern times.

L'Uomo Delinquente went through several revisions, and by 1897 it had grown to three volumes comprising 1,903 pages. With each edition Lombroso modified his theory from the dogmatic one of 1876 to a more flexible but still basically genetic version. In 1911 his daughter Gina summarized his last work and translated it into English; the publication of still another rendition, Crime: Its Causes and Remedies, was published a year later. Early Lombrosian theory asserted that all criminals met the physical dimensions and psychological characteristics outlined. Later, possibly responding to criticism, Lombroso concluded that the born criminal actually accounted for only about one-third of the criminal population (Lombroso-Ferrero, 1972). The other two-thirds consisted of a wide assortment of criminal types. Lombroso also suggested at this point that environmental factors were significant in the development of certain types of crime (Wolfgang, 1972).

Other criminal types identified by Lombroso included the habitual or professional criminal, who learns to violate the law systematically and engages in crime as a trade or occupation. The degrading influence of prisons (which he called "criminal universities") and the daily contact with other hard-core prisoners played a significant role in the development of this habitual criminal. Another type was the juridicial criminal, who violated the law not because of any "natural depravity" but simply by lack of prudence, care, and forethought—the impulsive type. Criminals of passion violated the law because of their "intense love, honor, noble ambition, or patriotism." In other words, they may have murdered to defend their honor, their loved ones, or their country. Criminaloids had "weak natures" and were highly susceptible to good and bad example. The criminaloid had innate characteristics very similar to those of the born criminal, but the environment was an important determinant of when he or she engaged in criminal actions. The born criminal, by contrast, was dictated by a strong organic predisposition to crime. Lombroso also recognized the morally insane and hysteric criminal types.

Born criminals, the biologically predisposed, exhibited a lack of guilt or remorse for any wrongdoing (although they often alleged repentance) and a peculiar inability to learn to distinguish between "good and evil." Lombroso reported they did not develop close acquaintances and were highly prone to betray companions and accomplices. They displayed "exaggerated notions of their own importance," were impulsive, cruel, and had a high tolerance for pain.

Lombroso at first considered the female offender to be very similar to the male offender, both in physical appearance and psychologically (Wolfgang, 1972). Singling out prostitution as representative of female crime, he saw it as an atavism (a throwback to more primitive times) and suggested that most women involved in prostitution were born criminals and lacked a "mother sense." He later modified this view to state that the born criminal woman did not clearly exhibit the same physical anomalies as the male born criminal, but psychologically she was more terrible and cruel than any man, almost monster-like (see Wolfgang, 1972). Lombroso concluded that women in general have many traits in common with children, such as revenge, jealousy, and an inclination toward "vengeances of a refined cruelty"!

An influential monograph published in 1913 by Charles Goring (1972) comparing the physical measurements of 3,000 English convicts to a like number of nonconvicts did not reveal the significant physical differences reported by Lombroso. This study, although plagued by numerous methodological flaws (as were Lombroso's own investigations) proved devastating to the Lombrosian position. Armed with Goring's findings and eager to put the genetic-crime issue to rest, many criminologists quickly wrote its obituary.

Although opinion varies about his positive or negative contributions to the field of criminology, there is little doubt that Lombroso had a considerable impact on research directed at the relationship between genetics and criminal personality. The late Stephen Shafer (1976, pp. 41–42), for example, has suggested that Cesare Lombroso could easily be called "the father of modern criminology" because his theories have stimulated research and empirical investigation "to include the criminal's personality and his social environment." Abrahamsen (1960, pp. 6–7) comments that Lombroso will be remembered "for disproving the assumption that a criminal committed a criminal act because his will was free and so was unquestionably responsible for his act." Abrahamsen adds that Lombroso paved the way for the examination of the criminal personality. Wolfgang (1972, p. 287) states: "The clinical, psychological and psychiatric analyses of today that report data on personality traits . . . are similar to, but much more refined and sophisticated than many of the findings reported by Lombroso."

Lombroso's research methods were faulty, especially in relation to the select population on which he based his original thesis. Considering his place in time, however, few would disagree that his contributions to the study of criminal behavior helped bring it out of philosophical and religious tenets and toward scientific investigation. The same criticisms of methodology leveled at Lombroso can just as validly be directed at the work of Sigmund Freud, the father of psychoanalysis.

PHYSIQUE AND CRIME

Physical characteristics and personality have been connected by theorists as far back as Hippocrates, who outlined a typology of physiques, tried to relate them to personality, and introduced the concept of humors or fluids within the body which influenced the personality (Hall & Lindzey, 1970). A more modern course in constitutional psychology was adopted by the German psychiatrist Emil Kretschmer (1925) who distinguished four types of body structures and tried to link them to specific mental disorders. He called one physique the *pyknic* and noted it was characterized by a short, fat stature. A second type, exhibiting tall and skinny features, was referred to as *leptosomatic* or *aesthenic*. The muscular, vigorous physique was called the *athletic* type. The fourth physique, the *dysplastic*, represented an incongruous mixture of different physiques in different parts of the body, making it appear "rare, surprising and ugly" (Hall & Lindzey, 1970).

More pertinent to our discussion on crime is the theory of William H. Sheldon (1949), who developed a similar but superior classification of body type in the United States and related physique to delinquency. Sheldon's method of delineating body type is called *somatotyping*. By extensively and painstakingly collecting physical measurements, documented by photography, Sheldon managed to categorize three basic body builds: the endomorph (fat and soft), the ectomorph (thin and fragile), and the mesomorph (muscular and hard) (see Figure 2–1). The reader with some background in embryology will recognize that the terms refer to layers of the embryo. The endodermal embryonic layer develops primarily into the digestive viscera, and thus individuals who are flabby and fat (endomorphs) are tied to the digestive system.

The mesodermal layer of the embryo develops into muscle and, therefore, the muscular body that is tough and well-equipped for strenuous activity is labeled the mesomorph. The ectodermal layer is developmentally responsible for the nervous system. The ectomorph has a large brain and central nervous system compared to the rest of his body, which is tall and thin.

It should be emphasized that Sheldon avoided making sharp distinc-

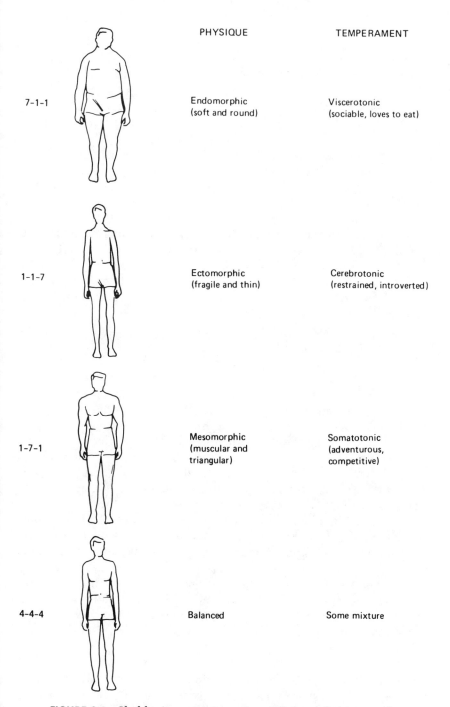

PHYSIQUE

TEMPERAMENT

7-1-1

Endomorphic
(soft and round)

Viscerotonic
(sociable, loves to eat)

1-1-7

Ectomorphic
(fragile and thin)

Cerebrotonic
(restrained, introverted)

1-7-1

Mesomorphic
(muscular and
triangular)

Somatotonic
(adventurous,
competitive)

4-4-4

Balanced

Some mixture

FIGURE 2-1. Sheldon's somatotypes in relation to physique and temperament

tions between body types or somatotypes. That is, rarely did an individual belong purely or absolutely to just one of the three somatotypes. Subjects were scored on the basis of three 7-point scales corresponding to the three somatotypes, with a 7 indicating that they were exclusively that body type. For example, a "pure" mesomorph would have a somatotype of 1-7-1, with the 1s denoting they were devoid of that particular body build. A 3-2-5 person would be primarily ectomorphic (5), but have some features of endomorphs (3) and mesomorphs (2). The average body build would be assigned a 4-4-4 index, indicating constitutional "balance."

Sheldon found a strong correlation between personality (or temperament) and somatotype, and he linked certain personality types with certain body types. One personality loves comfort, food, affection, and people. This type is usually even tempered and easy to get along with. Sheldon labeled this disposition *viscertonia* and, as you might have guessed, he connected it closely to the basic endomorph. A second personality type ordinarily needs muscular and vigorous physical activity, risk-taking, and adventure. A person with this temperament, according to Sheldon, is more likely to be aggressive and callous in relations with others, ruthless, and indifferent to pain (Lombroso's born criminal?). This cluster of personality traits was called *somatotonia* and was linked with the mesomorph. *Cerebrotonia* labels the person who is inhibited, reserved, self-conscious, and afraid of people; it correlates highly with the ectomorphic body build.

Sheldon began to test his delinquency theory in 1939 by exploring the relationship between delinquency and physique. His first study involved nearly 400 boys in a residential rehabilitation home (1949). The boys were assigned somatotype ratings, and biographical sketches—family background, medical history, mental and educational performance, and delinquent behavior—were drawn on each. Sheldon studied the delinquents for eight years, comparing them to a group of male college students. He found that the college students generally clustered around the average somatotype of 4-4-4. On the other hand, the group of delinquents was topheavy in the mesomorph category, but there were also signs of endomorphy. Ectomorphs were rare in the delinquent group. On the basis of his study, Sheldon concluded there were definite somatotypic and temperamental differences between delinquent and nondelinquent boys.

Subsequent investigations have provided additional support for Sheldon's findings, although the relationships in later studies have not been as clearcut as those he originally reported. Glueck and Glueck (1950, 1956) found that mesomorphs contributed far more than their share to the delinquent population (60 percent, with 30 percent endomorphs). In general, their findings established that delinquent boys were larger and stronger than nondelinquent boys. In a more recent study, Cortes and Gatti (1972) report that delinquent subjects (100 boys convicted by the court) were preponderantly more mesomorphic than nondelinquents (100 male high school seniors). Fifty-seven percent of the delinquent group could be easily classified as mesomorphic compared to 19 percent of the nondelinquent group. These percentages compare favorably with those cited by Glueck and Glueck (1950) in their study of 500 delinquents and nondelinquents.

Research by Staffieri (1967) has shown that ratings of attractiveness are significantly influenced by body build, with mesomorphs generally receiving the highest ratings. Comments from correctional personnel, however, indicate that the *faces* of inmates are generally more ugly than those of the general population. Norman Cavior and Ramona Howard (1973) took a closer look at the relationship between facial attractiveness and delinquency and found that both black and white delinquents were significantly less attractive than nondelinquents. These results suggest that facial unattractiveness may play a role in the development of crime and/or increase the probability of being adjudicated delinquent by the courts. Research has found that attractive children are favored by adults and other children. In fact, attractive children are less negatively evaluated than less attractive children, even when they both have committed identical antisocial acts (Dion, 1972; Dion et al., 1972). In one study using a simulated jury situation, good-looking criminals were treated more gently and were generally seen as less dangerous than a comparable group of unattractive criminals (Sigall & Ostrove, 1978). Furthermore, black skin, if considered less attractive than white skin, might prompt differential treatment in various sections of the judicial and criminal justice systems.

In an interesting pilot project designed to test the value of plastic surgery as a rehabilitative device, corrective surgery was offered to inmates with facial deformities at Rikers Island (Kurtzberg et al., 1978). The surgery was to be initiated at the time of their release from prison. After extensive medical and psychological screening, 425 inmates were divided into four groups. Depending upon the group, the inmate would receive either surgery, counseling, both, or neither (the control group). Overall, the results showed that nonaddict offenders receiving surgery were substantially less likely to engage in subsequent criminal offenses during a one-year follow-up period than a comparable group of disfigured offenders not receiving surgery. It is interesting to note that the group which received counseling alone committed higher incidences of detected crime than even the group which received neither surgery nor counseling. The results of the study are difficult to interpret, but they suggest that physical improvements also improve self-image and acceptance by others. Possibly, the subject has less need to defend or prove self-worth through criminal activities, or less need to give physical reactions to slights or challenges. And, possibly, the slights and challenges are fewer in number.

In summary, there appears to be a significant relationship between physique, or body build, and antisocial behavior. A relationship, however, does not establish what *causes* what. It only tells us that one thing appears when another thing does. Almost anything could be contributing to this relationship, and the most productive way to determine the cause is through well-designed experimentation. It is reasonable to assume, however, that boys and girls who are physically larger and more muscular than their peers are more likely to resort to physical means to get their way or gain material rewards, and that this pattern continues into adulthood. Moreover, it appears that the more attractive the person is, the greater will be the probability of a break or reprieve from the judicial system.

TWIN STUDIES

One of the principal methods used to determine what role genetics play in criminality has been to compare the incidence and type of criminal convictions among identical and fraternal twins. Fraternal twins (also called dizygotic twins) develop from two different fertilized eggs and are no more genetically alike than ordinary siblings (children from the same parents). Identical twins (or monozygotic twins) develop from a single egg and, therefore, they are always the same sex and share all the same genes. Theoretically, the twin method assumes that the environment exerts a similar influence on each member of a twin set. Therefore, differences or similarities between the twins are presumably due to genetic factors. Many investigators point out, however, that identical twins are so similar physically it is very likely they elicit more similar social responses from their environment than do fraternal twins. Although there may be some validity to this viewpoint, research has found that identical twins reared apart are more alike in some personality attributes than are identicals reared in the same home environment (Shields, 1962; Canter, 1973). It seems that when reared together identicals may make a conscious effort to accentuate their individual identities by being different from each other, whereas when reared apart they may have less need to be different.

Concordance, in genetics, is the degree to which related pairs of subjects both show a particular behavior or condition, and it is usually expressed in percentages. For example, assume we wish to determine the concordance of intelligence between twenty pairs of fraternal twins and twenty pairs of identical twins. Assume further that we found that ten pairs of the identical twins obtained approximately the same IQ score, but only five pairs of our fraternals obtained the same score. Our concordance for identicals would be 50 percent; for fraternals, 25 percent. Therefore, the concordance for identicals would be twice that of fraternals, suggesting that hereditary factors play an important role in intelligence. If, however, the concordance for identicals was about the same as that for fraternals, we would be obliged to conclude that genetic factors are unimportant, at least as represented by our sample and measured by our methods.

Numerous twin studies using this concordance method have strongly indicated that heredity is a powerful determinant in intelligence, schizophrenia, depressions, neuroses, alcoholism, and criminal behavior (Claridge, 1973; Rosenthal, 1970, 1971; McClearn & DeFries, 1973; Hetherington & Parke, 1975). The first such study relative to criminality was reported by the Munich physician Johannes Lange (1929) in his book *Crime As Destiny* (Rosenthal, 1971; Christiansen, 1977a). The title reflects Lange's Lombrosian conviction that criminal conduct is a predetermined fate dictated by heredity. Lange found a criminality concordance of 77 percent for thirteen pairs of adult identical twins and only 12 percent for seventeen pairs of adult fraternal twins. Not surprisingly, he argued that his finding strongly supported the fact of genetic programming for a criminal future. Auguste Marcel Legras (1932) then found a 100 percent criminal concordance for five pairs of identicals. Note that both of these studies used small samples. Subsequent studies, which improved in sophistication of design, twin identification, and sampling, continued to find a substantially higher criminal concordance for identical twins when compared to fraternals, although the concordance levels were not as high as those reported by either Lange or Legras. Table 2–1 summarizes these and other relevant investigations on criminal concordance. Although these tabulated investigations differed in method and definitions of criminality, the combined concordance levels demonstrate that identical twins differ significantly in concordance from fraternal twins.

Hans Eysenck, who also constructed tables using different studies, found similar concordances and concluded: "Thus concordance is found over four times as frequently in identicals as in fraternals, a finding which seems to put beyond any doubt that heredity plays an extremely important part in the genesis of criminal behaviour" (Eysenck, 1973, p. 167). Rosenthal (1975, p. 10) interjects a word of caution, stressing the many pitfalls of the concordance twin method and the ramifications of legal definitions of criminality, but allows: "Nevertheless, it is clearly not possible to rule out the potential fact that genetic factors may indeed be the primary source of the higher concordance rate in MZ (identical) as compared to DZ (fraternal) twins."

Eysenck further complicates the issue by pointing out that twin studies may actually have reported a *deflated* estimate of the true concordance rate, since it is likely that identical twins were often confused with fraternal twins, especially in the earlier studies. If twins are of the same sex, it is frequently difficult to distinguish identicals from fraternals from appearance alone. Today, we can make the differentiation by blood type, fingerprints (which are highly similar but not identical), and by examining various genetically determined serum proteins (Kretch, Crutchfield, & Livson, 1974). These methods, of course, were not available to earlier investigators, and thus Eysenck correctly contends that mix-ups may have confounded their results. Naturally, the concordance rates may just as easily have been inflated as deflated.

TABLE 2-1
Summary of Twin-Criminality Studies
Showing Pairs and Concordance Rates

Researcher	Identical Twins			Fraternal Twins		
	No. of Pairs	Pairs Concordant	Percent	No. of Pairs	Pairs Concordant	Percent
Lange (1929)	13	10	77	17	2	12
Legras (1932)	4	4	100	5	0	0
Ransanoff (1934)	37	25	68	60	6	10
Kranz (1936)	31	20	65	43	20	53
Stumpfl (1936)	18	11	61	19	7	37
Borgstrom (1939)	4	3	75	5	2	40
Rosanoff et al. (1941)	45	35	78	27	6	18
Yoshimasu (1961)	28	17	61	18	2	11
Yoshimasu (1965)	28	14	50	26	0	0
Hayashi (1967)	15	11	73	5	3	60
Dalgaard & Kringlen (1976)	31	8	26	54	8	15
Christiansen (1977b)						
Males	71	25	35	120	15	13
Females	14	2	21	27	2	8
Totals	339	185	55	426	73	17

As Table 2–1 reveals, twin studies have not *invariably* found high criminal concordance rates in favor of identical twins. One, in fact, found no significant difference at all between identicals and fraternals

(Dalgaard & Kringlen, 1976). The Dalgaard-Kringlen sample included all the registered male twins born between 1921 and 1930 in Norway. Thirty-two percent of the sample, however, were deleted from the analysis for various reasons, which might have affected the results in some way. Also, the researchers expanded the label "criminal" used in most twin studies to encompass traffic offenses, military offenses, and treason during World War II, as well as all actions against the penal code.

One of the most respected investigators in twin studies, the late Karl O. Christiansen, was at a loss to explain the lack of significant differences reported by Dalgaard and Kringlen. He advocated an additional study to determine whether "some special conditions exist in Norway that would dampen the expression of genetic factors . . ." (Christiansen, 1977a, p. 82)—a made-to-order doctoral dissertation for some enterprising Norwegian student, but to my knowledge it is not being attempted.

Overall, despite procedural and definitional problems and except for the Dalgaard-Kringlen data, the studies examining the concordance rates between twins have consistently indicated higher concordance for identicals. This clearly suggests that it might be wise to consider heredity as a powerful component in criminality.

ADOPTION STUDIES

Another method used to identify crucial variables in the interaction between heredity and environment is the adoption study, which is especially useful for determining what kinds of environments are most conducive to criminality. Unfortunately, there have been exceedingly few investigations of criminality using adopted children, and those have been fraught with methodological problems.

One of the first (although only remotely related to criminality) was carried out in Denmark by Schulsinger (1972), who checked out the incidence of "psychopathy" in the biological relatives of adopted adults. Schulsinger's sample included 57 adopted adults diagnosed as "psychopathic" whom he compared to a control group of 57 non-psychopathic adopted adults. The two groups were matched for sex, age, social class, and age of transfer to the adopting family. The study's direct implications for criminal behavior are questionable, because Schulsinger's diagnosis of psychopathy was based on his own loose criteria. Individuals who were "impulse ridden" and who exhibited "acting-out behavior" qualified. As we will see in Chapter 3, these descriptions do not necessarily connote either psychopathy or criminality.

In any event, Schulsinger found that 3.9 percent of the biological relatives of the acting-out adoptees could be classified as "psychopaths," compared to 1.4 percent of the control group's biological relatives. Although psychopathy was about two and a half times greater in the family backgrounds of acting-out adoptees, the results just failed to reach statistical significance, indicating that we should be very cautious about accepting the results.

Crowe (1974) conducted a more cogent examination, a follow-up of 52 persons relinquished for early adoption by female offenders. Ninety percent of the biological mothers were felons at the time of the adoptive placement, with the most common offenses being forgery and passing bad checks. Twenty-five of the 52 adoptees were female, and all the adoptees were white. Another 52 adoptees with no evidence of criminal family background were selected as a control group and matched for age, sex, race, and age at the time of adoption.

In the follow-up study, Crowe selected the 37 index and control subjects who had by then reached age eighteen. (Index subjects in research are those subjects who are of major concern.) Of the 37 index adoptees born of female offenders, seven had arrest records as adults, all seven had at least one conviction, four had multiple arrests, two had multiple convictions, and three were "felons." Of the 37 matching controls, two had adult arrest records and only one of these resulted in a conviction. Each subject's personality was diagnosed by three clinicians based on test results and data gathered in an interview; no family background was included. The clinicians made their diagnoses independent of one another and without knowing who among the subjects were indexes and who were controls. Six of the index adoptees were labeled "antisocial personality," whereas only one of the control group was diagnosed "probable antisocial personality."

Crowe's study found a positive correlation between the tendency of the index group to be antisocial and two other variables: the child's age at the time of adoptive placement and the length of time the child spent in temporary care (orphanages and foster homes) prior to that placement. The older the child of an offender upon adoptive placement and the longer the temporary placement, the more likely that child would be to grow up antisocial. The control group members were not affected by these conditions. This finding suggests that the two adoptee groups responded differently to similar environmental conditions, or else the adoption agency placed the offspring of female offenders in less desirable homes—and there were no indications that this was the case.

Let us look briefly at one more study which also underscores the importance of both genetics and environment. Barry Hutchings and Sarnoff Mednick (1975) reasoned that if there is a genetic basis for criminality, then there should be a significant relationship between the criminal tendencies of biological parents and those of their children who were adopted by someone else. In 1971 Hutchings and Mednick identified 1,145 male adoptees from the Copenhagen adoption files who were at the time of the study between the ages of thirty and forty-four. For purposes of comparison, the adoptees were matched for sex, age, occupational status of fathers, and residence by an equal number of nonadoptee controls. Fortunately, the researchers were also allowed to rifle through the Danish police criminal arrest files, a privilege not to be taken lightly!

The researchers were able to determine that 185 (16.2 percent) of the adoptees had criminal records, as compared to 105 (8.9 percent) criminal offenses for nonadoptees. A check on the biological fathers of the adoptees showed that they were nearly three times more likely to be involved in criminal activity than were either the adoptee's adoptive fathers or the fathers of the nonadopted controls. Furthermore, there was a significant relationship between the criminality of the sons and that of their fathers. If the biological father had a criminal record while the adoptive father had a clean record, a significant number of adoptees still became criminal (22 percent); but if the biological father had a clean record and the adoptive father had a criminal record, the number of adoptees who pursued criminal activities was less (11.5 percent). If both the biological father and the adoptive father were criminal, the chances were much greater that the adoptee would be criminal than if only one of the fathers were criminal. Hutchings and Mednick (1977) concluded that genetic factors continue to exert strong influences in the tendency toward criminality, even though environmental factors also play important roles.

One serious limitation to the Hutchings-Mednick data, as well as to any adoption study, is that agencies attempt to match the adopted child with the adoptive family on the basis of the child's biological and socioeconomic background. The Danish adoption agency used in the Hutchings-Mednick investigation confirmed that this was done. To their credit, Hutchings and Mednick not only recognized this problem, but also admonished that because the Danish society is largely homogeneous in cultural values and race, extrapolations to American society should be made cautiously.

In summary, twin and adoptive studies have suggested that genetic components may contribute significantly to a tendency to become criminal, but they have also found that environment is highly important. The available data so far indicate that certain human beings may be born with a biological predisposition toward behavior that runs counter to social values and norms, and that certain environmental factors either inhibit or stimulate it. To help pinpoint what this predisposition might be, we turn now to the theory and research of Hans J. Eysenck, a British psychologist.

EYSENCK'S THEORY OF PERSONALITY AND CRIME

Hans Eysenck (1977) proposes an *interactionist theory* of criminality: criminal behavior is the result of certain environmental conditions and *inherited* personality traits. He believes that we must examine the biological makeup and socialization history of the individual in order to form a comprehensive and effective theory of criminality. According to Eysenck, saying that crime is caused by social conditions of poverty, poor education, unemployment, or other factors in the social environment is as inaccurate as relying strictly on hereditary and biological explanations. "Crime cannot be understood in terms of heredity alone, but it can also not be understood in terms of environment alone" (Eysenck, 1973, p. 171). He also suggests that different combinations of environmental, biological, and personality factors give rise to different types of crime (Eysenck & Eysenck, 1970). This position implies that different personalities are more susceptible to certain crimes than others, an issue we shall return to later in the chapter.

Unlike most contemporary theories of crime, Eysenck's theory places heavy emphasis on genetic predispositions toward criminal conduct, or at least toward antisocial behavior. It is important to note at the outset that he is not suggesting that individuals are *born* criminal, but rather that some individuals are born with nervous system characteristics that are significantly different from the general population and that affect their ability to acquire social expectancies and rules. More specifically, Eysenck isolates features of the central and peripheral nervous systems to account for a substantial portion of the differences found in personality. The way each individual's nervous system functions may be as unique as his or her personality characteristics. Carrying it a step further, we could posit that some nervous systems are more likely to engage in criminal activity because of their reactivity, sensitivity, and excitability.

After many years of statistical analyses and empirical study, Eysenck has been able to delineate three major components of personality: *extraversion, neuroticism,* and *psychoticism.* He does not conclude that these components account for all the personality characteristics, but he does argue that they form the basic structure from which much of our behavior originates. Most of the research by Eysenck and others has been done on extraversion and neuroticism; they represent the core of Eysenckian theory. Psychoticism is a component he identified more recently to account for behaviors not fully explained by extraversion and neuroticism.

Eysenck visualizes these three personality factors on a continuum: most people fall in the intermediate or midpoint, while people at either extreme are relatively rare (see Figure 2–2). The extraversion dimension runs from the extreme pole extraversion to the extreme introversion, with the middle range called *ambiversion*. Thus, depending upon where a person falls on this dimension, that person may be an extravert, introvert, or ambivert. The neuroticism continuum runs from the polar ends of neuroticism to stability, with no middle label, although most people are at the middle. Psychoticism runs from tough-mindedness (high psychoticism) to tender-mindedness (low psychoticism), also with no label for the middle majority. The extraversion dimension is believed to reflect basic functions of the central nervous system (CNS), which consists of the brain and spinal cord, while neuroticism repre-

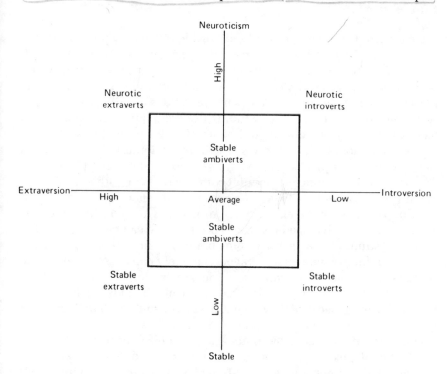

FIGURE 2–2. Illustration of Eysenck's personality dimensions for neuroticism and extraversion.

sents functions in the peripheral nervous system (nerve pathways out-side the central nervous system). As yet, no nervous system mechanism has been postulated for the dimension of psychoticism.

Eysenck developed several self-report questionnaires to measure these personality variables, and this has stimulated extensive research to test the validity of the questionnaires and his concept of personality. The British Maudsley Personality Inventory (MPI) and the American editions known as the Eysenck Personality Inventory (EPI) and the Eysenck Personality Questionnaire (EPQ) are the best known measuring instruments for classifying subjects along the three personality dimensions for research purposes. Overall, worldwide research findings have been highly supportive of Eysenck's general theory of personality. We will review the research related to this theory and crime in a later section of this chapter. But before we do that we must become better equipped with the basic concepts behind each dimension.

Extraversion

Behavioral Characteristics. The typical extravert is sociable, impulsive, optimistic, and has high needs for excitement and for a varied, changing environment. Extraverts tend to lose their temper quickly, become aggressive easily, and often are not very reliable. The extravert likes to have people around, enjoys parties, and is usually talkative. The typical introvert, on the other hand, is reserved, quiet, cautious, keeps feelings under close control, and generally tries to avoid excitement, change, and most social activities. The introvert tends to be reliable and unaggressive and places great value on ethical standards (Eysenck & Rachman, 1965). Ambiverts exhibit some features of both extraversion and introversion, but not to the extreme or consistency of those personality groups. Think of the extraversion dimension as a continuum representing a progressive need for stimulation, which can be defined as the "impact" stimuli have on areas of the brain. The impact is analogous to the taste of food. Some people have a relatively consistent tendency to prefer spicy, hot foods which provide greater impact on their taste centers, while others may more often choose bland foods (such as macaroni and cheese) because they do not desire the high taste impact. More generally, some individuals prefer and actively seek out more stimulation or stimulus impact from other areas of their lives as well—music, bustle, people, excitement, drugs, and so forth. People at the extraversion end of the dimension require higher levels of stimulation from their environment than those at the introversion end. If you conceptualize the dimension this way, you will realize that the popular usage of extroversion (sociability) takes on added meaning. Extraverts prefer lots of people and talk because of the added stimulation they receive. Remember, however, that our everyday, loose usage of the nouns extrovert and introvert are *not* the same as Eysenck's polar classifications.

The extraversion dimension can be measured by one of the Eysenckian personality inventories. Usually, two out of every three people will score in the "average" range, thus classifying them as the clinically uninteresting "ambiverts." Roughly 16 percent are extraverts and another 16 percent introverts.

Because extraverts have higher needs for excitement and stimulation to break the daily boredom, they are also most likely to run counter to the law. They tend to be impulsive, fun-loving, thrill-seeking people who are willing to take chances and stick their necks out. They enjoy pranks and practical jokes and find challenge in opportunities to do the unconventional or even the antisocial. In addition, features of the extraverted nervous system not only encourage stimulation seeking, but also inhibit the acquisition of society's rules, as we will see below.

Physiological Bases of Extraversion-Introversion. Eysenck (1967) hypothesized that people differ along the extraversion-introversion axis because of genetic differences in certain mechanisms in their central nervous system, particularly the tiny but complex network of neurons located in the central part of the brain stem called the reticular activating system (RAS) (see Figure 2–3). We shall discuss this mechanism in detail in Chapter 3. The RAS acts as a sentinel which awakens the portion of the brain called the cerebral cortex and maintains its alertness and attention. The cerebral cortex is that part of the brain where all the higher level functions occur, such as thinking, memory, and decision making (French, 1957). The RAS generates arousal in the cerebral cortex so that it will be alert to incoming stimuli. Nerve pathways communicating information to the cerebral cortex branch off into collateral pathways traveling to the RAS. In effect, these collaterals "tell" the RAS to alert the brain to incoming information.

Eysenck postulates that extraverts and introverts inherit an RAS which handles cortical arousal a little differently from the way it is handled in the majority of the population. Basically, the extravert's RAS does not generate cortical excitation or arousal as effectively as it does for the ambivert or the introvert. In fact, it appears to dampen down stimulation and the arousal properties of stimuli before they can reach the cortex. The introvert, on the other hand, is believed to have inherited an RAS that *amplifies* stimulation input, keeping cortical arousal at relatively high levels. So we have the extravert, who is cortically underaroused, seeking additional stimulation in an attempt to achieve an optimally aroused cortex, and the introvert, who is cortically overaroused, trying to *avoid* additional stimulation. The ambivert, who

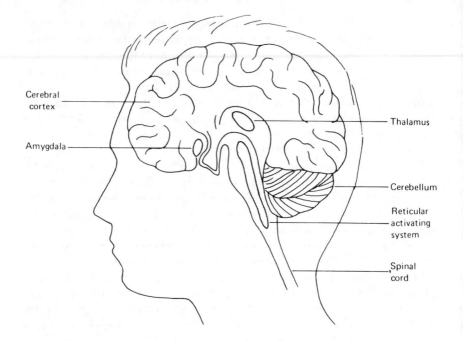

FIGURE 2–3. Location of the reticular activating system relative to other brain structures.

occupies an intermediate position of arousal, is apparently generally content with whatever amount of stimulation is received.

We shall also discuss in Chapter 3 the concept of optimal levels of stimulation or cortical arousal that human beings strive for. In other words, one of the motivations behind human behavior is the desire to achieve that "just right" level of stimulation and cortical arousal. Too much stimulation becomes aversive and even painful, while too little stimulation results in boredom and eventual sleep. It is assumed that the extravert, because of the dampening effect of the RAS, needs higher levels of stimulation to maintain that just right or optimal level of cortical arousal. The introvert, because of the amplifying effect of the RAS, desires relatively lower levels of stimulation. This explains why the typical extravert continually seeks adequate stimulation such as might be found in parties, loud music, vividly colored objects, spicy foods, sex, stimulating drugs, and other opportunities for excitement. Conversely, the typical introvert tries to avoid levels of stimulation comparable to those sought by the extravert, preferring soft music, cool and dark-colored objects, bland food, and generally sedate social gatherings.

The extravert's stimulation needs are well documented by numerous experiments (see Eysenck, 1967, 1976). As mentioned above, the greater tendency of extraverts to seek sensation is more likely to put them in conflict with the law, and this too is largely confirmed in the research literature. In fact, it has been suggested that a majority of the individuals involved in criminal activity are cortically underaroused and have a strong drive to obtain stimulation or sensation from their environments, such as risk taking, joy riding, and other activities of high stimulation value. Put quite simply, most criminals are extraverts.

Before we leave the section on extraversion, let's digress for a moment on the effects of alcohol on cortical arousal. Alcohol is a depressant. It lowers cortical arousal to the point where one may "pass out" or fall asleep. The extravert without alcohol is already "half in the bag," and with alcohol his or her alertness is lowered even more. Alcohol lowers the high cortical arousal of introverts to a point where they become more extraverted, behaviorally and physiologically. Thus, the normally quiet, reserved person may become very talkative and get up on the piano and dance after a couple of drinks. The drunken introvert now has an extraverted arousal level and seeks more stimulation. The correlation between alcohol and crime is a strong one and will be discussed in detail in Chapter 12, dealing with drugs.

Eysenck supposes that the active, aroused cortex is more effective in inhibiting activity than the poorly aroused one. Therefore, high cortical arousal leads to inhibition, while low cortical arousal allows subcortical regions of the central nervous system to function without restraint. In a sense, the human cortex lessens its censorship over the more primitive, subcortical regions of the nervous system when alcohol lowers its alertness. This opens the door to inappropriate, antisocial behaviors normally held in check by the cortex. Thus, under the influence of alcohol, introverts will do things they normally would not do. On the other hand, relatively small quantities of alcohol influence the extravert, who chronically functions at a low level of cortical arousal to begin with, toward uninhibited behavior.

The reader by now has gained some basic understanding of one of Eysenck's personality dimensions, but let's not forget that extraversion is not the whole story. We move on now to consider the second dimension, which is equally important.

Neuroticism

Behavioral Characteristics. Like extraversion, neuroticism is a significant variable in the relationship between personality and crime. Sometimes called emotionality, this dimension reflects an innate, biological predisposition to react bodily to stressful events. Basically, neuroticism deals with the intensity of emotional reactions. A person high on the neuroticism scale reacts intensely and lastingly to stress. In fact, even under low-stress conditions the person is likely to be moody, touchy, sensitive to slights, anxious, and often complains of various physical ailments such as headaches, backaches, and digestive problems. He or she tends to overreact to stress and have difficulty recovering to a normal, calm state. People high in emotionality have a strong propensity to develop neurotic features such as phobias and obsessions. Their opposites, persons at the other end of the continuum, display emotionally stable, calm, and even-tempered behavior. They tend to keep their wits about them under stress and intense excitement and to select appropriate reactions to emergencies. Researchers who test Eysenckian theory refer to high emotionality individuals as *neurotics*, while persons manifesting few neurotic features are labeled *stables*.

Physiological Bases of Neuroticism-Stability. The autonomic nervous system can be subdivided into the sympathetic and the parasympathetic nervous systems. The *sympathetic system* activates the body for emergencies by increasing heart rate, respiration flow, blood flow, pupil dilation, and perspiration. The *parasympathetic system* counterbalances the sympathetic by bringing the body back to its normal arousal state. According to Eysenck, differences in emotionality are due to variances in the sensitivity of these subdivisions, which are both under the control of the so-called "visceral brain" or *limbic system*. In addition to a complicated array of neuronal circuitry, the limbic system includes the neurological structures known as the hippocampus, amygdala, cingulum, and hypothalamus (see Figure 2–4). This hypothalamus appears to exert the greatest amount of control over the autonomic nervous system and thus represents the central mechanism in emotionality.

People who display high levels of neuroticism are believed to have unusually sensitive limbic systems so that emotionality is achieved quickly and lastingly. Theoretically, it may be that the sympathetic system is quickly activated, while the parasympathetic is slow in counterbalancing. In contrast, individuals low in emotionality (stables) may possess an underactive sympathetic system combined with an overactive parasympathetic system.

Although the autonomic activation appears to be a generalized state of arousal throughout the body, there is good reason to believe that each individual reacts to stress in unique ways. Some individuals tense the muscles in their neck, forehead, or back; others may respond with an increased heart or breathing rate. This tendency for "response specificity" may account for the various forms of neurotic behaviors found in human beings in reaction to stress. Some neurotics complain of headaches when tense, others of digestive problems or backaches.

SYMPATHETIC   PARASYMPATHETIC

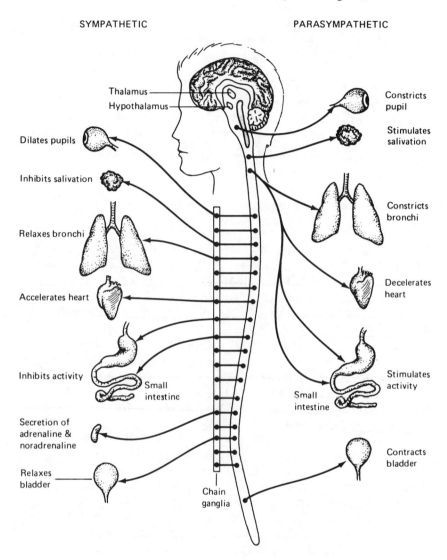

FIGURE 2–4. Illustration of the sympathetic and parasympathetic subdivisions of the autonomic nervous system.

Eysenck assumes that the individual who manifests high emotionality is more likely to engage in criminal activity than an individual with low emotionality. This assumption is based on the consistent research finding that emotionality can serve as a drive, pushing the person to perform in a certain way. If the person has "good" habits, a moderate level of emotionality motivates him or her to perform better than the person who is less motivated. On the other hand, if the person has "bad" or antisocial habits, a highly emotional person will be more motivated to engage in criminal activity than would a less emotional person with similar habits.

The two dimensions we have looked at thus far are usually combined in classifying an individual's personality. That is, based on Eysenck's personality inventories, the individual may be a neurotic introvert, a stable extravert, a neurotic ambivert, and so forth. If we accept Eysenck's views up to this point, we would also accept the idea that the neurotic extravert is the most likely to be involved in criminal behavior.

Psychoticism

Psychoticism is Eysenck's most recently formulated dimension, and although no physiological mechanism has been suggested to explain its characteristics, the dimension is highly similar to primary psychopathy, which we will discuss in Chapter 3. Behaviorally, "psychoticism" is characterized by cold cruelty, social insensitivity, unemotionality, disregard for danger, troublesome behavior, dislike for other people, and liking for the unusual. "Psychotics" are hostile toward others and enjoy making fools of them.[1]

Although the psychoticism dimension is too new to have gained much research attention, Eysenck hypothesizes that, like extraversion and neuroticism, it will prove to be a striking characteristic of the criminal population. He suggests that psychoticism will be especially prominent in the hard core, habitual offender involved in crimes of violence or sex (Eysenck, 1973; Eysenck, 1976).

Toward the end of this chapter we will put Eysenck on trial by trying to decide whether research to date has supported his theory. But the astute reader may realize that thus far we have merely defined extraverts, neurotics, and, to some extent, psychotics, and in the case of the first two we have isolated the physiological mechanisms that control them. We have not explained why, according to Eysenck, they are also apt to be criminal. The answer has to do with some very basic principles in psychology to which we now turn our attention.

Crime and Conditionability

We have thus far used the term "learning" rather loosely. It is important now to be more specific if we are to understand criminal behavior,

[1]It is important here that we make the distinction between Eysenck's "psychotics" and persons who are "psychotic" in the clinical sense of being out of touch with reality. Psychoticism as a classification of mental disorder and abnormality will be dealt with in Chapter 6.

since a basic premise of this book is that criminal behavior is learned. Psychologists have been able to delineate three major types of learning: classical or Pavlovian conditioning, instrumental or operant learning, and social learning. The student with a background in introductory psychology will recall Ivan Pavlov's famous experiments with dogs, in which they learned to salivate at the sound of a bell. Pavlov discovered that pairing a neutral stimulus (in this case a bell) with a significant stimulus (for example, food) would result in the dogs' eventually learning to associate the sound of the bell with food. How do we know the dogs learned to make that association? Because they salivated at the bell's sound, a response they normally reserve for food. The process of learning to respond to a formerly neutral stimulus (bell) which has been paired with another stimulus that already elicits a response (salivation) is basically *classical* or *Pavlovian conditioning* (Bourne & Ekstrand, 1976). In classical conditioning animals (or persons) have no control over the situation, even over what happens to themselves. The animal is "forced" to take the consequences. The bell is going to ring and food will appear, regardless of what it does. In addition, learning occurs not because of any reward or gain, but merely because of the *association* between the bell and the food. The sound of the bell always, or sometimes, occurs just before the arrival of food. In anticipation, the animal salivates.

In *instrumental learning*, the process is quite different. The learner must do something to the environment in order to obtain a reward or, in some cases, to avoid punishment. Instrumental learning is based upon learning the consequences of behaving in a certain way: if you do something, there is some probability that a certain rewarding event (or at least an avoidance of punishment) will occur. A child may learn, for example, that if she has a temper tantrum in the presence of her father, she will get a piece of candy, but her mother won't yield. The child will eventually learn to use temper tantrums when father is around, but not to use them in front of mother.

One important aspect of instrumental learning should be carefully noted. There must be a reason or goal driving the animal or person to operate on the environment. That is, the individual must have a purpose or expectation for his or her behavior; one expects a reward for the response. A reward or reinforcement is the event that increases the likelihood of a response. Classical conditioning, however, results from an association between stimuli, and it takes place without reward.

Social learning is more complex than either classical conditioning or instrumental learning because it involves learning from watching others and the organization of social experiences in the brain. Since Eysenck did not deal directly with social learning principles, we will reserve this topic for a later chapter.

Eysenck (1977) turns the question of criminal behavior around from the usual, "Why do people become criminal?" to, "Why don't more people engage in criminal behavior?" To answer this with the adage "crime doesn't pay" is nonsense, since there is evidence that for much of the criminal population, crime *does* pay. After all, one of the chief motivators of behavior is the desire to gain reward and pleasure (referred to as *hedonism*). "It would seem . . . that a person may, with a fair degree of safety, indulge in a career of crime without having to fear the consequences very much" (Eysenck, 1964, p. 102). Those caught, convicted, and incarcerated often represent that portion of the criminal population who are of lower intelligence, poorly taught, unable to afford an influential attorney, or simply unlucky. So, if instrumental learning is a major factor, there should be substantially more crime, because people usually would be rewarded for operating criminally on their environment. Moreover, punishment is frequently not provided, and when it is, it is so long in coming that it proves ineffective. Eysenck suggests, in fact, that delayed and sometimes arbitrary punishment may actually encourage criminal activity.

To explain why more people do not become criminal, Eysenck contends that classical conditioning has a stronger effect on most people than instrumental learning. That is, most people behave themselves because they have been classically conditioned during childhood about the rules of society. That guiding light, superego, conscience, or whatever it is that makes us feel uncomfortable before, during, and after a socially and morally disapproved act is, according to Eysenck, a *conditioned reflex*. In a traditional family environment the child is reprimanded or physically punished for a behavior that he or she wants to engage in, but which is against the social mores. Immediately after engaging in a socially or morally frowned upon act, say masturbating in public, the child usually finds that punishment quickly follows.

Let's return to Pavlov's dog experiments for a moment and substitute the food with painful shock. Immediately following the sound of the bell, the dog receives a severe electrical shock (punishment) through the grids in the floor of the cage. After a number of trials (bell followed by shock) the dog, rather than salivating, begins shaking in fear of what is to come. The animal has been classically conditioned to fear the sound of the bell, even when the shock no longer follows the bell.

Eysenck asserts that basically the same sequence occurs in childhood—inappropriate behavior followed by reprimand. Child masturbates, mother slaps. Following a few repetitions of this sequence, the thought of masturbation stimulates fear of the consequences prior to performing the act. In other words, the child associates masturbation with punishment, and this bonding between the behavior and the aversive consequences should deter the child from performing the act. Moreover, the nearer the individual comes to performing the act, the stronger the association (fear) becomes. Note also that the behavior the parent expects (stop masturbating) is not a behavior the child decides to engage in, such as we would find in instrumental learning.

Most people, Eysenck believes, do not participate in criminal activity because they have made a strong enough connection between deviant behavior and aversive consequences. On the other hand, those persons who have not made an adequate connection because of poor conditionability and/or unfavorable circumstances are more likely to emit deviant or criminal behavior. People prone toward deviant behavior do not anticipate aversive events strongly enough to be deterred; the association has not been sufficiently developed.

Pavlov observed that dogs differ widely in their conditionability to the sound of a bell and theorized that these differences come from properties found in their nervous systems. Eysenck makes the same observation concerning humans: extraverts are hypothesized to condition less readily than introverts due to biological differences in their nervous systems. In other words, introverts tend to have a better developed "conscience" than extraverts and are therefore less likely to engage in behavior contrary to society's laws and mores.

The principles of conditioning have been firmly established in the field of psychology as a valid explanation for many forms of behavior. The conditioning process appears to be a powerful force in the socialization of children, particularly in the suppressing of undesirable behaviors. There is every reason to believe that it may be a critical process in determining who becomes involved in deviant or criminal behavior.

Although the emphasis in this section has been on the conditioning process as an inhibitor of deviant behavior, there is also evidence that it can serve as an instigator of such behavior. As we shall see in later chapters, the association between *pleasurable* events and specific behavior is also an extremely powerful motivation toward criminal activity.

What part does neuroticism or emotionality play? Eysenck predicts that neuroticism functions as a drive strongly encouraging the performance of behavior previously acquired during childhood. That is, neuroticism amplifies existing habits in a person's repertoire of responses. If a neurotic extravert has not been properly conditioned to avoid stealing, neuroticism will function as a strong force or drive toward stealing. In other words, behavior (inappropriate or appropriate) = prior conditioning × (intensified by) emotionality. "We would expect that under strong emotion people would be more resistant to deterrence from pursuing the wrong course of action and would find it more difficult to learn the correct course of action" (Eysenck, 1964, pp. 142–143). In this sense, punishment may increase the degree of emotion present and, therefore, have a negative rather than a positive effect.

The Evidence for Eysenck's Theory

Now that we have gone through the rigorous intellectual exercise of digesting Eysenck's theory, can we find research to support it? Eysenck's prediction is that criminals as a group will score significantly higher on psychoticism, extraversion, and neuroticism than will non-criminals. Have studies borne this out? In some cases, yes, but in many respects the results are inconclusive. In some areas the research appears even damaging to the theory. This does not mean, however, that it is wrong or incorrect. Provided the experiments testing it have been carefully and soundly done, research findings which fail to support some parts of a theory suggest that it must be modified to account for the data more accurately. The theory can still be a very promising and useful one.

Before examining the specific findings, we should note some general problems about the research. Passingham (1972) presents a comprehensive review of the work done up to 1971, and posits that most of the experiments to that point were plagued by flaws in the basic experimental design. He points out that very few of the studies used adequate controls when comparing criminal and noncriminal populations. A control group is one in which all the relevant variables such as socioeconomic class, economic background, and intelligence are the same as those found in the experimental group which, in this case, refers to the criminal population. Otherwise, it is difficult to make meaningful comparisons and valid conclusions. Suppose we designed a study to determine whether the personalities of criminals are significantly different from those of noncriminals, and we used only college students as a control group. The most valid conclusion we can safely make, provided we found a significant difference, is that our criminal sample differed *only* from college students. It is clear that our college sample differs on some personality variables from the lower socioeconomic class (the class which is most representative of the criminal population) in general. The results, therefore, would reflect a difference between social classes and not between criminal and noncriminal behavior.

Most researchers have simply selected a hodgepodge of prisoners from one institution without discriminating subgroups of offenders. They have given them a questionnaire and made comparisons and conclusions based on responses from a poorly selected control group. It is quite obvious that prisoners are prisoners for a constellation of reasons and offenses. It is unlikely that they each made it to prison for the same reason. It makes better sense to try to discriminate among certain categories of offenses in an effort to determine whether in fact we can generalize about prisoners as a whole, or whether there are certain personalities prone to commit certain offenses.

Eysenck (1971, p. 289) recognized this when he commented: ". . . not all crimes are likely to be equally highly correlated with extraversion, and some types of criminal (behavior), such as the recidivist 'old lag,' lacking entirely in the social skills needed to make a success of living outside an institution, may in fact show introverted tendencies." In fact, many murderers and sex offenders do show strong introverted patterns. We must keep in mind that the above issues make firm, overall conclusions difficult. With this caution, let's take a closer look at research findings pertaining to the relationships between extraversion, neuroticism, psychoticism, and crime.

In general, Eysenck's prediction that the criminal and antisocial populations should score significantly higher on the extraversion scale has not been consistently supported (Passingham, 1972; Allsopp, 1976; Feldman, 1977). The results are especially inconsistent for male adult offenders and delinquents. While some studies (e.g., Price, 1968; Buikhuisen & Hemmel, 1972) report high extraversion scores for delinquents and adult male offenders, other investigations cite evidence that these groups score lower than the general population (e.g., Hoghugi & Forrest, 1970; Cochrane, 1974). Some found no difference between prisoners and delinquents compared to control groups (e.g., Little, 1963; Burgess, 1972). Other studies found evidence for significantly higher E-scores (extraversion) for violent offenders compared to other types of offenders (Gossop & Kristjansson, 1977). Studies dividing the extraversion characteristics into those which reflect impulsiveness and sociability have found that male adult prisoners score higher on impulsiveness than do male noncriminals, but score lower than the noncriminals on sociability (Eysenck & Eysenck, 1970, 1971). This suggests, among other things, that the sociability items on the extraversion scale are not pertinent for incarcerated prisoners, since correctional institutions are not particularly known for social events and parties.

The E-scale's failure to produce results consistent with Eysenck's hypothesis may reflect a weakness in his contention that a majority of criminals are poor conditioners. While many may have faulty consciences, the poor conditioning perspective is too limited in scope. It appears to be more accurate to say that a majority of criminals have offended partly because of poor conditionability, but also partly because they saw the antisocial behavior as one of the few choices available to them for some subjective gain. In other words, the E-scale reflects conditionability, but many (probably most) inmates are not in prison simply because of failure to associate social transgression with feelings of guilt and anxiety. Rather, they are incarcerated for a number of offenses prompted by a number of motivations in combination with a number of social situations. Because the E-scale is not sensitive enough to account for these various motivations and conditions, it would be more productive to test the theory on selected subgroups of offenders.

Howard Holanchock and I (Bartol & Holanchock, in press) administered the Eysenck Personality Questionnaire to 398 inmates at a maximum security prison in New York state. Sixty-two percent were black, 30 percent Hispanic, and about 7 percent white. The sample was divided into six offender groups according to conviction history: homicide, aggravated assault and attempted murder, rape and sexual assault, robbery, burglary, and drug offenses. Since it was crucial that the control group match the criminal group as closely as possible, subjects waiting in various employment agencies in predominantly black and Hispanic areas in New York City were asked to fill out the EPQ. We were able to find 187 such subjects, and from all indications, this control group's composition and background were equivalent to the criminal group's. The results showed that all six criminal groups scored *lower* than the control group on the E-scale. However, there were significant differences among the criminal subgroups themselves. Sex offenders, for example, were the most introverted, followed by burglars. Robbery offenders were the most extraverted among the offender groups. While demonstrating the ability of the EPQ to distinguish among offenders for this particular sample, the study does not support Eysenck's position on extraversion. Although there appeared to be a number of reasons for this lack of support, the most outstanding was the culture the inmates represented. That is, they were generally from the ghetto regions of New York City and were convicted of violent crimes. Eysenckian theory concerning the E-scale has been formulated primarily using European Whites convicted of property crimes. This observation stresses the importance of environmental considerations when dealing with heterogeneous criminal populations.

Research results for adult female offenders have been more promising, although the number of studies so far has been extremely small. Eysenck and Eysenck (1973) tested 264 female prisoners in Holloway Prison, London, comparing their responses to those of a control group of 357 women who were randomly chosen by a market research agency. Additional control groups were also used for comparison: 577 mothers of school children and 385 students in various adult courses. The results showed that female prisoners had a significantly higher extraversion score than any of the controls. Studies by Bartholomew (1963) and Saxby, Morris, and Feldman (1970) report a similar relationship between extraversion and female prisoners. Price (1968) reported that female delinquents (Borstal girls) scored significantly higher than the norms reported in the MPI manual. Interestingly, in the Eysenck and Eysenck investigation, the extraversion scores were somewhat lower in female prisoners than among male prisoners in the authors' previous studies.

The literature has consistently supported positive relationships between both neuroticism and psychoticism and crime and between those two dimensions and antisocial behavior (Allsopp, 1976; Feldman, 1977). Studies by Bartholomew (1959) and Fitch (1962) have found adult male offenders scoring significantly higher than controls on neuroticism, and Bartholomew (1963) and Eysenck and Eysenck (1973) found this to be the case for adult female offenders. Little (1963) reports higher neuroticism scores for male delinquents and Price (1968) for female delinquents. Eysenck and Eysenck (1970, 1971, 1973) have reported that psychoticism scores are substantially higher for both male and female prisoners than for male and female controls. Smith and Smith (1977) found that the P-scale (psychoticism) was positively correlated with the reconviction rate of persons on probation. Furthermore, this study also found the more "serious criminal tendencies" correlated with high P-scales.

Having people who were not convicts report offenses anonymously on a questionnaire and comparing their responses to the Eysenck scores is an interesting approach that has been used by Allsopp and Feldman (1975, 1976). Using nearly 200 school girls ranging in age from eleven to fifteen years, they found high scores on neuroticism, extraversion, and psychoticism significantly related to self-report offending.

Why have we spent so much time on the Eysenckian theory, especially since it is obviously a theory in a state of flux? Because, although much more research is needed before firm conclusions can be made, it offers great potential for a generalized testable theory of criminality, which the field of criminology desperately needs. For example, if we can someday say with confidence that neurotic extraverts (as defined by the EPI) are more likely to be involved in crime, if we can identify what types of crime, and if we can understand why this is so, then our chances of discovering how to prevent those crimes are increased. Also, treatment methods designed for certain offenses could be more effectively implemented.

Eysenk's theory is also important because it emphasizes the interaction of the environment, particularly classical conditioning, with characteristics of the nervous system. Of particular importance is the attention given to individual differences in nervous systems, which has received worldwide interest and much support as a biological basis for differences in personality and behavior (see Nebylitsyn & Gray, 1972). Integration of these findings into the field of criminology is needed to increase our understanding of criminal behavior. In addition, the theory is unique because it represents one of the very few attempts by a psychologist to formulate a general theory of criminal behavior.

At this point I would venture to suggest that Eysenck's heavy reliance on classical conditioning principles as a primary explanation for criminality, while avoiding other forms of learning, may prove to be one of his theory's damaging weaknesses. In a later chapter we will see much evidence to support social learning as a major determinant of some criminal behavior, but that is not to say that conditioning can be rejected. We will return to the Eysenckian view and the biological foundation for criminal behavior he proposes throughout the remainder of the text.

SUMMARY

Realizing that crime, like all human behavior, is a result of an interaction between heredity and environment, we have in this chapter looked at the research on the genetic makeup of persons who become criminal and at the conclusions that have been reached. A pioneer in genetic criminological research, Cesare Lombroso, asserted that there is a "born criminal" who is physically distinct from the general population and is predisposed to act antisocially. Lombroso's theory saw a number of revisions, but the final version retained the flavor of an innate criminal tendency in at least some offenders. Lombrosian theory was soon put to rest, but few would deny that he started theorists on the track of thinking that there might be more to crime than simply environmental and social factors.

Later theorists studied the relationship of body build (Kretschmer) or body type (Sheldon) to crime. Theirs and later studies supported some correlation with crime, but questionable methodology in many instances made it impossible to determine with high accuracy whether a causal relationship existed.

A number of studies of identical and fraternal twins have found a high concordance rate between identicals engaged in crime. That is, there is evidence that identical twins, even when separated at birth, tend to be alike in their pursuit of criminal careers, lending credence to genetic factors. Adoption studies have also been tried, but because of the difficulty in obtaining records, they have been scant. The adoption studies that have been done supported the genetic viewpoint, but also indicated that the environment can either stimulate or inhibit an inborn tendency toward criminality.

Hans J. Eysenck has come out strongly in favor of an interactionist approach to crime, seeing it as the result of environmental conditions (primarily conditioning experiences) working on inherited features of the nervous system. The core of his theory is that individuals with certain types of nervous systems (introverts) condition, or associate, more readily the mores of society with approval or disapproval than do individuals with other types (extraverts and ambiverts). In other words, introverts link transgressions with disapproval much sooner than others. However, as we shall see later, because of their quick association ability, introverts are also more likely to acquire sexual deviations than others.

Eysenck hypothesizes that neuroticism or emotionality tends to intensify existing habits, which in some cases may be antisocial habits. Thus, individuals with high emotionality may be more driven toward antisocial habits than individuals with low emotionality. Psychoticism appears to correlate with features of the psychopath, high recidivism, and "habitual offenders."

It is obvious that the Eysenckian position needs revision in some areas, particularly in distinguishing different types of offenders—the violent from the nonviolent, sex offenders from burglars, and so forth. The N and P dimensions have received considerable support in the research literature, while the E dimension needs much refinement. The theory, while still in a state of flux, offers promising possibility as a generalized, testable theory of criminality.

KEY CONCEPTS FOR REVIEW

Homo Delinquens
Somatotypes
Concordance
Extraversion
Neuroticism
Psychoticism
RAS
Autonomic Nervous System
Classical Conditioning
Instrumental Learning

MAJOR THEORISTS AND RESEARCHERS

Lombroso
Sheldon
Eysenck

SUGGESTED READINGS

Cortes, J.B. and Gatti, F.M. *Delinquency and crime: A biopsychosocial approach.* New York: Seminar Press, 1971.
A good study and review of the relationship between physique and crime.

Eysenck, H.J. *Crime and personality.* London: Routledge & Kegan Paul, 1977.
A comprehensive presentation of Eysenck's theory of personality as it relates to crime.

Mednick, S.A. and Christiansen, K.O. (eds.). *Biosocial bases of criminal behavior.* New York: Gardner Press, 1977.
A collection of recent studies describing the relationship between heredity, environment, and crime.

Plotnik, R. and Mollenauer, S. *Brain and behavior.* San Francisco: Canfield Press, 1978.
An unusually concise and readable presentation of the human nervous system.

THE PSYCHOPATH: THE UNDERSOCIALIZED OFFENDER

THREE

> . . . we are dealing here not with a complete man at all but with something that suggests a subtly constructed reflex machine which can mimic the human personality perfectly.*
>
> *Cleckley, 1976, p. 369*

HISTORICAL PERSPECTIVE

The psychopath, it seems, has been with us for at least as long as humans have recorded their own actions. Ancient writings and the classics allude to human behaviors that are strikingly similar to contemporary descriptions of psychopathy (e.g., Rotenberg & Diamond, 1972). Attempts to classify the psychopath began in the early 1800s when the French psychiatrist Phillippe Pinel coined the term *manie sans delire* (mania without insanity) to describe a constellation of behavior disorders characterized by asocial and antisocial actions, but without the features of "mental illness." In 1835 the British psychiatrist J.C. Pritchard renamed the clinically strange group of disorders "moral insanity," since he felt the behaviors manifested a "derangement" and a failure to abide by society's expectations of religious, ethical, and cul-

*From Cleckley, Hervey: *The Mask of Sanity*, 5th ed., St. Louis, The C. V. Mosby Co., 1976, p. 369.

tural conduct. Pritchard's terminology was widely accepted and used by both the public and the medical profession for over a half century. In 1888, however, the German psychiatrist J. Koch decided "moral insanity" had unwarranted negative connotations and proposed that a more acceptable designation would be "psychopathic inferiority."

Like his predecessors, Koch lumped a hodgepodge of behaviors into his diagnostic label, some of which are elements of the true psychopathic personality as we recognize it today, but many of which characterize neuroticism and personality disorders. The classifications had in common the belief that this social disorder without insanity was basically constitutional and likely inbred by a genetic strain which produced a basic flaw in the personality. There were implications, which in some respect continue today, that psychopaths were evil, human vessels of the devil, designed to destroy the moral fabric of society—"the devil made them do it."

Emil Kraepelin, who had an affinity for classification schemes, delineated seven categories of psychopathy in his Textbook of Psychiatry in 1913. The seven subtypes were the excitable, the unstable, the impulsive, the eccentric, the liars and swindlers, the antisocial, and the quarrelsome; all represented constitutional predispositions. Not to be outdone, Kahn (1931) suggested sixteen trait-syndromes for the psychopath. In 1930, G.E. Partridge considered psychopathy an exclusively social maladjustment and specified that "sociopath" was more applicable (Pennington, 1966).

To stem the proliferation of symptoms and labels and to check the resulting confusion and ambiguity, the American Psychiatric Association in 1952 dropped "psychopath" and officially adopted "sociopath," or, more specifically, "sociopathic personality disturbance." Contemporary researchers and clinicians use the terms interchangeably. The purist, however, considers the sociopath typically antisocial and most often criminal. The psychopath may or may not be criminal, but he or she demonstrates specific empirically verifiable behaviors and predispositions that differ from those of the general population.

Unable to resist its own propensity for labeling, the American Psychiatric Association in 1968 changed the 1952 classification "sociopathic personality disturbance, antisocial reaction" to personality disorder, antisocial type. The Group for the Advancement of Psychiatry (1966) suggested that the label tension discharge disorder, impulse ridden personality be used when diagnosing children who demonstrate features of their adult psychopathic counterparts. The Group also reserved the category "sociosyntonic personality disorder" for persons who exhibit aggressive, destructive behavior consonant with some subculture.

This text subscribes to "psychopath," more specifically "primary psychopath," as an experimentally and clinically useful designation. It is distinguished from "secondary" or "neurotic" psychopath, both concepts that can embrace the borderline and more common behaviors that have been loosely called "psychopathic." The primary psychopath is a unique breed of cat who is neither neurotic, psychotic, nor emotionally disturbed, as commonly believed, though he or she may obtain a high "psychoticism" rating in Eysenck's sense, as described in Chapter 2. This type of person is usually not volcanically explosive, violent, or extremely destructive, but is more apt to be outgoing, charming, and verbally proficient. The primary psychopath may be criminal, but many are not.

The inimitable Ferdinand Waldo Demara, Jr., the "Great Impostor," who forged documents and adopted dozens of occupations without stopping to obtain a high school education, is an example of a primary psychopath. Although he conflicted with the law because he persisted in faking identities, Demara actually performed valuable services for society. He once obtained the credentials of a Dr. French, the holder of a Harvard Ph.D. in psychology. Demara was in the U.S. Navy at the time, awaiting a commission on the basis of other "doctored" documents, but when he realized he was in danger of being exposed via a routine security check, he decided he would prefer the Dr. French identity. He dramatized a successful suicide by leaving his clothing on the end of a pier with a note stating that "this is the only way out." Naval officials accepted the "death" of their potential young officer, and Demara became Dr. French. With his impressive credentials in hand, he became Dean of Philosophy in a Canadian college, successfully taught an assortment of psychology courses, and assumed administrative responsibilities.

He became friendly with a physician named Joseph Cyr and learned the basics of medicine from long conversations with the man. Managing to borrow and duplicate the doctor's vital documents—birth, baptism and confirmation certificates, school records, medical license—Demara obtained a commission in the Royal Canadian Navy as "Dr. Cyr." He continued to familiarize himself with medicine by extensive reading.

During the Korean War, "Dr. Cyr" was assigned to a destroyer headed for the combat zone. The ship met a small Korean junk carrying many seriously wounded men, who were brought on board for emergency medical care. Three men were so critically hurt that only emergency surgery could save their lives.

Demara had never seen an operation performed, and he hurriedly reviewed available "how-to" books. For hours he operated with unskilled hands, relying only on what he could remember from the medical books. The operations continued throughout the night. By dawn, Demara not only had saved the lives of the three men, but also had successfully treated sixteen others.

Because the deeds were so noteworthy, they were broadcast over the ship's radio and the "miracle doctor" became world famous. The news, along with his picture, was flashed in the mass media. The real Dr. Cyr, shocked to find Demara's picture over his respected name, immediately exposed him. Demara was dropped from the Canadian Navy, but to save itself from embarrassment, the Navy allowed him to leave quietly, without prosecution. The interested reader may find a more extensive account of Demara's escapades in Smith's article (1968) or in Critchton's book, *The Great Impostor* (1959).

The public and the mass media generally associate the psychopath with criminality and bizarre perversions. The term "psychopathic killer" conjures images of a maniac gone berserk with a lust for wanton murder; "psychopathic rapists" supposedly torture and murder their victims because they hate their mothers and want to get back at women. These are gross misconceptions and inaccuracies; most crimes of primary psychopaths are in fact petty and without apparent rationale. Their criminal actions are often inappropriate and astonishingly immature pranks performed repeatedly without regard for the embarrassment or personal risks they entail. Repeating offenders who never learn the consequences of their petty crimes are a thorn in every law enforcement official's side.

Crimes committed repeatedly and without regard for risks and consequences are "second nature" to the primary psychopath, who seems to run in perpetual opposition to the law. The car theft for the ride, followed by probation, followed by another joy ride, a drunken brawl, or other "antisocial" actions is a typical sequence.

Some psychopaths, however, have perpetrated some of the world's most heinous and brutal homicides. Neville Heath—charming, handsome, and intelligent—committed in separate incidents two of the most brutal and sadistic sexual murders of two young English women ever uncovered (Critchley, 1951; Hill, 1960). Heath, like Demara, had an extraordinary career, much of it in the armed forces. In the course of ten years he managed to get himself commissioned and dishonorably discharged on three different occasions, once each in the British Royal Air Force, the Royal Armed Service Corps, and the South African Air Force. He flew with a fighter squadron in the Royal Air Force until court-martialed for car theft at age nineteen. After a series of thefts and housebreaking incidents, he was sentenced to Borstal Prison. Pardoned in 1939, he joined the Royal Armed Service Corps, where he earned another court-martial and dismissal for forgeries. Before reaching Britain from the Middle East where he had been stationed, he jumped ship, posed as a senior officer, and was commissioned in the South African Air Force until his past caught up with him. When not in trouble, Heath was regarded as a daring, confident, and highly charming officer—and a rake with women. After the third court-martial, he developed a taste for sadistic murder.

The notorious Charles Manson, who in the 1960s exhibited an uncanny ability to attract a devout cluster of unresisting followers, is another prototype of the psychopath at his worst. Still another is Henri Landau, also known as "Bluebeard," born in Paris in 1869 and hanged 51 years later, and who was said to have "loved" 283 women and murdered at least ten of them. Landau forged, swindled, seduced, and murdered, and he embarked on multiple occupational endeavors—including selling toys, practicing medicine and law, and engineering. His favorite procedure was to seduce women and charmingly persuade them to hand over their money and property for safekeeping.

Robert Hare (1970) outlines three subcategories of "psychopaths": the primary psychopath, the secondary "psychopath," and the dyssocial "psychopath." The latter two subcategories meld a heterogeneous group of antisocial individuals who comprise a large segment of the criminal population. Hare's secondary or neurotic psychopaths commit antisocial or violent acts because of severe emotional problems or inner conflicts. They are sometimes referred to as acting-out neurotics, neurotic delinquents, symptomatic psychopaths, or neurotic characters. The label "psychopath," as Hare agrees, is misleading because their behaviors and background have little if any similarity to those of primary psychopaths. The third group, dyssocial psychopaths, demonstrate the aggressive, antisocial behavior they have learned from their subculture, such as their gangs or families. They are also not true psychopaths. Hare's descriptions of the latter two categories match the socialized or subcultural delinquents or offenders and the emotionally disturbed offenders we referred to in Chapter 1; we will discuss them in detail later in the book. In the remainder of this chapter we will examine more closely the behavior, physiology, and background of the primary psychopath, whom we shall heretofore simply call the psychopath.

BEHAVIORAL DESCRIPTIONS

The most respected authority on the behavioral characteristics of the psychopath is Hervey Cleckley (1976), whose well-quoted text, The Mask Of Sanity, describes in clear and empirically useful terms the major behaviors demonstrated by the full-fledged psychopath, as distinct from the other psychopathic types referred to above.

Two of the psychopath's main features, Cleckley notes, are superficial charm and average to above-average intellectual ability, both of which are especially apparent during initial contacts. Psychopaths at first come across as friendly, outgoing, likeable, and alert. They often appear well-educated and knowledgeable, and they display many interests. Psychometric studies have indicated that they generally score higher on IQ tests than the general population (Hare, 1970), particularly on individually administered tests. In fact, Hare wryly comments, the psychopaths who were the sample for his studies were probably the least intelligent of their ilk, since they were not quite bright enough to avoid being convicted for their offenses. The tests were administered to imprisoned psychopaths.

Psychopaths also lack neurotic, psychotic, or emotional problems, such as excessive worry and anxiety, irrational thinking, delusions, severe depressions, or hallucinations. Even under high pressure conditions they will remain "cool" and calm, as did Ian Fleming's fictitious James Bond, a prime example. Feasibly, the doomed psychopath might enjoy a steak dinner with gusto just before being executed.

The infamous multiple murderer Herman W. Mudget, alias H.H. Holmes, retired at his normal hour the evening before his execution, easily fell asleep, slept soundly, and woke up completely refreshed. "I never slept better in my life," asserted Holmes to the cell guard after shaving and carefully dressing. He ordered and ate a substantial breakfast an hour before he was scheduled to be hanged. Throughout the entire ordeal, Holmes was remarkably calm and amiable, displaying no signs of depression or fear (Franke, 1975).

Closely related to this pattern is the psychopath's flat, emotional reaction and affect. Psychopaths may effectively mimic the appropriate emotions, but behind the façade there is no genuine feeling. Although they may relish practical jokes, they are often bizarre, inappropriate, or even cruel. Psychopaths lack genuine humor and, not surprisingly, the ability to laugh at themselves.

Psychopaths are unreliable, irresponsible, and unpredictable, regardless of the importance of the occasion or the consequences of their impulsive actions. This pattern is cyclical, and they may go for an extended period of time being responsible and reliable by paying bills regularly, being faithful to their spouses, or being reliable employees. They may even have great successes, be promoted, and gain honors, as did Demara and Heath. But suddenly, as skillfully as they have attained these socially desirable goals, they have an uncanny knack of unraveling their lives. They become irresponsible and may pass bad checks, embezzle money from the company computer with an impulsive, easily identifiable modus operandi, go on a drunken spree, or steal the boss's car and mate. Psychopaths may later say that they are sorry and plead for another chance—and most of them will probably get it. Invariably, if the psychopath is a young adult, the irresponsible behavior will return. Cleckley describes a potentially promising, brilliant physician in his early forties who was loved by his patients and had managed to develop a thriving practice during his "upswing" periods. His negative, psychopathic behaviors, however, were colossal blunders:

> This man's history shows a great succession of purposeless follies dating from early manhood. He lost several valuable hospital appointments by lying out sodden or by bursting in on serious occasions with nonsensical uproar. He was once forced to relinquish a promising private practice because of the scandal and indignation which followed an escapade in a brothel where he had often lain out disconsolately for days at a time.
>
> Accompanied by a friend who was also feeling some influence of drink he swaggered into his favorite retreat and bellowed confidently for women. Congenially disposed in one room, the party of four called for highballs. For an hour or more only the crash of glasses, scattered oaths, and occasional thuds were heard. Then suddenly an earnest, piercing scream brought the proprietess and her servants racing into the chamber. One of the prostitutes lay prostrate, clasping a towel to her breast, yelling in agony. Through her wails and sobs she accused the subject of this report of having, in his injudicious blunderings, bitten off her nipple. An examination by those present showed that this unhappy dismemberment had, in fact, taken place. Although both men had at the moment been in bed with her, the entertainer had no doubt as to which one had done her the injury.
>
> Feeling ran strong for a while, but, by paying a large sum as recompense for the professional disability and personal damage he had inflicted, the doctor avoided open prosecution. Before a settlement had been made, the guilty man attempted to persuade his companion to assume responsibility for the deed. It would be less serious for the other man, he argued, since his own prominence and professional standing made him a more vulnerable target for damaging courtroom dramatics and for slander. His companion, however, declined this opportunity for self-sacrifice with great firmness. (From Cleckley, Hervey: The Mask of Sanity, 5th ed., St. Louis, The C. V. Mosby Co., 1976, pp. 206–207.)

Impulsivity will prevent psychopaths who drift into criminal activities from performing like consistent, professional criminals. Lacking any long-term purpose in life, they will be unable to engage in professional, big-time crime, since they are likely to commit a major blunder before much time has lapsed. The professional criminal has purpose and a plan of action for his or her felonies; the psychopath is more likely to participate in capers and hastily planned frolics or serious crimes for immediate satisfaction.

Psychopaths have a remarkable disregard for truth and are therefore classic examples of the "pathological liar." They appear to have no internalized moral or ethical sense and cannot understand the purpose of being honest, especially if dishonesty will bring some personal gain. It should be emphasized that they have a cunning ability to appear straightforward, honest, and sincere, but their claims to sincerity are without substance.

One of the psychopaths' cardinal faults is their absolute lack of remorse or guilt for anything they do, regardless of the severity or immorality of their actions and irrespective of the traumatic effect of those actions on others. They often take considerable pleasure in the shock effects they engender with their admissions of guilt. They do not anticipate personal consequences and cannot appreciate predicaments. Psychopaths may engage in destructive or antisocial behavior with absurd risks and insignificant personal gain, such as forgery, theft, rape, brawls, and fraud. They will show no genuine remorse, whether they have bashed in someone's head, ruined a car, or tortured a child. They may well report they did it "for the hell of it."

Although above average in intelligence, psychopaths are usually incapable of learning to avoid failure and situations that are potentially damaging to themselves. In an effort to understand psychopathic behavior, some theorists have suggested that the self-destructive, self-defeating deeds and attitudes are a result of a need to be punished to mitigate the guilt psychopaths subconsciously experience, or more simply, that they are driven by a masochistic purpose. Evidence refuting these explanations will be elaborated upon later in the chapter.

Another principal trait of the psychopath is selfishness and an inability to love or give affection to others. According to Cleckley, egocentricity (self-centeredness) is *always* present in the psychopath and is essentially unmodifiable. Their inability to feel genuine, meaningful affection for another is absolute. Although outwardly likeable, they are seldom able to keep close friends and have great difficulty in understanding love in others. They are capable of likes and dislikes and may be highly skillful in pretending deep affection, but loyalty, warmth, and compassion are foreign to them. In addition, psychopaths usually do not respond to acts of kindness. They show capacity only for superficial appreciation. Paradoxically, they may do small favors and appear considerate; one prototype mowed the lawn for his elderly neighbor and slipped her some schnapps when she was ill—the next morning he stole her car.

Psychopaths have little capacity to see themselves as others perceive them. Instead of accepting the facts that would normally lead to insight, they project and externalize blame onto the community and the family for their misfortune. Interestingly, educated psychopaths have been known to speak fluently about the psychopathic personality, quoting the literature extensively and discussing research findings, but they cannot look into their own troublesome antics or mount a reasonable attack on their actions. They articulate their regrets for having done something, but the words are devoid of emotional meaning, a characteristic Cleckley calls semantic dementia. Johns and Quay (1962) remarked that psychopaths "know the words but not the music."

Small amounts of alcohol prompt most psychopaths to become vulgar, domineering, loud, and boisterous and to engage in practical jokes and pranks. Cleckley notes they choose pranks which have no appeal for most individuals and which at times seem directly calculated to place them in a "disgraceful position." The physiological reasons alcohol influences the behavior of the psychopath will be discussed in more detail later in the chapter.

Finally, an important behavioral distinction underlying much of Cleckley's description is what Quay (1965) refers to as the psychopath's profound and pathological stimulation seeking. According to Quay, the actions of the psychopath are motivated by an excessive *physiological* need for thrills and excitement. It is not unusual to see psychopaths drawn to such interests as race driving, skydiving, and motorcycle stunts.

SEX DIFFERENCES

Since the known population of psychopaths is dominated by men, little has been written about psychopathic women, although Hare did include them in some of his studies. One exception is a fifteen-year-long, extensive study by Samuel Guze (1976) on women in prison. The most frequent diagnosis of women felons, Guze notes, is psychopathy. A high percentage of the convicted female psychopaths were also regarded as alcoholic and/or hysterical. Hysteria is a personality disorder found almost exclusively in adolescent girls and young women. Its chief symptom is attention seeking, accompanied by an assortment of behaviors designed to obtain that attention: manipulative seductiveness, unusual friendliness, charm, and ostentatious grooming and dress. Guze reports that drug dependence was also significantly more frequent among arrested female psychopaths. Fifty-eight percent of them had drug abuse problems compared to 8 percent of the convicted female nonpsychopaths.

Guze found that the antisocial symptoms in the female psychopaths began around age eleven. Forty-two percent of the psychopaths had a history of juvenile arrests and records of frequent running away from home, and 65 percent demonstrated an arrest history for sexual misconduct, including prostitution, incest, homosexuality, and illegitimate pregnancies. Recidivism was greatest among psychopaths under age thirty. Seventy-two percent of the convicted female psychopaths who had ever married had been married at least once to a psychopath or an alcoholic.

There are few statistics on the ratio of male to female psychopaths. Robins (1966) reports that only 15 percent of the psychopaths in her study were female. They all followed the same behavioral patterns as males, except that they were more frequently involved in sexual misconduct. Seventy-nine percent of the females showed abnormally high sexual activity and "excessive" interest in sex matters. The median age of the onset of their psychopathic behavioral patterns was thirteen.

Cleckley (1976) describes "Roberta," a twenty-year-old psychopathic patient. The parents complained of their difficulty in understanding her. "'It's not that she seems bad or exactly that she means to do wrong,'" said her father. "'She can lie with the straightest face, and after she's found in the most outlandish lies she still seems perfectly easy in her own mind.'" Roberta stole small items from stores and relatives when she was ten, as if stealing were play. She often utilized ingenious ways of hiding and continuing her misdeeds. As an adolescent, Roberta began to buy dresses, cosmetics, candy, perfume, and other articles by charging them to her father without his awareness. Although her school work was mediocre, her intelligence was clearly superior. During her teens, she began to skip school and to stay out all night, alarming her parents, but admitting she was in the wrong. She demonstrated overt kindness to animals, but when her own dog was killed by a car she did not seem to care.

Roberta's truancy became intolerable to school officials, and she was expelled from high school. Her desperate parents sent her to a series of boarding schools, from which she was expelled or ran away. Back home, she added more habits to her repertoire—she borrowed money without paying it back and went to frequent late parties. Her father employed her as a bookkeeper in his business, where she used a good deal of ingenuity to embezzle considerable sums. Discussions with the family and friends did nothing to change her behavior, and she seemed entirely untroubled.

Up to this time, Roberta had had little interest in sex and had experienced only mild kissing and necking, which she said were "vaguely" pleasurable. She eventually ran away again, with no purpose except to wander around for extended periods of time. During this period, she discovered that prostitution was an effective way of obtaining money and a night's lodging. The police finally returned her to her home, and on meeting her parents she expressed affection, running to them and throwing herself in their arms. Although she said she was sorry for the distress she caused them, the penitence was free from actual feeling. She was unaffected by the inevitable gossip that surrounded her return to her small town. (From Cleckley, Hervey: The Mask of Sanity, 5th ed., St. Louis, The C. V. Mosby Co., 1976, pp. 46–55.)

BASIC PHYSIOLOGICAL CONCEPTS AND TERMINOLOGY

Contemporary research favors the view that psychopathic behavior results from an interaction between physiological and learning factors. It is important, therefore, that the student become familiar with some additional psychophysiological vocabulary and the basic structures of the nervous system, some of which we touched upon in Chapter 2. The concepts discussed here will lay the foundation for topics in later chapters as well.

The human nervous system can be divided into two major parts, either on the basis of structure or function. The easiest and clearest way to understand the nervous system is to make the divisions on the basis of structure, or "the way it looks physically."

Structurally, the nervous system includes the central nervous system (CNS) and the peripheral nervous system (PNS). The former consists of the brain and the spinal cord. The PNS refers simply to the nerve cells (called neurons) and nerve pathways outside the CNS. (See Table 3–1.) In other words, those nerves which leave the spinal cord and brain stem and travel to specific sites in the body comprise the peripheral (outside) nervous system. This outside system includes all the nerves connecting the muscles, skin, heart, glands, and senses to the CNS. The basic function of the PNS is to bring all the outside information to the CNS, where it is processed. Once the CNS has processed information, it relays the interpretation to the PNS if some action is necessary. When you place your finger on a hot object, the PNS relays this raw datum (it is not yet pain) to the CNS, which interprets the datum as the sensation of pain and, in return, relays a command to the PNS to withdraw the finger. The PNS cannot interpret, but only transmits information and communications.

TABLE 3-1
Divisions of Human Nervous System

I. Central Nervous System
   A. Brain
   B. Spinal Cord
II. Peripheral Nervous System
   A. Skeletal Nervous System (communicates with voluntary muscles)
   B. Autonomic Nervous System
      1. Parasympathetic (relaxes and deactivates after emergencies)
      2. Sympathetic (activates for emergencies)

Central Nervous System

Structurally, the CNS consists of the brain and spinal cord. Interpretations, thoughts, memories and images all occur in the cerebral cortex (the highest center of the brain). It is the processing center for stimulation and sensations received from the outside world and the body via the PNS. The cerebral cortex is the outer surface of the human brain and

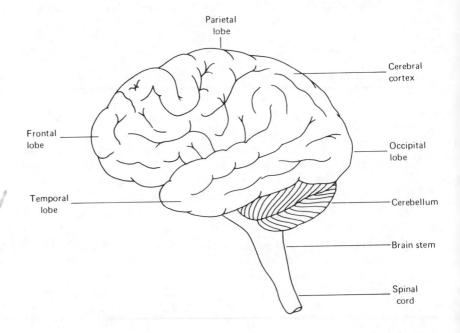

FIGURE 3–1. Illustration of central nervous system and major areas of cerebral cortex.

62

contains about 10 billion nerve cells or neurons (see Figure 3–1). Each neuron has a complicated communication link with numerous other neurons, creating an extremely complex and poorly understood communications network. The physical structures of the brain do not concern us here, but the electrical and arousal properties of the cortex are relevant to understanding the physiological electroencephalograms and psychological characteristics of the psychopath.

Electrical activity of the central nervous system was largely a curiosity until the German psychiatrist Hans Berger developed sophisticated equipment in the late 1920s enabling him to record oscillatory electrical potentials on the scalps of human subjects. This technique allowed researchers to study the electrical properties of the brain without discomfort to the subject and, eventually, accelerated investigations of the brain. Enthusiasm for Berger's work was slow in coming, however, and it was not until the early 1940s that electrical activity studies caught on. These electrical oscillations recorded from the cortex are known as electroencephalograms (EEGs): the device which records these EEGs is known as the electroencephalograph. Because of the oscillatory characteristics of the EEGs, they are commonly referred to as "brain waves."

Berger (1929) discovered that when EEG recordings were made of the relaxed adult, usually with eyes closed, the electrical activity generally oscillated between eight and thirteen cycles per second (CPS). This brain wave pattern appeared with some consistency under relaxed conditions, and Berger called the cycles *alpha* rhythms. Although these brain rhythms were easy to name and they occurred with some reliability, Berger was not sure what brain *function* he was actually recording. Investigators to this day remain uncertain as to the exact meaning of brain rhythms, despite the rapid technological advances in the capacity and potential of the recording hardware. Many researchers believe brain waves represent the synchronous, almost symphonic firing of billions of neurons, the purpose of which remains unknown. We do know, as did Berger, that the EEG is an everchanging reflection of the cortex's arousal levels and is sensitive to various changes in the external environment and mood and thought (internal environment) changes. By tapping this synchronous firing of neurons, researchers have learned the characteristics of the cortex during sleep, drug ingestion, development, and malfunction, such as epileptic seizures. Pertinent to our discussion here is the fact that EEG patterns have provided us with some clues about the psychopath's cortex functions.

Subsequent to Berger's findings, researchers were able to delineate several other cortical (adjective of cortex) rhythms. The *delta* rhythm spans one-half to three CPS, has high voltage, and indicates that the cortex is at its lowest stage of activity and arousal. The *theta* rhythm has four to seven CPS, less voltage than delta, and represents a stage slightly higher in cortical arousal than delta. Collectively, delta and theta are often referred to as *slow-wave activity* because of their relatively low frequency or oscillation rates. *Alpha* rhythms, which have eight to thirteen CPS, represent a higher level of cortical arousal than slow wave activity and are "normal" rhythm for the relaxed adult. *Beta* rhythms have nineteen to thirty CPS, low voltage, and reflect active cognitive processes, thinking, or general arousal states. Beta rhythms are sometimes referred to as "desynchronic" of alpha since they occur under conditions which block the occurrence of alpha. For example, if an EEG recording is being made while a person is relaxed with eyes closed and someone suddenly calls the person's name, there will be an immediate blocking of alpha with resultant beta rhythms. For our purposes, it is important to remember that beta reflects high states of cortical activity and arousal.

EEGs change with age, and the delta and theta rhythms that predominate in childhood give way to alpha and beta in normal adulthood, except during sleep, when the delta and theta patterns return. Throughout infancy, childhood, and adolescence the brain rhythms also become progressively more regular, and the cortex increases in potential for higher states of arousal. At birth brain rhythms are irregular and often nonexistent. During the first year, delta begins to occur with some regularity on both sides of the brain (Fois, 1961). After the first year, the theta rhythm dominates the EEG pattern, eventually giving way to alpha rhythms which begin to dominate at about age ten. The alpha gradually becomes regular and usually "matures" at around age fourteen. Beta rhythms develop at around age sixteen. The rhythms in the developing human are particularly susceptible to psychological stress and other factors in the environment. Highly irregular theta rhythms, for example, accompany older children having temper tantrums. They become more regular if the child lies down and calms down. The stages of sleep are also delineated on the basis of brain rhythms. The lighter stages of sleep are characterized by theta patterns while the deeper stages are reflected by delta patterns. Other things being equal, the more aroused and alert the cortex, the higher the frequency and the lower the voltage of the brain waves.

EEG Research on Psychopaths

The discovery that brain waves could be monitored prompted hypotheses about individual differences in those patterns, and experiments were devised to test them. In a pioneer study during World War II,

Hill and Watterson (1942) investigated the EEG patterns of 151 male British military personnel who were not adjusting to military service. The investigators divided the men into three classifications: 1. aggressive psychopaths, 2. mixed psychopaths, and 3. inadequate psychopaths. The groups actually represented heterogeneous clusters of personality disorders and obviously failed in many respects to meet Cleckley's criteria of psychopathy. However, one of the groups, the aggressive psychopaths, closely resembles our definition of the psychopath. This group also had a history of "violence to others regardless of the consequences, repeated destruction of property, or combinations of such kinds of aggressive impulsive behavior" (Hill & Watterson, 1942, p. 47). The results indicated that 65 percent of the 66 aggressive psychopaths demonstrated abnormal EEGs, compared to 15 percent for a group of "normals" used as controls. A majority of the abnormal EEGs were of a *slow-wave* variety—delta and theta; the control group exhibited the usual alpha and beta patterns.

This study prompted many other EEG studies on various kinds of behavioral disorders, including psychopathy. Subsequent studies of psychopaths have been consistent in revealing a significantly higher amount of EEG abnormality of a slow-wave variety in psychopaths (e.g., Craft, 1966; Hare, 1970). In a series of studies carried out by Knott, Platt, Ashy, and Gottlieb (1953), between 49 and 58 percent of the 700 psychopaths recorded had EEG abnormalities, mostly of a slow-wave variety. It should be pointed out that between 10 and 15 percent of the general population show abnormal EEGs, with "abnormal" being defined in a number of ways. Additional studies by Ehrlich and Keogh (1956) and Arthur and Cahoon (1963) also found that well over half of the psychopaths had abnormal EEGs, a majority reflecting slow-wave patterns.

Why slow-wave activity (immature brain-wave patterns) accompanies the EEG read-outs of a large number of psychopaths remains speculative and hypothetical. As mentioned earlier, what cortical functions the EEG represents remains an open question. It is also difficult to determine at present whether the EEG abnormalities generate psychopathic behavior or whether the psychopathic behavior causes EEG abnormality, because the studies have been correlational in design. It could be that neither one causes the other. Some researchers have argued that slow-wave activity represents delayed brain maturation (Hare, 1970). Since there is some evidence that EEG patterns of many psychopaths resemble the EEG pattern of children, it is arguable that the brain and cortical functioning of the psychopath is immature and childlike. Hare refers to this as the *maturation retardation hypothesis*. The hypothesis appeals because behavioral patterns of the psychopath—self-centeredness, impulsivity, inability to delay gratification, and inordinate stimulation seeking—resemble the behaviors of children. Interestingly, there is some evidence that, with increasing age, the immature EEG patterns of some psychopaths develop into mature ones, and there is a corresponding change toward more socially approved behavior (Gibbens, Pond, & Stafford-Clark, 1955). Robins (1966) found support for this observation, discovering that the change was most likely to occur between the ages of thirty and forty. It may be that the psychopath's cortical centers biologically mature later in life than those of the normal adult. It should be emphasized, however, that the EEG evidence to date is sketchy and fragmented, and considerably more data are necessary before a maturation retardation hypothesis receives widespread support.

Positive Spikes. In the late 1950s and early 1960s Niedermeyer (1963), among others, noticed that in highly aggressive individuals, including psychopaths, a brain rhythm of a different variety appeared with some regularity during sleep. Against a background of the usual slow-wave activity found in sleep, spontaneous bursts of brain waves with frequencies of six to fourteen CPS appeared in certain locations of the cortex (the temporal lobe) in 66 percent of the aggressive subjects. These people had a history of uncontrollable and violent episodes of destructive urges usually triggered by small, trivial slights. The aggressive explosions often resulted in extensive damage to property and injury or death to others. The brain-wave bursts are referred to as *positive spikes.* A number of researchers have suggested that positive spikes occur with some regularity in the EEGs of psychopaths who display explosive aggressive behavior (e.g., Kurland, Yeager, & Arthur, 1963). Most researchers have observed that following the aggressive episodes the perpetrator expresses no guilt for what he or she has done, although apparently fully aware of the violent act (Hare, 1970).

In summary, contemporary research focusing on central nervous system characteristics has revealed definite indications that the EEGs of psychopaths reflect inordinate amounts of abnormal brain-wave patterns, mostly of a childlike variety. These data further suggest that the psychopathic central nervous system is immature and does not develop fully until around age forty to forty-five.

Stimulation Seeking

Quay (1965) has suggested that the psychopath's behavior represents an extreme form of stimulation seeking. Physiologically, the psychopath does not receive the full impact of sensations from the environment. Therefore, in order to get the optimal amount of stimulation necessary to keep the cerebral cortex "satisfied," he or she must engage in greater amounts and more exciting forms of behavior.

A number of studies have supported Quay's hypothesis. For example, Wiesen (1965) found that psychopaths worked harder for visual (colored lights) and auditory (music on a radio) stimulation than did a group of nonpsychopaths. In a second experiment which provided continued bombardment of lights and music, Wiesen also demonstrated that nonpsychopaths worked harder than psychopaths to obtain three seconds of silence and relative darkness. In another study, Skrzpek (1969) delineated psychopaths and "neurotic delinquents" on the basis of a behavior rating list for psychopathy and neuroticism developed by Quay (1964). Skrzpek found that conditions that increased "cortical arousal" (e.g., where the subject was required to make difficult auditory discriminations) decreased preference for visual complexity in both the psychopathic and neurotic groups, but was most pronounced in the latter. On the other hand, a brief period of stimulus deprivation (presumably low cortical arousal) increased preference for complexity in both groups, but a significantly greater increase was shown by the psychopaths.

In an attempt to test Quay's hypothesis that pathological stimulation seeking derives from deficient responsivity of the nervous system, Whitehall (Whitehall et al., 1976) conducted an experiment utilizing 103 boring slides representing "concrete facades of a modern college campus building." Preadolescent subjects could control the rate of slide exposure while viewing them. From a group of 55 "disturbed" preadolescent boys, a group of eight psychopathic (antisocial) subjects and a group of eight neurotic subjects were selected by the professional staff at an institution. Another group of seven normals from outside the institution were chosen as controls. Ages were matched and averaged eleven and a half years. Results showed that the psychopathic and normal boys looked at the slides significantly less than the neurotic group. More importantly, the psychopathic preadolescents showed a significant decrease in viewing time earlier than the other groups, suggesting that they became bored more quickly than the other groups. The authors concluded that the data support the pathological stimulation seeking hypotheses and favored a physiological ingredient in the formulation of psychopathy. In another relevant project, Orris (1969) found that psychopathic boys showed poorer performance on a boring task requiring continous attention and that they engaged to a greater degree in boredom-relieving activities such as singing and talking to themselves.

Before continuing, it is important to have adequate understanding of two major concepts: 1. optimal arousal of the cerebral cortex and 2.

structures in the brain stem responsible for controlling the cortical arousal.

A number of theorists (e.g., Berlyne, 1960; Hebb, 1955; Fiske & Maddi, 1961) have postulated that organisms seek to maintain preferred or optimal levels of stimulation, where "stimulation" refers to the amount of sensation and/or information processed by the cortex. In effect, these theories argue for an inverted U-shaped function, with intermediate levels of stimulation most preferred and the extremes least preferred (see Figure 3–2). Insufficient amounts of stimulation lead to boredom, which can be reduced by an increase in stimulation-seeking behavior. On the other hand, exceptionally high levels of stimulation are also aversive and may promote behavior designed to avoid stimulation in an effort to bring the stimulus input to a more pleasurable level.

Cortical arousal appears to have a direct relationship with the amount of stimulation received by the cortex. Low stimulation produces a relatively low level of cortical arousal, whereas high levels of stimulation input initiate high cortical arousal.

Falling asleep requires that we lower the cortex's arousal level by minimizing external (noises, lights, etc.) and internal (thoughts) stimulation. If we do not wish to fall asleep, but our cortical arousal is low

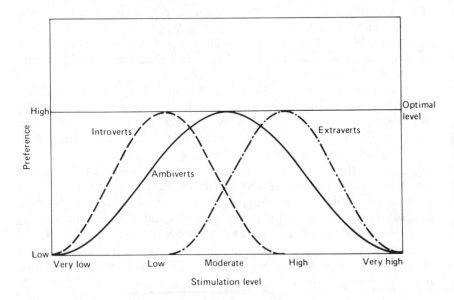

FIGURE 3-2. Optimal levels of stimulation for ambiverts, introverts, and extraverts. Note that introverts reach their optimal level sooner than ambiverts or extraverts do.

(e.g., boring lecture), we seek excitement to increase the arousal level. On the other hand, if stimulation becomes excessive, such as a loud, blaring TV, radio, or city street, we begin to "climb the walls" if we are unable to control the stimulus input. Some psychologists argue that a large segment of behavior can be explained as an attempt by the person to maintain optimal or "just-right" levels of stimulation—levels that are the most comfortable and pleasurable.

Just what constitutes an optimal amount of stimulation remains hypothetical, but there are certainly individual differences in the quality and quantity of stimulation necessary to reach the hypothetical optimum. Some of this individual difference may be a result of the functioning of certain physiological structures, particularly those mechanisms found in the brain stem. The reader will recall that Eysenck (1967) hypothesized that personality differences are in large part due to needs for stimulation, which are dictated by functional properties of the reticular formation.

The reticular formation can be conveniently divided into a number of anatomical areas. Chief among these is the reticular activating system (RAS), which is a tiny but complex nerve network located in the central portion of the brain stem. The RAS underlies our attentiveness to the world and acts as a sentinel which activates and maintains the general alertness of the cortex. Sensory signals or inputs from all parts of the body on their way to the processing center—the cortex—must first travel through the brain stem. Inside the brain stem, they branch into two major pathways (see Figure 2–3). One major pathway goes through a relay station known as the thalamus. The other travels through the RAS which, in turn, alerts the cortex for incoming information being routed through the thalamic pathway. The RAS-generated arousal is "nonspecific" in that it energizes the entire cortex and not any specific area. Therefore, any particular stimulation or sensation, from the outside world or from inside the body, has both a coded message (which travels through the thalamus) and a nonspecific arousing effect (which travels through the RAS). The RAS can also decrease cortical arousal. If certain incoming stimuli are no longer significant or relevant, the cortex dictates to the RAS to filter out that particular group of stimuli. The process is called adaptation or habituation. Therefore, repetitive and insignificant stimuli are prevented by the RAS from unnecessarily bombarding the cortex with meaningless detail.

Contemporary research and theory suggest that the psychopath has a pathological need for excitement and thrills because of some deficiency in or excessive habituation property of the RAS. The RAS either does not activate the cortex sufficiently to receive the full impact of the incoming information, or else it adapts too quickly, thereby shutting the cortex's activation down before it receives complete information. Either way, the psychopath is unable to reach optimal arousal levels with stimulation that normals find adequately arousing. So, the psychopath engages in behaviors that society refers to as thrill-seeking, chancy, antisocial, or inappropriate in order to reach satisfying cortical arousal.

The general concept of arousal has been used interchangeably with cortical arousal throughout the chapter. It should be noted, however, that many investigators refer to other forms of arousal, such as autonomic arousal (anxiety) or behavioral arousal in discussing psychopathy. Basically, they mean the same thing. Many states of activation or arousal involve overlapping systems (Korman, 1974). Thus, although there may be slightly different processes and mechanisms involved in different states of arousal, all arousal must involve the heightened arousal levels of the cortex. Therefore, the more general term "cortical arousal" is employed here to encompass all subclassifications of arousal.

In an interesting experiment, Chesno and Kilmann (1975) tested the arousal hypothesis of psychopathy by manipulating stimulation variables (aversive white noise and shock) and personality variables (psychopaths, neurotics, and normals). Ninety male offenders incarcerated in a maximum security penitentiary were selected for the experiment by various criteria. Psychopaths were classified according to Cleckley's criteria. The procedure involved an avoidance learning task, with electric shock being administered for certain incorrect choices by the subject. During the avoidance learning task, each subject received either 35, 65, or 95 decibels of white noise through earphones. White noise is an auditory stimulus which sounds like a hissing radiator.

If the arousal hypothesis is correct, the underaroused psychopath under low levels of stimulation should require some form of increased stimulation. Since errors in avoidance learning led to electric shock, psychopaths would be most likely to commit errors and benefit by the stimulation provided by the electric shock. Accordingly, as external stimulation increases (higher levels of white noise), the psychopath should have a decreased need for stimulation and, therefore, should learn to avoid the shock more effectively. The results of the study supported the hypothesis. Psychopaths made significantly more avoidance errors than the other groups as the stimulation decreased, which suggests they prefer punishment to boredom. The finding raises many questions about the well-known inability of psychopaths to benefit from punishment in situations low in stimulation, like prisons or even classrooms. That is, it might well be that the imprisoned psychopath would learn better in a stimulating situation.

Peripheral Nervous System

The PNS is subdivided into a *skeletal* division, the motor (movement) nerves that innervate the skeletal muscles involved in body movement, and an *autonomic* division, which controls heart rate, gland secretion, and smooth muscle activity. Smooth muscles are those muscles found in the blood vessels and gastrointestinal system; they appear "smooth" under a microscope in comparison to the skeletal muscles, which appear striped or textured.

The autonomic segment of the PNS is extremely important in our discussion of the psychopath, because here too research has consistently shown a significant difference between the psychopath's and the general population's reactivity or responsiveness to stimuli. The autonomic division is especially important because it activates emotional behavior and responsivity to stress and tension. Unfortunately for the student, the autonomic division can be further subdivided into the *sympathetic* and the *parasympathetic* segments. The sympathetic segment is responsible for activating or arousing the individual for "fight" or "flight" before (or during) fearful or emergency situations. The parasympathetic has the opposite effect of relaxing the individual after fearful or emergency situations. As the reader will recall, the psychopath presents a "James Bond coolness," even in times of very high stress. It is probable that either the sympathetic nervous system does not react sufficiently to stressful stimuli, or the parasympathetic system springs into action more rapidly than normal. As we shall see, there is support in the literature for both of these positions.

Before discussing in more depth the parameters of the autonomic nervous system which are found in psychopaths, we will go over the principles and techniques of measuring autonomic activity. Emotional arousal is largely under control of the autonomic nervous system, and it can be measured by monitoring the system's activity, such as heart rate, blood pressure or volume, and respiration rate. The most commonly used physiological indicator of emotional arousal, however, has been the skin conductance response (SCR), also known as the galvanic skin response (GSR). Since skin conductance response has been the label most advocated by contemporary researchers (Lykken & Venables, 1971) it will be used throughout this chapter.

SCR is simply a measure of the resistance of the skin to conducting electrical current. A number of factors in the skin influence its resistance, but perspiration appears to play a major role. Sweating corresponds very closely to changes in emotional states and has, therefore, been found to be a highly sensitive indicator of even slight changes in

71

the autonomic nervous system. Other things being equal, as emotional arousal increases, perspiration rate increases proportionately. Small changes in perspiration can be picked up and amplified by recording devices, known as polygraphs or physiographs. An increase in perspiration lowers skin resistance to electrical conductance. In other words, skin conductance increases as emotional arousal (anxiety, fear, etc.) increases.

We learned earlier that psychopaths lack the capacity to respond emotionally to stressful or fearful situations. Essentially, they give the impression of being anxiety-free and present a carefree, cool, devil-may-care demeanor. We would expect, therefore, that compared to the normal population, the psychopath has a comparatively underactive, underaroused autonomic nervous system. What has the research literature revealed?

Autonomic Nervous System Research. In a well-known study, David T. Lykken (1957) hypothesized that 1. since anxiety reduction is an essential ingredient in learning to avoid painful or stressful situations, and 2. the psychopath is presumed to be anxiety-free, then 3. the psychopath should have special difficulty learning to avoid unpleasant things. The reader will recall that two of the characteristic features of psychopaths are their inability to learn from unpleasant experiences and their very high recidivism. Lykken was careful to delineate his groups according to Cleckley's criteria. His psychopathic groups were drawn from several penal institutions in Minnesota (both male and female) and classified as either primary psychopaths or neurotic psychopaths. College students made up a third group called "normals."

The design of the experiment included an electronic maze the subjects were expected to learn as well as possible in twenty trials. There were twenty points of choice in the maze; each had four alternatives, only one of which was the correct choice. Although three of the alternatives were incorrect, one of these incorrect alternatives would give the subject a rather painful electric shock. Lykken was primarily interested in discovering how quickly subjects learned to avoid the electric shock (avoidance learning). He reasoned that avoidance learning would be rewarded by the reduction of anxiety upon encountering the point of choice, but since psychopaths are assumed to be deficient in anxiety, it was hypothesized that their performance would be significantly worse than that of normals. The hypothesis was correct.

Prior to the maze portion of the experiment, Lykken had measured the skin conductance changes of each subject while he or she tried to sit quietly for 30 to 40 minutes. During this time, the subjects would periodically hear a buzzer and occasionally receive a brief electric shock several seconds after the buzzer. Eventually, the buzzer became associated with the shock. In normal individuals the onset of the buzzer would come to produce an anxiety response in anticipation of the electric shock (classical conditioning) and would be reflected by a substantial increase in SCR.

The results clearly demonstrated that psychopaths were not only incapable of learning to avoid the painful electric shocks, but also that their skin conductance, compared to normals, was considerably less responsive to stress. The data indicate that psychopaths do in fact have an underresponsive autonomic nervous system and, as a result, do not learn to avoid aversive situations as well as most other people. Is this the basic reason that psychopaths continue to get into trouble with the law despite the threat of imprisonment?

Schachter and Latané (1964) pursued the finding further by using the same apparatus and basic procedure as Lykken, except for one major revision. Each subject was run through the maze twice, once with an injection of a harmless saline solution, and once with an injection of adrenaline, a hormone which stimulates physiological arousal. The subjects were prisoners at Stillwater State Prison in Minnesota and Bordentown Reformatory in New Jersey, selected on the basis of how closely they approximated Cleckley's criteria and how incorrigible they were, as measured by the number of offenses and time in prison. Prisoners high on these factors qualified as primary psychopaths, while those relatively low were regarded as normal prisoners.

The experiment found that injections of adrenaline dramatically improved the performance of the psychopath in the avoidance learning task compared to psychopaths who had received an innocuous saline solution. In fact, psychopaths with the adrenaline injection did better in learning to avoid shocks than did the normal prisoners with a similar injection. On the other hand, psychopaths who had saline injections were as deficient in avoidance learning as Lykken's psychopaths. Since anxiety is presumed to be a major deterrent to antisocial impulses, the manipulation of arousal or anxiety states by drugs has far-reaching potential in terms of effective treatment for psychopaths. Specific drugs apparently have the potential to increase the emotional level of psychopaths equivalent to that found in the general population.

Subsequent investigations by Robert Hare (1965a, 1965b) found that primary psychopaths have significantly lower skin conductance while resting than do nonpsychopaths. In a major study, Hare (1968) divided 51 inmates at the British Columbia Penitentiary into three groups— primary psychopaths, secondary psychopaths, and nonpsychopaths— and studied them under various conditions while constantly monitoring their autonomic functioning. The experimental conditions also permitted the observation of a complex physiological response known as the orienting response (OR).

The OR is a nonspecific, highly complicated cortical and sensory response to strange, unexpected changes in the environment. The response may take the form of a turning of the head, a dilation of the pupil of the eye, a decrease in heart rate, etc., and it is made in an effort to determine what the change is. Pavlov referred to the OR as the "what-is-it" reflex. It is an automatic, reflexive accompaniment to any perceptible change, and it can be measured by various physiological indices. The OR produces, among other things, an increase in the analyzing powers of the senses and the cortex.

Hare's experiment found that not only did psychopaths exhibit very little autonomic activity (skin conductance and heart rate), but also that they gave smaller ORs than did nonpsychopaths. His data suggest that psychopaths are less sensitive and alert to their environment, particularly to new and unusual events.

Hare has recently reported intriguing data relating to the heart or cardiac activity of the psychopath. The conclusions summarized above were based on skin conductance data, but when cardiovascular variables are considered, some apparent anomalies appear. While skin conductance is consistently low, cardiac activity (heart rate) in the psychopath is often as high as that found in the nonpsychopathic population (Hare & Quinn, 1971). Hare says ". . . the psychopaths appeared to be poor electrodermal (skin conductance) conditioners but good cardiovascular ones" (Hare, 1976, p. 135). That is, although psychopaths do not learn to react to stimuli as measured by skin variables, it appears that they learn to react autonomically as well as nonpsychopaths when the heart rate is measured.

Hare suggests that the psychopath might be more adaptive to stress by bringing into play "psychophysiological defense mechanisms," thereby reducing the impact of stressful stimuli. He and his colleagues designed experiments in which the heart rate could be monitored throughout the experimental session. In one experiment, a tone preceded an electric shock by about ten seconds (Hare & Craigen, 1974). In anticipation of the electric shock, psychopaths exhibited a rapid acceleration of heart beat, followed by a rapid deceleration of heart rate immediately before the onset of the noxious stimulus (a "normal" reaction is a gradual but steady increase in heart rate until the shock), but their skin conductance remained significantly lower than that found in nonpsychopaths. Therefore, psychopaths appeared to be superior conditioners when cardiac activity was measured, indicating that they do indeed either learn or inherit autonomic adaptability to noxious stimuli. Hare suggests that this accelerative heart response is adaptive and helps the psychopath tune out or modulate the emotional impact of noxious stimuli. This, he speculates, may be the reason that skin conductance responses are relatively low in the psychopath.

If psychopaths are generally underaroused, then we would expect that lie detection equipment and procedures, which are based on physiological reactivity to questions, would not be able to differentiate deceptive responses from truthful ones in the psychopath. Also, deceptive responses should be easy for psychopaths, since they are very adept at manipulating and deceiving others. In an early study, David Lykken (1955) found that psychopaths emitted similar skin conductance responses regardless of whether they were lying or telling the truth, which is exactly what we would expect. On the other hand, nonpsychopaths gave significant differences in reactivity. In other words, their lie ratios, as reflected by skin conductance, were larger than those of the psychopaths. Because of the artificial atmosphere of the laboratory compared to real-life situations, particularly highly stressful ones, Lykken admonished against uncritical acceptance of his findings until further testing. However, very few studies in recent years have directly examined the relationship between psychopathy and lie detection, and the matter was temporarily put aside.

More recently David Raskin and Robert Hare (1978) re-examined the Lykken study using more sophisticated equipment and better standardization for lie detection. Using 24 psychopathic prisoners and 24 nonpsychopathic prisoners, they found that psychopaths were as easily detected at lying as were nonpsychopaths in a mock crime scene involving a $20 "theft."

This contradictory finding underscores the fine tuning that is still needed for the understanding of the physiological characteristics of the psychopath. There is evidence, for example, that sufficiently aroused or motivated psychopaths will give physiological responses to interesting events which equal the reactions of nonpsychopaths (Hare, 1968). On the other hand, when it comes to highly stressful, serious occasions, psychopaths appear to have incomparable skill at attenuating guilt or fearful reactions (Lykken, 1978). The simulated crime scene in the Raskin-Hare experiment was not only relatively unstressful, but also the "game" may have interested the psychopath. It appears that the acid test for the lie detection hypothesis rests with carefully designed experiments under real-life, highly stressful situations. With the present data, conclusions cannot be made.

Let us sum up the experimental findings reviewed thus far on the autonomic functioning of the psychopath. First, results indicate that psychopaths are both autonomically and cortically underaroused, both under rest conditions and under some specific stress conditions. It appears that they are much more physiologically "drowsy" than nonpsychopaths. Secondly, because psychopaths lack the necessary emotional equipment, they appear deficient in avoidance learning, which might account partially for the very high recidivism they exhibit. Third, some data suggest that if emotional arousal can be induced, such as by adrenaline, psychopaths can learn from past experiences and avoid normally painful or aversive situations, such as jail, embarrassment, or social censure.

As noted earlier, psychopaths are profoundly affected by alcohol, even in small amounts. Alcohol is a general depressant, decreasing arousal levels in the nervous system. Research indicates that the under-aroused psychopath is already half asleep and "in the bag" and alcohol has the general effect of putting him or her entirely in the bag. Therefore, we would not only expect that the psychopath would get intoxicated more rapidly than a nonpsychopath of comparable weight, but also that the psychopath would have a greater probability of "passing out" sooner. We would also expect that the psychopath would have fewer sleep difficulties. Unfortunately, not enough data have been accumulated in these areas to make any conclusive statements.

CHILDHOOD OF THE PSYCHOPATH

We have discussed the behavioral descriptions and physiological components of psychopaths. Now, how did they get that way? The most popular notion about crime and behavioral problems is that they begin in the home, usually as a result of inadequate discipline or improper upbringing. From our discussion of the physiological components of psychopaths, however, it is obvious that the answer is not that simple. It seems that psychopathy is a result of a complex interaction between physiological factors, situations, and learning factors. Cleckley (1976) comments that relatively homogeneous classifications of psychopathy do exist, but he is not convinced of any common precursors found in family background.

The argument for the inclusion of neurophysiological factors as causal candidates in the development of psychopathy does not necessarily mean that these factors are hereditary. There is, in fact, very little evidence at present in support of a strong genetic influence. It is entirely possible, however, that psychopaths are born with a biological predisposition to develop the disorder. That is, similar to the Eysenckian position, it might be that psychopaths have a nervous system which interferes with rapid conditioning and association between transgression and punishment. Because of this inability, the psychopath fails to develop the usual anticipation of punishment and, hence, guilt. It is also possible, however, that certain aspects of the psychopath's nervous system have failed to mature; or, as another possibility, a lack of oxygen at birth may have adversely affected the RAS, independent of genetic predisposition.

It appears that psychopathy can be identified early. In a poll of Canadian psychiatrists, 12.7 percent were convinced that the psychopath could be diagnosed prior to age eight, and another 66 percent believed that the disorder could be identified before age eighteen (Gray & Hutchinson, 1964). In a longitudinal study conducted by Robins (1966), clinical records verified that 95 percent of the adult psychopaths investigated had demonstrated psychopathic behaviors 30 years previously, as children. After an extensive review of the literature, Quay (1972) notes that psychopathic behaviors found in adults are probably labeled "conduct disorders" or "excessive aggressiveness" in children. Childhood behaviors eliciting those labels include disobedience, disruptiveness, fighting, temper tantrums, irresponsibility, and attention seeking.

Earlier, we reviewed the evidence indicating that the psychopath is physiologically underresponsive and underaroused and thus has higher than normal needs for stimulation and stimulus input. If this behavior is based on some dysfunction of the nervous system, there is every reason to expect that we will find this same responsivity in children. Recent research has begun to link the psychopath's inordinate stimulation needs with the behavior of the hyperactive child, and it has been suggested that that child may be a *candidate* for psychopathy.

Hyperactivity

The hyperactive child is described as exhibiting excessive motor activity in situations which require less movement (such as in the classroom), impulsivity, temper tantrums, antisocial behavior, and learning difficulties, which usually result from the previous behaviors. A stimulant drug regimen is often prescribed to relieve the excessive activity. The use of stimulant drugs to control hyperactive children is referred to as having a "paradoxical effect," since it would be expected that stimulants would increase rather than decrease motor activity. Stimulants, however, appear to have the specific effect of influencing the RAS and other brain-stem structures by improving their efficiency and allowing more arousal and/or information to reach the cortex (e.g., Bartol, 1975).

If hyperactive children are plagued by low cortical arousal, they will require greater amounts of stimulation to reach their optimal level of arousal. Cantwell (1975) points out that hyperactive children do not display greater amounts of motor activity in the playground, but in such places as the classroom, where they are required to control stimulus input. During these periods it is likely that the arousal level drops below the normal requirement. Thus, the underaroused child will seek increased amounts of stimulation and excitement; one way of getting this is by "cutting up" in the classroom and by upsetting others. This behavior, the reader will note, is very similar to the behavioral pattern of the adult psychopath.

If the child receives adequate stimulus input, such as would be encouraged by stimulant drugs affecting the activity of the RAS, he or she would no longer need the surplus activity and would have less demand for stimulation and personal attention. This explanation would account for the fact that treatment of hyperactive children by using behavior modification in the classroom has been largely ineffective and why there has been a heavy reliance on drugs. In this regard, Feingold (1974) makes the provocative assertion that synthetic flavorings and coloring found in commercial foodstuffs affect the RAS by lowering its efficiency. It is Feingold's contention that hyperactive children have a negative reaction to these synthetic additives and need more stimulation than normal to reach proper levels of arousal. Could this also be the case for adult psychopaths?

In his extensive review of the literature on hyperactive children, Cantwell (1975) finds a common thread between adult psychopathy and childhood hyperactivity. He states, "Recent research on waking autonomic functions and EEG patterns in sociopathic adults and in hyperactive children suggest that both groups may have the same underlying neurophysical abnormality: lower levels of basal resting physiological activation than age-matched normals . . . . It would also suggest that . . . there may be a genetically transmitted neurophysiological abnormality that leads to hyperactivity in childhood and sociopathy in adulthood" (Cantwell, 1975, p. 199).

Mendelson (Mendelson et al., 1971) interviewed the mothers of 83 children, ages twelve to sixteen, who had been at a clinic several years previously and, at that time, were diagnosed hyperactive. Seventy-five percent of the children were still exhibiting hyperactive behavior at follow-up, and the chief complaints of their mothers were that the children had a "rebellious attitude" and general incorrigibility. Twenty-two percent of the children continued to demonstrate a long history of antisocial behavior and seemed destined to become psychopaths. Approximately 60 percent had had contact with the police, 17 percent on at least three occasions. Twenty-five percent of this group had been referred to juvenile court. More than a third of the 83 children had threatened to kill their parents, 7 percent carried weapons, and 15 percent had set fires. A similar finding was reported by Weiss (Weiss et. al., 1971), who conducted a five-year follow-up of hyperactive children when they became adolescents. The chief complaint of 70 percent of the mothers was "emotional immaturity." Thirty percent of the children had no steady friends at follow-up. Twenty-five percent continued to have a long history of antisocial behavior, 16 percent had been referred to court, and 3 percent were placed in a "reform school."

Thus, it appears very likely that childhood hyperactivity is a precursor of at least some adult psychopathy, underscoring the physiological involvement in the disorder. In general, however, there are disappointingly few studies directed at neurophysiological components of potential psychopaths during early childhood, unless we consider the expanding literature on hyperactive children. Several studies have found that 40 to 50 percent of the hyperactive children have abnormal EEGs (Satterfield, 1973; Capute et al., 1968; Hughes et al., 1971) with abnormal slow-wave activity being the most common finding. The reader will recall that this cortical feature is also common in adult psychopathy. In a series of studies, Satterfield (Satterfield & Dawson, 1971; Satterfield et al., 1974) found that many hyperactive children consistently demonstrated low skin conductance levels; the lower their skin conductance level the greater the restlessness, hyperactivity, and impulsiveness reported by their teachers. The children showing the lowest arousal (lowest skin conductance and cortical arousal as measured by EEGs) were most responsive to stimulants (methylphenidate). Following methylphenidate treatment, the underaroused children showed a significant increase in arousal as measured by skin conductance and EEGs and a decrease in motor activity.

Satterfield (1975, p. 78) hypothesized that hyperactivity results from "low arousal and insufficient inhibitory controls over motor outflow and sensory input." He believes that this lack of inner control results in an overwhelming increase in sensory activity reaching the cortex. Thus, the highly aroused cortex is overloaded by both relevant and irrelevant stimuli, and the individual loses control over what stimuli should dictate his or her behavior. It is difficult to accept this hypothesis, however, when we consider the conceptual gap between consistent findings of underarousal and Satterfield's contention of overarousal, plus the arousing effects of stimulant drugs on the RAS and cortical arousal. It would seem to be more a matter of stimulus deprivation than overstimulation.

Parental Loss

A significant portion of the research literature suggests that psychopathy is principally a result of a faulty family environment, and researchers have vied with each other to reach an appreciation of precisely what the fault is. In a background study done by Greer (1964) on subjects attending a psychiatric clinic in Perth, Western Australia, parental loss was found to have been experienced by 60 percent of the 79 psychopaths studied. That figure compared to 28 percent of the 387 neurotic subjects and 27 percent of the 691 normal subjects. Parental loss was defined as the complete loss or continuous absence of one or both natural parents for a least twelve months prior to age fifteen. It should be noted, however, that the psychopaths were classified according to the American Psychiatric Association's labeling in 1952, and thus probably included a rather heterogeneous group of "psychopaths." It is interesting that 1. significantly more female than male psychopaths had experienced parental loss, 2. a large proportion of the psychopaths experienced the parental loss before age five, and 3. psychopaths as a group were much more likely to have lost both parents. It has also been reported that the parental loss is more likely to be paternal than maternal (Oltman & Friedman, 1967), and that the more severe the psychopathic behavior, the more likely there is to be parental loss in the individual's background (Craft et al., 1964).

Although parental rejection or loss was found in a substantial number of other studies, many of these used different criteria in defining psychopathy. Hare (1970) also points out that most of the studies relied on biased and retrospective data, by obtaining background information from the psychopath (who is a far from reliable source), or parents, relatives, and friends. The information gathered is after the fact and likely to be distorted to make the facts fit the behavior.

Buss (1966) described two types of parental behavior which he felt are conducive to psychopathic patterns. In the first type, the parents are cold and distant to the child, allowing no close relationship to develop. In the second type of parental behavior, discipline, rewards, and punishment are inconsistent and capricious. Instead of learning right from wrong, the child learns to avoid blame and punishment by lying or by other manipulative means.

After an extensive overview of the subject, McCord and McCord came to the conclusion: "extreme emotional deprivation or moderate rejection coupled with other environmental conditions or with neural damage to inhibitive centers, best account for the development of psychopathy" (McCord & McCord, 1964, p. 87). In addition, it was the McCords' feeling that all psychopaths to some degree have experienced parental rejection, and that a substantial number have some undefined malfunction in the nervous system.

Cleckley (1976) rebels at this approach, asserting that the entire notion of parental loss and rejection has been oversold, and he is skeptical about any consistent family background pattern emerging from the research. A very large percentage of the psychopaths he has studied exhibit backgrounds which appear to be happy and conducive to excellent adjustment. Cleckley feels that, if there is a negative element in family background, it has been extremely subtle and abstruse. He suggests an incapacity on the part of the parents for simple warmth, for the "true intimacy that seems to be essential for biologic soundness (substantiality) in some basic relationships" (Cleckley, 1976, p. 411). He explains that parents may be fair, kind, and genial and demonstrate other superior qualities, but lack that one subtle but essential ingredient necessary to develop basic warmth and feeling in the child. Moreover, that one special quality may be nearly impossible to isolate for purposes of experimental study.

According to Phares (1972), one plausible explanation of psychopathy related to background is parental pampering and overindulgence. The child has been allowed to escape punishment for his or her antisocial and aggressive behavior by apologizing or promising not to do it again. Thus, the child learns to be exceptionally skillful in manipulating others by suitable verbalizations and by being "cute." Phares contends the main problem is that parents reinforce the antisocial behavior by allowing the child to receive rewards and escape punishment (also highly rewarding) for psychopathic behaviors. In addition, such a child rarely has to endure frustration or delayed gratification, since parents cater to every whim. The child will likely carry these useful behaviors into adulthood.

Although Phares' hypothesis is oversimplified, it appears likely that, in combination with a physiologically based need for stimulation, parental and other social response to those needs play a prominent role. In the extensive longitudinal study reported by Robins (1966) referred to earlier, the developmental history of 524 patients who had contact with a psychiatric clinic 30 years earlier was followed. One observation was that most of the psychopaths had fathers who were either psychopathic or alcoholic. Robins points out that three of the consequences of having an antisocial, ineffectual father are the inconsistent discipline he provides, marital discord, and a faulty model for the child. Interestingly, Robins did not find a significant relationship between parental rejection and loss and psychopathic behavior.

To sum up the family background data on the psychopath, it seems that if the parents were absent from the home, ineffectual or inconsistent in their discipline—or if they were psychopathic themselves—the chances were far greater that the psychopath would not have learned appropriate behavior, considering his or her difficulty learning in the first place. A typical developmental pattern would be hyperactivity in early childhood, probably accompanied by learning disability, a behavioral problem in the middle school years, juvenile delinquency as an adolescent, and a psychopathic or antisocial personality disorder in adulthood. While this pattern is emerging, the psychopathic personality learns, by reward, how to manipulate others verbally. The words "I'm sorry" or "I won't do it again" take on strong reinforcing properties, despite their insincerity.

Obviously, many children who exhibit these stimulation seeking, hyperactive behaviors do not become adult psychopaths. This is probably due, at least in part, to how their parents respond to their pranks, mischief, and excitement. It is likely that these parents are effective models who are consistent in discipline and, more importantly, do not use avoidance learning in their child-rearing practices. Rather than rely exclusively on punishment and threat, since the children do not respond to this approach, they apply reinforcement techniques in a consistent manner to reward appropriate behavior.

SUMMARY

The primary or true psychopath should be distinguished from people who may be classified as psychotic, neurotic, or emotionally disturbed. Primary psychopaths most often function in society as charming, daring, witty, intelligent individuals, high on charisma but low on emotional reaction and affect. If criminals, they become the despair of law enforcement officials, because their crimes appear to be without the usual motivation. Even worse, they show no remorse or ability to be rehabilitated. The research is consistent in portraying them as pathological stimulation seekers, even in childhood, and as individuals who possess a remarkable ability to adapt to stress.

We reviewed most of the physiological research which indicates that the psychopath is "different" from the rest of the population on a number of physiological measures. The psychopath is underaroused, both autonomically and cortically, a finding which may account for his or her difficulty in learning the rules of society. Recalling our discussion of Eysenck's theory in Chapter 2, it is clear that the psychopath would be a stable extravert with high psychoticism. The psychopath, like the extravert, is not aroused enough to profit as easily from the classical conditioning that sets most of us on the straight and narrow path in childhood. If, in addition to this physiological lack, the psychopath's family situation leaves him or her without effective models, then he or she is doubly cursed.

Many psychopaths also have abnormal brain-wave patterns, mostly of a slow-wave childlike variety, which suggestss that their nervous system is immature; it usually does not develop sufficiently until middle age. There are indications of more than the usual amounts of positive spikes, which are brain-wave bursts that correlate with aggressive episodes and impulsivity. Research has failed to discover, however, whether these abnormalities generate psychopathic behavior or vice-versa. There is also little evidence to support a strong hereditary influence, although we should not overlook the possibility that psychopaths may be born with a biological *predisposition* to the disorder.

Studies on the childhood of psychopaths indicate that it is likely that they followed the hyperactive syndrome as children causing chaos for parents and teachers (although it would be folly to maintain that the hyperactive child of today is the psychopath of tomorrow!). Partly because they are physiologically underaroused, psychopaths do not respond well to admonishment, threats, or actual punishment as do their nonpsychopathic peers. They do not learn society's expectations and the rules of right and wrong because anxiety-inducing discipline procedures are not at all anxiety-inducing. As we shall see in the chapter on treatment, however, psychopaths probably would respond well to positive reinforcement techniques.

There are still numerous gaps in our knowledge of the psychopath, one being in the area of sex differences. Research on female psychopaths is scant. The available data indicate behavioral characteristics for females are similar to those of male psychopaths, with slightly more emphasis among females on sexual acting-out behavior. This probably reflects a cultural bias, however, since women have been traditionally chastised more than men in that regard. Data on physiological measures of the female psychopath are simply not available and represent a rich potential for future research.

KEY CONCEPTS FOR REVIEW

Sociopath
Primary psychopath
Neurotic psychopath
Dyssocial psychopath
Slow-wave activity
Maturation-retardation hypotheses
Positive spikes
Cortical arousal
SCR
Underaroused autonomic nervous system
Hyperactivity
Parental loss

MAJOR THEORISTS AND RESEARCHERS

Hare
Cleckley
Guze
Lykken

SUGGESTED READINGS

Cleckley, H. *The mask of sanity*, (5th ed.) St. Louis: Mosby, 1976.
A well-written, fascinating presentation of the psychopath, primarily in the form of case studies.

Hare, R. *Psychopathy: Theory and research*. New York: Wiley, 1970.
A readable review of the physiological, psychological, and social research on the psychopath.

McCord, W., and McCord, J. *The psychopath: An essay on the criminal mind*. Princeton, N.J.: Van Nostrand, 1964.
A classic book on the distinguishing features of the psychopath.

Smith, R.J. *The psychopath in society*. New York: Academic Press, 1978.
A humanistic review of the research on the psychopath.

PSYCHOSOCIAL FACTORS: THE SOCIALIZED OFFENDER

FOUR

However petty a criminal act may be, it carries with it a promise of change in a favorable direction.

Halleck, 1967, pp. 76–77

Heredity and physiological elements play significant roles in the development of criminal behavior, as we saw in Chapters 2 and 3. In part, they account for individual differences in susceptibility to *classical conditioning*. Certain personalities (e.g., extraverts) do not condition as readily as other personalities (e.g., introverts). Moreover, we have seen that the capacity to be conditioned strongly affects fear of reprisal, which in turn inhibits socially undesirable or criminal behavior.

But using susceptibility to classical conditioning to explain criminality has its limitations. One problem is that it conceives of the human being as an automaton. Pair a neutral stimulus with a closely following painful event and the alert, intact "robot" will eventually associate or connect the stimulus with the painful event. Undoubtedly, this sequence is a very powerful factor in many behaviors, but it is by no means the whole story in the development of criminal behavior.

People do not come into situations empty headed, and any given situation is likely to differ from other situations in numerous respects. People have a vast store of living experiences and an extensive repertoire of ways to react to events. Thus, it is crucial that we regard criminals as active problem solvers who perceive, interpret, and respond to their environments in unique ways. The environment may include living conditions, opportunity to learn behavior, and the significant persons in one's life. If we consider criminal behavior as subjectively adaptive rather than simply "deviant," we might have even greater success discovering its causes. In this sense, illegal conduct is a response pattern which the person has found effective in a particular set of circumstances. Engaging in criminal behavior might be what one person sees as the only way to adapt or survive under physically or psychologically dire conditions. Another person may decide that violence is the only way to defend honor, protect self, or reach a personal goal. In either case, the person is deciding what is his or her best alternative for that situation.

Violent crimes of assault and homicide are often regarded as irrational, unpredictable, explosive, and therefore resistant to analysis (e.g., President's Commission on Law Enforcement and Administration of Justice, 1967). Holding this view is a serious mistake. The decision to act violently may be extremely quick, but it is not necessarily irrational or unpredictable—in fact, it rarely is. It is more often true that people behave violently because the violent approach has, for various reasons, proved effective in similar situations for themselves or for others they have observed. Under stressful or conflictful conditions, they may become disorganized in their response patterns, but it is important to realize that they have an expectancy about what the behavior—even disorganized, violent behavior—will accomplish. It is entirely possible that such persons have learned or observed that violence achieves certain personal goals a certain percentage of the time. Also, these persons may believe that they have very few alternatives in stressful, conflictful situations. Therefore, if they desire to alter what is happening, they may see violence as the only way. For example, lower socioeconomic or poorly educated people may not have acquired adequate verbal or social skills for dealing with conflictful situations, but they may have acquired the more primitive, physical, direct competencies, such as punching, stabbing, or shooting. In fact, it has been shown that often both the victim and assailant in a crime have in their pasts customarily relied on direct physical means to alter squabbles. Thus, what may appear to be explosive, irrational acts of violence to others may represent "natural" modes of conduct the person believes will work in resolving conflict.

All criminal behavior is learned, and some people, because of different personal attributes and experiences, learn it better than others. All three types of learning we shall examine shortly play substantial roles in the acquisition of criminal behavior and, depending upon the behavior, one type may play a greater role than the others.

The study of learning has had a long and sometimes controversial history. Learning theorists have discovered that what at first appears to be simple becomes increasingly complicated under empirical scrutiny. The problem we uncover is frequently greater than the problem we set out to solve. Voluminous data have been reported and analyzed, and numerous concepts have been developed and communicated in sophisticated and highly specific terminology. For our purposes, we will focus only on some of the more general aspects of learning as it relates to crime, avoiding most of the technical language, but keeping the basic content intact.

Most psychologists would accept the definition of learning advanced by Kimble (1961): *Any relatively permanent change in behavior produced by experience.* That rather general definition covers the three types of learning outlined in this book. The first, classical conditioning, was discussed along with Eysenck's theory of criminality. We also mentioned instrumental learning, but noted that, in Eysenck's view, it took a back seat to classical conditioning. In this chapter we will pay particular attention to the relationship between instrumental learning and criminal behavior. We will also discuss social learning, which is important because it helps us distinguish the reflexive and mechanistic learning characteristic of lower animals from the complex, varied processes of the human being. The three types of learning overlap and are far from being independent. Most complex human behaviors appear to be combinations of the learning types built up over years of practice and experience, and it is not easy to separate the learning process into neat components. Here we have divided learning into three segments for conceptual clarity and to organize the presentation, but it is important to remember that they interact and influence one another.

INSTRUMENTAL LEARNING

People do things to receive rewards or avoid punishment. This simple observation forms the basis of instrumental learning, which is probably the easiest type to understand. Behavior which enables us to obtain rewards or avoid punishing circumstances is likely to be repeated when similar conditions recur. The rewards may be either physical (e.g., material goods, money), psychological (e.g., feelings of significance or control over one's fate), or social (e.g., improved status). Even behaviors that society considers antisocial or criminal may be highly desirable for

ual if he or she gains reward from them and if the chances of
...ing the rewards are greater than the chances of being punished.
Rewards and avoidance of punishment are forms of *reinforcement for*
behavior. Physical, psychological, and social rewards are *positive reinforcements*, while the avoidance of something unpleasant or painful is a
negative reinforcement. An individual who successfully avoids a stressful event by feigning illness is getting negative reinforcement from the
malingering.

Sometimes the reinforcements for behavior appear obvious, but they
may be deceptively complex. For example, property crimes such as
shoplifting and burglary, or violent crimes such as robbery, appear to be
motivated primarily by physical rewards. However, these offenses may
also be prompted by a desire for social and psychological rewards such
as increased status among a peer group or an increase in self-esteem or
feelings of competence. It is a safe bet that all criminal behavior is
undertaken to gain the reinforcement (positive and/or negative) the
offender desires at that moment and in that particular context.

While positive and negative reinforcement increase the probability of
a response, the lack of reward and appropriate, well-timed punishment
decrease the probability of a response. If, instead of receiving reinforcement for a response, the person receives an aversive, noxious, or painful
stimulus (punishment), the person is less likely to repeat the response,
especially if there has never been reinforcement for the response in the
first place. Similarly, if a person does not receive reinforcement for a
response, the response is not likely to be repeated, particularly if the
response was never rewarded previously, or if it is emitted repeatedly
without reinforcement. If the behavior is occasionally reinforced in
combination with occasional nonreinforcement, then we have a response which is particularly resistant to suppression or extinction because the person hopes for a reward part of the time.

Theoretically, if criminal behavior is based primarily on instrumental
learning, then punishment or the withdrawal of reinforcement (called
negative punishment) should be a powerful way of dealing with offenders. The problem, as we shall see in detail in Chapter 13, is that so-called
punishment is not delivered or administered correctly. For the small
percentage of criminal acts in which a conviction results, punishment is
often delayed by court processes. If "punishment" is adjudicated, society cages the offender in a criminal subculture which encourages and
reinforces illegal behavior as part of its value system.

Even if society did administer appropriate punishment and could
withdraw rewards for criminal behavior, suppressing antisocial behavior does not automatically ensure legal behavior. The individual

must also receive and expect reinforcement for socially appropriate and legal behavior. And unless the individual is properly trained in social and occupational skills and rewarded by his or her important cultural or social group, then that person is very apt to revert back to former ways or develop new forms of illegal behavior.

So far, we have discussed how criminal behavior is *maintained* through the process of instrumental learning, which, in essence, is through reinforcement. In an earlier chapter we saw how criminal or antisocial behavior is *suppressed* through the process of classical conditioning. Through conditioning the child comes to link punishment with certain behavior and to anticipate that emitting that behavior will result in aversive conditions. The child, and eventually the adult, must decide which is more important: the reinforcement for the inappropriate or illegal behavior or the punishment which may follow. The subjective determination of which is more important will depend upon the individual's prior experience in that or similar situations. If the potential reward for that behavior offsets the potential discomfort, then the behavior is likely to be pursued. While we have discussed the features involved in the maintenance and suppression of criminal behavior, we have not yet dealt with how that behavior is initially learned or how the person determines which response to select.

SOCIAL LEARNING

Early learning psychologists worked in the laboratory, using animals as their primary subjects. Pavlov's theories on classical conditioning and instrumental learning, for example, were based on careful, painstaking observations and experiments with animals. The learning principles gleaned from his and other theorists' experiments could be generalized to apply to an enormous variety of human behavior. It was suggested also that if human behavior was largely learned, it could be modified through learning principles, which in many instances has proved to be true. Behavior modification and similar procedures based on our knowledge of clearly defined "laws" of learning have been extremely effective in changing some behavioral patterns. The power of reinforcement is one of the most soundly established principles in psychology today. This discovery has generated a plethora of behavior therapies and, unfortunately, a *zeitgeist* that all behavior is learned and, therefore, easily modifiable. Establish conditions which stimulate and encourage the maintenance of former behaviors and, *voila!* therapeutic success! The apparent simplicity of the procedures and methods was especially appealing to many clinicians, and the behavior modification package was rushed to correctional institutions in an effort to "modify criminal behavior."

However, oversimplification is dangerous when we are dealing with the complexities of human beings. There is little doubt that humans respond to reinforcement and punishment and that behavior therapy based on learning principles can change certain elements of behavior. There is also solid evidence that humans can be classically conditioned, although there are individual differences in their susceptibility. But when we lose sight of the person and overemphasize environmental or external determinants of behavior, we also lose another layer of valuable information. To repeat, the person is not a passive shell, swayed completely by external factors, as many environmental, social, and behavioral scientists would have us believe. The person is an active problem solver who perceives, encodes, interprets, and makes decisions on the basis of information the environment has to offer. If we are to understand criminal behavior, we must analyze the perceptions, thoughts, expectancies, competencies, and values of the individual. Social learning theory sets us in that direction. It not only takes the concepts and principles of learning out of the animal laboratory and applies them to complex interpersonal processes, but it also offers the conceptual tools for examining variables that affect a person's behavior. And, it also helps us to understand how one acquires the behavior in the first place.

There are several clusters of behavioral scientists who regard themselves as social learning followers, and each group has a somewhat different theoretical perspective. The social learning position presented here is generally regarded as the main and most influential one and is represented by the hypotheses and research of Julian Rotter and Albert Bandura; this body of work has been expanded and well integrated by Walter Mischel.

Cognitive Aspects of Social Learning

Rotter (1954, 1972) emphasizes cognition, a very important concept in the learning process. Cognition refers to "the psychological events involved in the formation and utilization of symbols and concepts associated with such varied activities as thinking, reasoning, and problem solving" (Kendler, 1974, p. 391). In simpler form, cognition refers to the process of thinking. Traditional learning theory fails to take into consideration what goes on between the time the organism perceives a stimulus and responds or reacts to that stimulus. Social learning theorists contend that this classical view is too simple and too general to allow precise prediction of behavior. The investigator of human behavior must examine more closely what goes on inside the organism in order to predict and understand human behavior.

Rotter stresses the importance of the individual's expectations (cognitions) about the consequences of his or her behavior and the rewards he or she will gain from it. In other words, before doing anything, a person subjectively evaluates: "What has happened to me before in this situation, and what will I gain?" According to Rotter, the probability of a specific pattern of behavior occurring depends upon the individual's expectancies regarding the outcomes of his or her behavior and the perceived values of these outcomes. Thus, to predict we must estimate the person's relevant expectancies, acquired from past experiences, and the perceived importance of the rewards gained by the behavior. The person will also often develop "generalized expectancies" which are stable and consistent across relatively similar situations (Mischel, 1976).

The personal evaluation process carried out by the individual may be exceedingly rapid and perhaps difficult for that person even to articulate clearly. Habits are good examples of behavioral patterns which the individual obviously realizes he or she performs, but does not think too much about.

The hypothesis that people enter situations with generalized expectancies concerning the outcomes of their behavior is an important one for students of crime. Rotter's contention would be that when he or she engages in illegal behavior, the individual expects the action to be productive in terms of a gain in status, power, affection, material goods, or living condition. The individual enters crime with certain expectancies. The violent criminal, for example, elects to behave that way because of a belief that something will be gained. The mass murderer might believe God has sent him on a mission to eliminate all "loose" women; the woman who "does in" an abusive husband looks for an improvement in her life style. Simply to label a violent person "impulsive," crazy, and lacking ego control fails to include other essential ingredients in the act. Although self-regulation and moral development are involved, the person who acts violently or illegally perceives and interprets the situation (including the victims) and selects what he or she considers is the most effective behavior at that time and place. If the person becomes violent and lashes out, he or she does so because that approach has been successfully utilized in past experiences for some kind of personal gain. Possibly the individual may have simply observed someone else gain when employing a similar procedure.

Imitational Aspects of Social Learning

Albert Bandura (1973b) introduced the concept of observational learning or modeling to the social learning process. An individual may acquire ways of doing something simply by watching others do it. Direct reinforcement is not necessary. The child may learn how to shoot a gun by imitating TV characters. With practice, the child "fine tunes" the behavioral pattern, and the behavior is maintained if peers also play with guns with enjoyment (see Figure 4–1). Even if the child has not practiced shooting, he or she has acquired some close approximation of how to shoot someone. It is likely, for instance, that just about every adult and older child in this country "knows" how to shoot a gun, even if they have never actually done so: "You point the gun and pull the trigger." The behavioral pattern exists in your repertoire even though you have never received direct reinforcement for acquiring it. Of course, shooting a gun safely and accurately is more involved, but the rudimentary know-how has been acquired through imitation.

Bandura contends that much of our behavior is acquired initially by watching others, who are called models. The more significant and meaningful these models are to us, the greater their impact on our behavior.

FIGURE 4–1. There is considerable evidence that children learn violent behavior through observation of adult models portrayed in the entertainment media.

92

Relevant models include parents, teachers, siblings, friends, peers, and even symbolic models such as TV or motion picture actors and book characters. The observed behavior of the model is more likely to be copied if the observer sees the model receive a reward for it, and it is less likely to be imitated if the model receives punishment. Once a person decides to use a newly acquired behavior, whether he or she maintains it will depend on expectancies for potential gain. If Penelope finds that slamming her father over the head with a baseball bat while he is asleep does not bring the same consequences as it did for Daffy Duck, then that behavior is likely to drop out of her repertoire for that particular situation. If, on the other hand, a modeled behavior does bring rewards—a well-timed temper tantrum in a crowded grocery store when refused candy, for example—it is likely to be kept for future occasions.

Bandura suggests that during the initial stage of behavior acquisition we learn "right" from "wrong" by observing the behavior of others, especially parents. In this sense, criminal behavior would be acquired initially by imitating or modeling relevant others and maintained by trying it. If the criminal behavior pattern develops a subjective expectancy of potential gain, and gain does occur, the behavior is kept and probably practiced with the expectancy of continued and/or greater gain and reinforcement in other situations. Of course, there will be individual differences in the behavior pattern, depending on sex, age, learning ability, body build, and nervous system characteristics (including differences in reactions to stress), conditionability, and information processing features.

Note that the concept of individual differences is one of the central elements in social learning theory. Individuals do not simply mimic or copy the exact behavior of models; everyone constructs his or her perceptions of reality in a highly selective and unique way. Research on the effects of models has consistently indicated that modeled behavior reflects a unique organization of the information by the observer and personal modifications of that observed behavior (Mischel & Mischel, 1976). The observer reconstructs aspects of behavior to dovetail with his or her style.

Bandura concentrated much of his research on the learning of aggressive and violent behavior, and we will return to his theory in Chapter 7. At this point, however, be aware that many experimental findings provide compelling support for his viewpoint (Walters & Grusec, 1977). For example, studies show that preschool children who watched a film of an adult assaulting an inflated plastic doll were significantly more likely to imitate that behavior than were a comparable group who viewed more passive behavior (e.g., Bandura & Huston, 1961; Bandura, Ross, & Ross, 1963). Many studies employing variations on this basic procedure have reported similar results, strengthening the hypothesis that observing aggression leads to hostility in both children and adults (Walters & Grusec, 1977). Apparently, people who observe aggressive acts not only imitate the observed behavior but also become more hostile in general. Carrying this observation one step further, we can suggest that people who observe the benefits of criminal action are more likely to engage in similar activity.

While the repression and maintenance of behavior is important in understanding crime, social learning adds another dimension. In a sense, it humanizes. Social learning provides clues about how behavior is initially acquired and what transpires inside the cortex. Another aspect of the psychosocial perspective is the *situation*. The physical and social environment are important components in the formation of behavioral patterns. All three learning positions emphasize the situation. However, while instrumental learning and classical conditioning pay particular attention to the physical situation (physical stimuli), social learning focuses more on the social environment and social relationships. In the next section, the situational factors will be outlined, beginning with frustrating conditions.

FRUSTRATION-INDUCED CRIMINALITY

Several learning investigators (e.g., Amsel, 1958; Brown & Farber, 1951) have noted that when an organism is prevented from responding in a way that had previously produced rewards, its behavior increases in energy level and vigor. These increased responses are assumed to be a result of an aversive internal state called *frustration*. Thus, any blocking of ongoing behavior directed at a specific goal will result in increased arousal and a heightened drive state. This drive state not only can energize behavior, but responses which lead to a reduction in the state may actually be strengthened or reinforced. These observations would suggest that people who employ violence to reduce frustrating events would, under extreme frustration, be more vigorous than usual, possibly even resorting to homicide. The hypothesis would also suggest that violent behavior used to reduce frustration would be reinforced because it reduced unpleasant arousal by altering aversive stimuli.

Leonard Berkowitz (1962) has been one of the most active researchers relating frustration to criminality. He proposed that criminal personalities could be divided into two main classifications: the socialized offender and the "individual" offender. The first is primarily a product of learning, conditioning, and modeling, the phenomena we have already looked at. Berkowitz believes the individual offender, by contrast, is principally the product of a long, possibly intense series of frustrations of not having his or her needs met. "Most lawbreakers may have been exposed to some combination of frustrations and aggressively antisocial role models, with the thwartings being particularly important in the development of 'individual' offenders and the antisocial models being more influential in the formulation of the 'socialized' criminals" (Berkowitz, 1962, p. 303). Hence, according to Berkowitz, both modeling and frustration are involved in the development of criminal tendencies, but with one set of life experiences favoring a particular criminal style.

Berkowitz defines frustration as the external interference with or the blocking of a person's ongoing goal-directed behavior. Frustration may occur, for example, when you would very much like a Coke but the Coke machine swallows your last quarter without delivering; or no matter how hard you study for exams you continue to get the same mundane "C" in a course. People living under low socioeconomic conditions may also feel frustrated, provided they have hopes for improving their situation. Hope and expectancy for attainment of goals are very important factors, as Berkowitz (1969) notes. People who anticipate or expect to reach a goal and who feel they have some personal control over their predicament are more likely to react strongly to interference in achieving that goal. Delay or blockage of goal attainment may generate intense anger and a violent response if the frustrated individual feels that response is the way to eliminate the interference.

The above theory helps to explain the upsurge in civil disorders experienced in Watts in the 1960s or in the New York blackout of 1977. We would expect that Watts demonstrators and the New York looters possessed hope for goal attainment (e.g., their fair share of middle-class materials or jobs), but had become impatient and frustrated in the delay and blockage they faced. In fact, a demographic profile of the 2,706 adults arrested for looting during the blackout revealed that the defendants had "stronger community ties" and somewhat higher incomes than the average defendant found in the criminal justice system (N.Y. Times, Aug. 14, 1977). Only about 10 percent were on welfare. Approximately half of the blackout defendants were gainfully employed. Sixty-five percent of those arrested were black and 30 percent were Hispanic. These data suggest that these defendants were, in general, eager to eliminate further delays in society's violations of their expectancy for a better life.

Berkowitz hypothesizes that the more intense and frequent the thwartings or frustrations in a person's life, the more susceptible and sensitive the person is to subsequent frustration. Thus, the individual who frequently strikes out at society in criminal or illegal ways may have encountered numerous severe frustrations, especially during early development, but that person has not given up hope. In support of this argument, Berkowitz notes the research findings on delinquency (e.g., Glueck & Glueck, 1950; Bandura & Walters, 1959; McCord, McCord, & Zola, 1959), which reveal that delinquent children, compared to non-delinquents, have been considerably more deprived and frustrated during their lifetime. Berkowitz also suggests that parental neglect or failure to meet the child's needs for dependency and affection are internal, frustrating circumstances that germinate distrust of all others in the social environment. This generalized distrust is carried into the streets and school, and the youngster may exhibit a "chip on the shoulder." The frustration of not having dependency needs met prevents the child from establishing emotional attachments to other people. The individual becomes resentful, angry, and hostile toward people in general.

Other researchers have also commented on the role frustration plays in spawning crime. Maier and Ellen (1959) distinguished criminal behavior which is economically motivated—theft, fraud, kidnapping, or tax evasion, for example—from criminal behavior which is frustration instigated, such as sex crimes and murder. In an experiment designed to engender frustration, Milgram (1977) found that teenagers were six times more likely to commit antisocial behavior, particularly theft and vandalism, when frustrated. Lefkowitz et al. (1977) report evidence that the frustrations of poor academic achievement and limited intellectual capacity may instigate violent, antisocial behavior. Similarly, a report by the National Institute for Juvenile Justice and Delinquency Prevention (1976) cites a possible link between the frustrations of learning disabilities and delinquency, but warns that further research needs to be done. Lunde (1976) cites clinical evidence that many murderers come from socially and economically disadvantaged families where extreme frustration was very common.

We will return to Berkowitz's hypothesis on the relationship between frustration and criminal behavior in Chapter 7. There we will deal with some of the problems the hypothesis faced and how Berkowitz adjusted his position in response to criticism. One of the major problems centers on what kind of frustration instigates antisocial behavior. Bandura (1973a), for example, reports evidence that people are more likely to respond antisocially to unwarranted than to justifiable hindrances, even though in both cases their goal-seeking behavior was equally thwarted. This observation again emphasizes that people's interpretation and outcome expectancies remain crucial in the understanding of crime, a point Berkowitz himself recognized in the later formulations of his theory.

Despite the problems of the frustration-criminality hypothesis, the concept provides us with some help in explaining so-called "irrational," impulsive violence and homicidal behavior. Frustration may result from a large range of conditions, including personal failures, interpersonal or material loss, personal limitations, lack of resources, feelings of guilt, and loneliness (Coleman, 1976). Furthermore, people lacking social competencies and education run out of means to cope more rapidly than do more privileged, educated, or socially competent people.

Under abnormal arousal levels, such as we might find in frustration, response selection ability tends to collapse (Broen, 1968); arousal seems to disrupt the orderly retrieval of appropriate response patterns. Therefore, the normally elicited response may not necessarily be the one the individual uses. Under extremely high frustration, the person may do the so-called "unexpected." He or she may fly off the handle, and may strike someone with a bottle. To those amazed people who know him or her to be a quiet, controlled person, the behavior may come as a complete surprise.

Early research (e.g., Mowrer, 1940; Maier, 1949) revealed that under frustrating conditions people tend to regress to earlier learned behavior which has been successfully employed in the past for similar events. In fact, research by Barthol and Ku (1959) suggests that under stress or frustration the person regresses to the earliest learned behavior that is appropriate to the situation. This implies that under frustrating circumstances adults tend to revert back to such childhood behaviors as temper tantrums, slapping, and kicking, particularly if these responses have been successful before. In addition, under the high arousal state of frustration they may administer the physical responses to their victim with greater vigor and strength, possibly to the extent that homicide or aggravated assault might result.

In sum, frustration, because of its arousal qualities, may be a significant factor in instigating crimes of violence. Extreme frustration may disorganize our response selection and cause us to regress to earlier, learned responses because the present way of responding is getting us nowhere. The point to be underscored here is that "crimes of passion" and other impulsive, enraged criminal actions should not necessarily be construed as unpredictable, instinctive acts of violence. It may well be that they are learned, predictable response patterns to extremely stressful conditions.

Violent acts prompted by frustration are reinforced because they reduce the arousal experienced and also change the person's situation. The nagging wife-victim can no longer taunt, since she is hurt, unconscious, or even dead. It should be realized, however, that frustration arousal does not accumulate over a period of time, as the psychodynamic point of view would have us believe. Rather, the available evidence indicates that arousal dissipates in time even without a response (Broen, 1968). Therefore, the psychoanalytic notion of accumulation of psychic energies which need to be drained off appears untenable.

THE SUBCULTURAL PERSPECTIVE
OF CRIMINALITY

Several sociological theories of criminology parallel some of the principles we have discussed thus far in this chapter. Subcultural theories are one collection of sociological points of view that appear particularly germane, because they stress the importance of learning, especially social learning.

Subcultural perspectives generally hypothesize that crime is partly a result of the subculture or group that an individual belongs to. The theories place considerable emphasis on the acquisition of criminal behavior by association with "criminally prone" group members, an idea very similar to the psychological theories of social learning. A subculture is a group which subscribes to a set of values that are different from those advocated by the societal mainstream or cultural majority. The group accepts, expects, and rewards the expression of shared values, beliefs, and roles which may be in conflict with society as a whole. Essentially, a subculture is a "culture within a culture" (Clinard, 1963).

According to most subcultural theories, crime is a product of social rather than individual "pathology." Individuals adopt behavior which is "normal" and adaptive to their own subculture, but which may be deviant in the eyes of the cultural majority. Most discussions of criminal subcultures center on the low socioeconomic or working class in an urban setting, since the official statistics continually show that crime rates are highest under deprived conditions. Although a number of sociological theories are concerned with the influence of subcultures, we will focus on three for illustration purposes: the Cloward-Ohlin theory, the Sutherland theory, and the Wolfgang-Ferracuti theory.

The Cloward-Ohlin Theory

The theory presented by sociologists Richard Cloward and Lloyd Ohlin (1960) is often referred to as the "opportunity theory." It divides subcultures in which crime flourishes into three types: the criminal, the conflict, and the retreatist subcultures. All three are based upon Robert Merton's (1957) observation that members of the lower class have limited opportunities for gaining success. According to the Cloward-Ohlin explanation, individuals living in poor, urban districts find their aspirations for success thwarted, become frustrated and angry, and attribute their troubles to the barriers erected by society rather than to personal inadequacy. While society encourages and rewards material success, it does not provide sufficient opportunity for lower-class citizens to achieve the well-advertised material and financial goods. Hence, these people feel justified in pursuing illegal careers and behavioral patterns in order to obtain their fair share of the highly visible material desirables.

The *criminal subculture* builds on illegitimate success models—persons who are not only highly visible to lower-class youths, but are also willing to establish relationships with them. The success models themselves are usually lower-class youths who became "successful" through one of the very few avenues available to them: theft, robbery, prostitution, drugs, and other illegal activities. Whereas middle-class youths have middle-class success models, such as lawyers, bankers, physicians, and other college or technical graduates to observe and emulate, lower-class youths usually have only "illegitimate" success models to imitate. Acquiring the values and skills of successful professional criminals who have managed to avoid deprived living styles is the way to get out of the dregs of continual deprivation and frustration.

Cloward and Ohlin note that learning values and skills of the criminal subculture is not sufficient to ensure successful performance of the professional criminal role. The person must also gain the support of the members of that subculture. He or she needs relationships with others in order to perform successfully as a criminal, such as appropriate middlemen, fences, lawyers, and bondsmen. Furthermore, not everyone is eligible to participate in the criminal subculture. In order to qualify, a person must be able to conform to the value systems of the group and to control undisciplined, unpredictable, erratic behavior. Impulsive acts do not belong in the pursuit of a successful criminal career. Therefore, stealing in this social context is a way of "expressing solidarity with the carriers of criminal values . . . and a way of acquiring the various concrete skills necessary before the potential criminal can gain full acceptance in the group to which he aspires" (Cloward & Ohlin, 1970, p. 309). In other words, the individual does not steal "for the hell of it," but in order to gain skill in the art of theft and acceptance by other members of the subculture.

It would seem from Cloward and Ohlin's observations that each criminal subculture screens for certain personality characteristics, especially those which indicate that a person thinks before acting, can conform to subcultural expectations, is reasonably stable, and can be relied upon. The best candidate is probably Eysenck's stable ambivert and introvert, or at least someone who can learn the values and skills expected by the normative group—overall, one who conditions, learns, and models well. Certainly, the criminal or delinquent who utilizes aggressive behavior with some discretion would qualify as a "socialized" delinquent.

In addition to the criminal subculture, a second subculture described by Cloward and Ohlin is the *conflict subculture.* Members of this group often endanger their own lives and the lives of others and cause extensive property damage for petty gain. In general, they are especially prone to "impulsive violence." These individuals, who have been deprived of both conventional and criminal opportunities to make it in their world, are essentially outcasts of both the criminal minority and the cultural majority. Their behavior reflects a kind of slashing out in frustration at society. The criminal activity of this subculture tends to be individualistic, unorganized, petty, poorly paid, and unprotected by powerful others.

The third subculture, the *retreatist,* typically comprises drug users and is characterized by social isolation and faulty social relationships. Social contacts are made only to secure sufficient chemicals or money to maintain the retreatist life style, which arises from "double failure." The individual's personality does not meet the requirements for the criminal subculture, nor does it allow the proficient use of violence characteristic of the conflict subculture.

Like all theories on human behavior, the Cloward-Ohlin position has been soundly criticized, mostly because it is limited to economically deprived delinquents and does not explain delinquency and criminal activity among other socioeconomic classes. Critics have asserted that delinquency among the low socioeconomic classes is more spontaneous and unstructured than what is implied in the Cloward-Ohlin delineation (Gibbons, 1977, p. 293). Katkin *et al.* (1976, p. 56) point out that the theory does not adequately take into account why some lower-class youngsters living in slum areas go on to achieve success through legitimate opportunities, while their peers revert to one of the three subcultures.

Overall, the Cloward-Ohlin theory seems to be explaining different opportunities for *learning* criminal behaviors inherent in delinquent subcultures. While not specifying the kind of learning mechanisms involved, the theorists imply that modeling and instrumental learning are the principal processes through which criminal behavior is acquired. Furthermore, the behavior appears to be maintained through reinforcement by group members by way of status, self-esteem, and other social and psychological rewards, plus the attainment of material goods for self and for the group. We might also surmise that "subcultural" moral development, a topic we will examine in a later chapter, is an important ingredient in the learning process. Second, though all three groups are frustrated with the social system, the conflict and retreatist groups appear to represent clusters of individuals who are highly frustrated as a result of personal failure, incompetence, poor interpersonal skills, and lack of opportunity. Both the conflict and retreatist groups reflect different coping behaviors in reaction to this extreme frustration.

The Sutherland Theory

The late Edwin Sutherland's theory of *differential association* presents a much broader view of criminal development by contending that, in general, all types of criminal behavior are learned through contact with criminal others, regardless of class boundaries. In fact, Sutherland specified that criminal behavior is learned in the same manner that all human behavior is learned (Sutherland & Cressey, 1974). That is, the many types of learning processes involved in the acquisition of noncriminal behavior are also involved in the acquisition of criminal behavior. Basically, it is who the person associates with, plus how long, how frequently, how personally meaningful the contacts, and how early in the person's development that makes the principal difference. According to Sutherland, individuals observe, imitate, internalize, and manifest the needs and values of a particular relevant criminal subgroup, a process he called "differential association." If the attitudes, values, and behaviors which are learned and which tend to be illegal outweigh the attitudes, values, and behaviors that are legal, then the individual is likely to engage in illegal activities.

It is important to note that Sutherland's formulation has dominated sociological criminology for the past four decades. The theory's popularity is not due to its newness or uniqueness but "it attempts a logical, systematic formulation of the chain of interrelations that makes crime reasonable and understandable as normal, learned behavior without having to resort to assumptions of biological or psychological deviance" (Vold, 1958, p. 192). However, because of their ambiguity, Sutherland's postulations about criminally inducing associations are not amenable to experimental verification and therefore have stimulated relatively few experiments designed to test them directly (see Gibbons, 1977, pp. 221–228). Also, as Donald Cressey (Sutherland & Cressey, 1974) admits, the theory has not specified what kinds of learning are important, nor is there adequate identification of personality variables. The heavy reliance on association appears to preclude the hypothesis that a person may become criminal not because of an overabundance of criminal associations, but because of poor conditionability and deficient internalization of social values.

The theory of differential association is an important one in that it is one of the better attempts at formulating a general theory of criminality. Also, it is valuable in directing attention toward an understanding of learning processes and suggesting the many varieties of acquisition modalities in the development of crime. In many ways, differential association stresses the potential usefulness of social learning theory or imitative learning and even suggests the possibility of subcultural moral development in contrast to the broader, culturally approved morality.

The Wolfgang-Ferracuti Theory

Similar to the Sutherland differential association hypothesis, the Marvin Wolfgang and Franco Ferracuti (1967) theory suggests that violent behavior and the attitudes favoring its use in interpersonal affairs are learned by living in a "subculture of violence." The Wolfgang-Ferracuti hypothesis depicts certain minority cultures as establishing a life style in which it is essentially *normal* to participate in violence, to expect it, and to be ready for retaliation. Furthermore, Wolfgang and Ferracuti attempt to relate the acquisition of violent values to social learning theory and try to integrate psychological principles with sociological ones. They posit ". . . we are convinced that these behavioral constructs of social learning not only are the most directly related to subculture theory but also are capable of generating an integrated theory in criminology" (Wolfgang & Ferracuti, 1967, p. 150). Unfortunately, while providing lip service to this need, they do not go much further in actually elaborating upon how this integration can be accomplished. In fact, it is difficult to determine whether the Wolfgang-Ferracuti position is really referring to instrumental learning or social learning, or both.

Although plagued by numerous shortcomings, subculture theories suggest that, in some cases, delinquency and crime are learned by modeling significant members within the subculture and being reinforced for peer-approved behavior. The subcultural group as a whole rewards behavior that it regards as "appropriate" and necessary. But, what of criminal behavior that might even be in opposition to the subculture's value system? Can we expect everyone in the group to behave the same way and to internalize the values equally? Wolfgang and Ferracuti stress that we can clearly expect individual differences within any criminal or noncriminal subculture. Why, then, do these differences exist? Is all criminal behavior a result of subculture influence?

The subculture theories of crime do not go far enough in their explanation of what type of learning and principles are important, and they do not adequately account for the wide variety of criminal behavior. Despite these limitations, they do emphasize the importance of learning and individual experiences in the development of criminal behavior, particularly concerning social relationships.

SITUATIONAL FACTORS

A number of behavioral and social scientists (e.g., Goldstein, 1975; Gibbons, 1977; Petersen, 1977) have complained that many studies and theories on crime have neglected situational variables in favor of motivational, personal, or individual variables. Some even suggest that criminality in some cases may be simply a direct result of being in the wrong place at the wrong time with the wrong people. For example, Don Gibbons (1977, p. 229) comments: "In many cases, criminality may be a response to nothing more temporal than the provocations and attractions bound up in the immediate circumstances out of which deviant acts arise." In another place Gibbons (p. 228) asserts: ". . . lawbreaking behavior may arise out of some combination of situational pressures and circumstances, along with opportunities for criminality, which are totally *outside the actor.*" The radical behaviorist B.F. Skinner (1971) contends that, apart from genetic factors, all human behavior is controlled solely by environmental contingencies and events. The situation automatically shapes and controls behavior—including, of course, criminal behavior.

There are many examples in which the situation does appear to be crucial in instigating criminal behavior. People are more likely to be assaultive and violent in a bar than in a church. If you were in a situation where you had a chance to embezzle $250,000 without any possibility of discovery, would you do it? What odds would you be willing to take in this situation? Given the appropriate circumstances, is there anyone who might not engage in criminal behavior? Does everyone have a price?

There is no simple answer to the above questions, because "it depends." It depends upon how the individual perceives the situation, what he or she expects the short-term and long-term effects will be, what his or her moral, ethical, and social values are. Generally speaking, the greater the situational pressure to perform a certain act, the greater the tendency for the individual to commit the act regardless of the personal factors involved. On the other hand, the fewer situational demands made on the person, the more likely that personal factors will play an important role.

Neither is the situation static, and this presents another set of variables. One's behavior shapes some of the environment; that is, people activate and create environments (Bandura, 1977). This is why criminologists are beginning to pay closer attention to the victims of crime (victimology), because victims often influence the course of the criminal actions, particularly in violent offenses. Bandura (1977) advocates that study of any human behavior must examine the *reciprocal interaction* of personal and environmental determinants. That is, while the study of the influence of the environment on behavior is important, equally important is the study of how behavior influences the environment.

To say that lawbreaking behavior is *outside* the perpetrator and is a direct result of environmental or situational influences does not represent the position of this book. Behavior rarely, if ever, occurs without some subjective purpose and expectancy which reside within the person. The offender does not necessarily enter a particular situation with the intention to commit an offense. In the course of the situation, however, the offender decides that the set of circumstances would be more in his or her favor if a behavioral alternative which has some probability of success is selected. Even if the individual engages in illegal action to please someone or some group, it is still performed with purpose and subjective gain in mind.

Psychologists have designed a number of experiments which emphasize situational determinants of criminal or "immoral" conduct. We will discuss four at this point to illustrate some situational variables. Keep in mind, however, that these experiments are using active problem solvers and cognitive creatures who are continually evaluating the situation. Thus, we will find individual differences even though the situational pressures to conform and participate may be strong.

One situational variable we will examine is authority, specifically the tendency to do something because someone with prestige or power said we must do it. The classic example of that is the My Lai incident of 1969, where American soldiers massacred women, old men, and children in a Vietnam village. Although a large number of troops participated in the massacre, there were many individual interpretations of why they performed what may appear to the outsider to be gruesome, extremely cruel, criminal, and immoral acts (see Hersh, 1970).

In an effort to delineate some of the variables involved in obedience to authority, Stanley Milgram (1977) designed a series of experiments using subjects who volunteered (for money) in response to a newspaper ad. The experiments were concerned with the amount of electrical shock a person is willing to administer to another person when ordered to do so. The subjects were adult males, ages twenty to fifty years, who represented a cross section of the socioeconomic classes. The subjects were told that the study was designed to determine the effect of punishment on memory. The experiment required a "teacher" and a "victim." Unknown to the volunteers, however, the victim was part of the experiment, a confederate of the experimenter who had been instructed to act in a certain manner as part of the experimental design. In a rigged drawing or coin toss, the naive subject always became the teacher and the confederate the victim. The victim (learner) was taken to an adjacent room and strapped into an "electric chair" in the presence of the naive subject.

The subject (or teacher) was led back to a room where there was a simulated shock generator, a frightening piece of apparatus with 30 switches which supposedly delivered 30 levels of electric shock to the victim-learner in the adjacent room. The 30 levels were indicated by volts (15 to 450) labeling the switches, along with phrases ranging from "slight shock" to "danger: severe shock," and beyond to the "XXX" level. The victim, of course, did not receive any shock, but the subject did not realize this. The subject was instructed to administer stronger and stronger shocks to the victim all the way to the XXX level each time the victim gave an incorrect answer on a learning task. The victim was not only trained to give incorrect answers but also to scream in agony, plead with the subject to stop, and pound on the wall at the higher levels of shock.

Milgram was interested in discovering how far people were willing to go under the orders of an apparent authority figure (the experimenter). Surprisingly, almost two-thirds of the subjects obeyed the experimenter and administered the maximum shock levels. In subsequent experiments under similar experimental conditions, but using different subjects, Milgram continued to find similar results.

Many of the subjects, although they unfailingly obeyed the experimenter's instructions to administer continued levels of shock, demonstrated considerable tension and discomfort. Some twitched, stuttered, bit their lips, twisted their hands, laughed nervously, sweated profusely, or dug their fingernails into their flesh, especially after the victim began pounding the wall in protest (Milgram, 1963). After the experiment, some reported that they wanted to stop punishing the victim but continued to do so because the experimenter would not let them stop. Milgram (1977, p. 118) observes: "The individual, upon entering the laboratory, becomes integrated into a situation that carries its own momentum."

In the subsequent studies Milgram modified the procedure in an effort to determine more precisely the conditions which inhibit or promote this extreme obedience. For example, he varied the "psychological" and physical distance between the subject (the teacher) and the victim (the confederate-learner). To *increase* the psychological distance between the two, Milgram eliminated the cries of the learner that had been programmed into the original experiment described above. In another experiment, to *minimize* the physical and psychological distance between them, the learner sat next to the teacher.

In general, Milgram found that the subjects displayed less obedience to the experimenter as the physical, visual, and auditory contact with the victim increased. Interestingly, the nearer the *experimenter* got to the subject, the more likely he or she was to obey. The psychological and physical distance variable presents us with some interesting implications.

If we were to analogize between the results of the Milgram studies and violent actions, we would expect that the more "impersonal" the weapon or situation (psychological and physical distance) the greater the likelihood for destruction and serious violence. Certainly, killing someone with a firearm at a distance versus killing someone with bare hands are two considerably different tasks. It would appear that the firearm offers a more impersonal and possibly easier way to eliminate someone, and thus is more likely to lead to violent behavior. Admittedly, this suggestion makes some quantum jumps from a serious psychological experiment in an artifical setting, but it is a point we should keep in mind when we discuss the relationship between weapons and violence in a later chapter.

Aside from the profound influence of commands from an authority figure on cruel, aggressive behavior, we should also pay closer attention to the reactions of the subjects in the experiment. There were considerable individual differences in the way subjects handled the situation. Some, of course, refused to go any further once they realized that they were hurting the victim.

A majority of the subjects, however, administered the full range of shock levels, although most displayed anxiety and conflict. Milgram noted a curious dissociation between word and action. Many subjects verbalized they could not go on, but nevertheless continued to do so. Some subjects interpreted the situation in a way which allowed them to conclude that this person of authority would not permit any harm to come to the victim. "He *must* know what he is doing." Other subjects expressed other interpretations and expectancies, such as the belief that the scientific knowledge gained by the experiment justified the method. It is interesting to note that students who have not undergone the ordeal are quite convinced they would be members of the defiant group who did not deliver extreme levels of shock. When they are placed in the situation, however, it may be a different matter.

Milgram suggests that our culture may not provide adequate models for disobedience. He admonishes (1977, p. 120) that his studies ". . . raise the possibility that human nature or, more specifically, the kind of character produced in American democratic society cannot be counted on to insulate its citizens from brutality and inhuman treatment at the direction of malevolent authority. A substantial proportion of people do what they are told to do, irrespective of the context of the act and without limitations of conscience, so long as they perceive that the command comes from a legitimate authority."

Deindividuation

Philip Zimbardo designed a number of studies which stress the importance of situational variables. In one paradigm he tried to focus on a process called *deindividuation* and its relationship to theft, looting, and vandalism. The development of deindividuation appears to require a complex chain of events. First, the presence of many other persons encourages the feeling of anonymity, which leads the individual to feel that he or she loses identity and becomes a part of the group. Under these conditions, the person no longer believes that he or she can be singled out for his or her actions. Apparently, this feeling further generates a "loss of self-awareness, reduced concern over evaluations from others, and a narrowed focus of attention" (Baron & Byrne, 1977, pp. 581–582). When combined, these processes lower restraints against antisocial, criminal behavior and appear to be basic ingredients in mass violence.

FIGURE 4–2. Middle-class white looters systematically stripped the above abandoned car within 26 hours in Manhattan. In Palo Alto, a similar car was left untouched during a seven-day period.

In one experiment, Zimbardo (1970) and a colleague purchased two used cars and left one abandoned on a street in New York City (Manhattan) and the other on a street in Palo Alto, California, a city of about 55,000 inhabitants. Zimbardo's deindividuation hypothesis predicted that due to the large population of New York, people were more likely to lose their identity and feel less responsible for their actions. Consequently, New Yorkers would be more likely to loot the abandoned vehicle, and this is exactly what happened. Within 26 hours, the New York car was stripped of battery, radiator, air cleaner, radio antenna, windshield wipers, side chrome, all four hubcaps, a set of jumper cables, a can of car wax, a gas can, and the only tire worth taking. Interestingly, the looting was not done by delinquents or some criminal subculture; all the looters were well dressed, middle-class Whites. On several occasions the looting was done by families: children and parents together in a family enterprise.

On the other hand, the car in Palo Alto was untouched during the seven days it was left abandoned. At one point during a rainstorm, a passerby actually lowered the hood to prevent the motor from getting wet. Why such a dramatic difference?

Zimbardo suggests that the process tested involved, among other things, the anonymity of the New York residents plus some situational cues which implied that they could get by without repercussions. In New York, who cares what you are doing as long as you are not bothering others or damaging a concerned party's property? Passersby in New York even stopped and chatted with the "looters." In Palo Alto, people could be more easily identified, and the expectancy for engaging in this kind of behavior would be social disapproval or gossip.

Deindividuation not only occurs in crowds, but may also be produced by one's being disguised, masked or dressed in a uniform like everyone else, or by darkness (Zimbardo, 1970). Research data indicate that people tend to be more abusive, aggressive, and violent when their identity is hidden. This phenomenon might explain why certain tribal customs include war paints, masks, and costumes for warriors during battle (Watson, 1973). It also helps explain the apparent ease with which members of groups such as the Ku Klux Klan are able to regress from apparently respectable citizens in daylight to violent, hooded terrorizers at night.

The process of deindividuation is vividly illustrated in a sobering experiment by Zimbardo (1973) known as the Stanford Prison Experiment. The researchers simulated a prison environment in the basement of the psychology building at Stanford University. The "prison" had all the physical and psychological makings of an actual prison: bars, prison drab, identification numbers, uniformed guards, and other features which encouraged identity slippage. Participants in the experiment were student volunteers who had responded to a newspaper ad for experimental subjects. The respondents were subjected to intensive clinical interviews and psychological tests prior to participation to ensure emotional stability and maturity. The subjects selected were "normal," intelligent college students from middle-class homes throughout the United States and Canada. They were paid $15 a day for participating.

The experiment required two roles—guard and prisoner. By way of coin toss, half of the subjects were randomly designated "guards" and the other half "prisoners." The preliminary screening and randomization assured that there were no significant differences between the guards and the prisoners and that the subjects did not differ from the normal population. The prisoners were unexpectedly picked up in a police car and brought to the simulated prison. There they were handcuffed, searched, fingerprinted, booked, and taken blindfolded to a location where they were stripped, deloused, given a number, and issued a prison uniform. Each prisoner was then placed in a six by nine foot cell which was shared with two other inmates.

The guards also wore standard uniforms and mirrored sunglasses to encourage deindividuation. In addition, they carried symbols of power: a night stick, keys to the cells, whistles, and handcuffs. Before the prisoners could do even routine things (e.g., write a letter, smoke a cigarette), they had to obtain permission from the guards. The guards made up their own formal rules (sixteen in all) for maintaining law and order in the prison, and they were free to improvise new ones.

Within six days both the guards and the prisoners had completely absorbed their roles: "In less than a week the experience of imprisonment undid (temporarily) a lifetime of learning, human values were suspended, self-concepts were challenged and the ugliest, most base, pathological side of human nature surfaced. We were horrified because we saw some boys (guards) treat others as if they were despicable animals, taking pleasure in cruelty, while other boys (prisoners) became servile, dehumanized robots who thought only of escape, of their own individual survival and of their mounting hatred for the guards" (Zimbardo, 1973, p. 163). Three prisoners had to be released during the first four days because of hysterical crying, confusion in thinking, and severe depression. Many others begged to be paroled with a willingness to forfeit all the money they had earned for participating in the experiment.

About a third of the guards abused their power and were brutal and demeaning. Other subjects did their jobs as tough but fair correctional guards, but none of these took the side of the prisoners by telling the brutal guards to ease off. Conditions got so bad that Zimbardo decided to terminate the experiment, which was planned for fourteen days, during the sixth day. The realism of the prison during that time was striking. "The consultant for our prison . . . an ex-convict with sixteen years of imprisonment in California's jails, would get so depressed and furious each time he visited our prison, because of its psychological similarity to his experiences, that he would have to leave" (Zimbardo, 1973, p. 164).

The experiment prompted Zimbardo to conclude: "Many people,

perhaps the majority, can be made to do almost anything when put into psychologically compelling situations—regardless of their morals, ethics, values, attitudes, beliefs, or personal convictions," (1973, p. 164).

Although the Stanford Prison Experiment does underscore the crucial importance of situational variables in determining behavior, there were still significant individual differences in the way the subjects responded to the conditions. For example, only a third of the guards became brutally enthralled with their power. Rather than making far-reaching conclusions on the basis of how a total of 21 subjects (both guards and prisoners) responded, it would be much more fruitful to give equal importance to personal variables.

It would also add considerably to our understanding of the process if we closely examined the values, expectancies, competencies, and moral development of the participants in combination with the situational factors. What developmental variables most likely predisposed individuals to act the way they did, and exactly how did they perceive the situation? What did they expect to gain by their behavior?

Situational variables have also been found to influence strongly what others do to assist a victim of a crime. Curious as to why people stand around and simply do nothing when someone is being murdered, beaten, or raped, social psychologists John Darley and Bibb Latané (1968) conducted an extensive series of experiments collectively known as bystander intervention research. Darley and Latané point out that one of the most distinctive features of an emergency or criminal event is that there are very few positive consequences in assisting. A person interfering when another is beating a third party with a tire iron risks harm and injury. Even to call the police is "getting involving" and risking threats. In addition, seeing an actual violent or criminal event is so unusual that a majority of people are not prepared for appropriate action and find considerable difficulty in deciding upon the best course of action. The presence of other persons also tends to inhibit one from taking responsibility for doing something for the victim. Many people assume others in the crowd know better what to do in an emergency: "There must be someone in the crowd who can administer first aid or is trained to fight better than I." "With this many people around, someone must have called the cops." "Why should I do anything when no one else is doing anything?" Hence, each bystander feels less personally responsible for the situation. By contrast, if you are the only one around to see the criminal action, it is more likely that you will feel responsible to do something.

Thus, individuals must consider their competencies and skills, the possible consequences of their actions, and what specific actions to take should they decide to become involved and take personal responsibility. At the same time the individual is influenced by the actions of others and by how near the phone is, whether a weapon is being used, and other physical characteristics of the incident. One positive consequence of assisting is the feeling the person will have about him or herself, particularly if that person is alone and therefore cannot "diffuse" responsibility to others.

SUMMARY

Although physiological factors play an important role in the development of both normal and deviant behavior, we have seen in this chapter that psychosocial factors play an even more crucial role. Psychological learning theories teach us that people are active problem solvers who stay with behavior they consider most effective. The criminal or antisocial person is no exception.

Social learning appears to be especially important in explaining how behavior is initially discovered, whereas instrumental learning provides an understanding of how it is maintained and altered. Instrumental learning takes place when an individual finds out that by acting a certain way he or she will receive rewards or avoid aversive circumstances. If a criminal gets reinforcement for his or her activity, and the reinforcements outweigh the possible punishment, then that person learns to continue that activity.

Thus far, we have restricted conditioning to refer to one of the processes involved in the elimination or suppression of undesirable behavior, especially in children. Specifically, undesirable behavior is avoided because it is associated with punishment or aversive events. Perhaps, at this point, the reader can see how the once-distinct boundaries between instrumental learning and classical conditioning are becoming blurred. One of the reinforcements for instrumental learning is the avoidance of aversive consequences, which is called negative reinforcement. Yet, certain behaviors in classical conditioning may also be avoided because they have become linked to aversive events. The distinction is that in classical conditioning the behavior (or images of the behavior) automatically conjures up physiological arousal and feelings of discomfort, called fear of reprisal. In instrumental learning, the behavior feels "good" because it helps the person avoid an aversive situation or gain a reward.

Subcultural theories of criminality parallel, in many respects, the principles of social learning. However, because they are limited to subcultures, they fail to account for other types of criminal behavior outside the subgroup. Moreover, their discussions of learning are vague and often circular.

The individual's experiences and learning opportunities only stress one side of the coin in the development of criminality. The other side involves aspects about the *situation* that encourage or discourage a particular behavior pattern. A person perceives, interprets, and responds to certain situations in certain ways which that person thinks are the most effective. A person usually does not respond the same way to all situations. Situations which thwart or in some way interfere with the expectancies of an individual may result in frustration, which in turn may set the stage for deviant behavior.

Situational factors have received much attention in psychological research. Elements in a situation such as authority, presence of others, psychological and physical distance, and deindividuation have all been found to influence some types of deviant and illegal behavior. Not to be neglected are the effects not only of the environment on behavior, but also of the individual's behavior on the environment. With that in mind, sociologists and psychologists alike are beginning to look at the effects of a *victim's* behavior on subsequent criminal action directed at him or her. All of these findings underscore well the interactional processes which occur between the situation and the personality in producing behavior.

KEY CONCEPTS FOR REVIEW

Classical conditioning
Instrumental learning
Reinforcement
Positive reinforcement
Negative reinforcement
Social learning
Modeling
Frustration-induced criminal behavior
Criminal subculture
Conflict subculture
Retreatist subculture
Differential association
Subculture of violence
Reciprocal interaction
Deindividuation

MAJOR THEORISTS AND RESEARCHERS

Rotter
Berkowitz
Cloward and Ohlin

Sutherland
Wolfgang and Ferracuti
Bandura
Milgram
Zimbardo
Darley and Latané

SUGGESTED READINGS

Bandura, A. Social learning theory. Englewood Cliffs, N.J.: Prentice-Hall, 1977.
A contemporary and comprehensive introductory presentation of social learning theory.

Berkowitz, L. Aggression: A social psychological analysis. New York: McGraw-Hill, 1962.
A classical treatment of the contributions of frustration theory to aggression and crime.

Houston, J.P. Fundamentals of learning. New York: Academic Press, 1976.
A good, broad and detailed survey of learning theory and relevant research.

Zimbardo, P. "The human choice: Individuation, reason and order versus deindividuation, impulse and chaos," in W.J. Arnold and D. Levine (eds.), Nebraska symposium on motivation 1969. Lincoln: University of Nebraska, 1970.
An excellent, well-written article reviewing the theory and research on deindividuation.

DEVELOPMENTAL FACTORS: JUVENILE DELINQUENCY

FIVE

In the United States, risk-taking, rebellion, and the conscious violation of social norms are part of the rites of passage for the adolescent. Some criminal activity on the part of the young is almost universal in the transition from adolescence to adulthood. Most adolescent crime is not serious, not repetitive, and not predictive of future persistent criminal careers.

Zimring, 1978, p. 15

While it is true that most juvenile offenders do not pursue persistent antisocial or criminal lives, a majority of people who do display antisocial behavior as adults also demonstrated it as youths. This chapter deals with the persistent offender who continually functions counter to the social mores, rather than with the age-specific delinquent described above by Zimring. Therefore, we shall be concerned primarily with the juvenile delinquent who later becomes an adult criminal, not with the juvenile "going through a phase" of development.

Persistent antisocial behavior does not emerge suddenly in the adolescent. It begins to develop in early childhood (Bandura & Walters, 1963). Deviant behavioral patterns are learned through a gradual process of watching, trying, and modifying the patterns that will gain the highest return in reinforcement. Behaviors which do not bring satisfactory returns are dropped out and those that deliver gains are retained. In this chapter we shall examine some of the developmental processes which appear to contribute to criminal and persistent antisocial behavior. We will also try to determine whether and how the socialization process of the criminally-prone person differs from that of the law-abiding person. Socialization is the general term used for the learning that takes place during development.

After some discussion of family background, the development of impulsiveness, and the relationship between persistent offending and intelligence, we shall look at moral development, which brings us away from the strict socialization perspective and helps us understand how values, attitudes, feelings, and behaviors are internalized. Then we will direct some attention at the more common offenses committed by juveniles: vandalism, auto theft, and running away from home. Serious offenses involving substantial threat to the life or physical security of victims will be covered in later sections of the book, in conjunction with adult offenses.

DEFINITIONS

Juvenile delinquency is an imprecise, nebulous legal and social label for a wide variety of norm-violating behavior. There are as many legal definitions as there are jurisdictions. Broadly, a *juvenile delinquent* is one who commits an act defined by law as illegal or delinquent and who is adjudicated "delinquent" by an appropriate court. The legal definition is usually restricted to persons under age eighteen, but in some jurisdictions the age is different. Unlawful acts which may be committed by juveniles are divided into four major categories: felonies, misdemeanors, drug offenses, and status offenses. Felonies, drug offenses, and misdemeanors are usually defined the same way for juveniles as for adults. Status offenses are acts the statutes declare as offenses which only juveniles can commit and which can be adjudicated only by a juvenile court (U.S. Department of Justice, 1978). Typical status offenses are violations of curfew, running away from home, truancy, possession of alcoholic beverages, and leading an immoral life.

In popular usage, the term "juvenile delinquent" defines the boy or girl who "gets into trouble" but may or may not have been adjudicated delinquent by juvenile court. This social label may carry peer and social status, or it may designate its carrier an anathema, to be avoided because of the potential bad influence he or she may have on the conduct of other youths.

The reader should be aware of differences in the judicial system's philosophy with regard to the delinquent in contrast to the adult offender. The system provides a juvenile court for child and adolescent offenders and criminal courts to deal with persons over a designated age. Juvenile courts are built on the philosophy that offending children should be protected and rehabilitated rather than subjected to punishment (Task Force on Juvenile Delinquency, 1967). Preventive efforts are most needed for them because they are not yet set in their ways. Implicit in this belief is the feeling that the older offender has become too hard core and habitual to respond well to rehabilitative efforts.

Some states, in fact, extend this concept to cover the youthful offender, who is older than the juvenile delinquent but still relatively young, usually under age twenty-four. Youthful offender statutes try to allow more flexibility in the judicial system to process the young adult, emphasizing more rehabilitation-oriented sentencing alternatives. Again, the philosophy is that the young offender is not yet too far gone to be rehabilitated and redirected. In some states, like California, correctional facilities are established specifically for youthful offenders.

INCIDENCE

According to statistics (Task Force on Juvenile Delinquency, 1967), one in every nine children will be referred to juvenile courts for delinquency before the eighteenth birthday. If we look only at boys, the ratio rises to one in every six. Persons under eighteen constituted about 25 percent of all arrests in 1976, and 8 percent of all persons arrested were under fifteen (Kelley, 1977). It is estimated that in 1974 over 1 million (1,252,700) juvenile delinquents were handled by courts having juvenile jurisdiction in the United States (U.S. Department of Justice, 1977).

Table 5–1 reveals some of the offense frequencies reported to the FBI during 1976. Nearly half of all arrests for property crime were of persons under eighteen, over three-quarters of these being male. Arrested youths were frequently involved in motor vehicle theft, arson, vandalism, running away, curfew violations, and selling or receiving stolen property.

Facilities for juveniles at the end of June 1973 held 45,694 persons: 35,057 males and 10,637 females (U.S. Department of Justice, 1978). Table 5–2 shows the types of offenses for which adjudicated juveniles were sent to public detention and correctional facilities in June, 1973. Forty-three percent were being detained for felonies, 27 percent for status offenses, 23 percent for misdemeanors, and 7 percent for drug offenses.

Research and statistics often differentiate between the serious and the nonserious juvenile offender. Zimring (1978) proposed that the serious

TABLE 5-1
Arrests of persons under 15 and under 18 years of age during 1976*

Offense	Total (All ages)	Under 15	Under 18
Murder and nonnegligent manslaughter	14,113	190	1,302
Forcible rape	21,687	915	3,745
Robbery	110,296	10,156	36,990
Aggravated assault	192,753	9,552	32,678
Burglary—breaking and entering	406,821	78,275	209,396
Larceny—theft	928,078	173,535	399,235
Motor vehicle theft	110,708	14,726	58,279
Arson	14,534	4,626	7,601
Vandalism	175,082	60,569	109,712
Narcotic drug laws	500,540	15,514	119,522
Liquor laws	302,943	9,679	108,934
Curfew and loitering law violations	88,601	24,217	88,601
Runaways	166,529	65,173	166,529
Other assaults	354,010	25,907	69,904
Stolen property: buying, receiving, possessing	92,055	8,142	28,940

*Source: FBI Uniform Crime Reports, 1977, p. 183.

offender is one who engages in criminal activity that involves serious threats to life or to personal safety and security. Serious juvenile offenses include rape, homicide, aggravated assault, robbery, and arson. Although other definitions vary and often lack precision, most reports are fairly consistent in suggesting that the proportion of such offenders is small (Hudson & Mack, 1978). Arrest records of persons under age

TABLE 5-2
Adjudicated Delinquents and Persons in Need of Supervision Held in Public Juvenile Detention and Correctional Facilities, by Type of Offense and Sex, Midyear 1973*

Type of Offense	Both sexes	Male	Female
Total	38,356	30,944	8,312
Felony	9,270	8,606	664
Misdemeanor	4,834	4,115	719
Drug offense	1,400	1,074	326
Status offense	5,850	3,439	2,411
Information not available	17,002	12,810	4,192

*Source: U.S. Department of Justice, Children in custody, 1978, p. 20.

eighteen reported by the FBI for 1976 suggest that the serious juvenile rate is 6 percent of the entire juvenile offender population.

However, the estimated number of delinquency cases disposed of by juvenile courts is increasing at a significantly faster rate than the population for that age group (see Figure 5–1). Even if only a small percentage of youths continue their antisocial activity into their adult years, the adult offense rate also will likely increase at an uncomfortable pace.

DEVELOPMENTAL CORRELATES
OF DELINQUENCY AND CRIME

Since we shall deal with the origins of normal and deviant behavior in this section, we must be a bit more precise about our understanding of instrumental learning and social learning. A firmer grasp of the two

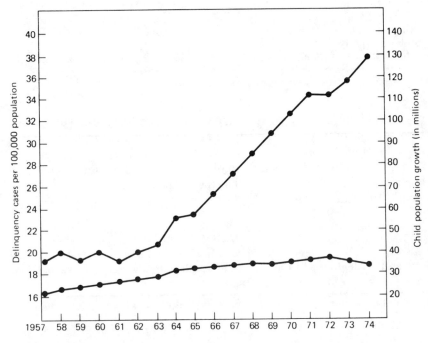

FIGURE 5-1. Estimated rate of delinquency cases disposed of by juvenile courts, United States, 1957–1974. Chart is based on children ages 10–17.

Source: Corbett, J., & Vereb, T.S. *Juvenile Court Statistics: 1974*, Washington, D.C.: U.S. Government Printing Office, 1977.

learning processes will enable us to understand the developmental sequences more easily and accurately.

New behaviors can be acquired either through direct experience or by observation. The instrumental learning position argues that new response patterns are learned through direct experience by the rewards or punishment received. In other words, holders of this position believe that most novel responses are acquired through trial and error. You try the behavior, and if it brings a positive return you will try it again. In a sense, this view of learning sees learning by reinforcement as a mechanical process in which responses are acquired and modified by their immediate consequences.

Social learning contends that a very large portion of human behavior, probably most, is acquired by observing models. But there is more to it than that. All behaviors seen are not modeled. If this were the case, the child would be so overwhelmed that he or she could hardly function at all. Rather, the child imitates those models he or she considers important and worth emulating. In other words, the child is selective about models. Models who are judged to be lacking in pleasing characteristics are generally ignored or rejected (Bandura, 1977).

As the child gets older, he or she tends not to imitate immediately—as a young child does—but stores the observed behaviors for a future occasion. Bandura (1977) reports that the evidence shows that this storage is most often verbal, specifically in the form of symbolic codes requiring some degree of cognitive or intellectual capacity. Thus, we have an attention process which revolves around who is worth watching—and a retention process which is concerned with the manner and how well observed behavior is stored in the brain.

A third process involves the reproduction of the observed behavior. At some point in time the occasion may occur in which the behavior will be tried out. When this happens, the individual gains some information about the behavior and also learns about the gains it provides. If the reproduced behavior delivers satisfactory reinforcement, it will become a stronger response alternative reserved for certain situations.

There is good evidence to show that delinquency patterns begin in early childhood (Conger & Miller, 1966; Conger, Miller & Walsmith, 1965; Lerman, 1968). Learning experiences begin early and build upon themselves. Conger and his colleagues noted differences between future delinquents and nondelinquent children during their early school years, in impulsiveness, social skills, and feelings for others. Delinquents were less friendly, less considerate in dealing with others, negative toward people in authority, more impulsive, and generally less responsible. During the middle school years, poor academic performance became increasingly evident, especially as displayed by underachievement, poor work habits, and faulty planning (Conger, 1977). School became increasingly aversive for the delinquents, and they began to rely on alternative behaviors, especially attention-getting ones. By the end of the ninth grade, many were manifesting the more common delinquent acts: vandalism, running away, joyriding, incorrigibility, and like behavior. The consideration and empathy for others had not advanced much beyond the stage it was at during their early childhood, and they became increasingly antagonistic toward authority and resentful of school regulations.

Many theorists and researchers have reported relationships between certain developmental-background variables and delinquency. Broken homes, inconsistent discipline, impulsivity, and below average intelligence emerge with consistency in the backgrounds of delinquents, but there is also evidence that they occur frequently in those of nondelinquents. However, although correlational studies must be viewed guardedly and with the usual warning that a correlation is not a cause, the consistency of the findings emphasizes that they are, in some way, important factors in developing antisocial behavior.

Family Background

Studies regularly find delinquents coming from broken homes (one-parent homes which become that through divorce or separation) more often than do nondelinquents (Glueck & Glueck, 1950; Eaton & Polk, 1961; Monahan, 1957; Rodman & Grams, 1967). Using 500 matched pairs of delinquent and nondelinquent boys, the Gluecks reported that 60.4 percent of the delinquents and 34.2 percent of the nondelinquents came from broken homes. There is also some evidence that delinquent girls are more affected in a negative way by broken homes than are delinquent boys (Rodman & Grams, 1967), and that younger children are more affected than are older children (Clarizio & McCoy, 1976).

While studies continually find the correlation between broken homes and delinquency, the variables contributing to this relationship remain unclear. McCord, McCord, and Zola (1959) have reported that the emotional atmosphere in the home is more important than the one parent aspect. They suggest that a home full of emotional conflict, marital discord, and negligence is more likely to generate a delinquent youth than the loss of a parent. Still, this suggestion does not tell us precisely why emotional upheaval and conflict in a home should promote more delinquency than an emotionally stable one.

In line with the socialization process and the social learning position, it is reasonable to assume that homes with inadequate or faulty models for parents would produce children who have not witnessed a wide variety of socially desirable behavior. For example, homes with an unavailable, alcoholic father and an abusive, neglecting mother, both of whom are overwhelmed with frustration and financial woes, would not provide a solid collection of models to emulate. Furthermore, it is entirely possible that a child may not even wish to imitate the parent if he or she views the parental model unfavorably. This tendency often becomes a problem during the adolescent years when parental models do not measure up to certain standards required by the adolescent.

Under situations where inadequate models are present, the child can either resort to direct experience (instrumental learning) or observational learning via peers or media characters. However, direct experience (or trial and error) is a very inefficient way to acquire responses (Bandura, 1977), and therefore, the learning is probably observational to a large extent. Imagine learning how to drive a car, without having seen one driven before, through trial and error. Therefore, it is very likely that in some so-called broken homes, the real culprit is the breakdown of the modeling process and not simply the emotional upheaval or the marital conflict.

Discipline seems to be a very important ingredient in the development of delinquency. Inconsistent or physically harsh discipline within the home seems to produce more delinquency than do consistent and "reasoning" forms of discipline. Button (1973) found a very high correlation between the severity of physical punishment used and the amount and severity of antisocial aggressiveness displayed during adolescence. Also, a repetitive complaint by delinquents is the lack of fairness and objectivity demonstrated by parents in their administration of discipline (McCord et al., 1959; Glueck & Glueck, 1950), a complaint voiced much less frequently by nondelinquents.

Inconsistent discipline usually also reflects inconsistent dispensation of reinforcement. This means that reproductions of the behaviors observed would not be consistently strengthened or weakened in the home environment. In addition, the atmosphere of severe, harsh punishment, which is often not contingent upon any specific behavior but rather randomly assigned at the whim of the parent, engenders an unpleasant environment to be in for any length of time. Third, physical punishments of slapping, hitting, and punching provide a pattern to be modeled when frustrated and disenchanted.

A child's home situation may prove so unbearable, aversive, and unreinforcing that the child may be forced to find models and reinforcement outside the home and within the peer group. Unfortunately, many of the peers are in the same boat. Disenchanted with home, they also seek other sources of reinforcement and knowledge, which they find only in the peer group. Thus, the group becomes a subculture, with fragments of its own values and attitudes it has adopted with varying degrees of fervor. If some of the behaviors of the group are considered illegal or antisocial by society, the members of the group are often referred to by theorists as *socialized* or *gang delinquents*. They have learned well the expectations of their peer groups, even though from society's standpoint they are deviant. It appears that most early and mid-adolescent delinquency is carried out in groups (Hood & Sparks, 1970), which suggests that a large part of the delinquent acts are committed by delinquents "socialized" by their peer groups—which in turn suggests breaks in the modeling process in many delinquent homes.

While certainly not restricted to lower socioeconomic class families, juvenile delinquency does occur far more frequently in urban families hobbled by limited financial and social resources (Task Force on Delinquency, 1967). The lower socioeconomic class also tends to have substantially more one-parent families. Generally, broken homes with limited resources are less likely than two-parent homes to offer adequate socializing environments. There is, of course, a variability in this contention. Some one-parent families provide far better socializing environments than most two-parent families; and research has yet to examine the effects of the growing phenomena of "shared custody" between divorced parents or adoption of children by single persons. On the whole, however, the frustrated, depressed, or overwhelmed single parent is not likely to provide adequate dispersion of reinforcements, punishment, and discussion which encourage socialization and the development of social skills. Poor socialization climates are excellent breeding grounds for disenchanted, frustrated, and misguided youth—misguided in the sense that they have not been sufficiently "indoctrinated" into middle-class social attitudes and skills.

The Development of Impulsiveness

"Impulsive" is one of the most shopworn descriptors of the juvenile delinquent. This frayed concept implies that youths are more inclined to act on sudden urges than on thought. It suggests that delinquents do not think about what they are doing, but are reflexive creatures who immediately respond to the urge of the moment, unpredictably and uncontrollably.

Impulsiveness is often referred to as the inability to delay gratification, which suggests that the individual shows little in the way of socialization and internalization of social values. Inability to delay gratification is, in fact, a hallmark of the *undersocialized* or *psychopathic* delinquent and offender. McCord and McCord (1964, p. 9) state that "the psychopath is like an infant, absorbed in his own needs, vehemently demanding satiation." The undersocialized delinquent, therefore, would appear to be the most impulsive, while the socialized and disturbed delinquents tend to demonstrate features of greater self-control.

There is good evidence (e.g., Quay, 1965; Ross, 1974; Mischel, 1961; Rosenquist & Megargee, 1969; Stumphauzer, 1973), however, that delinquents as a whole are more often willing than comparable groups of nondelinquents to take immediate gratification in favor of larger but delayed rewards. As a group they have found it most expedient to take what is available and not wait for future contingencies. In part, this strong orientation for the present may be a result of broken promises or lack of reinforcement for working toward future goals. It is not surprising, therefore, that some delinquents' backgrounds often show academic failure (Trojanowicz, 1978). The reinforcements for academic achievement are not readily apparent and are too far into the future to be of major concern. Moreover, while waiting for the promised future dividends from education, the individual may find the delay period highly aversive and punishing.

Children exhibit the same degree of self-control and delay of gratification as the model or models to which they have been exposed (Bandura & Walters, 1963). Parents and other adults who verbalize the need for delaying gratification but display little self-control themselves provide poor social models for their children. "Listen to what I say and don't do what I do" is a faulty parenting adage.

Also, inconsistent discipline and reinforcement create an atmosphere of noncontingencies where certain behavior and social consequences are interpreted as unrelated. In an environment where reinforcing and punishing events often happen unpredictably and inconsistently, the child develops a sense of lack of control over his or her fate. There is little appreciation for the consequences of one's own actions, whether antisocial or socially desirable. The socialization process based on punishment of undesirable acts breaks down, and the threat of punishment becomes largely ineffective. The child learns to take his or her chances and develops a "get-what-you-can-now-and-don't-worry-about-the-un-predictable-consequences" philosophy of life.

Mischel (1976) brings additional considerations to the discussion of delay of gratification, which he sees as a two-part process. First, the individual must decide to wait for more attractive rewards sometime in the future. Among the many determinants of the decision-making process is the expectancy the individual has about the realization of the promised rewards. If, from past experiences, the person has learned that the promised and delayed rewards failed to materialize, it is unlikely that he or she will make the decision to wait. If the decision is made, however, the individual must *maintain self-control* throughout the waiting period. From the evidence so far, it appears that self-control during the waiting period requires the ability and skill to generate distractions (both cognitive and behavioral) in order to reduce the frustration and aversiveness of waiting. The decision to wait requires trust in one's social environment and some positive experiences with delayed reinforcement. Self-control demands skill in keeping oneself occupied in a satisfying way until the delivery of the expected reward; one must also be able to tolerate and deal with frustration. Growing up in an environment which offers little opportunity for the development of this two-stage process would promote a desire for immediate gratification of needs to the detriment of long-term rewards. Therefore, dropping out of school might win out over tolerating the grind: "earning" money through thievery might win out over spending time in a job-training program.

While the notion of impulsiveness, therefore, is important for the understanding of delinquency and adult crime, it should not be simplistically viewed as meaning irrational or uncontrolled behavior. Rather, impulsiveness reflects a lack of concern for the future consequences of one's present behavior. It can be thought of as a dimension: at one pole we have the individual who is not at all concerned beyond immediate gratification; at the other pole we have the excessively self-controlled person who is so chronically concerned that he or she cannot make decisions. The impulsive person at the one extreme believes that the best policy is to enjoy the *now* regardless of the consequences; the excessively controlled person at the other extreme does not feel comfortable about most present behavior. At each end, the individual considers present behavior in comparison to delayed consequences. The importance a person places on present behavior depends upon past learning experiences.

Lack of appreciation for the delayed consequences of one's behavior, especially when it comes to violent crime, prevents the threat of punishment, jail sentence, or even of capital punishment from being an effective deterrent. The highly impulsive delinquent or the psychopath who gets more reinforcement for antisocial behavior patterns presents a formidable foe for society and law enforcement.

Comment: The Disturbed Delinquent

Thus far we have concentrated on the features of the *socialized* and *undersocialized* delinquent or offender without directing much attention toward the *neurotic* or *emotionally disturbed* delinquent and offender, who will be given some attention in the next chapter. Some of the behavioral features which distinguish the disturbed delinquent from the other types are feelings of inferiority, social withdrawal and introversion, and anxiety (Quay, 1972). In essence, the disturbed delinquent appears to have an inadequate supply of response alternatives for dealing with his or her environment. This young person adapts to situations by withdrawing because of an inadequate response repertoire for the events at hand.

Social introversion and anxiety are the keys here. Eysenck's position is that introverts develop stronger associations between behavior and reprimand. Thus, the introverted child is particularly fearful of doing the wrong thing, especially outside the family. In a sense, he or she becomes self-conscious. Another aspect to consider is the introverted child's general avoidance of stimulation—including social contacts— and lack of curiosity, perhaps both due to nervous system characteristics. Because of these tendencies, introverts are less likely to develop a large assortment of knowledge and skills for dealing with the environment. Therefore, the withdrawn introvert lacking adequate social skills and competencies has few opportunities to be noticed, appreciated, or to feel generally significant. One avenue available for the acquisition of significance is to demonstrate notable behaviors, such as delinquency.

The disturbed delinquent prefers to violate social mores and laws on his or her own; hence, the oft-cited label "solitary delinquent." A common observation is that many disturbed delinquents come from the middle class. A common explanation for this delinquency is that the youth wants to get caught and punished to satisfy deep-rooted feelings of guilt (Clarizio & McCoy, 1976). However, an alternative explanation might be that neurotic delinquents commit antisocial acts to feel significant. That is, their deficiency in behavioral patterns promotes a sense of insignificance and ineffectiveness; a steady diet of this inadequacy and insignificance may prompt a desperate attempt to be noticed and recognized. One way to obtain this recognition is to do well in academic pursuits or other activities that do not require much social skill and involvement. Another approach would be to engage in illegal conduct where parents, peers, and authorities show concern and interest.

Delinquency and Intelligence

Criminologists (and many psychologists) have been all too eager to label invalid and spurious the relationship between intelligence and delinquency. Even to mention the connection in the presence of some precipitates a derisive reaction previously reserved for Lombroso's theories. Hirschi and Hindelang (1977, p. 572) write: "Today, textbooks in crime and delinquency ignore IQ or impatiently explain to the reader that IQ is no longer taken seriously by knowledgeable students simply because no differences worth considering have been revealed by research." As Hirschi and Hindelang note, these textbooks are wrong, since one of the most consistent findings in the delinquency literature is that delinquents do, as a group, score lower on standard intelligence tests than nondelinquents do. Why the difference exists is at the heart of the controversy.

The explanation in vogue contends that standard intelligence tests are really barometers of cultural and socioeconomic differences and not of "native ability." Standard IQ tests, the argument goes, are Western civilization, white, middle-class inventions designed to measure some vague and ill-defined concept the majority calls "intelligence." Intelligence tests are simply not sensitive to the less fortunate members of society. Black or Hispanic ghetto children or poor, lower-class children are at a substantial disadvantage on the standard IQ test because they have not been properly indoctrinated into the middle-class mainstream, which relies heavily on verbal skills for achievement. Anti-IQ arguments tell us that delinquents and criminals as a rule score lower on IQ tests not because they are intellectually inferior, but because they have, as a rule, grown up in the lower socioeconomic classes of society where intellectual enrichment is generally unavailable.

However, in an incisive review of the relevant literature, Hirschi and Hindelang argue that the available evidence strongly suggests that there is a strong relationship between IQ and delinquency *independent* of socioeconomic class. That is, upper-class delinquents have also been found to have lower IQs than upper-class nondelinquents; and lower-class delinquents have scored lower than lower-class nondelinquents. In fact, IQ is a more accurate *predictor* of delinquency than either social class or race. Even when social class and race are controlled for, IQ continues to emerge as a significant variable distinguishing between delinquent and nondelinquent youths.

The question that many "experts" and investigators fail to address is: "Which comes first, the low socioeconomic status or the low IQ?" It is very probable that people who do not function intellectually to an average level in a complex, technological society will be found at the lower levels of the socioeconomic ladder in many cases. By the same token, people who are not exposed, do not have the opportunity, or are not encouraged to develop intellectual competencies because of the restrictions imposed by low social status or racial bias, will not as a rule do particularly well on conventional IQ tests based upon middle-class standards. But to favor one relationship while completely discarding the other is poor scholarship, and it is unscientific. Until more evidence is collected and carefully sorted, we must assume that intelligence, or whatever the concept IQ tests measure is, along with social class plays a role in the development of delinquency and crime.

Research has shown that about 10 percent of all incarcerated inmates can be classified as mentally retarded (IQs below 70) (Brown & Courtless, 1970) and that 10 to 12 percent of incarcerated delinquents could be so classified (Santamour & West, 1977). About 1.6 percent of the adult prison population have IQs below 55, which suggests moderate to severe intellectual retardation (Brown & Courtless, 1970). These statistics suggest that these individuals were limited in the number of options available to them for adapting in their environment. Also, they were more likely to get caught and convicted.

Possibly, those convicted and incarcerated have not been able to adapt as readily as their counterparts because of limited ability to model effectively. Recall the discussion presented on social learning theory earlier in this chapter. The ability to learn from one's social environment is dependent in large part upon symbolic coding capacities. It may be that the storage for observational learning is not as efficient for some as it is for others, and thus the cognitively limited person will be at a definite disadvantage when it comes to social learning, even of criminal behaviors.

The entire issue of the relationship between intelligence and delinquency must be exhumed and re-examined. Perhaps criminologists, sociologists, and psychologists have been too hasty in their reactions against IQ tests. There is little doubt that the standard tests are primitive, crude measures of some aspect of human thinking. Whatever these instruments measure, the ingredient appears to be necessary for most people to achieve in this society. Of course, there are numerous variables that are necessary for achievement, such as opportunity, motivation, and persistence. Intelligence and cognitive ability in general are also closely related to moral development and maturation, a topic to be covered in the following section.

The material we have presented under the developmental factors must remain tentative. Most of the studies done on delinquency have been correlational and require that we think of the relationships as merely suggestive of causal factors. We have tried to coordinate social learning principles with the research findings in an effort to find explanations for delinquent behavior. In this way, the reader not only gains a better grasp of social learning but also learns some testable hypotheses for the origins of criminal behavior.

SELF-CONTROL: INTERNALIZATION
AND MORAL DEVELOPMENT

How people acquire and "internalize" the norms and values of the external social world is a key question in the study of criminal behavior. *Internalize* here implies that people accept events or beliefs and make them a part of their own thinking. The assumption prevalent among social scientists is that norms which were once alien and outside the individual eventually become part of the individual's way of thinking about what is right and wrong. At first, the norms are imposed; ultimately they become internalized, but not for all people. Some individuals internalize the social expectations more easily than others, and in this section we will attempt to understand why. Theoretically, we might expect that the most troublesome criminal would be the one who has had the most difficulty internalizing society's regulations.

One of the first major psychological studies on moral character was carried out by Hugh Hartshorne and Mark May (1928–1930). It focused on such behaviors in children as honesty, generosity, and self-control, and its results proved temporarily devastating to those who believed that people could be classified according to consistent personality traits of morality or immorality. The data showed that moral behavior appeared to be largely situation-specific! That is, because a child conducted him- or herself morally or honestly in one situation did not mean that this same commendable behavior would continue in a different situation. In fact, the researchers found that a child who was dishonest or ruthless under one set of circumstances was likely to respond differently under a different set of circumstances. The disappointing conclusion that a situation appears overwhelmingly more important in determining moral behavior than does personality temporarily slowed efforts to delineate moral-immoral traits. However, more recent, sophisticated statistical analysis has revealed that this was perhaps an unjustified conclusion (Burton, 1963, 1976; Eysenck, 1977). General personality factors are now believed to play a more significant role in determining moral behavior than was originally concluded, but the data still indicate that situational factors exert a very potent influence.

Investigations centering on moral development have been primarily concerned with moral *judgment* and reasoning. The Swiss psychologist Jean Piaget (1932) was an early pioneer in studying how people mentally symbolize organized social rules and how they make judgments based on that organization. He hypothesized that morality develops in a series of steps or stages. Each moral stage depends upon previous stages, along with the intellectual or cognitive equipment and the social experiences of the individual. The developmental psychologist Lawrence Kohlberg

(1976) revised the Piagetian formulation substantially and generated a considerable amount of research interest in the area.

Similar to Piaget, Kohlberg postulates that moral development evolves in a sequence of stages. The sequence is invariant; each individual must develop the features and skills of a lower moral stage before attaining a higher one. Kohlberg identifies three primary stages: *preconventional* morality, *conventional* morality, and *post-conventional* morality. Within each primary stage there are two additional substages which we will refer to here as early and late. During the early *preconventional stage*, one behaves solely on the basis of obtaining rewards and avoiding punishment. The individual has not yet developed any notion of right and wrong and, therefore, is essentially not moral at all. This orientation toward reward and punishment and unquestioning deference to superior power is principally characteristic of children below age seven.

During the late preconventional stage, the right action consists of that which satisfies one's own needs. This stage reflects a selfish orientation which considers the needs of others only to the extent that favors will be returned: "You scratch my back and I'll scratch yours." According to Kohlberg (1976, 1977), human relationships are viewed similarly to those in a marketplace, not of loyalty, gratitude, or justice, but of using others to gain something. The person develops some understanding that in order to obtain rewards one has to work with others. Note that the emphasis is still on meeting one's own needs. This moral orientation appears to resemble the morality found in psychopaths and under-socialized delinquents.

The early *conventional morality stage* is referred to as the "good boy" or "good girl" orientation. The individual's behavior is directed toward gaining social approval and acceptance, and there is much conformity to stereotyped images of what the majority regards as good behavior. In order to obtain social rewards and avoid punishment, one has to be "nice." During this stage the conscience, or the ability to feel guilt, begins to emerge. At the late conventional stage the orientation is to do things out of duty and to respect the authority of others. The person becomes especially aware that certain rules and regulations are necessary to ensure the smooth functioning of society; socially approved behavior is motivated by anticipation of dishonor and blame if one is derelict in performing one's duty. Guilt feelings arise principally out of doing concrete harm to others. This particular substage, late conventional, is often labeled "law and order" morality because of the strong orientation of unquestioning respect for authority, conventionalism, and rigid rules of conduct.

The final and highest stage of moral development—the *post-*

conventional–is probably reached by only a small sector of the population. It requires the ability to be reasonably abstract and possess good cognitive organizational ability. During the early post-conventional stage, correct action is determined by an understanding of the general rights of the individual as compared to the standards which have been critically examined and agreed upon by the whole society. In addition to taking into consideration what is constitutionally and democratically agreed upon, one must also consider the rightness or wrongness of behavior on the basis of personal values. Kohlberg believes that this stage reflects considerable emphasis upon the "legal point of view," but with the orientation that laws can be changed if they are not rational or socially useful. While the late conventional stage stressed fixed rules of conduct, the early post-conventional person sees flexibility in the laws and individual convictions as paramount.

The late post-conventional person demonstrates an orientation "toward the decisions of conscience and toward self-chosen ethical principles appealing to logical comprehensiveness, universality, and consistency" (Kohlberg, 1977, p. 63). The moral principles are abstract and ethical, and they reflect universal principles of justice, of the reciprocity and equality of human rights. The person relies on his or her own personally developed ethical principles and shows respect for "the dignity of human beings as individual persons."

People progress through the stages at different rates and at different ages in their lives, and many never reach the post-conventional stage. The development of moral judgment depends on the intellectual capacity of the person and the life experiences he or she has been exposed to. If the person possesses the cognitive ability to develop high stages of moral development, lack of sufficient social experience may prevent him or her from reaching the higher stages. On the other hand, despite adequate moral upbringing, the individual may lack the cognitive ability to abstract and generalize moral principles necessary at the higher stages.

The reader should realize that Kohlberg did not suppose that most people's moral judgments fit neatly into a single stage. Rather, many people will demonstrate a wide range of moral judgments, with the majority of the judgments clustering around a single stage. This seems to recognize that situational factors can have an influence on a person's judgments and is similar to, although not as pessimistic as, the early May-Hartshorne findings.

Kohlberg's hypothesis is important because it suggests that the search for the development of criminality should pay attention to the intellectual development of the individual as well as to learning and external social factors. To conclude that delinquency springs from lower classes only because of frustrations, disparity in opportunities, social expectations, or learning from association with criminal elements, neglects the potentially powerful role of cognitive developmental factors as *mediators* of criminal conduct.

Intelligence and maturation alone, of course, cannot account for the whole story in moral development. Bandura (1977) cites research evidence to document the observation that moral behavior can be acquired and modified through imitative and observational learning procedures. Also, although cognitive learning is certainly a factor in moral development, we should also bear in mind that people vary in what they teach, model, and reinforce in children of different ages (Bandura, 1977). For example, people explain things differently to a three-year-old than to an eleven-year-old.

The point advanced here is that the internalization of what is judged to be right or wrong in a given society must be examined in any explanation of criminality. The nature of the mental representations of society's expectations, mores, and regulations strongly influences the course of criminal behavior preferred by an individual. However, knowledge of what is right or wrong is not enough to encourage one to behave morally or legally. You may realize that one course of action is clearly immoral and another course is moral, and yet choose the immoral one without a tinge of guilt. Certainly, the affect or emotional component of morality is an important one, perhaps even the most crucial. Without feelings of anxiety, shame, or guilt to accompany moral knowledge, the effectiveness of moral training and expectations would be highly inadequate. And finally, what you believe and feel still may not jibe with what you actually do in a situation.

It appears that each of these three stages of moral development depend, in varying degrees, upon the three types of learning we have discussed. The emotional aspect of moral development seems to depend primarily on classical conditioning (Brown, 1965; Aronfreed, 1976), while the acquisition of moral knowledge and conduct is achieved principally through instrumental and social learning (Brown, 1965; Kohlberg, 1976; Mischel & Mischel, 1976).

The affective dimension of moral development appears to be especially noteworthy. The primary learning mechanism of associating feelings about morality is classical conditioning. Emotions may be classically conditioned to mental representations. For example, a memory may initiate strong emotional reactions. The significance of the affective features of morality is that a child may be conditioned in what behaviors are approved or disapproved before he or she has the cognitive ability to understand, even remotely, the reasons. You can train an infant not to stick a wet fork into the nearest electrical outlet before that infant cognitively understands why. For example, a sharp hand tap every time the child reaches for the outlet will lead him or her to associate the outlet with the tap, and this will hopefully inhibit the behavior. Naturally, if the infant manages to jab the fork in, the electrical shock will in all likelihood be sufficient punishment to prevent a recurrence. The child will associate the outlets with the painful shock and avoid the behavior of jabbing forks into outlets.

Aronfreed (1976) believes that the association of fear and anxiety to mental representations is one of the most influential processes in establishing socially desirable behaviors in human beings. Specifically, the emotional anticipation of punishment (fear) is extremely crucial in learning to inhibit immoral, inappropriate, or antisocial behavior. Aronfreed argues that cognitions assume their power over conduct because fear becomes attached (through conditioning) to the cognitions themselves. Eventually, through the basic mechanisms of classical conditioning, punishment begins to induce control of conduct in the absence of others.

We learned in Chapter 2 that individuals differ in their predisposition to react to fear-inducing situations. People who do not condition particularly well may, under the same learning conditions, not acquire the affective loadings of moral cognitions as well as do other more conditionable individuals. Although these less conditionable individuals may intellectually "know" right from wrong, they will connect less "feeling" to these cognitions. Therefore, the individuals would be less morally inclined than would a comparable group. The psychopath and, in many respects, the stable extravert would certainly qualify for these characteristics.

In sum, moral development theory, which stresses the cognitive internalization of standards and attitudes, offers another point of view on the development of criminality. Presumably, people who internalize social rules should be less likely to violate them. In view of the Kohlberg scheme, this would especially apply to acts which harm or injure another person, psychologically, socially, or physically. Unfortunately, while there is an abundance of theory on moral reasoning (e.g., Lickona, 1976), studies directly testing the relationship between criminality and morality are sparse.

Certainly, the undersocialized delinquent or the psychopath demonstrates a primitive level of moral reasoning in his or her actions. Such a person believes only in self-gain, with little understanding of the feelings of others. One of the few studies that directly examines this relationship (Fodor, 1973) found that psychopathic delinquents appear to be operating at a preconventional level of reasoning, while a comparable sample of nonpsychopathic nondelinquents clustered between the preconventional and conventional stages.

Also, people who are violent toward others and express that in the form of rape, murder, assault, or other violent acts for personal gain are also likely to be at the lower stage of morality. Until research adequately investigates this relationship, however, this point must remain speculative.

The remainder of this chapter will focus on some of the more common offenses committed by juveniles. In order to illustrate the complexity of and various reasons for these offenses, some motivational typologies will be presented. To the extent that research supports it, we shall try to link types of juvenile offenders with motivational features of the offense.

JUVENILE OFFENSES

Vandalism

Vandalism is the willful or malicious destruction of public or private property. The term comes from the behavior of an early Germanic tribe called the vandals, who invaded Western Europe during the fourth and fifth centuries and ruthlessly destroyed property (Cohen, 1968a). Today, it is predominantly a juvenile offense and is very often done in groups. It is also frequently directed at public places, particularly schools. In 1976 vandalism was estimated to be responsible for $600 million in property damage to the nation's public schools (*Time*, July 11, 1977, p. 20). Cohen notes that the highest rate of vandalism occurs in schools with obsolete facilities and equipment, low teacher morale, and high levels of disenchantment and boredom among students. Since schools often represent sources of frustration and symbols representing and providing more painful circumstances than reinforcing ones for many youths, they are likely targets for destruction.

While vandalism has drawn exceedingly little research attention, the press does provide periodic and, occasionally, emotional coverage of the topic. We often read statements made by town or police officials to the effect that the destructive act was "pointless, aimless, wanton, senseless, or meaningless." Very often, so-called meaningless acts are associated in the minds of the public with "mental illness" or psychological problems. "Anyone who would do something like that has to be crazy," or "I can't understand what kind of person would do such a thing," are commonly heard statements.

Two important points should be stressed. First, it appears that most acts of vandalism are deliberately done for some purpose or expectation. Second, there is no evidence that vandalism is perpetrated by emotionally disturbed delinquents who are acting recklessly and savagely. Vandalism, like all criminal behaviors, is not a homogeneous activity, but is an offense committed under different situations for different reasons and by different personality types.

Cohen (1968b) outlined six types of vandalism, each reflecting a different motivation. Since a description of their features encourages the reader to realize the complexity involved in this activity, it is worthwhile to examine the typology briefly. One of the dangers of any typology, however, is that individuals must be found to fit into it, which is not always an easy task. Also, since there is apt to be much overlap, the categories are not mutually exclusive; some youths may have more than one motivation when they vandalize.

1. *Acquisitive vandalism* takes place for the purpose of gaining money or property. Examples include breaking open telephone coinboxes, stripping wire from buildings, breaking parking meters, and stripping hubcaps.

2. *Tactical vandalism* is damage done to obtain a more personal goal. For example, breaking a window to secure a place to sleep, jamming a machine in a factory to get a prolonged rest period, or destroying a valuable art work to gain attention.

3. *Ideological vandalism* is intended to deliver a message or draw attention to an ideological cause. Examples include breaking embassy windows, painting on the walls of a federal building, or damaging an ROTC building.

4. *Vindictive vandalism* is damage done in order to gain revenge. Damages to school buildings and public places represent good illustrations of this type.

5. *Play vandalism* is destruction done in the context of a game. Who can break the most street lights? Who is the strongest in tipping over gravestones?

6. *Malicious vandalism* is an expression of anger or frustration generally directed at some symbol which the offender associates with the source of anger. For example, middle-class property or a white person's business may be damaged by frustrated lower-class, nonwhites.

It appears that we would need another category, *excitement vandalism*, which would resemble to some extent play vandalism. In this case the damage occurs as a result of an effort to break the boredom. Instead of just "messing around" all day, juveniles turn to vandalism which offers the possibility of some excitement and kicks and may be pursued primarily for that purpose (see Figure 5–2).

The fact that vandalism is largely a group phenomenon indicates that the process of deindividuation discussed in the previous chapter may be an important contributing factor. Wade (1967) refers to vandalism's "mutual excitation" property—i.e., a kind of "behavioral contagion" encouraged by spontaneous imitation takes place. Since it is especially important to the adolescent to be a part of a gang and not be labeled a "chicken," the deindividuation process is encouraged. The gang engenders feelings of anonymity and diffusion of responsibility, initiating a kind of "group mind" where the group acts as a self-stimulating, mindless whole. We will return to this topic under mob violence in Chapter 8.

In addition to different motivations for vandalism, there are probably also different personalities engaging in it. For example, extraverts may be more prone to excitement vandalism, while introverts may engage in vindictive vandalism. It is most likely that the socialized delinquent participates in forms of vandalism because of material rewards (acquisition vandalism), because others are doing it (deindividuation), and/or because he or she feels a need to prove his or her worth to peers (play vandalism). The undersocialized delinquent is likely to engage in van-

FIGURE 5–2. A large percentage of vandalism is directed at school buildings. The photo above shows extensive damage to windows of a high school during a winter holiday.

dalism because of boredom and an immediate need for stimulation and gratification (e.g., play or excitement vandalism). The disturbed delinquent may be more involved in vindictive or malicious forms of vandalism because of personal frustrations and feelings of low self-esteem and inadequacy; or he or she may be involved in tactical forms to gain attention. Research is seriously lacking in this area, however, and discussions concerning offender types must remain speculative.

There is no evidence that vandalism marks the first stage in a delinquent or criminal career (Cohen, 1968b). In fact, in one 30-year follow-up study, it was found that vandalism was one of the few offenses that showed no relationship with later criminal activity (Cohen, 1968b). Vandalism in conjunction with other juvenile offenses, however, is a precursor of adult crime. That is, the persistent youthful vandal who also steals cars, is involved in drug traffic, and/or commits violent offenses is likely to become the serious offender we are concerned about.

Auto Theft

Another common offense among juveniles is motor vehicle theft. Over half of all persons arrested for this offense in 1976 were under age eighteen (Kelley, 1977). It also appears to be an offense which is relatively safe from detection, with only 14 percent of all the reported incidents resulting in any arrest. Unlike other stolen property, stolen cars are frequently retrieved: 59 percent of locally stolen cars are eventually returned to the owner (Kelley, 1977). However, when the vehicle is recovered it is usually damaged and stripped of some items.

The sociological literature generally contends that auto theft is predominantly a white, middle-class, adolescent offense (e.g., Gibbons, 1977; Sanders, 1976; Cavan & Ferdinand, 1975). Gibbons (1977, p. 310) writes: "car thieves . . . are usually from middle-class, comfortable economic backgrounds. They live in single family dwellings in middle-income areas. Their parents are usually white-collar or other types of middle-class workers." However, other research (e.g., McCaghy et al., 1977) suggests that the contention that auto theft is largely a favored-class phenomenon may be overstated. Based on data from sections of Virginia and Toledo, Ohio, McCaghy and his colleagues found that Blacks and economically deprived individuals were over-represented in auto theft in relation to their proportions in the population for those communities. For example, in the Toledo data, 55.9 percent were white and 42.2 percent were black; however, Blacks made up only 13.8 percent of the Toledo population. In addition, about two out of every three auto thieves resided in areas where the median income was under $10,000.

The sociological literature also concentrates on auto theft as primarily motivated by joyriding and kicks, or less frequently by professional resale possibility. McCaghy and his colleagues, however, proposed a useful typology which includes a number of important motivational considerations. The same warning given in the vandalism section about pigeonholing juvenile or criminal offenses into neat packages also holds here, however, and it should be kept in mind that the McCaghy typology is based on *arrest* data.

1. *Joyriding*. This motivation appears to be a factor in one out of every four auto thefts. The vehicle is stolen to have a good time, to break the boredom, to achieve excitement and thrills. We should also include in this category cars stolen because of "dares."

2. *Short-term transportation*. This motivation seems to play a role in approximately one of every three auto thefts. Adolescents take the car as a means of getting from one place to another.

3. *Long-term transportation*. This motivation seems to be the primary reason in about one out of every four offenses. In this case, the individual takes the car for personal use for an extended period of time, painting it, repairing it, and using it until he or she decides to steal another.

4. *Profit*. The motive here is primarily resale value, and it occurs in an estimated 6 percent of all auto thefts.

5. *Commission of another crime*. This motive is rare (occurring in about 3 percent of the arrests for auto theft). It involves stealing a motor vehicle for use in the commission of another crime such as robbery, burglary, larceny, rape, or abduction. Stolen vehicles also hamper police detection of the criminal.

We could add at least one other category to the McCaghy typology: auto theft due to status- and image-building among peers. The adolescent is constantly seeking identity and a place among peers, and a car theft venture which includes "hot wiring" should increase this status, provided the particular group perceives this activity in a positive way.

Similar to the vandalism typologies, each of the motivations listed above has a basic goal and objective, which indicates that auto theft is not prompted by meaningless, aimless, or senseless psychological forces. We should stress that there is probably much overlap between the categories, and it is feasible that an individual might steal a motor vehicle for a combination of several of the above reasons.

Research is scarce with regard to the types of personality most prone to steal motor vehicles, although one factor appears with regularity: like vandalism, auto theft among youths is principally a gang activity

(McCaghy et al., 1977). This suggests that group dynamics and deindividuation may play significant roles in both vandalism and auto theft among youths.

Runaways

A runaway is a youth under the age of eighteen who voluntarily leaves home with some objective in mind. The objective may be immature or poorly organized, but it is an objective nevertheless. The youth expects to change his or her predicament in some way by running away.

Running away is strictly a juvenile or status offense. While the FBI statistics (Table 5–1) show a reported incidence in 1976 of 166,529, a number of publications have estimated that the actual number is probably somewhere between 500,000 and 1 million per year (Walker, 1975). This rate amounts to about 1.5 to 3 percent of the total youth population between the ages of ten to seventeen in the United States. It is also estimated that at least half of the runaways are girls with an average age of fifteen. Most often, runaways are one-episode affairs, that is, the general tendency is not to run away more than once. About two-thirds of runaway episodes end within 48 hours (Shellow et al., 1967).

Youths who repeatedly run away are often referred to as "splitters." At least half of all runaways stay in the town or general vicinity in which they live (Beyer et al., 1973; Butler et al., 1974) and, in general, the length of time a youth stays away increases with age (Brennan et al., 1975). Most episodes occur during the summer months or near vacation times (Levine, 1962). In institutions, the highest number of runaways occur within the first six months after admission (Levine, 1962).

Theoretical explanations for runaways range from staunch beliefs of psychopathological causes to equally intense beliefs of social causes. Early research was primarily of the former variety (Walker, 1975). The psychopathological position argues that the basic causal factors in runaway behavior reside within the youth, who is either mentally deficient, is highly impulsive, has a weak ego, is neurotic, or possesses other characteristics of instability. Leventhal (1963, 1964) contends that runaway behavior results from a fear of total loss of environmental control and having feelings of powerlessness. Psychoanalytic viewpoints generally stress the importance of the Oedipal conflict in their explanations. For example, Robey et al. (1964, p. 763) argue that one of the causes of female runaway behavior is "the unconscious threat of an incestuous relationship with the father."

On the other end of the continuum we have advocates of the strict social-environmental causation position. This view holds that youths run away because of poor home environments or intolerable environmental pressures. Hildebrand (1963, p. 216), for example, described the runaway as "a second generation delinquent" who is "often the seed of the future felon," primarily due to a poor home environment and lack of family discipline. Family rejection and neglect are also often related to runaways (Walker, 1975).

Robins and O'Neal (1959) report that a diagnosis of "sociopathic personality" is common among runaways, accounting for nearly a third of the cases they examined. This finding suggests that a large number of runaways may be extraverted, poorly socialized youths seeking new experiences and/or avoiding boring or aversive situations at home. Homer (1974) has proposed a distinction between runaways: they either "run from" intolerable home situations or "run to" something outside the home. It should also be mentioned that it is not unusual for the parents of "run froms" not to want them back *(U.S. News & World Report,* May 12, 1975, pp 49–50).

The repetitive theme which emerges from the literature is that runaways, compared to nonrunaways, have often been subjected to inadequate parent-child relationships and to other conditions which are unconducive to normal development (Walker, 1975). Before we jump on the social-environmental bandwagon, however, it should be understood that some youths living in dire family conditions run away, some do not, and some even resort to suicide. Environmental conditions interact with personality factors such as biological predispositions and previous learning experiences. It is entirely possible that youths who run away still feel that they have some control over what happens to them and feel that by running away they can improve their situation. They are still relatively hopeful, optimistic youths who feel that things can get better. On the other hand, youths who continue to reside in poor social and emotional surroundings may be those who are too fearful to venture out. Others may be too depressed, apathetic, and pessimistic to leave. The alternatives are too scary, unknown, and hopeless to try. To label runaways simply as "impulsive" is a way of explaining by naming, and it fails to advance our understanding of the behavior. It is most feasible to assume that youths leave home for a specific, subjective purpose—however misguided or quick it appears to others. The research seems to indicate that the intention to leave was frequently expressed by the child prior to the actual act (Walker, 1975). It is also likely that many runaways are extraverted youths seeking more exciting alternatives.

One of the most frequently mentioned secondary reasons that youths run away is school problems (Walker, 1975); conduct problems have also appeared often, both at home and in the school (Goldemeier & Dean, 1973; Foster, 1962). These findings also suggest we should take a closer look at personality factors along the lines of extraversion.

Numerous typologies have been proposed for runaways, but all seem to have serious limitations. In an extensive review of the typological schemes, Deborah Walker (1975, p. 30) concludes: "all of these schema can be criticized for incomplete development, vaguely defined categories, and inadequate validation." Because of these inadequacies, it does not appear that the presentation of these runaway typologies would advance our understanding of the phenomenon at this stage of our knowledge.

SUMMARY

In this chapter we looked at some of the developmental factors consistently found in the backgrounds of persons who engage in criminal behavior. We stressed that most youths who participate in delinquent activity do not follow a criminal career. On the other hand, adult criminals very likely were involved in antisocial behavior as youths, since deviant behavior usually begins early.

The literature reports with regularity that delinquents tend to come from broken homes, are behaviorally impulsive, and generally show cognitive limitations. After re-defining impulsiveness we integrated each of these findings into a social learning frame of reference.

Participants in delinquency can be divided into rough categories paralleling the three adult-offender types: the *undersocialized*, the *socialized*, and the *disturbed* delinquent. The undersocialized delinquent engages in antisocial behavior because of inadequate socialization and parenting, compounded by a lack of concern for future consequences. The socialized or "gang" delinquent participates in illegal behavior as part of the group, prompted by the expectations and regulations established by the group. In other words, he or she has been "socialized" by peers into their subculture. The disturbed offender can be best described as one who lacks appropriate or adequate skills for developing self-worth and significance. A bulk of this type's delinquent action is probably designed to gain some importance and significance.

The importance of the internalization of external standards and values was stressed. Special emphasis was directed at Kohlberg's moral stages of development, which depend upon cognitive maturation and experiences. Social learning theorists question the validity of the stages concept, arguing that social learning can account for moral reasoning as well as can the theories of the cognitive-developmentalists.

Vandalism, auto theft, and running away, as typical juvenile offenses, were examined. Some typological motivational schemes were outlined to illustrate the complexities involved in even some of the less serious offenses.

KEY CONCEPTS FOR REVIEW

Observational learning
Socialized delinquents
Impulsiveness
Undersocialized delinquents
Disturbed delinquents
Intelligence
Internalization
Moral development
Preconventional morality
Conventional morality
Post-conventional morality
Vandalism
Auto theft
Runaways

MAJOR THEORISTS AND RESEARCHERS

Bandura and Walters
Glueck and Glueck
Piaget
Kohlberg
Cohen
McCaghy

SUGGESTED READINGS

Clarizio, H.F., and McCoy, G.F. *Behavior disorders in children,* 2nd ed. New York: Thomas Y. Crowell, 1976, Chap. 8.
A comprehensive and balanced view of the psychological position on juvenile delinquency.

Glueck, S., and Glueck, E. *Unraveling juvenile delinquency.* New York: Harper, 1950.
A classical and detailed report of the well-known investigations of the authors.

Lickona, T. (Ed.). *Moral development and behavior.* New York: Holt, Rinehart & Winston, 1976.
An excellent review of the current research and theory on moral development written for the upper-level undergraduate or graduate student.

Savitz, L.D., and Johnson, N. (Eds.). *Crime in society.* New York: Wiley, 1978.
A collection of articles which present a contemporary, balanced, and well-integrated perspective on crime, particularly juvenile delinquency.

"MENTAL ILLNESS" AND CRIME

SIX

A person cannot be held morally culpable if he cannot do what he ought to do, nor can he be blamed if he cannot refrain from doing what he ought not to do.

Ronald Bayer, 1978, p. 222

Scientific investigations of abnormal behavior and criminal behavior have much in common. Attempts to differentiate abnormal from criminal behavior produce vague and controversial definitions, classifications with a string of exceptions, unwieldy and complex variables—and they are all hampered by the pitfalls inherent in the process of brains trying to understand other brains. In addition, both abnormal and criminal behavior are "deviant" in the sense that they stray from what the in-group considers normal, expected, and average for its culture. In this sense the criteria for determining what behaviors constitute "normality" are fluctuating, philosophical, and often self-serving for the majority or for some powerful controlling group.

Despite the complexities of definition and criteria, there has been some slow, laborious, occasionally circular progress toward the understanding of the "deviant" human mind. Researchers have learned, for example, that deviant behavior is acquired through the same fundamental processes as nondeviant behavior. Deviant behavior (both abnormal and criminal) represents learned response patterns for coping with perceived threats, fears, and stressful situations and, generally, for surviving in the world (real or imagined). Problems arise when we try to classify and simplify individual response patterns, however, because we lose sight of the fact that in an effort to survive each individual has uniquely discovered what works best for him or her. As many clinicians are too well aware, human behavior rarely follows a set, predictable pattern where it can be catalogued or will correspond neatly to a description out of a textbook of abnormal psychology. Nor do taxonomies and typologies of human behavior follow clearly delineated categories. Labels commonly used in the mental health professions, therefore, represent only rough approximations of dominant human response patterns. More importantly, diagnostic labels explain nothing; they are only shorthand descriptions of behaviors. A statement that a young man murdered because he was schizophrenic fails to explain why he murdered; it tells us only that he demonstrated some "unusual" behavior patterns before, during, or after the murder.

This chapter will examine the relationships between psychologically abnormal behavior and criminal behavior. This analysis requires a brief presentation of the concepts and terms traditionally used by the behavioral, social, and legal professions in describing abnormal behavior. We will also take a close look at the meaning of the legal designations "criminally insane" and "dangerous."

"MENTAL ILLNESS" DEFINED

During the past century, determining what constitutes abnormal behavior has been a medical enterprise, particularly a psychiatric one. Because of the distinguished success of the medical model in dealing with physical disease—obtaining symptoms and diagnosis and providing treatment based on that diagnosis—it was assumed that the conceptualization used in physical diseases would also be effective in describing behavior problems. Thus the terms "mental illness," "mental disease," "sick," "treatment," "patient," "diagnosis," "mental hospital," and "mental health" permeate even the scientific study of abnormal psychology. The courts, the public, patients, the media, and clinicians have all used these terms with regularity. Abnormal behaviors are called "symptoms" and are allegedly due to some internal malfunction ("the disease process"). The disease or medical model continues to exert influence on our present conceptions of abnormal behavior, with the implicit suggestion that *only* medicine has the knowledge to classify and treat illness and disease, physical or mental.

Few would argue with this substantial decision-making power in matters involving physical disease, but the determination of "mental illness" is another matter. Granted, the disease or medical model did bring behavior disorders out of the realm of witchcraft and evil spirits, prompting more humane treatment of "abnormal" people. Today, however, the overwhelming bulk of research strongly indicates that no virus or disease is involved in the majority of cases of abnormal behavior. For example, Millon and Millon (1974, p. 5) note that ". . . with few exceptions, notably those due to brain damage or infections such as syphilis, a hundred years of intensive research has failed to uncover bodily diseases that are causally involved in psychological abnormalities." There is some research evidence, however, that some of the more serious behavior disorders are, in part, linked to *genetic* factors (e.g., Rosenthal, 1971). For instance, there is some reason to believe that genetic causes have a significant role in the degree of the nervous system's sensitivity to stress and stimulation (Eysenck, 1967), and this might result in certain individuals' propensity to develop certain disorders under specific conditioning or learning situations. Both schizophrenia and severe forms of manic depression have been linked to biological factors. It should be emphasized, however, that we are referring to genetic or hereditary actions and not disease, virus, or physical trauma.

Some professionals (e.g., Szasz, 1970, 1974; Mowrer, 1960) have argued that the concept of "mental illness" and most of its accompanying terminology are archaic and have outlived their usefulness. Thomas Szasz, an outspoken psychiatrist, calls the psychiatric notion of mental illness a myth and a propaganda stunt perpetrated by psychiatrists on the public and the courts. "Their aim is to create in the popular mind a confident belief that mental illness is some sort of disease entity, like an infection or a malignancy," he asserts (Szasz, 1970, p. 19). Others say psychiatry still clings to the disease notion in order to maintain ultimate control over determining who is mentally ill and who is not. Presumably, many psychiatrists wish to guard that power within their profession, thus determining not only who are the mentally ill but also who should treat them. By continuing to subscribe to the myth that abnormal behavior is a disease and, therefore, a medical problem, society will continue to turn to psychiatry for definition, determination, and treatment.

Although the term "mental illness" is inaccurate and outdated, it does permeate the mental health and criminal justice systems in describing deviant or abnormal offenders. As long as we remember that it does not refer to some physical illness or sickness to be treated solely by physicians, we can use the term loosely while discussing some psychiatric and legal issues concerning insanity, criminal responsibility, and dangerousness. Otherwise, however, we should avoid the term and use instead the general label "behavior problem."

Regardless of the debate, there is no denying that the determination of insanity, although basically a legal issue, is strongly influenced by psychiatry. The judicial system has traditionally relied heavily on psychiatrists to determine who is "mentally ill" and generally seeks and accepts their testimony as expert witnesses (often excluding other professionals) in cases involving criminal responsibility and competence. Although the court always makes the final determination, studies (e.g., Vann, 1965; Pfeiffer et al., 1967; Steadman & Cocozza, 1974) have found that the court agrees with the recommendations of psychiatrists about 90 percent of the time. Attempts by other professionals to infringe on or challenge this legal territory are often attacked in force by the American Psychiatric Association.

To illustrate: In the classic 1962 Supreme Court Case of Jenkins vs. U.S., the question was raised as to whether the testimony of a qualified and certified clinical psychologist could be regarded as expert concerning the presence or absence of mental disease or mental defect (Bazelon, 1974). The American Psychiatric Association argued that a psychologist is not competent to give opinions on mental disease or illness, and therefore that testimony by anyone other than a physician or psychiatrist should be invalid. Fortunately, the court disagreed and found a qualified psychologist's opinion fully admissible in cases involving the determination of mental illness or defect. In the Rouse case in 1966, the American Psychiatric Association issued another statement concerning treatment of mental illness: "The definition of treatment and the appraisal of its adequacy are matters for medical determination" (Bazelon, 1974, p. 22). A group of psychiatrists also recently noted, in relation to the assessment of criminal dangerousness, "According to virtually all legislation with respect to dangerous persons, an individual cannot be legally identified as dangerous until psychiatry has diagnosed him as such" (Kozol, et al., 1972, p. 374). It is interesting to note, however, that in a recent case before the California Supreme Court, the American Psychiatric Association submitted a brief which informed the court that: "The newly imposed duty to warn is also inconsistent with the finding of scientific research that no special professional ability or expertise has yet been demonstrated in the prognosis of dangerousness. Instead, the few studies which have been done strongly suggest that psychiatrists are rather inaccurate predictors; inaccurate in an absolute sense, and even less accurate when compared with other professions" (Schwitzgebel, 1977, p. 145).

The judicial system has become increasingly disenchanted with the behavioral sciences and the concepts, appraisal methods, and terminology of mental illness. Consider an illustrative statement by Judge Bazelon (1974, p. 18) who, after 25 years of experience in the U.S. Court of Appeals, concludes: "My experience has shown that in no case is it more difficult to elicit productive and reliable expert testimony than in cases that call on the knowledge and practice of psychiatry." This statement could apply equally well to psychologists who employ diagnostic labeling and psychodynamic concepts of mental illness in assessments and explanations of criminal behavior.

The disenchantment begins with the fact that the judicial system requires expert testimony based on reliable, valid evidence which emphasizes the observable. Neither psychiatry nor psychology has progressed to a point where it can determine *post hoc*, or after the criminal act, what an offender was thinking or feeling at that time. Nor are psychology and psychiatry able to group individuals into neat clusters of mental or emotional competence and answer with confidence that an offender was not in control of his or her behavior or mental processes at the time of the criminal act. The professionals can give opinions, and they can challenge each other's opinions—which they do with fervor and which gives rise to much of the judicial cynicism. Seldom are ballistics or fingerprint experts pitted against one another in the courtroom; with behavioral experts, the practice is commonplace. The embarrassingly high amount of disagreement about diagnostic labels, competency, and criminal responsibility has prompted Brendan Maher (1966, p. 21) to comment: "In many court areas there tends to develop a body of clinicians who frequently find psychosis (defense clinicians) and a body of clinicians who do not find it (prosecution clinicians)."

Because of the importance of the entire issue of mental illness, insanity pleas, appraisal of dangerousness, and criminal responsibility, it is instructive for the student of criminal behavior to be familiar with the present state of the art. Therefore, much of the remainder of this chapter will be concerned with taking a good, hard look at the available scientific evidence on these issues. First, however, we need to review the diagnostic labels commonly used by clinicians in both the mental health clinic and the courtroom.

LABELING ABNORMAL BEHAVIOR

Since the classification system outlined by the American Psychiatric Association in 1968 and presented in the *Diagnostic and Statistical Manual of Mental Disorders* (commonly known as the DSM-II) represents the official diagnostic format for psychiatry, it is important to be familiar with its diagnostic labels and what kinds of behavior they describe.[1] A brief outline of the classification system is presented in Table 6–1. These labels are freely used by the news media, clinicians, the public, and the judicial system to "explain" why murders take place. For example, the infamous "Son of Sam" who terrorized young women in New York City with a .44 revolver in the mid-1970s was labeled a probable "paranoid schizophrenic who had been rejected by a woman and took out his sexual rage at night with his .44" (*Newsweek*, July 11, 1977, p. 18). This diagnosis was attached to him on the basis of sketchy samples of behavior and very vague clues, before he was even apprehended or evaluated by a professional. What is a paranoid schizophrenic? Can clinicians diagnose an individual without even having had contact with the person or obtaining information about his or her background?

Diagnostic labels do not represent neat parcels of behavior patterns that do not overlap. Individuals do not choose a cluster of abnormal behaviors and follow a definitive pattern. For example, in most cases of neurosis or psychosis, the individual is manifesting behavior patterns

TABLE 6-1
Selected Abnormal Behavior Classifications

I. Psychoses
    A. Schizophrenia
        1. simple type
        2. paranoid type
        3. hebephrenic type
        4. catatonic type

    B. Major or severe affective (mood) disorders

    C. Paranoid psychoses
        1. paranoia
        2. paranoid states

II. Neuroses

III. Personality disorders
    A. Antisocial (or psychopathic) personality disorder
    B. Schizoid personality disorder
    C. Paranoid personality disorder
    D. Explosive personality disorder

---

[1]It should be pointed out that the DSM-II is presently undergoing revision and should be released sometime in late 1979 or early 1980. The revised edition will be called DSM-III.

which he or she has learned will provide temporary relief from the perceived stress and strain of living. While these unique coping behaviors offer some relief, they also often generate additional problems in work-study habits, personal habits, and interpersonal relationships. Some of these behavioral patterns may even bring the individual into conflict with the law and society's expectations of appropriate behavior. Often, "disturbed" individuals exhibit overlapping behaviors; many show features found in several diagnostic categories.

We shall pay particular attention to three major diagnostic categories—psychosis, neurosis, and personality disorders—primarily because these are the most common labels used in describing or explaining criminal behavior. Psychosis is the diagnostic category most often associated with discussions and judgments involving the legal term "insanity" or with criminal responsibility and competence. Note that an individual may be diagnosed psychotic and not be legally regarded insane; similarly, a person may be legally designated insane without being clinically regarded as psychotic. We shall return to these distinctions later in the chapter in our discussion of legal considerations.

Psychosis

The chief characteristic in psychosis is loss of contact with reality, because the individual appears to have extreme difficulty in distinguishing between it and fantasy. Perceptually, the person may see, hear, smell, or otherwise sense things that are not correspondingly apparent to others in the environment. These perceptual distortions and misinterpretations are known as *hallucinations*. Often, the hallucinations are auditory—the person may hear voices, music, or peculiar sounds. The person may also grossly misinterpret the intentions and behavior of other people (real or imagined). These apparently unsupported beliefs, claims, and complaints are known as *delusions*, and the entire array of these distorted thoughts and beliefs is called the *delusional system*. In order to deal with mounting stresses and overwhelming discomfort, the person may also develop bizarre behavioral patterns or isolate himself or herself completely from the social environment. The deterioration of daily activities may be so profound that hospitalization or professional care may be necessary. Psychotic patterns which are believed to be primarily due to psychological causal factors are called *functional psychoses*. Psychotic behaviors assumed to be the result of identifiable organic factors, such as tumors, malnutrition, infections, toxicity, or injury are usually referred to as *organic psychoses*. However, the overlap and interactive features of the causal agents between these two divisions sometimes makes the distinction meaningless (Coleman, 1976).

Psychoses may be further subdivided to distinguish whether the behavioral features primarily represent a thought disorder called *schizophrenia*, a mood disorder labeled *affective disorder*, or specialized categories of psychotic disorder characterized by delusional systems known as *paranoia* and *paranoid states*.

Neurosis

This is a behavioral problem which plagues an estimated 20 million persons in the United States alone (Coleman, 1976). The chief ingredient for the disorder is the expression of excessive anxiety, or autonomic arousal. In large doses, feelings of anxiety are highly unpleasant, prompting the person to take certain measures to alleviate the discomfort. For example, a person may become extremely fearful of germs and avoid all physical contact with people, wipe all public doorknobs before touching them, and wash his or her hands thoroughly every hour of the day. Another example is an extreme fear of elevators. The person's unique adaptive behavior in this case might be to avoid elevators completely, even after obtaining a well-paying job on the fiftieth floor of an insurance building. Despite the long, tedious, 45-minute stairwell climb every morning to get to work, and the 35-minute struggle back down, the person finds himself or herself unable to alter the painful dread of elevators and therefore avoids rather than copes with the problem.

Neurotic individuals, in contrast to psychotics, are aware of their problems, and unless their habitual ways of responding to stress handicap them socially, emotionally, or economically, they usually do not seek professional help. Furthermore, neurotic behaviors, in contrast to psychotic behaviors, do not demonstrate "gross distortion or misinterpretation of external reality, nor gross personality disorganization" (DSM-II, 1968, p. 39). Neurotic individuals are usually "anxious, ineffective, unhappy, and often guilt-ridden people" who do not typically require hospitalization but who may require psychotherapy (Coleman, 1976).

Personality Disorders

This third diagnostic division is especially important in our discussion of criminal behavior. It involves a hodgepodge of behaviors which do not fit into the more traditional categories. According to the DSM-II (1968, p. 41), "this group of disorders is characterized by deeply ingrained maladaptive patterns of behavior that are perceptibly different in quality from psychotic and neurotic symptoms. Generally, these are lifelong patterns, often recognizable by the time of adolescence or earlier." Personality disorder patterns are not regarded as behaviors that deal with internal feelings of anxiety, but rather as behaviors directed at meeting one's own needs "in unethical ways at the expense of others" (Coleman, 1976). Personality disorders are a result of "immature development" and the behaviors tend to be childlike, impulsive, selfish, and acting out. Persons with personality disorders do not feel guilty because they bring distress to others, and they often fail to recognize their faults and their disruptive behavior. They regard their actions as "normal." They habitually exhibit the same socially maladaptive behavior from situation to situation, with little or no attempt to vary it to fit the circumstances. They appear rigidly set in their ways, manifesting little flexibility in mending them. For example, the individual exhibiting a personality disorder may be consistently aggressive, suspicious, or ineffectual across situations. Typically, personality disorders are not responsive to the traditional forms of psychotherapy.

Comments on Abnormal Behavior

Some behavioral patterns within each of these major classifications are more applicable than others to mentally ill offenders. Personality disorder, particularly antisocial (or psychopathic) personality, is a very common diagnosis in court-referred evaluations of offenders. Among the more severe behavioral problems or psychoses, paranoid schizophrenia appears frequently in psychiatric impressions of offenders, particularly of the more violent ones.

Neurosis is a clinical designation reserved for a heterogeneous class of behaviors featuring some expression of apprehension and anxiety, commonly called "nervousness." Neurotic behaviors are response patterns designed to reduce uncomfortable levels of anxiety. The reader will recall that Eysenck postulated that criminals, as a group, exhibit higher levels of neuroticism than do noncriminals. Neuroticism is not quite synonymous with neurosis, just as Eysenck's psychoticism is not synonymous with psychosis. Neuroticism is a hypothetical dimension reflecting responsivity of the autonomic nervous system. If the person's autonomic nervous system overreacts to stress (high neuroticism), he or she is more susceptible or predisposed to neurotic behaviors than is a person low on neuroticism. The clinical diagnosis of neurosis is different. That is, the traditional diagnostic rules usually require that 1. the patient express discomfort and anxiety about some stimulus or set of stimuli and 2. the reaction to coping with the anxiety-provoking stimuli be inhibitory or a hindrance to adaptation. Individuals who score high on the neuroticism scale are not *clinically* neurotic until they qualify for the diagnostic rules of discomfort and prevention of adjustment. Later in this chapter we shall return to the relationship between clinical neurosis and crime, and the reader should remember then that we are not referring to the neurotic susceptibility as hypothesized in Eysenck's neuroticism dimension.

For now, our task is to become better acquainted with the psychiatric descriptive jargon used in certain subcategories of psychosis and personality disorders that are encountered most frequently in the criminal justice system, specifically schizophrenia and paranoid reactions (both psychoses) and explosive, paranoid, schizoid, and antisocial personality disorders.

SCHIZOPHRENIA

Schizophrenia is a catch-all diagnosis reserved for emotional states and behavioral patterns of psychotic proportions. The label represents a constellation of varied behaviors which may include extreme social withdrawal, unpredictability, severe speech disorder, disorders in perception and attention, gross mood disturbances, and, most importantly, gross disturbances in thinking. When the Swiss psychiatrist Eugen Bleuler (1857–1939) introduced the diagnostic term "schizophrenia," it was intended for individuals manifesting a notable split in thought processes. In contemporary usage, it indicates a split between reality and thought (Rimm & Sommervill, 1977).

In the U.S., Europe, and Japan, an estimated 1 percent of the population may be expected to develop some form of schizophrenia during its lifetime (Page, 1975). The incidence rate is about the same for both sexes. The onset of schizophrenia normally occurs around late adolescence and early adulthood, with a majority of hospital admissions occurring between the ages of twenty-five and thirty-five. Fifty percent of the residents in mental hospitals today are diagnosed schizophrenic, with paranoid type the most common subdivision (Coleman, 1976).

No specific behavior pattern appears consistently in people suffering the disorder. For example, only one-third report hallucinations, and the content of these hallucinations differs from individual to individual (Page, 1975). Each individual selects his or her unique behavioral pattern in an effort to withdraw from the painful or stressful effects of reality. Schizophrenia is represented by such a wide variety of behavioral patterns that Roger Brown (1973) comments that persons called schizophrenic are as diverse as persons called normal.

Certain chemicals (e.g., LSD), sensory deprivation conditions, and prolonged loss of sleep can also induce schizophrenic-like reactions. However, the chemically-induced reactions dissipate with the chemical, whereas the disordered behavior of schizophrenics persists for many years. In a substantial number of people the schizophrenic behaviors remain for a lifetime.

One of the principal and diagnostically essential symptoms of schizophrenia is an irrational and bizarre thought process. In a case described by Page (1975, p. 196), a young woman diagnosed schizophrenic was asked to report her associations to the word "day." She responded: "Night, April 15, Immaculate Conception." When asked, "Are you married?" she answered, "Yes, There are many bad women in the world who should be punished. The Lord is the father to my child." Many schizophrenics complain that thoughts rush through their minds, seemingly all at the same time. Their thoughts seem to be out of control and become frightening as well as confusing.

Another important behavioral characteristic of schizophrenia is speech disturbances. Often speech is unintelligible, strange, or nonexistent. For example, one man I treated developed an elaborate but cryptic system of numbers for communication, so that when asked a question he would respond in digits, never words. Although it took many months to decipher the code, it became quite apparent that this individual had actually constructed a somewhat meaningful language of digits. Certain number combinations were used for each word. In another case, a man would tersely say, "Gonna cut your throat" whenever he was in the presence of other people; this was apparently the only phrase he had used for nearly eight years. Some schizophrenics verbally withdraw completely and refuse to utter any intelligible speech patterns. Other schizophrenics may "flip in and out" of intelligible and unintelligible speech, often unpredictably.

A third distinguishing characteristic is extreme social withdrawal and detachment from the social environment. The schizophrenic may view other people as hostile, threatening, and not to be trusted. The person may literally seek a corner where he or she can stand facing the wall with his or her back to the world.

Inappropriate emotional response is a fourth relatively common characteristic. Schizophrenics often giggle when the normal response in a particular situation would be sadness or fear. They may cry without apparent reason. Many appear to suffer a diminished capacity for experiencing joy or pleasure under any condition.

Several of these characteristics may be present in one person, but rarely do you see a "walking textbook" description of schizophrenia. The behaviors vary from individual to individual, place to place, and time to time. Often the behavioral pattern is on the fringes of schizophrenia, and the behaviors occasionally appear in combination with other abnormal behaviors characteristic of another disorder. The variability of symptoms may make a "precise" diagnosis exceedingly difficult, and clinicians may disagree on what specific behavior pattern is being demonstrated by the person. Problems of this sort prove to be rather embarrassing in the courtroom, especially if "proper diagnosis" turns evasive.

The Schizoid Personality Disorder

This has many of the same features as schizophrenic reaction, but there is an absence of delusions, hallucinations, and thought disorders. According to the DSM-II (p. 42), the schizoid personality "manifests shyness, oversensitivity, seclusiveness, avoidance of close or competitive relationships, and often eccentricity." As noted by Page (1975, p. 298) schizoid personalities are "detached from reality but not out of touch with it." Their fantasy and daydream life is rich and intense, and they prefer an inner world to an outer world. They are described as introverted, cold, aloof, and emotionally detached, and on occasion are considered odd and peculiar. Sometimes they do exceptionally well in intellectual or creative pursuits.

PARANOID REACTIONS

Quite often the mass media will aver that a certain murderer or rapist was paranoid schizophrenic at the time of the offense. What does that label mean? "Paranoid" is used loosely and widely by professionals and the public. "Paranoia," a Greek word meaning "to think beside oneself," can be traced back over 2,000 years in the medical literature (Millon & Millon, 1974). Although it has functioned throughout history as a "wastebasket" category, the terms *paranoia* and *paranoid reaction* have been refined to pertain to a pattern of behavior whose prominent ingredient is an unwarranted suspicion of the motives of others.

Clinicians use several diagnostic names for paranoid reactions: paranoid schizophrenia, paranoid state, paranoia, and paranoid personality disorder. The specific paranoid designation depends upon the intensity to which the individual is sensitive to the motives of others plus the complexity, logic, and organization of the suspicious beliefs or delusional systems he or she develops. The major determinant of the diagnosis is the delusional system, which may range from a jungle of vague, poorly conceived suspicions to an elaborate, logically convincing set of prejudices or imagined plots. If the paranoid features are pronounced and severe in the sense that they dictate the person's daily activities, the individual will qualify for either paranoid schizophrenia, paranoid state, or paranoia. If the features are "deeply ingrained," habitual, and interfere with the person's ability to maintain satisfactory interpersonal relationships, but do not impede his or her ability to function adequately, the person may be diagnosed paranoid personality disorder.

Paranoid schizophrenia is used when the delusional system strongly and severely interferes with contacts with reality. The suspicion-oriented delusions may be supplemented by hallucinations, usually auditory in nature, where the persons "hear" people calling them bad names, talking about them, and/or threatening them (Page, 1975). The delusional system becomes enmeshed into other behavioral patterns of the individual, promoting problems in interpersonal relationships, moods, and thinking. The person's attitude is frequently hostile and aggressive in line with his or her delusions.

Paranoid schizophrenics are assumed to be potentially very dangerous if they obsessively suspect that others are beginning to plot to threaten their personal survival. Under these conditions, paranoid schizophrenics may consider that their only alternative lies in "getting" the others first. Coleman (1976) cites the example of a school principal who showed many paranoid features and who was convinced that the school board was discriminating against him. The principal's solution was to shoot the school board members—and he promptly did just that, killing most of them.

In cases where the delusional system or beliefs are carefully organized, internally consistent, logical and convincing, and are the outstanding and only seriously deviant feature of the personality, the person may qualify for the phenomenon of *paranoia*. Paranoia is extremely rare and is "characterized by the gradual development of an intricate, complex, and elaborate paranoid system based on and often proceeding logically from misinterpretation of an actual event" (DMS-II, p. 38). If one accepts the individual's distorted perception of the initial event, the delusional system built upon that event develops with compelling logic. In fact, the logic may be so compelling that the paranoid person may draw a group of others to join him or her in some strange cult, sect, or movement in religion or politics. Often, the person has convinced himself or herself that he or she is endowed with unique and superior ability (often referred to as delusions of grandiosity).

A tragic example of the power of one man's delusional system was illustrated in 1978 in Jonestown, Guyana, where the self-proclaimed spiritual leader Jim Jones persuaded hundreds of people to join him in his own "humanitarian" visions for a better life. Eventually, his delusions of grandeur ended in the mass suicide or murder of 900 men, women, and children, including Jones himself. The delusional system developed by Jones is clearly portrayed in an article by Carey Winfrey (1979) in the *New York Times Magazine*.

The major difference between paranoia and the *paranoid state* is the degree to which the delusional system is organized, consistent, and logically developed. Like paranoia, the paranoid state is relatively rare; it is unusual for people to behave in a purely paranoid fashion while not showing other psychotic behavioral patterns. The decision as to whether the delusional system follows a paranoia, paranoid state, or paranoid schizophrenic pattern is often a "judgment call" and a gray area which generates considerable disagreement among clinicians.

One last paranoid category, the *paranoid personality disorder*, is explained in the DSM-II as a "behavioral pattern characterized by hypersensitivity, rigidity, unwarranted suspicion, jealousy, envy, excessive self-importance, and a tendency to blame others and ascribe evil motives to them. These characteristics often interfere with the patient's ability to maintain satisfactory interpersonal relationships" (DSM-II, p. 42).

The paranoid personality is argumentative and does not like to be criticized. To defend his or her stance, this person may become highly aggressive and assaultive. The individual rigidly adheres to this mode of conduct, regardless of the difficulty it gets him or her into. The paranoid personality's general view of the world is that people are basically malevolent and out to get you if they can; most of his or her problems are misfortunes, the person feels, and are due not to his or her own behavior but to the malicious behavior of others. Thus, paranoid personalities are unlikely to take the blame for assaults, since they feel they have to defend themselves from the onslaughts of others. They are constantly on the alert for slights which they translate into personal attacks. For example, if the paranoid walked into a room full of people who began to laugh as he or she entered, it is highly likely that the person would assume and be immediately convinced that they were laughing at him or her. Although this suspicion extends to many phases of the individual's life, it is particularly directed at interpersonal relationships. Thus, most of the relationships are volatile, and paranoids are frequently on the verge of explosive anger directed toward friends.

Paranoid personalities are emotionally restrained, stiff, humorless, and unwilling to compromise. Stubbornly, they insist on their views, yielding no ground, and if pushed to the wall on a point they may explode in angry outbursts regardless of the consequences. Since jealousy permeates their life style, they develop extremely few close involvements or friendships.

EXPLOSIVE PERSONALITY

Only a few of the dozen personality disorders are of concern to the criminal psychologist. We have already discussed three: the paranoid personality disorder and the schizoid personality, which we looked at above, and the antisocial personality disorder, synonymous with psychopathy, which was covered in Chapter 3.

At this point we shall examine the *explosive personality*, also known as the *epileptoid personality disorder, aggressive personality* or, as suggested by Mark and Ervin (1970), the *dyscontrol syndrome*. The explosive personality disorder is described as one in which unpredictable outbursts of physical or verbal aggression occur in a person normally showing good control. Moreover, these episodic behaviors appear inappropriate for the situation. In some cases, the aggression reaches violent proportions, resulting in serious injury to others. Usually the individuals express guilt and remorsefulness following the aggressive episode, often explaining they do not know what came over themselves, or that they seem to be "driven."

Although the individual regrets his or her actions, this regret does not prevent their repetition when the person is again frustrated (Page, 1975). Mark and Ervin (1970, p. 126) note that individuals with explosive personalities usually exhibit four characteristics (not necessarily present at the same time): "1. a history of physical assault, especially wife and child beating; 2. the symptom of pathological intoxication—that is, drinking even a small amount of alcohol triggers acts of senseless brutality; 3. a history of impulsive sexual behavior, at times including sexual assaults; and 4. a history (in those who drove cars) of many traffic violations and serious automobile accidents."

This brief informational sojourn through some of the major diagnostic classifications of behavioral problems has introduced the reader to some common terms and definitions used by clinicians in describing and, sometimes, in explaining criminal behavior. Despite the clinical thinking that certain types of behavioral problems should be considered more prone to criminal activity and also more potentially dangerous than others, the question we must address ourselves to in this chapter is whether the evidence justifies that belief. What is the incidence of criminal behavior among people evaluated as being deviant or behaviorally abnormal? And, do persons in certain clinical diagnostic categories in fact commit more criminal acts than the normal population?

BEHAVIOR DISORDERS AND CRIME

It is a common misconception that some crimes, particularly heinous, violent acts such as brutal and senseless slayings, are almost always committed by people who are "mentally ill." That misconception, perpetuated by the news and entertainment media and often accepted by the criminal justice system, has become ingrained into American society to the point where the "crazy" person is to be feared and should be confined for society's protection. A man who sexually molests and kills a four-year-old child has to be "sick." Why else would he do it? Popular literature editorializes that contemporary society is "sick," murderers are "sick," and our criminal youth is "sick."

The problem here is the popular tendency to view deviant, seemingly irrational behavior as psychologically abnormal behavior. The public confuses socially deviant behavior with "mental illness," and in this sense, the psychotics, the schizophrenics, and the personality disordered are guilty by association. Unpredictable, irrational, bizarre, disoriented people are frightening and, thus, dangerous. It is important to note, however, that murderers and violent offenders, although socially deviant, are not necessarily psychotic or "crazy." In fact, the research literature is highly consistent in pointing out that psychotic or severely disturbed individuals are no more likely to commit serious crimes against others than the general population (Lunde, 1976; Brodsky, 1973, 1977; Henn et al., 1976a; Gulevick & Bourne, 1970). The TV, movie, or mystery novel portrayal of a killer gone berserk with bloodthirsty delusions is sensational, frightening, and perhaps entertaining, but in truth the phenomenon is rare.

Fritz Henn and his colleagues conducted an extensive series of investigations on all the defendants referred to by the court in St. Louis for psychiatric assessment over a period of years (Henn et al., 1976a). Their one major conclusion was that psychotics are no more likely to commit sexual crimes or other crimes against persons than the general population. In fact, of the nearly 2,000 persons arrested for homicide in St. Louis between 1964 and 1973, only about 1 percent qualified as psychotic. Data comparable to this were also reported by Hafner and Boker (1973) on the German population and by Zitrin et al. (1975) and Rappeport and Lassen (1965) on the American population.

In a separate sample using 1,195 defendants accused of a variety of crimes, the St. Louis project found that the most frequent diagnosis was personality disorder, accounting for nearly 40 percent of all the diagnoses. Two-thirds of those classified personality disorders were specifically designated "antisocial personality."

The second most frequent diagnosis was schizophrenia (which also included those labeled "probable" schizophrenia) comprising 17 percent of the total diagnoses. The other diagnostic designations were evenly distributed and of low frequency. It was interesting to note, however, that 93 percent of those defendants referred were diagnosed something, which probably reflects, in part, the biases of the court in their referrals and the apparent obligation of the evaluation team to tag on a diagnosis of some sort.

About one-quarter of the defendants received an additional or secondary diagnosis, the most common being alcoholism, followed by drug addiction. The Henn findings support those reported by Guze (1976) who found alcoholism prevalent among criminal offenders. Alcoholism in the St. Louis survey appeared to cut across all diagnostic categories, with the notable exception of schizophrenia, where only a few cases of a secondary diagnosis of alcoholism were found. The combination of alcoholism and drug addiction as a secondary diagnosis was common in persons diagnosed antisocial personality.

A recent review by Rabkin (1979) of the criminal behavior of discharged mental patients sheds some further light on the relationship between crime and abnormal behavior. She reports that, unlike earlier research, a significant number of recent studies have found that the arrest rate for discharged mental patients was higher than the rate for the general population, especially for assaultive behavior. However, closer examination of these research data reveals that the disproportionate arrest rate for mental patients was predominantly the result of two factors.

First, a small subset of patients who had criminal records prior to hospital admission continued their antisocial ways soon after discharge from the mental institution. Their high arrest rates substantially inflated the arrest rates for all mental patients. On the other hand, patients who did not possess prior criminal records were substantially below the arrest rates for the general population. Rabkin suggests that the upward trend in arrest rates is partly due to the increasing tendency of courts to refer many of the criminally prone to a mental institution rather than to process them through the judicial system. Policy changes in many mental institutions which allow patients to return to the community much sooner than before also affect this upward trend.

The other factor accounting for the disproportionate arrest rates is a diagnostic one. Rabkin found that a majority of the criminal offenses after discharge were committed by individuals who had diagnoses of alcoholism, addiction, or personality disorder. As we have seen, these diagnostic categories have been reported with consistency in other studies. We have seen, too, that many "personality disorders" are really antisocial behaviors, but classified personality disorder because the clinician could find no other label to pin on the individual acting "antisocially." Of course, alcoholism and addiction are in the fringe areas of traditional diagnoses of behavior problems or mental illness. The arrest rate for other diagnostic classifications was found by Rabkin to be highly similar to that reported in the general population.

In summary, the research literature fails to support the widespread and enduring myth that psychotics or the severely disturbed tend to be killers or other violent offenders. It is possible, however, as some clinicians believe, that although the incidence rate of violent offenses among psychotic people is about equivalent to that found in the general population, the more bizarre violent offenses are committed by psychotics. Yet, there has been no research to delineate offense "bizarreness" as a function of behavioral problems in the research literature, and this possibility must remain speculative. Research does indicate, however, that alcoholism, chemical addiction, and personality disorder do appear with some regularity among offenders. In the case of personality disorders, antisocial personalities (psychopaths) are overrepresented, but it is difficult to determine how much bias or subjective criteria enter into the assessment and diagnosis. Upon judicial referral, the evaluating agency realizes at the outset that the individual is "antisocial" because of his or her deviant behavior, and this prior knowledge may contaminate the final diagnosis.

The incidence and nature of behavioral disorders among convicted populations is difficult to determine. Inmate populations are considerably different from the population at large because they have been filtered through the judicial process, and prison life is likely to have had some effect on their mental state. However, a review of nine studies on prisoner populations found that the overall incidence of psychosis is small, occurring in only 1 or 2 percent of the entire population (Brodsky, 1973). Clinical neurosis also appears infrequently, occurring in about 4 to 6 percent of prisoner populations. Personality disorders, on the other hand, are diagnosed very frequently. For example, Schands (1958) found that 56 percent of 1,720 North Carolina prisoners could be classified as personality disorders of some variety. Although the incidence of psychosis in prison populations appears to be small, we should keep in mind that a substantial segment of prison inmates exhibiting psychotic behaviors are transferred to institutions for the "criminally insane" and therefore not included in statistical counts of prison populations.

THE CRIMINALLY INSANE

The term "criminally insane" has traditionally encompassed a variety of behavioral categories and judicial determinations. The label has generally been reserved for those individuals involuntarily committed to a security section of a mental institution or "hospital prison," and often more for custodial reasons than for treatment purposes. Although state statutes vary, there are four basic avenues available for entry into a broad definition of the criminally insane community. They are 1. not guilty of some serious crime by reason of insanity, 2. incompetent to stand trial, 3. mentally ill prisoners transferred to a hospital prison, and 4. the "dangerous" mentally ill patient.

The best known, due to the wide publicity it draws, is the insanity plea and the subsequent judicial determination of "not guilty by reason of insanity," often abbreviated NGRI. NGRI determinations are based on the assumption that the person who committed a criminal act is not guilty of malicious criminal intent because of some degree of mental "disease," "illness," or "defect." The main issue of NGRI cases centers around the defendant's mental state during the time the offense was committed, which might be months or even years prior to a court-requested psychological or psychiatric evaluation. Presumably, the NGRI individual was not acting of his or her own free will at the time of the offense: the person's actions were beyond his or her willful control.

Despite the fact that NGRIs have been found not criminally responsible for their acts, the public generally believes, and the state statutes often presume, that NGRIs are unpredictable, bizarre, and potentially dangerous individuals who pose a serious threat to society. Therefore, NGRIs become "dangerously mentally ill" individuals, who must be committed and securely held until their mental condition improves to a "nondangerous" level through some kind of effective treatment.

Although NGRI cases receive extensive press coverage, it is a rare defendant who pleads and is subsequently adjudicated NGRI. Valid estimates indicate that in only about 4 percent of all U.S. criminal cases does the defendant use the insanity plea (Steadman & Cocozza, 1974; Scheidenmandel & Kanno, 1969). In addition, NGRIs are estimated to make up only 4 percent of the entire committed "criminally insane" population (Steadman & Cocozza, 1974).

One of the major reasons for the low ratio of insanity defenses to criminal proceedings appears to be that confinement to a mental institution for an indefinite period of time is no better a bargain than incarceration in a correctional facility for a specified time period (Monahan, 1977). Moreover, confinement to a special section for the criminally insane in a mental hospital has usually offered little in the way of psychological improvement or effective treatment, and by and large has not been a place for doing "easy time." Therefore, defendants and their attorneys have usually used the insanity plea only where the nature of the alleged offense presented a real and uncomfortable possibility of life imprisonment or death.

The second pathway to the criminally insane designation is to be evaluated by clinicians and ruled by the court as "incompetent to stand trial," abbreviated IST. IST means that the individual is considered to be so intellectually and/or psychologically impaired that he or she is unable to understand the criminal proceedings against him or her or to cooperate with counsel in his or her own defense (Sleffel, 1977). An individual may be diagnosed psychotic, schizophrenic, or mentally retarded and still be evaluated by the judicial process as competent to stand trial.

In an extensive study of the criminally insane in New York State institutions in 1966, Henry Steadman and Joseph Cocozza (1974) found that approximately 40 percent of the so-called criminally insane population were IST defendants. What this means is that over one-third of the persons involuntarily confined in security hospital-prisons were only *charged* (not convicted) with crime and were ordered by the court to be confined to an institution for an indefinite period of time until somehow found or rendered "competent." Steadman and Cocozza discovered (as have other investigators) that a shockingly large number of IST defendants had been confined against their will before being tried—for periods which sometimes far exceeded the maximum sentence allowed for their alleged offenses. More significantly, the Steadman-Cocozza data showed that ISTs had not received any treatment which would enable them to achieve competency, nor were there any criteria which precisely defined competency.

Until recently, the standard judicial procedure for determining incompetency required the confinement of defendants to a maximum security institution for a lengthy psychiatric-psychological evaluation (usually 60 to 90 days). Following the evaluation, the defendant was subjected to a special hearing to determine incompetency "eligibility." If the court found the defendant incompetent to understand the charges brought against him or her, the judicial proceedings, or to help counsel in his or her defense, then the defendant would be automatically committed to a security hospital for an indefinite period of time until "competent." Theoretically and realistically, this indefinite time period could extend—and sometimes did—into a lifetime of involuntary commitment. Effective treatment was either not provided or could not be offered, and it was anyone's guess what actually constituted "competency."

In an effort to dramatize the inadequacy of treatment for the so-called criminally insane, Kirkland Schwitzgebel (1977) cites the case of a defendant who received a suspended sentence for third degree assault, but then violated parole. He was sent by the court to a state hospital where he was evaluated IST, and he spent the next fourteen and one-half years at that state institution awaiting trial. During that time the defendant received a fractured nose, a fractured right leg, fractured ribs, an injured back, burns on his face and chest, and numerous other injuries as a result of beatings from patients and hospital personnel. He also suffered rectal bleeding and headaches. His hospital files indicated that he not only failed to receive any kind of psychotherapy during his years of confinement, but the only prescription he apparently did receive during that time was for vaseline and rectal suppositories. And yet, the hospital ultimately discharged him as "improved," with the approval of the court.

Not only do criminally insane patients receive, as a group, very little psychotherapy, but when it is provided its effectiveness is very much open to question. For some behavioral disorders such as schizophrenia, no consistently effective therapy has been discovered.

Although still a long way from providing valid and reliable solutions, recent court rulings are beginning to ameliorate injustices perpetrated by the numerous disparities between criminal law and mental health law (Wexler, 1977). For example, the limits of legal confinement for incompetence are more clearly delineated (e.g., Jackson vs. Indiana, 406 U.S. 715, 1972), and the length of incompetence evaluations has been restricted. Similar legal clarifications have been made in cases regarding NGRI. Perhaps one of the most far-reaching U.S. Supreme Court rulings on this issue occurred in 1966 in Baxstrom vs. Herold. Chief Justice Earl Warren, speaking for the majority of the court, held that mentally ill patients should be given equal protection of the law. That decision directed that there be equality in the procedures used to commit individuals to mental hospitals, whether they be convicted criminals or "civilians." We will discuss the Baxstrom decision in greater detail in the next section, since the ruling is especially relevant to the legal and psychological definitions of dangerousness.

A third way a person may attain criminally insane status is to exhibit psychotic or severely disturbed behavior while incarcerated in a prison or correctional facility. The Steadman-Cocozza analysis found that 40 percent of the criminally insane population consisted of these "mentally ill" inmates, who were transferred out of prison and into hospital settings. Finally, a small segment (about 10 percent) of the criminally insane population consists of individuals who acted violently during their stay in a civil mental institution and were transferred to a security institution ostensibly for the staff's or other patients' safety.

SEXUAL PSYCHOPATHS

In addition to the four broad categories of criminal insanity, there is in some states a separate category that seems to exist primarily to deal with one type of criminal or potential criminal, the psychopath. Because the great majority of these states specify sexual deviancy, the laws as a group are called the *sexual psychopath statutes*. As of December 1976 there were criminal sexual psychopath statutes in 25 states and the District of Columbia (Sleffel, 1977). In general, these state statutes depict the "sexual psychopath" as a legally sane but "mentally disturbed sex offender" who is particularly dangerous to children, women, or both. Unfortunately, the psychological definitions of what kind of person constitutes a "sexual psychopath" are vague, inconsistent, and circular (Sleffel, 1977). The qualifying behavior may range from indecent exposure to forcible rape. In some states, a person *thought* to be dangerous as a potential molester or assaulter would qualify as a sexual psychopath. Among the sexual psychopath statutes is the well-known Maryland Defective Delinquent statute, which in addition to a number of sexual offenses also includes a wide assortment of other kinds of criminal behavior committed by juveniles.

Like the criminally insane, persons found to be sexual psychopaths are usually committed to a mental institution for an indeterminate period of time. This involuntary deprivation of liberties raises ethical, philosophical, and legal questions which are beyond the scope of our present discussion. However, two very important features about the criminally insane and the sexual psychopath labels should be noted.

First, the classifications are based on the assumption that certain members of the mentally ill population are dangerous to the community. Implicit in these designations is the belief that behavioral scientists and clinicians can determine, predict, treat, and prevent dangerous behavior. We shall wait to elaborate on this issue in the next section of this chapter.

Second, state commitment codes relative to "dangerous" people often badly confound the *parens patriae* and the police power functions of the state (Shah, 1977). *Parens patriae* refers to the remedial, therapeutic, and care-giving responsibilities of the state, whereas police powers pertain to such authority as involuntary confinement of people adjudicated to be dangerous to the community or themselves (preventive detention). A majority of state commitment codes demonstrate vague, imprecise terminology which confuses and fails to delineate where *parens patriae* functions begin and police powers stop. Very possibly, the lawmakers' inability to formulate adequate statutes concerning the "mentally ill criminal" reflects a basic and pervasive misunderstanding of the relationships between abnormal and criminal behavior and the concept of dangerousness. They have plenty of company. As we shall see in the next section, behavioral scientists and clinicians themselves have had a difficult time not only evaluating and predicting dangerous behavior, but even defining it.

DANGEROUSNESS

In August 1966, Charles Whitman, a University of Texas student majoring in architectural engineering, carried his personal arsenal in a footlocker to the observation deck of the 307-foot-tall University tower. He proceeded to load a number of high-powered, scope-equipped rifles and began randomly shooting at confused people near the observation deck and on the ground far below. Whitman managed to shoot 44 victims, killing 14, before a policeman and a citizen climbed to the tower and put an end to the ordeal by shooting Whitman himself. Among his victims were his mother and wife, whom he had murdered the previous evening.

An investigation revealed that the twenty-five-year-old Whitman had consulted a psychiatrist five months before the incident and, during a two-hour interview, had described "overwhelming violent impulses" and a fear of his inability to control them. He had also revealed a compelling need for "going up on the tower with a deer rifle and start shooting people." Although Whitman did not return for further consultation after the initial two-hour session, knowledge of his consultation and confession brought on a public outcry and questioning of why he was not treated, confined, or referred to the proper authorities. These questions assume that clinicians can predict which individuals the public should be protected from. Are behavioral scientists really able with a high degree of accuracy to determine which individuals are most likely to be murderers, rapists, or other violent assaulters?

The judicial system apparently believes that clinicians do have such predictive ability. Although the number of commitments has been substantially reduced over the past two decades, approximately 50,000 persons every year are legally committed to mental institutions on the basis of assessed potentially dangerous behavior to others and/or themselves (Rubin, 1972). About 5 percent of the total population in mental hospitals in the U.S. are kept in maximum security based on potentially dangerous behavior. There are another estimated 60,000 persons arrested every year for crimes against persons (homicide, aggravated assault, forcible rape, and robbery) and referred by the court for evaluation for dangerous behavior, an evaluation which plays a major role in determining length and type of incarceration or hospitalization (Steadman, 1976; Rubin, 1972). Is this judicial confidence in clinicians justified?

Among the potential predictors of dangerous behavior suggested in the traditional psychiatric-psychodynamic literature are latent homosexuality, excessive aggression, a poor capacity for relationships with others (emotional coldness), and a desire for attention (MacDonald,

164

1976, p. 145). Except for aggression, these "predictors" of dangerous behavior have not stood up under empirical scrutiny.

The triad of enuresis, firesetting, and unusual cruelty to animals in children as predictive indicators of eventual adult violence has received particular attention. Enuresis refers to uncontrolled, unintentional voiding of urine past the age of three, usually during sleep, and is commonly known as bedwetting (Herbert, 1974). According to the psychodynamic literature, enuresis is considered to have a sadistic significance, with the act of urinating being equivalent to fantasies of damaging and destroying, and it is thus an overt demonstration of hostility in retaliation to parental rejection (Hellman & Blackman, 1966). Therefore, the logic goes, it is likely that violence-prone adults were enuretic as children; the prediction for future violence increases in accuracy if the child also manifested a propensity toward setting fires and was cruel to animals. "From phantasies of destruction through the act of voiding, the child proceeds to the active destruction of fire with its magical omnipotence and then to direct violence against good animals—animals which are accepted by adult figures whereas the child was not" (Hellman & Blackman, 1966, p. 1,434). The consequence of this behavioral pattern is a generalization of violent aggressiveness toward society. The triad itself is a "pathognomonic sign" that the child is seriously disturbed and a menace to the community.

In an article examining the relationship between the violence triad and 84 offenders (31 violent and 53 nonviolent), Hellman and Blackman (1966) claim to have found that three-fourths of the violent offenders had the triad, compared to the appearance of the triad in only 28 percent of the nonviolent offenders. Closer examination of the data, however, reveals that only 45 percent of the violent offenders had *all* three components of the triad, as compared to 13 percent of the nonviolent group. In addition, the experimental procedure was vague and questionable. It appears, for example, that all the examiners were fully aware of the hypothesis and the kinds of offenders they were dealing with. Under these conditions, the obvious bias of the examiners would possibly contaminate the data collection and interpretation. Numerous other methodological flaws in the study prevent confident acceptance of the findings.

After an extensive review of the literature between 1950 and 1971, combined with 779 taped interviews with professionals in 25 fields dealing with troubled youths, Justice, Justice, and Kraft (1974) were forced to conclude that the so-called violence triad was a poor predictor of adult violence. Rather, they found a history of fighting, temper tantrums, truancy, and other school problems appearing substantially more frequently than other behaviors. MacDonald (1968, 1976) found that among three matched groups—hospital patients who made homicidal threats, convicted homicide offenders, and a control group of hospital patients—the violence triad was a poor predictor of violence. Overall, the violence triad has yet to be proved capable of predicting violent behavior.

Another deeply entrenched prediction hypothesis in the psychiatric literature is fantasy characterized by violent content. Rubin (1972) notes that psychiatry and psychoanalytic theory ambiguously base predictions of dangerousness on the individual's fantasy and daydreaming processes. Accordingly, if there are certain elements or indicators of destructiveness or violence in an individual's imaginational or fantastical content, then he or she is more likely to engage in those acts and should be regarded as dangerous. Empirical evidence also fails to support this position. In fact, Jerome Singer (1975, p. 114–117) hypothesizes and cites supportive evidence that fantasy, if anything, may work to reduce overt episodes of aggressive action.

Psychological tests as predictors of violence have fared no better. In an extensive survey of the research literature, Megargee (1970) reports that he was unable to find any psychological test which can predict with acceptable accuracy the probability of violent behavior. That situation still exists to date (Monahan, 1976). The so-called projective techniques of testing, such as the Thematic Apperception Test (TAT) and the Rorschach (inkblots), which are used by many psychiatrists and clinical psychologists to predict and diagnose behavior, repeatedly have been found to possess questionable predictive powers or utility (Mischel, 1968; Maloney & Ward, 1976; Anastasi, 1976; Zubin, Eron, & Schumer, 1965). Although some objective personality inventories, such as the Minnesota Multiphasic Personality Inventory (MMPI) and the California Psychological Inventory (CPI), are among the most carefully documented and studied psychological instruments, predictions are not their forte. Their strengths lie in the assessment of *immediate* psychological states and conditions. It is unfortunate that many clinicians will hide behind the false security of the apparent objectivity and quantification of psychological tests to support their predictive claims when the instruments have not been proven to have predictive validity, particularly related to criminal behavior.

You are probably wondering at this point if clinicians can predict dangerous behavior at all. The answer is, only to a very limited extent. In an excellent critique of clinical prediction, Mischel (1968) notes that the best predictor of any behavior we now have at our disposal is whether and how often the individual has engaged in the behavior in the past. If the individual has a history of frequent violent episodes, then there is a

better-than-chance probability that he or she will engage in that behavior in the future, especially if the situations are the same, or nearly so,
and the individual is young (Steadman & Cocozza, 1974). Before discussing how accurate we can expect the clinician to be, we will examine
why the question of predictability of dangerousness has been such a
problem.

Problems in Predictions of Dangerousness

First, predictions assume a keen understanding of the "natural" laws
of human behavior, a goal which behavioral scientists are a long way
from reaching. Even in relatively simple tasks under specified, controlled experimental conditions, our batting average is often not very
impressive. When we move into highly complex behaviors engineered
under highly complicated situations, such as dangerous behavior, predictability drops to a disappointingly low "hit" record. What complicates the issue even more is that most behaviors are determined as much
by situational circumstances as by personality dispositions. Prediction
of dangerous behavior requires that we be able to foresee environmental
events as well as detect personality factors. A majority of predictions of
dangerousness are based on notions that the propensity to be violent
resides entirely within the individual. As we saw in Chapter 4, concentrating on personality while neglecting environmental factors fails to
provide a complete picture of any behavior and its determinants.

Second, the concept of dangerousness is murky. No one seems able to
agree on which particular behaviors should be included in the term, nor
have many empirical investigations delineated precisely what is meant
by it. The courts have tried to limit dangerousness to include a propensity to "attack or otherwise inflict injury, loss, pain, or other evil"
(Steadman, 1976, p. 57). Furthermore, the dangerous act must occur in
"the community in the reasonably foreseeable future" (Rubin, 1972, p.
399). In addition to the stipulation that the dangerous behavior must
occur soon, it also must be based on a "high probability of substantial
injury" (Rubin, 1972). The judicial expectation is that clinicians' fore-
cast of dangerous behavior must be "virtually certain" rather than
merely likely. Far from clarifying the issues, the legal terminology of
"substantial," "pain," "evil," and "virtual certainty" create more controversy and subjectivity than they eliminate. In addition, Steadman
(1976) argues that not only are these judicial terms insufficient for actual
judicial application, but also that the courts rarely press expert witnesses to explain and document the reliability or validity of the measuring instrument or the crystal ball they are using. If the judicial system
did press, it would likely find many clinicians relying on hunches,

speculation, vague clinical judgment, and ethereal intuition based principally on psychiatric and psychological folklore.

Like the judicial system, behavioral and social scientists have also had their problems with the concept of dangerousness. Some define "dangerous" to include only those behaviors which actually injure or destroy persons (e.g., Rubin, 1972); others extend the term to encompass destruction of property as well (e.g., Mulvihill & Tumen, 1969); and still others even include fantasy or ideation (e.g., Ervin & Lion, 1969). Many investigators use the terms "violent" and "dangerous" interchangeably. A number of behavioral scientists (e.g., Monohan, 1976; Sarbin, 1967; Steadman, 1976) have argued that the term *violence* be restricted to action and behavior, while *dangerousness* be reserved for the relationship between the present or past status of the individual and future violence or destruction.

A third problem is that violent or dangerous behavior has a low base rate compared to many other behaviors. That is, it occurs so infrequently that the prediction odds are against the predictor, since the very probability of occurrence is low. Obviously, if you are trying to predict behavior which is likely to occur with a high frequency, the "hits" would be very much in your favor. On the other hand, if you are trying to predict behavior that rarely occurs, your "hits" will be relatively low, even with sophisticated predictors.

Clinical Accuracy in Predictions of Dangerousness

Many recent investigations are highlighted by statistical predictions. Research directed at determining accuracy of behavior prediction employs regularly the terms "false positives" and "false negatives." False positives refer to those individuals who we predict will engage in a certain behavior (in this case dangerous behavior) and do not. False negatives refer to those who we predict will not engage in dangerous behavior but who do. If we predict 50 persons out of a group of 200 will be violent and only two eventually demonstrate violent behavior during some prescribed period of time, we have on our hands 48 "misses" or false positives. In addition, if three of the remaining 150 who we do not predict to be dangerous do manifest violent behavior during our time interval, we also have three false negatives.

The public is especially concerned about false negatives—those "dangerous" individuals who have been tested and have been "turned out on the streets" because they are supposedly no longer a threat to society. The news media are especially sensitive to this issue and are quick to note when a former mental patient or parolee judged to be cured is suspected to be a brutal slayer. Behavioral scientists are more interested in false positives, since they are more amenable and meaningful to study in terms of determining accuracy in predictions. Psychiatrists are particularly prone to have a high ratio of false positives, probably because of enormous pressures from the judicial process and the public (Steadman, 1972, 1974; Toch, 1977). A high proportion of false positives tends to minimize the risk of any false negatives.

Kozol, Boucher, and Garofalo (1972) found that even after intensive background sampling and clinical examinations made independently by at least two psychiatrists, two psychologists, a social worker, and other professionals, these clinicians still had two false positives for every three persons they predicted would be dangerous. Moreover, because of the weak methodology, the odds were very much in their favor (see Monahan, 1973; Steadman, 1976).

Johnnie Baxstrom was convicted of second degree assault in April 1959 and sentenced to a two-and-one-half- to three-year term in a New York prison. In June 1961 he was assessed "insane" by a prison physician and transferred from the prison to Dannemora State Hospital for the criminally insane. Despite his continual petitions to be transferred to a civil institution, the Department of Mental Hygiene determined ex parte that Baxstrom was not suitable for care in a civil hospital. As a result of these actions, he remained institutionalized beyond the time his prison sentence had expired. In 1966 the U.S. Supreme Court ruled (Baxstrom vs. Herold, 1965) that Baxstrom had been denied equal protection of the law by being confined in an institution for the criminally insane, without the benefit of a new hearing to re-evaluate his "potentially dangerous" classification.

The high court's ruling influenced the confinement of at least 967 other patients held under similar circumstances in hospitals for the criminally insane in New York State. These patients, known as the "Baxstrom patients," were transferred against the advice of psychiatrists to civil mental facilities. The Baxstrom patients were predominantly nonwhite, of the lower socioeconomic class, and middle aged. Although most had previous arrest records and many had previous convictions, very few had any sex crime offenses, and only 58 percent had been convicted of violent crimes (Steadman, 1976, p. 63). On the average, the patients had been institutionalized continuously for fourteen years.

Keeping in mind that the Baxstrom patients were evaluated as among New York's most dangerous, let us look at follow-up reports, all of which found that the level of predicted dangerousness to be expected from these patients was apparently grossly overstated (Monahan, 1976, p. 19). For example, in a follow-up survey of 85 Baxstrom patients reported by Steadman and Cocozza (1974), it was discovered that 20 percent were re-arrested, but only 7 percent were convicted, and these were for minor offenses such as vagrancy and intoxication. An examination of both in-hospital and community behaviors revealed that only 20 percent of the extremely dangerous patients were assaultive toward others during the four-year follow-up period (Steadman, 1976, p. 63). One of the most crucial variables determining whether the Baxstrom patients demonstrated assaultive behavior was age: the younger the patient, the more likely he or she was to manifest assaultive behavior. Steadman and his colleagues also used their Legal Dangerousness Scale (Cocozza & Steadman, 1974), a measure of four criminal background characteristics, and found that they had two false positives out of every three patients predicted to be assaultive, again dramatizing the inaccuracy of prediction.

Monahan (1976) notes that the Supreme Court decision on the Baxstrom case affected a similar group of "mentally ill offenders" in Pennsylvania (*Dixon vs. Attorney General of the Commonwealth of Pennsylvania*, 1971). Following the procedure in the New York case, the patients were transferred to civil hospitals for re-evaluation. A four-year follow-up on 438 Dixon patients by Thornberry and Jacoby (1974) found that only 14 percent of the patients were reported for assaultive behavior, with the younger patients showing a higher probability than older patients. Thus, the false positives were 86 percent.

In an effort to predict violent recidivism among parolees, the California Department of Corrections Research Division in 1965 tried to develop a violence-prediction scale based on background information such as age, commitment of offense, number of prior commitments, opiate usage, and length of imprisonment of each offender released on parole (Wenk, Robison, & Smith, 1972). By using the above-mentioned "predictor" variables to divide the parolees into groups, the researchers isolated about 3 percent of the parolee population as the most violent. However, only 14 percent of these individuals actually violated parole by engaging in a violent or potentially violent act, compared to a 5 percent violation rate for parolees in general. Although the most violent group was considered nearly three times more likely than the other groups to break parole by involvement in violence, it should be stressed that a majority (86 percent) of those high violence parolees did not actually engage in violent activity while on parole. Of course, it is possible that a significant number of the high violent group who did not violate parole by violent means might have reverted to violence after parole, or that their violence went undetected during the parole period.

In another procedure developed by the California Department of Corrections Parole and Community Services Division, all parolees released to supervision were classified into one of six categories, according to past aggressive behavior (Wenk, Robison & Smith, 1972). Categories ranged from the most serious aggressive category (those who committed one or more acts of major violence) to the lowest level aggressive category (no recorded history of aggression). The classifications were based on offender histories and psychiatric evaluation of violence potential. This procedure revealed that those regarded as most potentially aggressive (two highest aggressive groups) were no more likely to be violent than the less potentially violent groups (two lowest aggressive groups). The rate of actual violence for the potentially aggressive groups was 3.1 per thousand, compared to 2.8 per thousand for the potentially least aggressive groups, an insignificant difference.

In a third project, Wenk, Robison, and Smith (1972) studied a sample of 4,146 youthful offenders admitted to the Reception Guidance Center at Deuel Vocational Institute, California, during the period from 1964 to 1965. The study was primarily aimed at determining which background data were most useful in predicting violence during a fifteen-month parole period after the offenders' release from the institution. During the fifteen-month period, 104 or 2.5 percent of the youths had been involved in a violation of parole because of violent (assaultive) behavior.

In an effort to search for predictive variables of violent behavior, the authors combined and divided the background data in a number of ways. One research procedure revealed that general recidivism (any violation of parole) and violent recidivism (violation of parole by violence) were highest for youthful offenders who had been admitted to the institution on several occasions (multiple offenders). In another research procedure, youthful offenders who had a history of "actual" violent behavior (which may or may not have resulted in legal commitment to the institution) were three times more likely to be involved in violence recidivism during the fifteen-month parole period. Although this is an impressive finding by itself, the authors admonish that if they were to make predictions based on the same background data they would be accurate only once in twenty times, since only a relatively small proportion of the youths with violent backgrounds demonstrated a violent violation during parole.

In summary, the research data indicate that clinicians have a tendency to overpredict dangerous behavior. That is, there are far more false positives (misses) than correct positives (hits) in their predictions. Since the populations in the projects reviewed here were highly selective, mainly convicted offenders in institutions for the criminally insane, it is possible that the number of false positives might be substantially higher in different samples. Also, about the only predictor variables which emerged as reasonably accurate were previous history of dangerous behavior and age.

THE NOTION OF FREE WILL

In Chapter 1 we pointed out that one of the basic assumptions generally accepted by behavioral scientists (but with varying degrees of conviction) is that human behavior is lawful. If one believes in the lawfulness of behavior, one also accepts that behavior is the inevitable result of prior events and experiences. That is, what a person does in any particular situation depends upon the events and experiences which have transpired sometime previously. The belief in antecedents as the determinants of present behavior is called determinism, or more specifically *psychological determinism.*

The judicial system views behavior differently. Deeply embedded in criminal law is the notion of *free will.* Persons are free to choose among any number of competing behavioral options in any given situation. They freely select their responses and hence are held responsible and culpable for their actions. While social and psychological forces must be considered, the major determinants are the individuals themselves. However, in exceptional cases, where psychosocial forces or mental impairment "cause" a person to violate the law beyond his or her control, then that person cannot be held responsible. Presumably, the forces or impairment interfered with the person's freedom to choose between right and wrong. Implicit in this argument is that the concept of lawful behavior does not exist for abnormally functioning persons. This is reflected, for example, in the frequent habit of the judicial system of making referrals to mental health clinics for the assessment of dangerousness in offenders believed psychologically abnormal. In order to establish and predict dangerousness, you must assume that behavior is lawful and is determined by antecedents—or at least that the offender's "free" will is lawful!

The position taken in this book is that behavior is principally determined by the situation and the person's expectancies about the potential gain that certain behavior will bring, regardless of whether the behavior is considered normal or abnormal. The learning principles involved in the development and maintenance of normal and abnormal behavioral patterns are the same. While the person is not a robot, in both cases the individual goes with his or her best hunch about reaching a desired goal. Thus, to speak of free will for one person and determinism for another does not seem logical.

For example, a young man who has been diagnosed a paranoid schizophrenic may sincerely believe that people are plotting against him, possibly even to do him physical harm. Let's say that the belief is pure delusion, without any basis in fact. Fearing that those who are out to get him are ready to move in, he decides that his best alternative under

172

those *imagined* circumstances is to kill his "enemies." The question is, what gives this person any more license to kill than the so-called "sane" person who murders under a *real* threat to safety—for example, an embezzler gunning down a blackmailer? Should the mentally ill or insane person be held as responsible as the normal or sane person?

At the present time the judicial system appears to operate under a double standard. Those evaluated insane or mentally ill are considered not to be functioning under the guidance of their own free will when the crime was committed and thus are not held responsible for their actions. The normal or sane person, on the other hand, is held completely responsible for his or her action because that person went with the best hunch—albeit a highly deviant one—in a particular situation. In addition those assessed insane receive treatment to re-establish their free will, while those supposedly operating on free will receive punishment.

Before concluding this section, we should look at the issues of free will and determinism (or lawfulness) from a different perspective. Possibly, in most human behaviors, both are operating to some degree. That is, to some extent free will may be partially weakened by the external environment. Easterbrook (1978) points out that the all-or-none assumption that human behavior is either lawfully determined or a result of free will may be a very limiting position for psychologists to take. Easterbrook defines free will as the ability to master or control what happens in a situation. If an individual influences and controls what happens in a particular situation, then he or she is exercising free will. If, on the other hand, the environment controls what happens and what behavioral events take place, the individual has little free will under that set of circumstances. Easterbrook argues that in most day-to-day behavioral events, the individual has some control over the environment, and the environment in turn exerts some control over the behavior of the individual. In line with his definition, free will and the environment interact to produce behavior in a majority of cases.

If kidnappers force a father to rob a bank in exchange for the life of his five-year-old daughter, the case is relatively straightforward. The environment is controlling the individual's behavior, and it has severely limited the number of choices the individual can make of his own volition. Traditionally, the judicial process has found little difficulty in resolving the free-will issue in cases where external control is clearly evident. Control by the environment precludes free will and personal responsibility.

The relationship between free will and "sane" or "insane" behavior is far more complex, because the determination is basically subjective or relies heavily on the statements of experts who generally do not agree with one another. Normally, the argument revolves around how much free will or control the individual is believed to have had over his or her fate and the fate of others.

Easterbrook explains that free will depends upon, among other things, the cognitive ability and competence of the individual. Competent people are more likely to exert more mastery over their environment: "A free person is one who strives to master his environment in accordance with personal standards and recognizes his responsibility for his deeds. By contrast, a 'pawn' . . . yields to the forces and structures that he perceives in his situation, regardless of his personal ideals, and denies personal responsibility for his action or inaction" (Easterbrook, 1978, p. 12). Anxiety, stress, and depression are indicators that the person does not feel that he or she has control over events. The environmentally controlled person tends to react to events rather than try to master them. Anxiety, depression, and "reacting" behavior are features of a maladjusted or emotionally disturbed person. In this sense, the highly anxious, conforming individual is one who does not feel mastery or control over his or her own environment. Moreover, it is the individual who lacks the cognitive equipment, learning experiences, and social skills who is most likely to feel this way. The more limited the competence, the more widespread the external control and loss of freedom.

In the above sense, if we think of insanity status as signifying absence of free will, it is the most severely depressed and anxious person who would qualify. However, the individual who exhibits psychopathic behavior, antisocial tendencies, other personality disorders, and criminal behavior often *feels* some sense of control, mastery, and free will, and this often is the reason for engaging in deviant acts. Using this measure, the serial murderer playing "catch me" games with police and press would not be considered insane. Nor would the husband who uses a shotgun on his wife after twenty-one years of marital discord; the killing could be viewed as a deliberate way of gaining control of his situation.

The above discussion, of course, is essentially theoretical. But until we obtain a better handle on what we mean by free will and the loss of freedom of choice in the emotionally disturbed individual, the legal concept of insanity will be applied arbitrarily. The question of insanity (as the absence of free will) revolves around the issue of personal control, or whether the individual was in control of his or her behavior during the offense. In cases involving environmental control that is strong enough to be clearly observable to others, the lack of freedom is evident, although insanity is not the issue. In cases involving personal control, the situation is complex and ambiguous because we are dealing with subjective interpretations of control over events: that is, did the accused believe that he or she had personal control?

Psychology, at present, is in no position to determine the degree of personal control demonstrated during some past incident. Therefore, we cannot determine whether an individual involved in a crime was functioning under free will or "lack of control" in any particular situation. When court experts attempt to do so, they are actually acting on vague hunches with which other experts may completely disagree.

SUMMARY

We have attempted in this chapter to examine the relationships between psychologically abnormal behavior and criminal behavior. The tendency to associate behavior disorders, particularly the more unusual and socially reprehensible ones, with "mental disease" or "mental illness" is a habit that dies hard. It lends itself well to pigeonholing human behavior and to placing more weight on the judgments of psychiatrists and other clinicians who embrace the medical model.

Human behavior seldom allows itself to be placed into neat classifications, and although society assumes that some of its more heinous crimes are committed by people who are "mentally ill," research has shown that the most severely mentally ill are no more likely to commit crimes than are members of the "normal" population. There is, however, evidence to support the belief that paranoid schizophrenics—who make up a small percentage of the mentally ill—may commit serious, bizarre crimes. On the other hand, bizarre crimes are also committed by psychopaths and other nonpsychotic individuals.

The diagnostic categories which do tend to be represented in the criminal population are the personality disorders, which generally do not qualify an individual for "insanity" status. The antisocial personality, the explosive, the paranoid, and the schizoid are all classifications that appear when criminals are referred by the courts for clinical diagnosis.

We have seen that there are four avenues by which a person may attain criminally insane designation. The first is by being legally determined not guilty by reason of insanity (NGRI), a designation that draws considerable publicity but that actually occurs rarely. A second avenue is to be determined incompetent to stand trial (IST), a rubric which may include physical as well as mental ailments. A deafmute, for example, if unable to help in his or her own defense, may be judged IST. Generally, IST refers to defendants who are believed so emotionally unstable or mentally retarded that they are unable to assist their attorney. Grave injustices are done when such persons are relegated to institutions until rendered competent, and seemingly forgotten there. Fortunately, in the wake of the Baxstrom case, many state statutes have tightened the IST rulings to limit the amount of time persons spend in institutions and to force periodic reviews of their situations. "Criminally insane" is also used to refer to prison inmates transferred to hospital settings because of abnormal behavior and to persons in mental institutions who exhibit violent behavior during their stay and are transferred to a special security wing.

There is also in some states a separate category of criminals or potential criminals—the sexual psychopaths—who, like the criminally insane, are remanded to mental institutions for the protection of society.

Closely related to the issue of determining who are criminally insane is the matter of predicting who are likely to commit a serious crime and, therefore, are dangerous to society. Courts and the public frequently call on the clinical practitioner to make such determinations, but we have seen in this chapter that prediction is a tenuous thing. Criminal behavior, like other behavior, is learned, and one of the best predictors is whether a person has engaged in such behavior in the past, although that by no means guarantees that he or she will continue. Clinicians are more likely to have false positives than false negatives in their predictions. That is, they are more likely to err in predicting a person to be dangerous, perhaps under the assumption that "it is better to be safe than sorry."

It would be too presumptuous to say the term legal insanity is outmoded. But perhaps a moratorium should be called on its use, until such time as issues such as free will and personal control are better defined and incorporated into the criteria. As it is presently used, legal insanity reflects a double standard approach in the treatment of alleged criminals. Almost all behavior, whether normal or "abnormal," is determined to some extent by past learning experiences, so that the notion of free will in its purest sense appears mythical. Until the issue of personal control becomes clearer, it is not logical to judge some persons as being out of control of their actions and others as acting with complete freedom.

KEY CONCEPTS FOR REVIEW

Psychosis
Neurosis
Personality disorders
Schizophrenia
Hallucinations
Delusions
Affective disorder
Paranoid reactions
Paranoid schizophrenia

Explosive personality
NGRI
IST
Sexual psychopaths
Parens patriae
Dangerousness
Violence triad
Free will

MAJOR THEORISTS AND RESEARCHERS

Coleman
Easterbrook
Steadman and Cocozza

SUGGESTED READINGS

Coleman, J.C. *Abnormal psychology and modern life* (5th edition). Glenville, Ill.: Scott, Foresman, 1976.
An unusually comprehensive and well-written text on abnormal behavior with some emphasis on criminal behavior.

Easterbrook, J.A. *The determinants of free will.* New York: Academic Press, 1978.
A provocative presentation of the empirical and philosophical positions on the determinants of free will.

Sales, B.D. *The criminal justice system.* New York: Plenum Press, 1977.
An excellent book of readings pertaining to the relationships among the psychological, legal, and public policy perspectives on the dangerous offender, obscenity, insanity, prison environment, and parole decision making.

Steadman, H.J. and Cocozza, J.J. *Careers of the criminally insane.* Lexington, Mass.: Lexington Books, 1974.
A well-documented presentation of the background and disposition of the Baxstrom case.

HUMAN
AGGRESSION
AND VIOLENCE

SEVEN

The long history of man, besides its enobling features, contains also a disruptive malice which continues into the present. Since the rise of the first neolithic cultures, man has hanged, tortured, burned, and impaled his fellow man. He has done so while devoutly professing religions whose founders enjoined the very opposite upon their followers. It is as though we carried with us from some dark tree in a vanished forest, an insatiable thirst for cruelty.

Loren Eiseley, 1971, p. 85.

There is ample evidence to illustrate the long history of human involvement in aggression and violent behavior. Aggression has been instrumental in helping people survive. Human beings have learned from centuries of experience that aggressive behavior and war enable them to obtain material goods, land, and treasures; to protect property and family; and to gain prestige, status, and power. In fact, it is difficult to imagine the survival of the human species without aggression. Today, with the rapid advance of technological information on how to destroy, aggression presents the most dangerous behavior known and threatens the very existence of society. Because of its destructive possibility, aggression has drawn a heavy concentration of psychological research.

Aggression warrants an entire chapter, because it is the basic ingredient in violent crime. A good understanding of aggressive behavior should provide us with a better picture of violence and perhaps with the material to identify its determinants. Violence is, after all, the extreme, physical form of aggression.

Is human aggression instinctive, biological, learned, or some combination of these patterns? If aggression results from an innate, biological mechanism, then the methods designed to control, reduce, or eliminate aggressive behavior will differ significantly from methods based on the perspective that aggression is learned. Drugs, brain stimulation, surgical intervention, or encouragement of appropriate outlets may be in order. If aggression is largely a learned behavior, then methods using the principles of learning should prove most effective.

By all accounts, a large portion of animal aggression appears to spring from innate, biological programming carried from generation to generation to ensure the survival of the species. Humans, however, with their enormously complex and sophisticated cerebral cortex, rely heavily on thought, associations, beliefs, and, in the long run, *learning* as a primary determinant of behavior. How much does animal programming contribute to human behavior, if at all? Are people aggressive and violent because their animal "instincts" continue to direct this particular behavior? If the evolutionary aggressive drives still reside within the subcortical (below the cortex in the "old" brain) structures, as some physiologists tell us they do, are they modifiable? If not modifiable, what are the best ways of preventing people from attacking and killing one another?

DEFINITION OF AGGRESSION

The task of defining human aggression is surprisingly difficult, as many social psychologists have discovered. Forcibly jabbing someone in the midsection is certainly defining it by example. But what about jabbing someone more softly, in jest—is this an example of aggression? In the latter case it probably depends upon how the act is interpreted by the victim. If someone refuses to speak to you after you ask a question, is that an example of aggression? What if someone spreads malicious gossip about you? If a burglar breaks into your home and you take out your trusty but rusty handgun and point it at the intruder, pull the trigger, but it doesn't fire. . . is yours an act of aggression? If someone passively sits on your doorstep and blocks your way, is this aggression?

All of the above may be legitimate examples of aggression, but they represent different forms. Some social psychologists have attempted to define aggression as the intent and attempt physically or socially to harm another individual or, in some cases, to destroy an object. This definition seems adequate for many situations, but it has several limitations. Refusing to speak does not fit well into the definition, since it is not an active attempt to harm someone. A person staging a sit-down strike on your doorstep also is not trying to injure you. Most psychologists put these two behaviors into a special category of aggressive responses and call them "passive-aggressive behaviors," since they are generally interpreted as being aggressive in intent, while the behavior itself is passive and indirect.

It is useful to recognize two general types of aggression, distinguished by their goals or the rewards they offer the perpetrator: *hostile aggression* and *instrumental aggression* (Buss, 1971). *Hostile aggression* occurs following anger-inducing conditions such as insults, physical attacks, or beatings; the perpetrator's goal is to make the victim suffer. Most homicides, forcible rapes, and other violent crimes directed at harming the victim are precipitated by hostile aggression. This class of aggressive behavior is characterized by the intense and disorganizing emotion of anger, with "anger" defined as an arousal state elicited by certain stimuli, particularly those evoking attack or frustration.

Instrumental aggression begins with competition or the desire for some object or status that someone else possesses—jewelry, money, territory, spouse—where the perpetrator wants to obtain the desired object, sometimes regardless of the cost. Instrumental aggression is often reflected in robbery, burglary, larceny, and various "white-collar crimes." The obvious goal in a robbery is for the thief to obtain cash value items, usually without the intent to harm anyone. However, if someone interferes with the thief's objective, the thief may feel forced to harm the person interfering or else risk losing the desired goal. Instrumental aggression is usually also a feature of calculated murder by a paid, impersonal killer.

In an effort to conceptualize the many varieties of human aggression, Buss (1971) attempted to classify them (see Table 7–1). It is fairly easy to pick out exceptions and overlaps in the Buss scheme, but the exercise emphasizes how hard it is to categorize human aggressive behavior, and it epitomizes the many problems which have hampered social psychologists for several decades.

Most definitions, as Bandura (1973a) notes, imply that aggression is solely concerned with behaviors and intentions which reside within the perpetrator (or performer). Going a step further, Bandura includes both the performer and the victim. Adequate definitions of aggression must consider both the "injurious behavior" of the perpetrator and the "social judgment" of the victim. To avoid what Bandura refers to as the "semantic jungle" of aggression, we shall define aggression here as *the intention and attempt to harm another individual physically or psychologically or to destroy an object.* This definition includes all the behaviors

TABLE 7-1
Varieties of Human Aggression

	Active		Passive	
	Direct	Indirect	Direct	Indirect
Physical	Punching the victim	Practical joke booby trap	Obstructing passage, sit-in	Refusing to perform a necessary task
Verbal	Insulting the victim	Malicious gossip	Refusing to speak	Refusing consent, vocal or written

*Source: Buss, A.H. Aggression Pays. In J.L. Singer (ed.), The Control of Aggression and Violence. New York: Academic Press, 1971, p. 8.

described in Buss's typology. We shall refer to violence as destructive aggression. Often it is intense and uncontrolled behavior that injures or destroys the recipient or is intended to do so (Daniels & Gilula, 1970).

THEORETICAL CAUSES OF AGGRESSION

The question of whether a human being is born an aggressive, naturally violent animal who must defend self, family, and territory from intruders, or whether the human is born relatively free of aggressive tendencies, but acquires aggressive modes of action from society, has generated a raging controversy among psychologists and other behavioral scientists for more than 30 years. This debate is often referred to as the "nature-nurture" controversy, and it has touched every school of thought in human behavior.

Psychodynamic Viewpoints

Sigmund Freud, the father of psychoanalysis, was convinced that human beings are from birth constantly susceptible to a build-up of aggressive energy, which must be dissipated or drained off before it reaches dangerous levels. This is known as the *psychodynamic* or *hydraulic model*, since it bears a close resemblance to pressure build-up in a container. If excessive pressure accumulates in the container—the human psyche—an explosion is likely to occur, as demonstrated by violent tirades of behavior. According to Freud and others who subscribe to the psychodynamic point of view, people who have tirades are blowing off the excessive steam of aggressive energy.

Freud suggested that destructiveness and murder are manifestations of this aggressive energy discharge. Aggressive energy accumulates to dangerous levels in people when they have not had ample chance to discharge this internal energy more appropriately. The discharging process is known as *catharsis*, and it constitutes one of the most important components in psychoanalytic psychotherapy. Catharsis of aggressive energy, according to the model, may be accomplished by actual behavior (playing football, for example) or vicariously (watching football). Thus, the psychodynamic position predicts that children who participate in or avidly watch school sports will be ultimately less aggressive than children who do not. Additionally, the orthodox psychodynamic followers would predict that people involved in hostile aggression such as violent crime have not had sufficient opportunity to "blow off steam" and keep their aggressive energies at manageable levels. Psychodynamic recommendations for violent crime control are based on the assumption that humans, by their very nature, are always -going to be prone to aggressive impulses. Thus, the human animal must be provided with multi-channels for catharsis and taught appropriate ways for achieving it (e.g., adequate recreational facilities). Psychotherapy for excessively aggressive behavior, according to the psychodynamic model, would allow the child to blow off steam under the guidance of a therapist. In this way the child (or adult) would learn how to dissipate aggression in socially approved, appropriate ways.

Ethological Viewpoints

A group of scientists known collectively as ethologists have published a number of books and articles in the area of aggression which have proved interesting, readable, and popular in the eyes of the layperson. The more cogent writings of the group include Konrad Lorenz's *On Aggression* (1966), Robert Ardrey's *The Territorial Imperative* (1966), and Desmond Morris's *The Naked Ape* (1967). Lorenz is the chief spokesperson for the theoretical formulation of ethology as it relates to aggression. Ethology studies animal behavior in relation to the animal's natural habitat and compares that behavior to human behavior.

Lorenz, a Nobel laureate in biology, sees aggression as an inherited instinct found in both humans and animals. One of the principal purposes of aggression in animals, and presumably in humans, is to defend and protect "staked out" territory—a territory which ensures a sufficient quantity of food and water, of space to roam and to reproduce. Lorenz argues that if this space is violated, the instinctive or genetically programmed response is to attack, or at least to increase aggressive behavior toward the intruder, to prevent violations against the preferred distance or territory.

This tendency to attack space violators is generally referred to as *territoriality*. Lorenz believes that territory-based aggression is an innate propensity developed through the lengthy, complex process of evolution. Innate aggressive behavior between members of the same animal species (intraspecific) prevents overcrowding and ensures the best and most powerful mates for the young. Moreover, the more deadly the animals' evolutionarily developed weaponry (e.g., fangs, claws, physical size, and strength), the more intense the innate inhibitions against participation in physical combat with members of its own species. Lorenz asserts that this innately programmed inhibition ensures the survival of the species, since constant intraspecific physical combat would eventually promote the extinction of that particular species. Instead, intraspecific aggression is accomplished by a complicated display of force such as a show of teeth, size, or color array rather than actual combat; such displays are commonly referred to as *ritualized aggression*. Through an intricate communication system not yet clearly understood by scientists, the aggressing animals transmit signals, after which the more powerful, dominant animal generally wins out. The losing animal demonstrates defeat by various appeasement behaviors, such as rolling over on its back (characteristic of puppies), lowering of tail or head, and defeat cries; it then leaves the territory of the dominant animal.

What does all of this have to do with human aggression? Lorenz believes that it is important to understand animal aggression before we can understand human aggression, since humans are part of the animal world and probably follow many of the same basic principles of nature. Other ethologists also assert that humans are programmed to follow nonhuman principles. From their studies on personal space invasion in human subjects, Efran and Cheyne (1975, p. 225), for example, observed that "human society may operate through mechanisms which are less uniquely human than is currently fashionable to suggest." But Lorenz also explains that human beings have outdistanced the evolutionary process in terms of inhibiting aggression. Instead of developing natural weapons and the corresponding species-preserving function of innate inhibitors through ritualized aggression, humans have developed technological weaponry. Thus, many ethologists feel they can provide at least a partial answer to why human beings wantonly maim and kill members of their own species: they have not developed the ability to engage in the species-preserving behavior of ritualized aggression, yet they have developed the capacity, through superior learning ability, to annihilate.

The implications of the ethological view of aggression as instinctual are staggering. If violence, greed, and criminal action follow instinctive inclinations, there is little point in trying to change them by social means, such as education, welfare, equal job opportunities, rehabilitation of convicts, and preventive mental health programs. These programs would be wasteful and illusory.

Except for a few scattered studies, however, the overwhelming bulk of the research literature has not supported the ethological theory on human aggression (Anderson & Lupo, 1976; see also Montagu, 1973). One of the major problems is the excessive argument from analogies between animals and humans. Lorenz argues, for example, that the Greylag goose is remarkably similar to the human species (Berkowitz, 1973). However, the human brain has made us remarkably unlike the Greylag goose and considerably less likely to rely on instinct for determining behavior. In fact, research has yet to delineate any instinctive or *invariant* genetically programmed behavior determinant in humans.

The ethological position also fails to acknowledge and interpret the vast body of existing research that has tested it. This curious failure to integrate evidence from the scientific community undermines the validity of the ethologists' whole presentation. Some critics, in fact, have referred to ethological theorizing as "scientific-sounding misinformation" (Leach, 1973). Zoologists, biologists, and psychologists have tried to apply tenets to humans and simply have not found support for their validity. To date, there is little evidence to justify portraying humans as innately dangerous and brutal, or as instinct controlled. The reader who is interested in pursuing this argument further will want to consult Ashley Montagu's *Man and Aggression* (1973).

Population Density

Closely related to the ethologist's point of view is one based on population density; it sees aggression as a result of overcrowded conditions. In areas of high concentration of people, personal space is continually being violated. In urban areas, crowded mass transit systems and overcrowded apartment complexes infringe upon personal space and territory. Is overcrowding a principal factor in the instigation of violence and crimes against personal property?

A series of provocative studies conducted by John B. Calhoun (1961, 1962) with domesticated rats suggest interesting analogies between rats and humans. Calhoun, a research psychologist at the National Institute of Mental Health, allowed groups of rats to propagate freely in a limited physical space, but with adequate quantities of rat chow and water. Eventually, the rat colonies became overpopulated to such an extent that they demonstrated behaviors which were considered "abnormal."

The normal style of living for this species of rats includes the male rats finding one or more mates, building a nest, producing young, and raising them. Although the males roam freely, they normally do not show interest in another nest. The ecollect their own harem and family, select a plot or cage, and defend it. Calhoun's study found that when the population increased, males either no longer cared about building a nest or were not strong enough to defend it from bands of marauding male rats. The marauders would enter the nests, attack the females, and tear up the nests. The females became so harassed by the marauders that they lost interest in caring for their young. The marauding rats were those who could not build nests because of lack of space, and they developed a life style based on attacking other males and females physically and sexually.

There was also a group of "juvenile delinquents," consisting of males and females without a nest who were usually too weak to defend one or have a mate. They would gather in large clusters and spend the day milling around the floor of the cage, sometimes engaging in severe fighting, sometimes simply sleeping, or sometimes harassing other rats in the vicinity. Rather quickly, the rat society deteriorated and the population declined considerably. Calhoun's studies have been replicated by other studies and, in general, similar results have been reported.

Although there is no evidence of a relationship between overcrowding and crime among humans, some work has suggested a link between overcrowding and aggression. It is tempting to analogize from rats to humans, but the research evidence concerning crowding effects on human aggression is not clearcut. Experimentation in overcrowding with human subjects would not be encouraged by society and would obviously be fraught with legal and ethical questions.

Some investigators have exposed people to various high populations combined with various room temperatures (Griffith & Veitch, 1971). In general, as population density and temperature increased, so did subjects' negative feelings toward one another. Other investigations (Freedman et al., 1972) have indicated that population density has different effects on men and women. In crowded conditions, males tend to demonstrate more aggressive, hostile behavior than do men in uncrowded conditions. The reverse is true for females. These behaviors were observed only in same-sex groups—all male or all female groups—and the groups were together for only four hours. In mixed-company situations, the differences in aggressive behavior did not occur. Thus, available evidence suggests that men are uncomfortable and hostile in crowded same-sex conditions, while women tend to become more affable and friendly in crowded same-sex situations. To what extent crowded men become antisocial remains very much an open question and depends upon a constellation of factors.

A number of correlational studies conducted in various geographical areas throughout the U.S. by Freedman (1975) strongly indicate that there is no relationship between population density (people per square mile) and crimes of violence, such as murder, rape, and aggravated assault. When populations were matched for socioeconomic class and other relevant variables, crimes of violence actually decreased as population density increased. Freedman believes that part of this phenomenon is due to the large number of potential witnesses in high density areas.

In sum, firm conclusions that population density contributes directly to human aggression cannot be made by psychologists with present evidence. While population density may play a significant role in engendering aggressive behaviors in animals, in the human population the situation is far more complicated.

Frustration-Aggression Hypothesis

Around the time of Freud's death in 1939, a group of psychologists at Yale University proposed that aggression is a direct result of frustration (Dollard et al., 1939). According to Dollard and his colleagues, people who are frustrated, thwarted, annoyed, or threatened will behave aggressively; and people who exhibit aggressive behavior are frustrated, thwarted, annoyed, or threatened. The Dollard group postulated that aggression is a natural, almost automatic response to frustrating circumstances.

Because of its simplicity and important implications, the frustration-aggression hypothesis drew considerable research, accompanied by criticism on several fronts. Psychologists found it difficult not only to decide what "frustration" was, but also to determine how it could be measured accurately. Research also began to reveal that aggression is a much more complicated phenomenon than Dollard's first conception would have us believe. Frustration does not always lead to aggression; and aggressive behavior does not always signify "frustration." Experiments began to indicate that people respond to frustration and anger differently. Some respond with aggression, but others may have a wide variety of responses. Also, other emotional states besides anger have been found capable of instigating aggression (Berkowitz, 1973).

A chief spokesperson for a revised, contemporary version of the frustration-aggression hypothesis is Leonard Berkowitz, whose general views on the causes of criminality were presented in Chapter 4. Berkowitz continues to revise and modify the frustration-aggression hypothesis to keep it more in line with current research findings. Basically, he believes (1962, 1969) that frustration increases the probability that an individual will soon act aggressively. He defines aggression as a behavior whose goal is to inflict damage or injury on some object or person. The behavior may be overt (physical or verbal) or implicit (for example, wishing someone dead). Berkowitz says frustration results when behavior directed at anticipated goals or expectations is thwarted in some way. In a sense, any nonfulfillment of expectations may result in frustration. Thus, to be frustrated a person must have been expecting or anticipating the attainment of a goal or achievement. Deprivation of goals, achievements, or goods by itself does not necessarily qualify as a frustrating agent. People who are living under deprived conditions are not necessarily frustrated unless they actually expect something better. "Poverty-stricken groups who have never dreamed of having automobiles, washing machines, or new homes are not frustrated because they have been deprived of these things; they are frustrated only after they have begun to hope" (Berkowitz, 1969, p. 15).

According to Berkowitz, aggression is only one common response to frustration. The individual may learn other ways of responding, such as withdrawing, doing nothing, or trying to alter the situation by a more compromising approach. Therefore, Berkowitz not only acknowledges and emphasizes the importance of learning, but he also stresses the importance of individual differences in reacting to frustrating circumstances.

One other factor, aggression-eliciting stimuli, is important. The presence of appropriate "aggressive stimuli" in the external environment (or internal environment represented by thoughts) also increases the probability of aggressive responses. Before elaborating on this point, let us go back and review Berkowitz's basic position: Frustration occurs when a person is blocked from obtaining an expected goal; frustration generates anger; anger predisposes or readies the person to behave aggressively. Whether the person actually engages in aggressive actions will depend, in part, on the availability of aggression-inducing stimuli or cues in the environment, and in part on his or her learning history and individual way of responding to frustration.

A good example of an aggressive stimulus is a weapon. For most people in our society, a firearm is automatically associated with aggression. According to Berkowitz's theory, the presence of a gun is more likely to generate aggressive action than is the presence of a more neutral object, even when the gun is not used. An experiment by Berkowitz and LePage (1967) revealed that male subjects who were angered were more likely to engage in aggressive action in the presence of a gun than were similarly angered subjects in the presence of a badminton racket. The experiment suggests that the presence of a gun (such as on a visibly armed police officer) may actually facilitate a violent response rather than inhibit it—at least for people who get "turned on" in the presence of a weapon or similar aggressive cue.

Berkowitz states that anger is only one potentially aggressive emotion. Other heightened arousal states can also stimulate aggression. He cites evidence where unpleasant states such as pain or pleasant states such as sexual arousal also may lead to aggressive behavior (Berkowitz, 1973).

In summary, the Berkowitz hypothesis calls aggression a function of a generalized state of arousal combined with appropriate, aggression-eliciting stimuli. Once the person is aroused, the presence of aggression-associated stimuli or cues increases the probability of aggressive or violent action. In most cases both arousal and the appropriate cues must be present for aggression to occur. The cues are those stimuli which the individual has previously associated with aggression, and association comes about through either reward and punishment (instrumental learning), simple association in time (classical conditioning), or, as we shall learn in the next section, social learning.

Recent research suggests that the effects of frustration on aggression are strongly influenced by two additional mediating factors: 1. the magnitude of frustration experienced by the potential aggressor, and 2. whether the frustrating event is perceived as arbitrary or unexpected (Baron, 1977). While much research is still needed, it appears that the greater the frustration, the higher the probability that a person will aggress. In fact, low levels of frustration appear to generate little in the way of aggressive behavior (Baron, 1977; Ebbesen et al., 1975). In addition, there is some solid evidence that people are more aggressive in reaction to arbitrary or unexpected aggression (Baron, 1977; Worchel, 1974; Zillman & Cantor, 1976). That is, if the person interprets the frustrating event as justified, or feels that the event is at least partially under his or her control, then he or she will be less predisposed to act aggressively. These two factors suggest that unless the frustrating circumstances are evaluated as intense and seen as outside a person's control, aggression is unlikely to occur.

As the research evidence accumulates, the once simple frustration-aggression hypothesis becomes more complicated and riddled with exceptions. The science of human behavior does not provide simple answers.

Aggression and Temperature

So far in this chapter we have progressed from the biological, individual factors theorized to be determinants of aggression toward the more environmental and situational positions. Not surprisingly, one environmental factor which has been related to violence is atmospheric (ambient) temperature. Presumably, as temperature increases, violence increases. This heat-of-the-night assumption was proposed as partial explanation for the riots and civil disturbances during the late 1960s and early 1970s (Baron, 1977). Recent research, spearheaded by Robert Baron (Baron & Ransberger, 1978; Baron & Bell, 1975; Baron & Lawton, 1972; Baron & Bell, 1976; Bell & Baron, 1977), has found evidence to suggest that there is a relationship between ambient temperature and aggression. However, the relationship appears to be a highly complex one, as illustrated in Figure 7–1. Extremely low and high temperatures tend to inhibit aggression, while intermediate levels tend to be associated with aggression. Baron suggests that when the temperature becomes very unpleasant (too hot or cold), the person's major concern is to do something about reducing or raising the temperature, such as getting a cold drink or putting on heavier clothing. However, lower levels of discomfort tend to enhance the likelihood of aggression in some people. Specifically, the discomfort produced by intermediate levels of temperature (compounded by unpleasant odors and other environmental variables accompanying the increases) serves to induce irritability and hostility in potential aggressors. After a determinable point, however, these effects gradually become so aversive that the person's dominant response is to escape or reduce them.

Baron's proposal suggests that collective or individual violence may

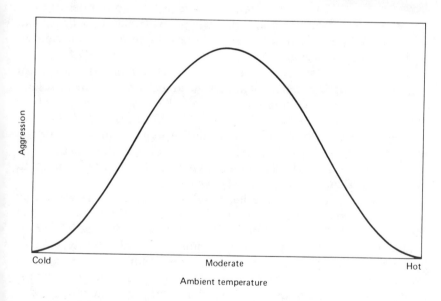

FIGURE 7-1. Hypothesized relationship between aggression and ambient temperature.

become prominent during intermediate, in comparison to cold or hot, environmental temperatures. He has also hypothesized a similar relationship between noise levels and aggression (see Baron, 1977).

Social Learning

Why do some people behave aggressively when intensely frustrated or uncomfortable while others change their tactics, withdraw, or are seemingly not affected at all? As we discussed in Chapter 4, the research to date strongly indicates that a major factor in the way an individual responds to frustration is his or her upbringing and past learning experiences. The human being is, of course, very adept at learning and maintaining behavior patterns that have worked in the past, even if they only worked occasionally; this learning process begins in early childhood.

As we have seen, children develop many behaviors merely by watching their parents and "significant others" in their environment, a process known as modeling or observational learning. More specifically, a child's behavior pattern is often acquired through the modeling or imitation of other people, real and imagined, whom the child observes and hears about (Bandura, 1973a).

For example, suppose that you return home after a harried day which was also hot and humid (frustration) and you find an official-looking letter from the IRS in the mailbox. You open it, perhaps muttering mild obscenities under your breath, and find that the IRS claims that you have shortchanged the U.S. government by several hundred dollars over the past three years, although you know that you have not (more frustration). You are due for a careful audit in two days (even more frustration). In response to this frustration, you slam your fist on the table, exclaim "Damn it!" or some colorful variation, and kick the nearest chair (just enough not to damage your toe, since you have learned the painful consequences from past violent episodes). Unknown to you, your son observed your reaction to frustration. Several hours later, when his block tower crumbles, little Harris pounds his fist, kicks the living room chair, and curses, "Damn it!" . . . one trial learning!

When the child's imitative behavior is reinforced or rewarded by praise and encouragement from significant models, the probability that the rewarded behavior will occur in the future is increased. There is evidence that American parents (consciously or inadvertently) encourage or reinforce aggressive behavior in their children. For example, in the case of little Harris, the child's behavior may be reinforced by the parents' drawing attention to it, "Isn't that cute?" or by laughing. Harris is also expected or encouraged to be like a hard-hitting middle linebacker, or to take care of himself against the neighborhood bully, provided he is approximately the same size. He also learns that the child who aggresses successfully against others is often rewarded by status, prestige, and the most attractive toys or material goods.

Although parents represent the major models for learning, there are many other sources in the social environment which provide imitative models for learning and reinforcement of aggressive behavior. Other children are very powerful influences on learning. Other members of the family, friends, and television characters are all potential models to be imitated by the child.

Since parents are powerful models, we would expect aggressive parents to have aggressive children. In an old but classic study, Sears, Maccoby, and Levin (1957) interviewed 400 mothers of kindergarten children about the disciplinary techniques they used, their attitudes about children's aggressiveness, and the children's expressions of aggression toward peers, siblings, and parents. One of the major findings was that aggressive, physical punishment by parents was related to aggressiveness in their children. This behavioral pattern was especially true when this disciplinary tactic was supplemented by high permissiveness toward aggression. Siegel and Kohn (1959) found that preschoolers played more aggressively when they were watched by a permissive adult than when no adult was visible.

A leading proponent of the social learning-aggression position is Albert Bandura (1973a), who argues persuasively that aggressive behavior can be most productively understood and modified by learning principles. As psychologists learn more about human behavior, the bulk of the scientific data tilts toward the learning view. However, most psychologists today believe that understanding aggression requires an interactive combination of antecedent events, including physiological, cognitive, and environmental factors. The trend is definitely away from psychoanalytic and instinctive explanations.

Social learning theory hypothesizes that most aggressive behavior is initially acquired through observation of aggressive models or on the basis of direct experience. Its expression is maintained by reinforcement. The social learning system acknowledges the fact that biological structures set limits on the types of aggressive responses which can be learned, and that genetic endowment influences the rate at which learning progresses (Bandura, 1973a). In the main, however, most behaviors displayed by people are learned by observation, either deliberately or inadvertently, through the influence of example.

Lest we oversimplify the issue too much, we should keep in mind that mere exposure to aggressive models does not guarantee that the observer will engage in similar aggressive action at a later date. A variety of conditions may prevent observational learning from taking place. Individuals differ widely in their ability to learn from observation. For instance, some people may fail to notice the essential features of the model's behavior, may not care to imitate the model, or may have a poor symbolic or visual memory. Bandura suggests that one important component of observational learning may be the motivation to rehearse what has been observed. He notes several examples where mass murderers originally got the idea from descriptive accounts of the other mass killings. The incident remains prominent in the mind of the prospective mass killer long after it has been forgotten by others. The person continues to mull it over and rehearse the scenario until, under appropriate conditions, it serves as the script for his or her own murderous action.

Another restriction on observational learning is what happens to the observed model. If during an aggressive episode the model is reprimanded or punished for acting aggressively, this will inhibit the observer's behavior. Thus, the "bad" guy should not get away with it if we are to discourage antisocial behavior via the entertainment media.

Berkowitz (1970) thinks that aggressive and violent behaviors are more reflexively or impulsively based than do the social learning theorists. He suggests that in many cases the individual reacts violently in a particular situation, not because that person anticipates pleasure or displeasure from the action, but because "situational stimuli have evoked the responses he is predisposed or set to make in that setting" (Berkowitz, 1970, p. 140). That is, the individual has been conditioned—specifically, classically conditioned—to react violently in that situation simply because of prior experiences in that particular situation.

The maintenance of aggressive behavior requires at least periodic reinforcement for its continued expression. Social learning sees aggression as being maintained by instrumental learning. More specifically, observational learning is an important factor in the *initial* stages of learning, but reinforcement is necessary for the behavior to be maintained during the later stages. The reinforcement may be positive, as for example in obtaining material or social rewards, or the reinforcement may be negative, as reflected in its ability to alter aversive conditions such as teasing. If aggression gains subjectively important rewards for the person, then he or she is likely to continue it. Moreover, in American society aggression is rarely punished during the early formative years. Aggressive, young children often receive social approval for sticking up for their rights with other children, although aggression directed at adults is not usually condoned.

Another reinforcement consideration is *control*. Aggressive behavior helps the aggressor control the social environment and the situation. Through aggressive actions, he or she affects others and the events that are taking place. If things are not going his or her way, or if the person is being taunted by others, aggression provides a means to gain some control over the events by changing them. The psychological reinforcement of control is an important one and will be considered in greater detail in later chapters.

Effects of Mass Media

Within the last two decades, more research has been directed at the effects of mass media on aggression than at any other potential instigator (Goldstein, 1975). There are good reasons for this. By the age of sixteen, the average child has spent more time watching television than in the school classroom and has witnessed more than 13,000 killings (Walters & Malamud, 1975). In addition, there are four scenes of violence portrayed on the television screen to every one expressing affection. Not surprisingly, experimental studies have revealed that, in general, television violence has a significant effect on the frequency and type of aggressive behavior expressed by both adults and children.

In a classic study by Bandura (1965), 66 nursery school children were divided into three groups and shown one of three five-minute films. All three films depicted an adult verbally and physically assaulting a plastic BoBo doll, a large inflatable doll with a sand base. One group observed the adult model rewarded with candy and a soft drink at the end of her aggressive behavior. A second group saw the adult model spanked and verbally reprimanded for her behavior. A third group witnessed a situation in which the model received neither punishment nor reward.

Following the film showings, the children were permitted to free play for ten minutes in a playroom of toys, including a BoBo doll. The group which had witnessed the adult model being rewarded for the aggressive behavior exhibited more aggression than the other two groups, with boys demonstrating higher frequencies of aggression than girls. The group which saw the adult model punished exhibited the lowest amount of aggression in the playroom.

Bandura's findings imply that children's aggressive behavior is significantly influenced by what they see on television. Goldstein (1975) notes that Bandura's study also underscores children's ability to learn aggressive behavior without reinforcement or reward—observational learning. Numerous follow-up studies have not only replicated Bandura's findings, but also have been consistent in demonstrating that media violence has a strong influence on real-life violence in many situations (Baron, 1977). On the other hand, exceedingly few studies have found support for the cathartic or psychodynamic viewpoint, which argues that television and other vicarious methods should "drain off" aggressive urges.

There is also some evidence that television has a "contagious" effect.

For example, the film "Fuzz" was shown on national television in October 1973. It depicted youths dousing tramps with gasoline and setting them afire. Two nights later a young woman was driving through the Roxbury section of Boston when her car ran out of gas. Returning to it with a two-gallon can of gas, she was met by six young men who forced her into a backyard, beat her, and ordered her to douse herself with the gasoline. Imitating the "Fuzz" scene, one of them struck a match and threw it at her. She immediately became a screaming human torch and died several hours later. The helicopter escape of a prisoner in the film "Breakout" was also imitated, as evidenced by two actual attempts in different parts of the world shortly after it was released. Airline hijacking is another example of the contagious effect; reports in the mass media of hijacking incidents have been frequently followed by other attempts.

As far back as 1912, the French sociologist Gabriel Tarde wrote about "epidemics of crime" which were prompted by a spectacular crime story (Berkowitz, 1970). He noted, for example, that a lurid crime in one community was often followed by similar crimes in other communities, not long after the *modus operandi* was publicized. Tarde pointed out that the case of Jack the Ripper inspired female mutilations in several English provinces. Berkowitz (1970) cites evidence that suggests that the Richard Speck murder of eight student nurses and the Charles Whitman shooting spree in the University of Texas tower may have stimulated similar violent crimes. At least five homicides in Arizona were apparently influenced by the Whitman killings. In November 1966 an eighteen-year-old walked into an Arizona beauty school and shot four women and a child. The offender said he got the notion from the Speck and Whitman murders.

Chaffee and McLeod (1971) cite evidence to suggest that television violence has substantially less effect on families where parents do not rely on aggressive behavior as a life style to solve problems. The Chaffee-McLeod results suggest that to a large extent parental models override violent models on television. Parental models also appear more influential than television, even in young children (Goldstein, 1975).

Exposure to media-portrayed violence does not, of course, automatically promote aggression. Some individuals are affected more than others. Children from low-income families have been found to be more influenced by media violence than are middle-class children (Eisenhower, 1969), and aggressive children watch more television than do nonaggressive children (Lefkowitz et al., 1977). Berkowitz (1970) suggests that individuals who rely heavily on aggression for getting their needs met are considerably more influenced by media violence than are people less prone to violent solutions to problems. Several studies have shown that it is the extremely aggressive adolescents who are most strongly attracted to violence portrayed in media entertainment (Berkowitz, 1970; Eron, 1963; Halloran, Brown, & Chaney, 1969). So far, the evidence indicates that violence in the media has its greatest effect on individuals who have already learned that aggressive action pays.

In general, most of the evidence to date supports the social learning explanation of aggression and violence. The proponents of social learning are among the first to admit, however, that the theory still needs extensive refinement, which could take many years. It is possible that the theory will be replaced by a more comprehensive one. Social learning's present strength lies in its consideration of *both* the individual factors, such as expectancies and learning history, and the social situations in which aggression occurs. Its weakest link may lie in its failure to explain the physiological determinants of aggression.

One important point should be introduced concerning the social learning position, a point that will be crucial in the understanding of many criminal offenses. We have emphasized that criminal behavior cannot be properly understood by examining the personality or the situational variables alone. However, personality and situational variables are not functioning as independent determinants which simply combine to produce behavior (Bandura, 1977). Rather, *they are continually determining each other*. The person's behavior affects the situation, and the situation affects his or her behavior. For example, in crimes directly involving the victims, such as assaults and homicide, we will find that the offenders affect the victims and the victims (who are part of the situation) affect how the offenders respond. The reciprocal relationship is one that deserves mention again here because it often comes into play in violent crime.

Victim-Precipitated Aggression

The preceding sections of the chapter have stressed that aggression is principally a learned behavior. In addition, the evidence indicates that aggression, while being influenced by numerous variables, is largely acquired through modeling and maintained through various forms of reinforcement, particularly social reinforcement. But we have not yet paid sufficient attention to one more crucial parameter: the victim of the aggression. Although temperature, noise, personal expectancies, reinforcement, models, frustration, and situational cues are all important variables, we shall learn in the next chapter that, in a large number of homicides and aggravated assaults, the victim played a prominent role in instigating the attacks upon him- or herself. Specifically, what started as a heated argument developed into a physical, violent brawl—a process known as *escalation*.

Put yourself in a situation where you are at a party. Suddenly, someone begins making derogatory remarks about your appearance, adds other verbal insults, and eventually begins to shove you. What is your mood at this point? Most of the research reviewed by Baron (1977) shows that most people respond to provocation by returning provocations of their own (see Taylor, 1967; Epstein & Taylor, 1967; Hendrick & Taylor, 1971; O'Leary & Dengerink, 1973). Furthermore, the reciprocated response approximates in intensity the one received. Also, the research is consistent in demonstrating that verbal attacks often lead to physical retaliation and violence. The implication is that in some crimes, the behavior of the victim may have had a role in escalating the offender's actions.

Before leaving the topic of aggression and examining this phenomenon in greater detail with relation to specific offenses, it is important to look at some of the research on the relevant physiological components of aggression. Earlier in the chapter we referred to some innate and instinctive features of aggression, but until now we have not looked at research findings.

THE PHYSIOLOGY OF AGGRESSION

Although there is little research to suggest that physiological factors play a role in *instrumental* aggression, there is a growing accumulation of experimental evidence that the nervous and endocrine systems, both in animals and humans, contribute significantly to *hostile* aggression. The endocrine system is involved in the internal secretion of hormones into the blood or lymph.

For example, many violent crimes committed by women occur during the premenstrual week (Moyer, 1971; Goldman, 1977). In one study in which the investigators used prison records for data, it was found that 62 percent of the crimes of violence by the women of that institution were committed in that phase (Morton et al., 1953). The "premenstrual syndrome" has also been studied by Dalton (1961), who reported that 49 percent of all crimes by women occurred during the premenstrual week or during menstruation. Clinical observations report that a majority of women complain of some irritability or depression prior to or during menstruation (Janowsky et al., 1967).

According to K. E. Moyer (1971), the premenstrual syndrome is associated with a fall in progesterone levels in the blood; administration of progesterone to women alleviates symptoms of irritability and tension.

Another study shows that women taking birth control pills containing progesterone demonstrate less irritability and hostility than do women not on any pill (Hamburg et al., 1968).

On the other hand, the male hormone testosterone facilitates hostile aggression in both males and females (Moyer, 1971; Goldman, 1977). This fact may, in part help explain why males overwhelmingly commit more violent crimes than do females. For example, males in 1974 outnumbered females in arrests for aggravated assault about six to one (Kelley, 1977). In addition, the relationship between the secretion rate of testosterone and the level of overt hostility correlates well in young men, but not in older men (Goldman, 1977). This relationship was especially notable between male adolescents who had a history of assault or attempted murder. It must be stressed, however, that learning and social expectations play an extremely powerful role in these statistics. We shall return to this point when we examine female criminality.

It is fairly well documented that castration lessens the tendency for animals to be aggressive. In very rare instances, castration of human prisoners convicted of sex crimes has significantly reduced aggressive episodes (LeMaire, 1956; Hawke, 1950). Injections of the female hormone estrogen or similar agents (e.g., diethylstilbestrol) have substantially reduced aggressive or antisocial behavior in prisoner populations. Compulsory castration was a legal procedure in some areas of the United States until as late as the 1950s, and it continues to be practiced to a very limited extent in some other countries (Johnson, 1972).

Research in the biological sciences depends on the development of sophisticated, advanced technology. Because of the recent rapid increase in instrument sophistication, biologists have been able to pay closer attention to the potential influence of molecular components, especially substances known as neurotransmitters, in exciting and inhibiting aggression. Neurotransmitters are biochemicals directly involved in the transmission of neural impulses. Without them, communication within the nervous system would be impossible. Recent investigations have found that a number of neurotransmitters, namely norepinephrine, acetylcholine, and serotonin, may influence the cortical and subcortical mechanism responsible for aggression and violence in important ways. Norepinephrine and acetylcholine appear to be especially important in the excitation of aggression, while serotonin appears to play a part in the inhibition of aggression (Goldman, 1977).

No single neurotransmitter solely excites or inhibits aggression and violence. Neurotransmitters are the basic chemicals for all behavior, and modification of their levels in the nervous system is likely to affect a rather large range of behavior and emotions. Yet the considerable potential of drugs in the control and reduction of aggression cannot be overlooked. Drugs primarily affect the neurotransmitters. If certain neurotransmitters are implicated in aggressive behavior, it is not too farfetched to consider drug regimens for its control.

Abundant evidence shows that aggressive and violent behaviors can be facilitated or prevented by the stimulation or destruction of certain mechanisms and bioelectrical circuits in areas of the brain. The research on laboratory animals is especially convincing in this regard. Although precise "aggressive centers" remain relatively unknown, most of the investigations have concentrated on a general area of the brain stem known as the limbic system, which consists of a diverse group of complicated brain structures and circuitry. The scientific search for aggressive centers of the brain has specifically focused on a small almond-shaped, complex group of nerve cells in the brain stem called the amygdala, another structure called the hypothalamus, and on a portion of the brain called the temporal lobe. It is interesting to note in this connection that Charles Whitman, the notorious Texas tower sniper, was reportedly found in an autopsy to have a large tumor in the area of the amygdala (Mark & Ervin, 1970, p. 148). Richard Speck, who brutally murdered eight student nurses in Chicago, reportedly displayed symptoms of a serious brain disease (Valenstein, 1973).

Even so, routine postmortem examinations on chronically antisocial, violent persons have generally found no noticeable lesion or malformation in the limbic system or other areas of the central nervous system (Goldman, 1977). Possibly, the instrumentation utilized in postmortem analysis may not be sophisticated enough, or else the neural involvement is more functional than structural. That is, the problem might be more a result of biochemical or neurotransmitter substances than malformation of or damage to certain neural structures.

Researchers examining the relationship between aggression and the brain typically drill a small hole in the skull (usually in experimental animals) which enables them to penetrate the brain with small insulated wire electrodes for electrical stimulation or minute glass hollow tubes (cannulae) for chemical stimulation of specific sites of the brain and stem. This "stereotaxic" procedure allows the precise implantation of needle electrodes or of cannulae, and many researchers believe it has profound possibilities for the control of hostile aggression in the future. The needle electrode, once properly implanted, may be permanently attached to the skull with screw fittings, allowing a small segment of the electrode to protrude from the skull for the attachment of wires, or in some cases to receive radio transmission from a distance (see Figure 7-2). This procedure of "wireless" communication is known as telemetry. The external portion of the electrode is small enough to be covered with hair and thus not be noticeable. The subject feels no pain from the procedure.

Small electric currents are passed through the insulated needle electrodes to the brain site, stimulating the brain structure (or destroying it, if necessary, with direct current or high frequency alternating current), much as the brain itself stimulates the structure through its highly complex circuitry. Aggressive and violent behavior may be either generated or inhibited, depending on whether the site has an excitatory or inhibitory function. If the location has an excitatory function, low frequency alternating current may excite the person to behave aggressively. King (1961) reports the classic example of this phenomenon: A female subject became hostile and threatened to strike the experimenter when she was electrically stimulated in the region of the amygdala. Once the current was terminated, the patient quickly returned to normal and displayed no signs of aggressive behavior. Each time the experimenter turned on the electrical current, the subject again demonstrated a hostile reaction.

On the other hand, aggression may also be *inhibited* by stimulation at a location that inhibits hostile reactions. It is now technologically possible for behavioral scientists to implant an electrode in a specified region

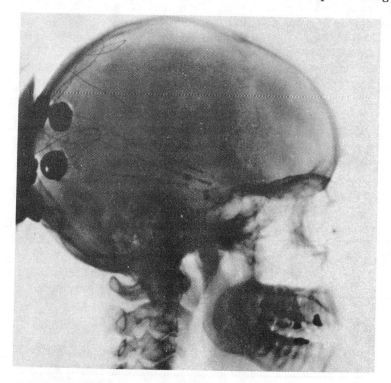

FIGURE 7-2. Diagramatic representation of electrode implants into the amygdala for control of aggression.

of the human brain and monitor the brain wave patterns by a computer some distance away, even without direct wire connections. When a specific brain wave configuration occurs which is known to be associated with violent behavior for the particular individual, a radio transmission is sent to the receiver, or implanted electrode, activating an electrical stimulation to the brain site. Once the inhibitory brain mechanism is activated, the subject's tendency for hostile action is dissipated.

Substantial research indicates that a significant number of prisoners who have committed violent crimes show abnormal brain-wave patterns (Valenstein, 1973; Mark & Ervin, 1970). As we have seen in Chapter 3, one category of abnormal brain-wave pattern, technically known as slow-wave activity, is especially apparent in the temporal lobe region of the brain. Hare (1970) estimates that 2 percent of the general population exhibits abnormal brain waves, compared to 8.2 percent of the population of convicted murderers, and 14 percent of aggressive psychopaths.

Another type of abnormal brain-wave activity discussed previously is positive spike activity, occurring in less than 2 percent of the general population. People with a history of impulsive, aggressive, and destructive behavior may have positive spike activity as high as 20 to 40 percent (Hare, 1970). These destructive and violent responses are often precipitated by relatively mild provocations and sometimes result in severe damage to property and injury or even death to others. These findings are simply correlations; they do not signify cause and effect. It is impossible to determine from the data whether abnormal brain waves cause violent behavior or whether violent behavior causes abnormal brain-wave configurations.

Violence is also controlled by producing permanent alterations of brain tissue (lesions) by surgical, electrical (direct current), or chemical procedures. Lesions in the temporal lobe of the brain were performed on several prisoners in California (Valenstein, 1973). The Japanese neurosurgeon Hirataro Narabayashi claims success with amygdala operations on a diversity of patients plagued by, among other things, aggressive, uncontrollable, destructive, and violent behaviors. Dr. Narabayashi reports that about 68 percent of his patients showed a significant decline in aggressive, violent behavior (Valenstein, 1973).

Some investigators have proposed that we control the antisocial elements in our society by any perfected biochemical, electrical, or surgical means available. For example, Kenneth B. Clark, former president of the American Psychological Association, asserted in his presidential address that psychology "can no longer afford to rely solely on the traditional, prescientific attempts to contain human cruelty and destructiveness" (Clark, 1971, p. 1,055). Clark believes that biological research in psychology is rapidly developing to the point where the criminal brain can be controlled by various biochemical and surgical procedures, which he refers to as psychotechnology:

> The implications of an effective psychotechnology for the control of criminal behavior and the amelioration of the moral insensitivities which produce reactive criminality in others are clear. It would seem, therefore, that there would be moral and rational justification for the use of compulsive criminals as pretest subjects in seeking precise form of intervention and moral control of human behavior. This suggestion is based on the assumption that no human being who is not impelled by some forms of internal, biochemical, or external, social forces—or some combination of both—would choose to be criminal if he were provided with options (Clark, 1971, p. 1,056).

Clark also suggests that world leaders should be required to submit themselves to the most perfected forms of psychotechnological and biochemical intervention for the control of their potentially aggressive, hostile impulses in order to prevent the mass destruction of civilization.

The potential medical, legal, moral, and ethical ramifications of such proposals are obviously overwhelming. It is true that biochemical intervention and surgical techniques on the human brain are rapidly becoming a reality, but who decides what to do to whom? Who will be the big brother who makes the decision about what individuals will be required to submit to psychotechnology? What are the constitutional rights of the subjects? It is also highly likely that the biological alleviation of aggressive behavior will affect other socially desirable behaviors. There is evidence to suggest that aspects of the individual's emotional, cognitive, and intellectual functioning may be significantly affected by biological manipulation of the brain. Neuronal networks in the central nervous system do not function in physiological isolation. It is estimated that the brain contains 10 billion brain cells (neurons), and the infinitesimal intercommunication network between these cells constitutes the most complex system in the known universe. Each nerve cell or neuron appears to play some role in behavior. Scientists talk about areas or structures in the brain in a kind of conceptual shorthand, but the delineated regions do not exist as separate entities with only one function each. Therefore, surgical, electrical, or chemical intervention not only affects certain dimensions of aggressive behavior, but elements of other behaviors as well.

It is also extremely unlikely that a majority of criminals in our society

ring from some kind of brain pathology or dysfunction. There is
ve evidence that some small proportion of violent crime, especially that precipitated by hostile aggression, may be committed by
individuals with brain pathology, but it would be foolhardy to conclude
that brain dysfunction accounts for an appreciable amount of aggression.

HEREDITY AND THE XYY CHROMOSOME

A number of early investigators believed that criminal behavior and the
predisposition to be violent were a result of heredity. As mentioned
earlier, the most prominent among the proponents of the view was
Lombroso, who played a major role in establishing the "Italian school of
criminology." Lombroso was convinced that the criminal "type" could
be identified by a number of specific physical characteristics, such as the
unsymmetrical shape of the head and jaw, a low forehead, protruding
ears, and bushy, connected eyebrows.

A more recent field of inquiry relating genetics to criminality has been
in the area of the so-called XYY chromosomal syndrome. A number of
investigators have hypothesized that the chromosomal anomaly XYY is
closely related to violent criminal activity found in males. Much of the
impetus in the research field was generated after a study by Jacobs and
his associates (1965) reported that an extra Y chromosome is significantly associated with tall stature, mental retardation, and an unusually
high level of aggressive behavior.

Chromosomes are chains of genetic material known as DNA, which
contain hereditary instructions for the growth and production of every
living cell in the organism. They control physical traits such as eye
color, hair color, and height, and they possibly have substantial influence on many psychological predispositions and temperaments. Each
cell in the human body normally possesses 46 chromosomes, or 23 pairs.
One pair in each cell is responsible for sex determination and sex
characteristics. One member of the pair is always an "X," whereas the
other member may be either an "X" or "Y," depending on the sex of the
individual. They are named "X" or "Y" because of their physical appearance under a microscope. In the normal woman, cells have two X
chromosomes, while in the normal man the cells consist of one X and
one Y. In rare instances, however, a genetic anomaly occurs in males in
that two Y chromosomes pair with a single X—hence the phenomenon
XYY. Rather than the normal 46 chromosomes, the individual has 47.

Although there are many exceptions, the principal characteristics associated with the presence of an extra Y chromosome include unusual height, episodes of violent aggression, and borderline intelligence. Severe acne or scars from acne are also a characteristic. A number of infamous murderers have been found to have XYY abnormalities, the first being Robert Peter Tait, who was convicted of beating to death a seventy-seven-year-old woman in Australia (Fox, 1971). The XYY characteristic, however, was discovered after his trial and did not have appreciable effect in delaying his execution. The XYY genotype was first used as a basis for defense in 1968 at the trial of Daniel Hugon in Paris. Hugon was charged with the brutal murder of an elderly prostitute. Although Hugon was convicted of murder, he received only seven years imprisonment, but the effect of XYY abnormality on the sentence is unclear (Fox, 1971).

The mass murderer Richard F. Speck was convicted and sentenced in 1966. Because he physically resembled the XYY syndrome, a number of researchers later decided to examine his chromosome structure. Although there was considerable confusion at the time of the results, it has been concluded that Speck's body does not contain the XYY abnormality.

"Big Bad John" (Sean) Farley, a six-foot, eight-inch, 240-pound giant who was accused of murdering and mutilating a Queens, New York woman in 1969, was convicted of first-degree murder, in spite of his lawyer's defense of insanity from a chromosomal imbalance.

Is there empirical support for the relationship between XYY chromosomal abnormality and crime, or even between the XYY structure and violence? In an extensive review of the world literature, Jarvik, Klodin, and Matsuyama (1973) concluded that the presence of the XYY configuration in the general population averages between .11 and .14 percent; among mental patients it is significantly higher, averaging between .13 and .20 percent. More importantly, when Jarvik and her colleagues combined 26 different studies (5,066 subjects) conducted on criminal populations, XYY occurred in 1.9 percent of the cases. This frequency, they noted, is 15 times that found in the general population.

So far, the data provide strong support for the relationship between criminal behavior and the extra Y chromosome, but there is still little evidence that violence and XYY go hand in hand. The 1.9 percent found by Jarvik and her colleagues constitutes a very small proportion of the prison population and therefore very little of the violence in our society. One more important point should be made: XYY prisoners have been found to have a lower incidence of assaults against persons than comparable groups of "normal" XY prisoners (Price & Whatmore, 1967). Actually, a vast majority of the XYY crimes were against property.

EPILEPSY AND VIOLENCE

Vague statements concerning the relationship between epilepsy and violence are sometimes encountered in the literature (e.g., Mark & Ervin, 1970). This noted relationship is believed to involve, in most cases, temporal lobe or psychomotor epilepsy. Presumably, the person plagued with psychomotor epilepsy is prone to uncontrollable periods of violence and destruction. The available research, however, fails to support a general epilepsy-violence relationship (Valenstein, 1973; Blumer, 1976).

Although angry, irritable behavior between seizures is commonly reported in chronic temporal lobe epileptics, physical harm is rarely inflicted (Blumer, 1976). In rare cases, some violence may occur in the confusional state which takes place immediately after an epileptic seizure if the individual is provoked. During the rage attack, the individual appears to lose control, is frightening, and may even destroy some furniture or strike a family member, but he or she rarely injures someone. Although this is disruptive for the family, the attack rarely leads to criminal charges. Furthermore, effective medication for epileptic seizures is so readily available today that the likelihood of these seizures not being controlled is very small. The incidence of criminal offenses among persons with epilepsy is not significantly higher than that found in the general population (Gunn, 1971).

SUMMARY

Aggression has been endemic in the human being's history and has been instrumental in helping the species to survive. Paradoxically, it now represents a threat to human comfort and existence. We defined aggression in this chapter as the intention and the attempt physically or psychologically to harm another individual or to destroy an object. As such, it is the basic ingredient in violent crime.

In an effort to decide whether aggression is instinctive, biological, learned, or some combination of these, we examined the theories propounding each of the viewpoints. Proponents of the psychodynamic view believe human beings build up aggressive energy and need to discharge it in socially approved channels, or it will reach dangerous levels. Ethologists, led by Konrad Lorenz, see aggression as an inherited instinct found in both humans and animals. They attribute to humans the same mechanisms for dealing with it as they do to animals, with the difference that humans have not developed the lower species' way of inhibiting it, but rather have developed more sophisticated aggressive maneuvers. Neither the psychoanalytic nor the ethological viewpoints have been supported to any considerable extent in the research literature.

Population density has also been proposed as a cause of aggression, and we saw that although some works found a link between over-crowding and aggression in animals, little definitive work has been done with humans. Some studies have even found a decrease in crimes of violence as population density increases.

The frustration-aggression hypothesis was found inadequate to account for the complexities of human behavior. Berkowitz has tried to modify the theory to accommodate much of the research findings, but gaps still exist. At the present time, social learning most adequately encompasses the scientific evidence and observed behavior, both in terms of the acquisition of aggressive behavior and its maintenance. Modeling or observational learning plays a crucial role in response discovery; reinforcement, especially in the form of social approval, appears to be the best explanation of why and how aggressive behavior is maintained. There are still numerous conditions that must be further examined, particularly on issues surrounding aggression-provoking environments and situations.

The relationship between violence and aggression portrayed by the mass media and the tendency to behave accordingly appears to be a strong and consistent one. This finding lends considerable support to the social learning position on the acquisition of aggression. We also stressed in this chapter that victims often play a significant role in precipitating violent and aggressive attacks upon themselves.

The physiology of aggression is often overlooked in the literature, but we saw that physiological variables can have significant effect on violent and aggressive behavior. In extreme cases, violent criminals have been found to have tumors or lesions on neurological structures believed to be partially responsible for aggression. It is highly unlikely, however, that an appreciable segment of the violence-prone population is suffering from similar brain damage or forms of neurological impairment.

It has also been shown that the increases in the male hormone testosterone and decreases in the female hormone progesterone promote irritability and hostility. Drugs, therefore, have considerable potential for controlling aggression. Similarly, research has been done in attempts to alter electrically and surgically the portions of the brain that control aggression. The danger with both drugs and surgical intervention, however, is the probability that other areas and functions of the brain will also be affected. Until more refined techniques are available, as well as more information about the working of the brain, using either of these methods for controlling aggression is questionable. Also, the ethics involved are probably more complicated than the understanding of the neurological mechanisms themselves.

In recent years the relationship between the chromosomal structure known as XYY and criminal behavior has drawn increasing empirical interest. Research data to date show that individuals possessing an XYY abnormality are overrepresented in the prison population. However, an important aspect of this finding is that a large majority of XYY persons have been convicted of property crimes and not of violent crimes as originally believed.

A relationship between epilepsy and violence has not been supported.

KEY CONCEPTS FOR REVIEW

Hostile aggression
Instrumental aggression
Psychodynamic theory of aggression
Ethological viewpoints
Ritualized aggression
Frustration-aggression hypothesis
Temperature and aggression
Population density and aggression
Social learning and aggression
Effects of media-portrayed aggression
Escalation
Premenstrual syndrome
Testosterone
Neurotransmitter
Limbic system
XYY chromosomal syndrome

MAJOR THEORISTS AND RESEARCHERS

Freud
Lorenz
Berkowitz
Bandura

SUGGESTED READINGS

Bandura, A. *Aggression: A social learning analysis.* Englewood Cliffs, N.J.: Prentice-Hall, 1973.
An upper-level treatment of aggression from a social learning perspective.

Baron, R.A. *Human aggression.* New York: Plenum Press, 1977.
An up-to-date, comprehensive review of the recent research on human aggression.

Goldstein, J. H. *Aggression and crimes of violence.* New York: Oxford University Press, 1975.
A good review of all the theories of aggression and a perspective on violent criminal behavior.

Johnson, R. N. *Aggression in man and animals.* Philadelphia: W.B. Saunders, 1972.
A highly readable book on the study of aggression in animals and humans from a wide range of viewpoints.

CRIMINAL HOMICIDE
AND ASSAULT

EIGHT

Violence is part of a struggle to resolve stressful and threatening
events—a struggle to adapt.

Daniels and Gilula, 1970, p. 405

If the entertainment media represent a reasonably decent barometer of
human interests, homicidal violence must rank as one of the most
fascinating subjects known to Western civilization and, along with sex,
the most marketable. It also seems that the more bizarre, senseless, or
heinous the murder, the more likely it is to receive extensive press
coverage, followed shortly thereafter by books, television specials, and
movies. Unusual mass murders and so-called "motiveless" killings are
especially popular.

Homicides, however, make up only about 2 percent of the total violent
crimes reported to the FBI (Kelley, 1977). Numerically, this amounts to
approximately 20,000 murders in the United States. Explanations of the
disproportionate amount of attention criminal homicides draw are multiple. One of the principal reasons appears to be the same reason that the

occult, mysterious monsters, strange tales, UFOs, and haunted houses are popular. Human beings need a certain amount of excitement and arousal in their lives to prevent them from being mundane, inane, and boring (Berlyne, 1960). This stimulation need partly explains why some people try roller coasters, sky jumping, race car driving, and gambling, and look at films of chain-saw massacres, vampires, werewolves, and torture chambers. These activities add a bit of excitement and spice to life. Criminal homicide, perhaps because of its reality, represents the ultimate terror if it is performed with ingenuity. This stimulation craving may partially explain some people's apparent need to know the more sensational details of a murder. Of course, a very large proportion of murders are rather straightforward in that they are not unusual, intricately planned events, or even very exciting, as we shall see in this chapter. But doing, seeing, and hearing the same things day in and day out is boring, and one needs change. Novel things produce arousal and excitement and break the monotony. Theoretically, some bored persons may even take their cues from the entertainment media and create their own excitement by murdering, torturing, or raping.

Curiosity or exploratory behavior, which is very closely related to excitement and arousal, may also help to explain the marketability of murder. One of the purposes of curiosity appears to be that it allows organisms to adapt and adjust to the environment (Butler, 1954). Curiosity about murders might permit us to prepare ourselves for the possibility that the event might happen to us at some time in the future. Reading about bizarre, seemingly irrational homicides might help us to identify signals to watch out for in similar circumstances. Information about the incident provides us with cues about what kinds of people murder, what kinds of people get killed, and under what kinds of situations. With this information, we might feel better equipped to deal with violence in the future.

In this chapter we will examine the situational, environmental, and psychological factors which occur with some consistency in homicide and assaultive offenses. Sociological research has supplied solid data concerning the demographic and situational variables surrounding the aggregate numbers of homicides and assaults reported officially to various agencies. This material will be presented shortly and will be necessarily statistical (see Table 8–1). Next, we will make a brief sojourn through the psychiatric literature on homicide, with the intention only of providing the reader with a flavor of the past and present thinking in that area. Then, we will focus on the research findings regarding *individual* or personality factors in murder and violence, a topic we hardly touched upon in the aggression and violence chapters. Following this

TABLE 8-1
Homicide Rate per 100,000 Inhabitants of Selected Countries
Around the World in the Year Reported

Country	Rate	Year	Country	Rate	Year
Angola	4.8	1970	Ireland	0.4	1967
Australia	1.5	1967	Israel	1.7	1968
Austria	0.9	1968	Italy	1.0	1967
Belgium	0.8	1968	Japan	1.4	1967
Canada	9.7	1968	Mexico	19.5	1967
Chile	26.4	1967	Mozambique	2.9	1970
Columbia	21.5	1967	Netherlands	0.4	1968
Cuba	5.1	1965	Nigeria	3.0	1969
Czechoslovakia	1.1	1967	Northern Ireland	0.7	1967
Denmark	0.6	1968	Norway	0.6	1968
Finland	2.2	1968	Panama	4.9	1967
France	1.3	1967	Philippines	27.7	1972
Greece	0.7	1967	Poland	0.9	1968
Guatemala	18.8	1968	United Kingdom	0.7	1967
Hungary	2.3	1968	United States	6.8	1967
Iceland	1.5	1968	Uruguay	5.7	1967

Source: Data obtained from United Nations. *Demographic Yearbook—1974*. New York: United Nations, 1975, and adapted to tabular format.

presentation, we shall look at some miscellaneous but important areas of homicide and violence—mass murders, homicides in prisons, and mob violence.

Up to this point in the book, broad, theoretical issues have been introduced in an effort to lay a solid foundation upon which specific offense categories can be viewed. The offense features presented in the remaining chapters will be interwoven with the concepts outlined in the previous chapters.

DEFINITIONS

Before getting into this chapter, we have to cover some of the dry essentials by defining criminal homicide and aggravated assault. For our purposes we will use the definitions supplied by the FBI in the *Uniform Crime Reports* (UCR), keeping in mind that state statutes may limit or extend these definitions.

Criminal homicide includes both murder and nonnegligent manslaughter. The definition excludes suicides, accidental deaths, or justifiable homicides. *Justifiable homicides* refer to "1. the killing of a person by a law enforcement officer in line of duty, and 2. the killing of a person in the act of committing a felony by a private citizen" (Kelley, 1974, p. 6). Negligent *manslaughter* is limited to deaths judged to be caused by "gross negligence" of some individual other than the victim. *Aggravated assault* refers to "assault with the intent to kill for the purpose of inflicting severe bodily injury by shooting, cutting, stabbing, maiming, poisoning, scalding, or by the use of acids, explosives, or other means" (Kelley, 1974, p. 6).

Aggravated assault generally has been studied in conjunction with homicide. Many assaults are viewed as homicide attempts that have failed because of prompt medical attention, efficient communication systems, the unavailability of a lethal weapon, or pure luck (Dunn, 1976). In a project report by the Criminal Justice Research Center, Albany, N.Y., in 1976, it was held that the practice of assuming complete equivalence of murder and aggravated assault was largely unwarranted (see Dunn, 1976). The report noted that in 1970, the aggravated assault rate was twenty times greater than that of murder and nonnegligent manslaughter. "Given this disparity in rates, it is difficult to imagine that even one-quarter of all aggravated assaults were attempted homicides or would have been homicides except for the intervention of medical care," (Dunn, 1976, p. 10). Moreover, the report suggests that knowledge of aggravated assault may be limited by the tendency to link it with homicide.

It may well be that aggravated assault is a phenomenon different from homicide in terms of several important variables, such as the motives and intent of the behavior. Still further, the "assaultive personality" may represent a different breed from the "homicidal personality"—if there is such a thing as a characteristic personality within each offense category. To maintain an assault-murder distinction would be a clever thing to do in this chapter, for it would allow an organized presentation of the two categories and add to conceptual clarity. Realistically, however, this ambition is difficult to achieve. Most studies have collapsed both categories into one because the research literature has shown that a substantial segment of the people who commit murder have also displayed a history of assaultive behavior. From all indications, at least one cluster of murderers rely fairly consistently upon assaultive methods in dealing with conflict, which certainly clouds the murder-assault distinction. Also, the major difference between homicides and aggravated assault might be in the type of weapons used by the assailant. The high-powered bullet is, in most cases, more lethal (and more impersonal) than the knife (Gillin & Ochberg, 1970; Block, 1977).

Block (1977) contends that murder is a highly plausible outcome of any violent crime, including robbery and rape, and as such should be considered in a general subcategory underlying *all* forms of violent crimes. According to Block, murder is in most ways no different from criminal violence that does not result in death. Essentially, he believes that murder is often an outcome of an aggravated assault, rape, or robbery which progressed beyond the consequences intended by the offender. We might ask at this point: Then what was the offender's reason for shooting or stabbing in the first place? The intention might not have been to see a dying victim at the end of the action, but we might surmise that the offender did have a specific intent to "terminate" the victim's behavior, or at least change the events that were happening at that particular moment. We will return to this point later in the chapter, but for now it is assumed in this book that violent behavior which results in criminal homicide possesses many of the same features as aggravated assault.

SOCIOLOGICAL CORRELATES OF HOMICIDE

Race

One of the most consistent findings reported in the sociological litera- ture is that in America, Blacks are involved in criminal homicide at a rate that far exceeds their numbers in the general population. On the basis of an extensive investigation of some of the parameters involved in 588 homicide cases reported in Philadelphia during the years 1948 to 1952, Marvin Wolfgang (1958, 1961) found that about 73 percent of the offend- ers and 75 percent of the victims were black. Furthermore, in almost all the reported cases (about 94 percent) Blacks killed Blacks, or Whites killed Whites, indicating that homicide is largely an intraracial affair.

Recent investigations have indicated that race-homicide relationships still prevail. In a ten-year study of criminal violence in Chicago between 1965 and 1974, Richard Block (1977) found that, although the incidence of homicide more than doubled during that time, the proportion of black involvement in the homicide rate changed very little. Specifically, in 1965, 72 percent of all homicide victims in Chicago were black, com- pared to a 70 percent victimization rate in 1974. The percentage of homicides attributed to black offenders in 1965 was identical to the percentage reported in 1974: 78 percent. In addition, 90 percent of the homicide victims and offenders were members of the same race in 1965, compared to an 88 percent intraracial incidence rate reported in 1974.

The FBI *Uniform Crime Reports* (Kelley, 1977) show that in 1976 Blacks made up 53 percent of all the arrests for murder, while they constituted only about 18 percent of the U.S. population. Moreover, 71 percent of the prisoners incarcerated for homicide in state and local correctional facilities in 1972 were black (Hindelang et al., 1976).

Sex

Although not quite as strong as the relationship between race and homicide, the relationship between homicide and sex is also consistently high. Wolfgang reported that 82 percent of the murderers in Philadelphia were male, and 76 percent of the victims were male. More specifically, the homicide offender rate per 100,000 was 41.7 for black males, 9.3 for black females, 3.4 for white males, and only .4 for white females. Notice how the race factor emerges strongly in combination with the sex factor. That is, proportionally, a very large segment of homicides are not only committed by males, but by black males. The UCR reports that in 1976 males outnumbered females nearly six to one in criminal homicide arrests. Other studies in Houston (Pokorny, 1965), in Chicago (Voss & Hepburn, 1968; Block, 1977), in England (Gibson & Klein, 1961), and in Israel (Landau et al., 1974) have repeatedly confirmed the very high ratio of males to females in homicide offenses.

In reference to homicide victim rates, the English study found that 60 percent of the victims were females, while U.S. studies have hovered around the 25 percent mark for female victims. The Israeli study reports that 51 percent of the victims of Jewish killers were female, compared to only 34 percent for non-Jewish offenders. These data illustrate the importance of considering cultural determinants and the nature of personal relationships in any discussion of homicide rates.

Victim-Offender Relationship

Research has also consistently shown that in at least two-thirds of all homicides the offender and the victim knew one another well (Wolfgang, 1958; Bullock, 1955; Svalastoga, 1956; Driver, 1961; Hepburn & Voss, 1970; Wong & Singer, 1973). In the Wolfgang data, the victim and offender were strangers in only about 14 percent of the cases. In a more recent investigation in Chicago, Hepburn and Voss (1970) found that the victim and offender unfamiliarity was slightly higher, at 19 percent. From all indications, these findings appear to hold across all cultures.

There are some recent indicators, however, that more people are now being killed by strangers than was reported in previous years. In Chicago during 1974, the murder victim and the offender were acquainted in only 58 percent of the incidents (Block, 1977). One of the major hypotheses for this dramatic increase in the number of people being murdered by strangers is based on the very rapid increase in armed robberies and the tendency to use firearms during the robbery attempt.

Weapons

Guns and knives are the two preferred instruments for inflicting death, but this preference is somewhat influenced by sex, race, geographical, and other parameters. For example, Philadelphia during the early 1950s had stabbing as the most common killing method (Wolfgang, 1958), while in Chicago during the 1960s and early 1970s, shooting was the preferred method (Hepburn & Voss, 1970; Block, 1977). Furthermore, more recent homicide incidents in Chicago due to firearms have increased by almost three times the firearms deaths reported in 1965 (Block, 1977). However, death inflicted by other weapons has increased only slightly. This finding suggests that the increase in homicide rates may be due in part to the greater availability of firearms. Nationally, firearms were used in 64 percent of the total murders reported in 1976; this figure compares to 18 percent of the cases where a knife or sharp instrument were used (Kelley, 1977).

Other Factors

Most research has found that homicides tend to increase during the summer months. In addition, weekends, especially between 8 p.m. Saturday and 2 a.m. Sunday, are clearly the times when homicides most often occur (Wolfgang, 1958; Hepburn & Voss, 1970; Block, 1977).

The Wolfgang data show that of total homicide offenders, nearly two-thirds had previous arrest records. More importantly, when an offender had a previous record he or she was more likely to have a record of offenses against persons than against property, and they were usually serious assault offenses. You will recall that in our discussion of predictability of criminal offenses, we commented that the past track record of the offender is the most useful in determining future offenses. The Wolfgang study suggests that in a large number of homicides, the offender has displayed a strong preference for engaging in violent behavior as a way of resolving conflicts. Perhaps at the time of the homicide the victim precipitated a greater violent reaction than had been necessary in past episodes.

Wolfgang found that about 26 percent of the cases could clearly be regarded as victim-precipitated. Hepburn and Voss (1970) found that among Chicago homicides about 38 percent of the cases seemed provoked by the victim. Sociological studies also point out that offenders' motives for killing are often based on reported minor altercations and domestic quarrels in which both parties were actively aggressive. Recall the phenomenon of escalation discussed in the previous chapter, where people tend to retaliate on a level comparable to the insult or blow they receive, and, also, where vrebal quarrels very often escalate to physical blows. Sociologists have also generally observed that to people outside the particular cultural context in which the offense took place, the precipitating factors for the argument may appear rather trivial causes for the killing of another human being.

The influence of alcohol in homicides continually crops up in a wide range of investigations. Wolfgang reports that in nearly two-thirds of the cases, either the victim, the offender, or both had been drinking immediately prior to the slaying. This correlation appears to be especially true in homicides involving Blacks (Wolfgang, 1958; Hepburn & Voss, 1970). The relationship between alcohol and violence is an especially important one and will be dealt with more thoroughly in Chapter 12.

In summary, the sociological data demonstrate that a large portion of the homicides take place between people who know one another, usually well, and that the offense frequently takes place following an argument in an environment where alcohol has been consumed. Almost always it is an intraracial affair perpetrated by males against males.

AGGRAVATED ASSAULT

Aggravated assault has not drawn nearly the amount of research, publication, or popular interest that murder has. And yet, in 1976 there were an estimated 490,850 reported aggravated assaults in the U.S. (Kelley, 1977). These statistics show that the aggravated assault rate is 25 times greater than that of homicide. Overall, aggravated assaults accounted for 50 percent of the crimes of violence. In addition, the number of arrests for aggravated assault increased 40 percent between 1972 and 1976, while the incidence of murder increased 1 percent during the same period. For every 100,000 inhabitants in this country, 225 were reported victims of aggravated assault, with rural ratios (128 per 100,000) considerably below metropolitan ones (255 per 100,000). These statistics and the fact that the legal definition of aggravated assault includes the "intent to kill" indicate that the lack of studies specifically directed at that offense is quite remarkable—and puzzling.

A number of reasons might account for the scarcity of the research. Most notable is the common complaint that aggravated assault is very difficult to classify or categorize (Pittman & Handy, 1964). Whether or not the assault incident qualifies for aggravated assault depends on a number of things, including the seriousness of the injury, the type of weapon used, and the intent of the offender. Assaults carried out without a weapon and not causing serious harm to the victim are traditionally classified as "simple assault." On the other hand, if an assault is carried out without a weapon but inflicts serious injury on the victim, the offense would be classified aggravated assault. We have a problem in this case, however, in deciding what constitutes serious harm. In reference to intent, police records have revealed that in as many as 40 percent of the aggravated assault cases, the intent of the offenders is reported as "unknown" (Dunn, 1976). Also, the intent of the victim is very often conjecture on the part of the arresting officer (U.S. Department of Justice, 1976). And finally, classification procedures appear to differ widely among police departments (Task Force Report, 1967).

Sociological Correlates of Aggravated Assault

Blacks made up 41 percent of the total arrests for aggravated assault in 1976, while 57 percent of the remaining arrests were of Whites (Kelley, 1977). Although the arrest rate relationship between race and assault is not as strong as the one for homicide, the lower assault rates might reflect a greater resistance of Blacks to having law enforcement officials involved in personal squabbles. Similar to the homicide pattern, however, assaults continue to be an overwhelmingly intraracial phenomenon (Dunn, 1976; Block, 1977).

The victim and offender normally know one another or are relatives in at least 50 percent of the reported cases (Dunn, 1976; Mulvihill, Tumen, & Curtis, 1969). As might be expected, the lethal gun is significantly less often employed in aggravated assault than in homicide occurrences. Block (1977) found in his Chicago study and Dunn (1976) in a Westchester County (New York) project that the weapons most commonly used in assault incidents were hands, fists, or feet—although the use of firearms is becoming increasingly popular. The utilization of the personal weapons of hands, fists, or feet in assault is also largely a national preference (Kelley, 1977).

About half of those arrested for assault in 1976 were under the age of twenty-five. In addition, males outnumber females seven to one in total arrests for aggravated assault.

Sociological research has provided us with considerable information about some of the social situations in which murder and assault are likely to occur, the weapons used, and some of the demographic variables of the offender and victim. Still, the data do not clearly tell us why. Why did this particular person aggress against another person at this point in time and with this weapon? We could convince ourselves that it is because the person is a member of a subculture that advocates violence, or that the person became violent because of association with other violent persons. However, these explanations are not quite satisfactory, because they do not tell us why some people within the violent-prone subculture do not become violent or why there are numerous individual differences in the time, place, and threshold for violence. They do not tell us what process learning by association refers to—classical conditioning, instrumental learning, modeling, or cognitive processes? In order to change the learned behavior, you must understand the process by which it is acquired and what precisely is maintaining that behavior.

Mainstream psychiatry has attempted to understand the internal states of the individual who exhibits a propensity toward violence and has postulated a number of theoretical models to explain these internal states, traits, and forces. These models have influenced the "internal perspective" for many years, and it is worthwhile to examine some of the theories briefly.

PSYCHIATRIC CORRELATES OF VIOLENCE

While sociological criminology concentrates upon and emphasizes the importance of environmental factors in the development of violence, mainstream psychiatric criminology contends that violence is primarily a result of parameters *within* the individual that propel him or her toward violent acts. Traditional psychiatry with a Freudian or psychoanalytical orientation perceives the human species as driven by innate antisocial urges which society must control by providing ways for them to be channelled and drained off in an approved manner. In contrast, mainstream sociological criminology generally perceives human beings as being "victims" of the numerous inadequacies of the social and physical environment.

In oversimplified terms, the Freudian orientation in psychiatric criminology is especially prone to view murder as a result of unconscious urges and conflicts, often sexual in nature, while the situation, the victim's behavior, or the general circumstances are seen as only secondary contributors to the killing. For example, in this discussion on murder, the criminal psychiatrist John MacDonald (1961, p. 94) asserts: "External circumstances very often do not motivate the deed at all, and the doer . . . would mostly have to acknowledge that he really did not himself exactly know what impelled him to do it. . . ." MacDonald advocates searching for deeper meanings and unconscious wishes within the individual's psyche rather than readily accepting apparent, obvious explanations for murder. Similarly, David Abrahamsen (1960,

p. 186) contends: "The unconscious motivation, which is by far the major driving force in a homicide and of which the culprit is usually unaware, is one of the reasons why he is unable to give a logical explanation of his act."

In order to delve into the unconscious, psychiatric criminology concentrates on discovering commonalities of the criminal "mind," and in this section we will be concerned with the "mind of the murderer," a phrase which has been used several times by psychiatrists in naming their books on the subject. Before we proceed further, however, and at the risk of sounding tautological, we must understand this very important point: *There is no way devised in which one human being can determine what another human being is or was actually thinking at the time of a crime.* Behavioral scientists and clinicians are not mind readers and do not have some mystical power they have picked up in the course of their training for *accurately* pegging people after a few professional or social contacts. In fact, research in social psychology has yet to find any particular personality type which can accurately perceive what other people are "really like" or what they think about.

Any determination of what a person was thinking at the time of a murder is based on the verbal and motor behavior of the defendant and/or what was "seen" by witnesses; behavior is an indirect, assumptive way of assessing what goes on in the human brain. As many of us have come to realize, what a person says may be completely different from what that person actually does or thinks. Clinicians and behavioral scientists subjectively infer what a person is thinking, or was thinking, by observing behavior as objectively as possible. Presumably, one of the major advantages of "objective" psychological tests is that they provide samples of behavior under standardized or controlled situations. If a clinician states that murderers who kill older women are fixated at the Oedipal stage of psychosexual development, there is no way to prove that he or she is wrong in the assessment. However, will other equally competent clinicians arrive at the same conclusions? If there is considerable and varied disagreement, then we must ask ourselves about the value of the conclusions. Moreover, we must look at the *utility* of these clinical observations for prevention, police detection and apprehension, rehabilitation, and the establishment of solid, well-documented theories of criminality. If observations prove to have utility in discovering commonalities and causal variables, they will also improve our predictive ability.

Here is a case in point. According to *Newsweek* (July 11, 1977), New York police psychologist Harvey Schlossberg interpreted the infamous .44 revolver used by the Son of Sam killer to be "a surrogate penis and the shooting a macabre form of orgasm." This statement makes good press copy, but how is it useful? How does it help apprehend the criminal? By the same token we could state that everyone who owns a gun needs a surrogate penis, and every shot at an inanimate object represents a benign orgasm, while shots at animate objects represent malignant orgasms. Prove that statement wrong. The question we should ask ourselves is, how useful is the statement in deciphering the complexities of murder?

In reviewing the psychiatric literature on homicide this author struggled with the same basic problems that Wolfgang and Ferracuti (1967) complained about several years ago. Most of the psychiatric research is based on case studies. The instruments used (usually projectives) lack demonstrable validity and often call for intuitive interpretations. Classifications are inconsistent. There is a preoccupation with medico-legal implications, and an overwhelming desire to "prove" Freudian orthodoxy. Overall, I agree with Wolfgang and Ferracuti that the vast majority of these studies have very limited value in helping us construct an understanding of the genesis of crime. Many of the psychiatric contributions in book form, although often upheld as classics in criminological literature, are not significantly more conclusive. In commenting on the psychiatric literature on murder, Wolfgang and Ferracuti write: "Consistently . . . they show little or no awareness of etiological and dynamic factors in homicide other than those which appeal to the particular psychiatric hypothesis upheld by the author. The theoretical contributions are sometimes negligible and often consist of a rewording of the basic tenets of Freudian orthodoxy. The generalizations are loose, and the practical treatment or prevention techniques which are advocated are often shallow, unrealistic and contradictory . . . their scientific value and their practical impact remain quite doubtful" (1967, p. 203).

It may be instructive, nonetheless, to review briefly some of the more general positions of psychiatry on homicide and try to relate these observations to what other social and behavioral scientists have also observed.

One school of psychiatric criminology sees the murderer as not being vastly different in personality from the nonmurderer. For example, Bromberg (1961) contends that the one major difference between the law-abiding citizen and the murderer is that the former is merely a dreamer wallowing in fantasy while the latter acts out the fantasy. Bromberg believes that murderous impulses and sadistic fantasies reside in all of us, consciously and unconsciously, but murderers act them out because of "weak egos" and inadequate repressive mechanisms. In other words, the murderer does not possess sufficient self-control to prevent the emergence of destructive and violent impulses drawn from fantasies. Both Manfred Guttmacher (1960) and David Abrahamsen (1960) basically agree with this interpretation, but Guttmacher admits that "psychoanalysis has no answer as to what it is that makes man succumb or give in to his fantasies so that they become criminal acts" (p. 11).

Although it is highly questionable as to whether or how often everyone entertains murderous thoughts, consciously or "unconsciously," it is a common point of agreement among students of violence that murder, in a majority of cases, *appears* to be a result of an explosive, spontaneous, and impulsive act featuring very little in the way of forethought. The psychiatric point of view of homicide as an act demonstrating inadequate ego control and repressive mechanisms, while not adding anything significantly new to the literature on homicide, does support the observation made by other disciplines. Interestingly, Bromberg perceives murder and violence as necessary evils in society, prompted and encouraged by people who wish, again consciously or unconsciously, to see their fantasies acted out by others: ". . . society, for its own equilibrium, needs the criminal it spawns" (1961, p. 11).

Manfred Guttmacher (1960) suggests that murderers kill because they do not appreciate the deprivation they inflict upon others. This observation sounds highly similar to the stage of moral development discussed in Chapter 5 called the preconventional stage. The reader will recall that the preconventional person operates principally on the selfish motive of gaining rewards and avoiding punishment, without considering the feelings and welfare of others. The common psychiatric observation concerning violence-prone people and their propensity toward cruelty to animals even after most children outgrow this tendency fits well into this moral scheme. It is likely that abnormal cruelty to animals and peers reflects a retarded moral development in that the person does not appreciate pain and discomfort in others. Guttmacher also notes that many murderers have "a reckless disregard for human life," including their own.

The presentation here has been selective, fragmentary, and excessively brief. Moreover, it is important to note that there is an increasingly large number of psychiatrists of criminal behavior who accept only some or none of the psychodynamic or psychoanalytical model as a valid explanation of murder. However, the views of the psychiatrists presented here are still very much regarded as expert views in the psychology of crime by the criminal justice system and the legal profession. The reader must decide for him- or herself whether the traditional psychiatric theories offer a clear, practical, precise explanation of criminal homicide. The wise reader, of course, will go directly to the sources themselves to supplement this presentation.

VIOLENCE AND PERSONALITY

Violent Individuals

As we have mentioned, many views and theories consider violence and homicide to be results of impulsive, spur-of-the-moment, and unpredictable actions of enraged individuals. The person who savagely assaults and sometimes kills is operating on impulse, the theory goes, and slashes out at a taunting victim without forethought or planned strategy. This point of view, of course, partly supports the argument for gun control. If the gun were not available, the perpetrator would not have wounded or killed the victim—at least not as easily.

It is unlikely, however, that the availability of a weapon explains the whole story. Certain personalities are more likely to react violently in certain situations than others. In his book *Violent Men*, Hans Toch (1969) suggested that a majority of violent episodes are a result of well-learned, systematic strategies of violence that certain personalities have found to be effective in dealing with conflictful interpersonal relationships. In other words, violence is not the act of a person gone berserk, but possibly of one who has *habitual* response patterns of reacting violently in particular situations which encourage a violent response. It is Toch's impression that, if we examine the history of violent individuals, we will find consistency in the approaches they use to interpersonal relationships. These individuals have learned, probably in childhood, that violence works for them; violent responses are successful in obtaining various goals and goods.

Toch formulated a typology of violence-prone offenders based upon consistent tactics people use in interpersonal situations which develop into violent events. He catalogues ten different personality styles under two major orientations: 1. the orientation to manipulate others with violence or the threat of violence in an effort to satisfy personal needs, and 2. the orientation to react violently toward others when feeling threatened or vulnerable to manipulation.

It would not be worthwhile at this point to describe each of the personality types outlined by Toch. The classification scheme is vague and overlapping, and research data to support them is meager. Nonetheless, Toch's approach represents an attempt to bring criminal violence and homicide out of the realm of unpredictability and into the potential area of lawful, predictable behavior.

Overcontrolled and Undercontrolled Offenders

Perhaps one of the more heuristic formulations in explaining "assaultive personalities" has been suggested by Edwin Megargee (1966), who

221

identified two distinct personalities in the highly assaultive population: the *undercontrolled* and the *chronically overcontrolled* aggressive types. The undercontrolled aggressive person has very low inhibitors against aggressive behavior and frequently engages in violence when frustrated or provoked. The notion of low inhibition for antisocial acts is exactly what Eysenck has suggested in his explanation of criminal behavior. The violently prone person has failed to learn to restrict his or her antisocial behavior because of faulty conditioning. Similarly, the undercontrolled type follows many of the same peculiarities of the psychopath or the undersocialized offender. The reader may also note the similarities with the psychiatric contention of poor impulse control or insufficient ego strength. Another side to this is the possibility that, not only has the undercontrolled person not been properly socialized to restrict antisocial, assaultive behavior, but also he or she might have gained reinforcement for assaultive behavior, such as increased status or material rewards.

The chronically overcontrolled type presents some interesting differences. Here, inhibition against aggressive behavior has been well established and rigidly adhered to regardless of the provocations. This individual has learned (or been conditioned) all too well about the consequences (real, imagined, or implied) of engaging in violence. In other words, he or she is the socialized, or perhaps oversocialized person who, through conditioning, has readily associated violations of social mores and regulations dictated by others with potentially punishing consequences. The introvert is the prime candidate for the overcontrolled, while the extravert is the best qualified to exhibit features of the undercontrolled.

There comes a point where frustration and provocation become overwhelming, and the overcontrolled personality strikes out with violent behavior, perhaps even exceeding that normally displayed by the undercontrolled type. Still further, this typology suggests that the more brutal slayings are often performed by the normally inhibited, restricted person. We have all heard cases where neighbors, friends, and relatives are shocked about a homicide committed by a "nice, quiet, well-mannered boy," the "disturbed delinquent" we met in Chapter 5.

> A 16-year-old choir boy described as a "hell of a nice kid" was arraigned here Thursday as funeral services were held for three girls he is accused of stabbing to death.
>
> . The girls' bodies were found Monday, face down in a stream in deep woods about a quarter of a mile from their homes.
>
> The state medical examiner said two of the girls were

stabbed 40 times each and the third eight times. The death weapon was believed to be a hunting knife (Tom Stuckey, Associated Press Release, October 14, 1977).

A plausible explanation for the extremely assaultive behavior exhibited by the overcontrolled person might lie in the high arousal level generated by frustration. High arousal is typically accompanied by muscle tension and other physiological changes. Punching, stabbing, or beating someone is likely to reduce muscular tension. Thus, assaultive behavior becomes reinforcing in and of itself. Each stab reduces arousal and tension to such an extent that the next one reduces it even more, producing a long series of brutal stab wounds. Possibly, the tension-arousal levels do not reach the peaks in the undercontrolled person as they do for the overcontrolled person because of the constant release characteristic of the undercontrolled's behavior.

In an empirical test of Megargee's hypothesis, Blackburn (1968) divided a group of violent offenders into extreme assaultives and moderate assaultives. Extreme assaultives were operationally defined as those who were convicted of murder, manslaughter, or attempted murder. Moderate assaultives included persons convicted of wounding with intent to cause serious bodily harm, malicious or unlawful wounding, and assault. On the basis of personality measures, extreme assaultives were found to be significantly more introverted, conforming, and overcontrolled, and less hostile than moderate assaultives. Moreover, extreme aggressive behaviors occurred only after prolonged or repeated provocation (real or imagined).

In another study reported by Tupin et al. (1973), convicted murderers with a history of habitual offenses were found to have a much higher incidence of hyperactivity, fighting, temper tantrums, and other extraverted features during childhood than a comparable group of murderers without a previous criminal record. On the other hand, clinical studies on "sudden murderers" without a previous record (e.g., Weiss et al, 1960; Blackburn et al., 1960) have found them to be introverted and plagued by feelings of inadequacy, loneliness, and frustration.

Ronald Blackburn (1971) was able to distinguish British murderers on the basis of four personality variables. However, almost half of his sample demonstrated behavior features which were consistent with Megargee's overcontrolled personality. The other proportion of the murder sample could easily be classified as undercontrolled and/or psychopathic.

Lee, Zimbardo, and Berghold (1977) reported a limited but pertinent study using a small group of murderers. Ten of the murderers were classified as "sudden murderers" because their background reflected no other criminal offenses, while another group of nine murderers were regarded as habitual offenders with prior arrests for violent acts. The Stanford Shyness Survey and the Minnesota Multiphasic Personality Inventory (MMPI) were administered to the groups. On the Stanford Shyness Survey, eight of the ten sudden murderers reported themselves as "shy," while only one of the nine habitually violent offenders considered himself so. The MMPI indicated that the sudden murderer group tended to be significantly more overcontrolled and passive than the habitual offenders, who tended to be more undercontrolled and assertive. These results combined with other observations suggested to the authors that people who are overcontrolled are capable of more extreme violence when "inner restraints" are broken down than are individuals who hold their behavior under looser controls.

At the present time there is consistent evidence to indicate that murderers appear to differ along a continuum of undercontrolled-overcontrolled, with a majority at the extremes. Moreover, undercontrolled murderers tend to display a habitual offense record, while overcontrolled murderers, showing few criminal incidences in their backgrounds, are more likely to engage in a quick, violent murderous episode characterized by an apparently quick decision to injure or kill. It should also be carefully noted that the undercontrolled person highly resembles the extraverted personality and the psychopath. The overcontrolled, restricted, socially withdrawn person appears identical to our well-conditioned introvert who has overlearned inhibitions against aggressive behavior.

The over- and undercontrolled dimension offers some exciting possibilities for future research, and it stresses the importance of considering individual differences in criminal conduct. However, it remains unclear what importance situational parameters play in the dimension. For example, it is highly possible that passive, unassertive people not only are more likely to experience intense frustrations, but also likely to find themselves in many situations where they feel threatened, desperate, and/or powerless. The Lee-Zimbardo-Berthold group has attempted to relate the lack of social and verbal skills so characteristic of shy people to the sudden murderer. Specifically, they suggest that the sudden murderer is typically a shy individual who has not acquired the necessary social skills which permit most people to assert themselves in social situations. If a person lacks the skill and techniques to at least modify some of his or her social experiences, this would be likely to precipitate a feeling of helplessness. Situations which promote feelings of powerlessness, lack of control of one's own fate, and helplessness are likely to engender two primary response patterns: approach (attack) or avoidance (withdrawal). The withdrawal response to feelings of helplessness, as cogently presented by Martin Seligman (1975), is often referred to as depression and feelings of hopelessness. There is nothing you can do about the situation, so why bother? This response pattern is vividly illustrated by people in dire poverty conditions characterized by little opportunity for change.

On the other hand, an alternative response is to attack, to lash out in desperation, especially if previous response patterns have failed to change the circumstances. Very possibly the sudden murderers, who have been passive and pushed around all their lives, are using a last ditch effort to change what is happening to them. Their homicidal violence may be a very desperate response to gain control over their lives. Sudden murderers may be murderers out of desperation. An interesting question could be posed at this point: Which is more adaptive under helpless conditions—depression, hopelessness, and suicide, or violence?

A life punctuated by numerous varied and intense frustrations has been commonly observed by researchers examining the background of the murderer (Berkowitz, 1962; Palmer, 1960; Henry & Short, 1954). Stuart Palmer noted that murderers, in comparison to their siblings, were subjected to significantly more physical illnesses, physical beatings, social and academic frustrations in school, and psychological frustrations from parents. Some researchers have even suggested that individuals who have suffered extreme frustration are more likely to commit suicide, while individuals experiencing moderate frustration are more likely to commit homicide (Henry & Short, 1954).

Internal-External Control

Another personality variable which appears to influence propensity toward violent, assaultive behavior is one's perceived control over environmental events. If a person feels in control over what happens to him or her in the world and if that person feels that his or her responses affect the rewards and punishments that come along, then he or she can be called an *internal*. If, on the other hand, a person feels that he or she has very little effect on personal conditions and events and that everything is a matter of fate, that person is an *external*. These expectancies about controlling one's fate can be placed along a continuum running from absolute belief in one's influence on the world to a belief that no matter what one does it will not make any difference. It has been hypothesized that internals, because they firmly believe that they influence external events, will be more predisposed to use aggression and violence to alter situations than will externals (Baron, 1977). Evidence relating to the validity of this hypothesis has been reported by Dengerink and his colleagues (Dengerink, O'Leary, & Kasner, 1975). It suggests that people who are haunted by feelings of hopelessness and helplessness about their fate are less likely to engage in violent behavior. This phenomenon may account partially for why violence is principally an offense committed by the young. Older people living under dire economic and limited conditions may perceive their future as hopeless and fall prey to apathy. The younger persons in those conditions, however, continue to view their future with hope and feel that they can do something to change their lot—even if it requires illegal and violent maneuvers.

Type A and Type B

David Glass (1977) has delineated two clusters of behavioral patterns which he calls Type A and Type B and which differ on three major dimensions. Type A is characterized by extremes in: 1. competitive achievement striving, 2. time urgency, and 3. aggressiveness. Type B, by contrast, is low on these dimensions. Type A persons work on most tasks at near maximum capacity and will push themselves to great limits to achieve success. They nearly always appear to be in a hurry and are constantly scurrying around to meet self-appointed deadlines and time pressures. Interference with their bustling activity is met with aggressiveness and hostility. Because of these behavioral patterns, Type A individuals are most susceptible to coronary heart disease and high blood pressure (Jenkins et al., 1974). In addition, the hard-driving Type A is an individual who often suppresses fatigue and works to near exhaustion (Carver, et al., 1976).

The research results so far suggest that Type As tend to be more aggressive than Type Bs when exposed to situations which threaten their sense of competence and mastery (Carver & Glass, 1978). However, in situations which do not hinder their strivings, they do not differ from Type Bs in aggression. Although too new a concept to have received much attention from criminologists, this analysis of personality may have considerable value in future research on aggression and violence.

Environmental Control

The theory and research on violence and personality reviewed thus far suggest that one of the major factors affecting violence and aggression is environmental control. People who interpret a situation as a threat to their control over their fate appear to be more prone toward violence than those who do not see the events similarly. Of course, there have to be a number of qualifiers attached to this statement. Individuals who lack adequate social and verbal skills with which to deal with social threats and conflict may have a greater tendency to resort to physical violence as a way to gain competence and mastery over events. Also, the tendency to be violent depends upon 1. reinforcement history of aggressive behavior, 2. the kinds of behavioral patterns acquired through modeling, and 3. the associative strength between aggressive behavior and aversive, negative consequences.

Moral Development

There is at least one additional factor which needs to be mentioned in this context: the *moral development* of the person. Moral development, as you will recall, includes the personal internalized standards and attitudes an individual carries around from situation to situation. In this sense, values and attitudes are personality variables which are assumed to have some consistency across various situations. Unfortunately, research directed at the relationship between violently prone persons and moral development is virtually nonexistent, but there is reason to believe that people who violently attack others as a way of resolving conflict or threat are less morally developed than those significantly less prone to violent attacks. Highly moral people, or at least those with a well-developed standard for human life and dignity, would be less inclined toward violence.

Some indirect evidence for this assumption is provided by Baron (1977). He reports evidence which suggests that highly prejudiced people will generally behave more violently than those with less prejudice. Donn Byrne (1974) also cites research which demonstrates that authoritarian personalities (those whose personality characteristics include a high degree of prejudice) are much more likely to be aggressive toward people they consider lower in status or background than themselves. Recent work focusing on the prejudice-aggression relationship has been conducted by the Donnersteins (see Donnerstein & Donnerstein, 1976), and the general findings have supported the connection.

The link between moral development and violence is illustrated in the following case example:

> F. is a twenty-year-old Black presently serving concurrent sentences of 25 years to life in a maximum security prison for armed robbery and three counts of murder. His convictions center around an armed robbery of a small grocery store—an act that he "pulled off" by himself. During the robbery, the owner refused to hand him the money and F. began to strug-

gle with the man. During the struggle he lost his disguise and shot the victim; he also stabbed the victim several times with such force that the knife broke off. Concerned that the two frightened customers in the store might identify him, he poked their eyes out with a screwdriver. Although F. claimed that he only wanted to blind them, both victims died almost instantly. "I guess I used too much force," he later commented without apparent remorse. He was identified leaving the store and arrested shortly thereafter.

F's arrest history shows a first arrest at age thirteen for brutally beating to death a resistive victim he tried to mug. At that time, he was placed in a juvenile institution but released thirteen months later. At age fifteen he was arrested for aggravated assault, convicted, and placed on probation. Later that same year he was arrested for disorderly conduct, but was continued on probation. F. brags that he has murdered six other persons during the course of fights and robberies, but none of the murders has been proven.

His family background reflects a perpetually absent, alcoholic father and an abusive, assaultive, but "highly religious" mother. His prison file contains a psychiatric summary which reads: "Repetitive psychotic episodes in reality testing combined with delusional perceptions and hallucinations, but does not follow the normal schizophrenic process. He is a very disturbed and dangerous man." He has a twelfth grade equivalency diploma gained through the prison program and scores as average on intelligence tests. In his spare time he lifts weights and works out in the prison gym. Physically, he is a muscular six feet two inches tall and weighs 210 pounds; he thoroughly enjoys making people afraid of him.

F. conceives of the world as a vicious dog-eat-dog place, and survival is for the fittest and the con man, he believes. When asked what prompted him to kill in the grocery store, he replied: "Look, ya can't understand where I'm coming from so don't feed me this why did I do it crap. It's easy to kill. Really easy, man. I've killed many times and I'll kill again. I figure it's usually them or me. Where I'm coming from, toughness is what gets respect. Hell, even the guards respect you if you're mean . . . really mean. I get what I want here. No one messes with me. Not the guards, no one. I don't care what happens to the other guy. Just me, ya know . . . That's what it's all about."

MASS MURDERERS

Based on clinical observations and experience, the criminal psychiatrist Donald T. Lunde (1976) attempted to distinguish between the personality of the single murderer and that of the mass murderer. The single murderer, of course, is the individual who takes one human life over a long period of time. The mass murderer, on the other hand, kills a number of people during a single episode or kills several people over a period of time. Lunde suggests that we reserve the term "mass murderer" for the multiple killer during a single episode and refer to the individual who commits several murders over a period of time (perhaps even years) as a serial murderer. Other than the temporal distinction between mass and serial murderers, however, Lunde fails to suggest other distinguishing characteristics. Therefore, we will refer to both serial and mass murderers as mass murderers for the remainder of this section.

According to Lunde, mass murderers "are almost always insane," and usually kill for no apparent reason or for an apparent but perverse (often sexual) reason. He notes that mass murders in the United States are almost always performed by white males, while, as we have seen, single murders are frequently committed by Blacks. The mass murderer is rarely intoxicated during the episode, while single murders are often associated with alcohol consumption in offender, victim, or both. Also, Lunde notes, mass murderers rarely know their victims well. However, the choice of victims is not random or coincidental; the killer usually selects victims possessing specific attributes. There is some significant psychological or physical feature about the victims that is connected with the criminal's predilection for murdering them.

Lunde believes that most mass murderers fall into two personality categories: *paranoid schizophrenia* or *sexual sadism*. We have already discussed the salient features of paranoid schizophrenia in Chapter 6, and we will not review that particular syndrome here. Sexual sadism ". . . in its extreme form is a deviation characterized by torture and/or killing and mutilation of other persons in order to achieve sexual gratification" (Lunde, 1976, p. 48). Unlike the paranoid schizophrenic mass murderer, the sexual sadist usually does not exhibit psychotic behaviors and skillfully tries to avoid detection by the police. However, Lunde warns that of all types of murderers, the sexual sadists are the most likely to murder again. Characteristically, they are younger males (under age thirty-five) who have few normal social and sexual relationships. The victims are almost always female, who are apparently viewed as objects to be used only for pleasure.

The British psychiatrist Robert Brittain (1970) also made numerous clinical observations on the sadistic murderer, many of which are in basic agreement with Lunde's notes. Brittain further observed that sadistic murderers are typically shy, withdrawn, quiet, mild-mannered, and rarely show anger. They have very few friends and prefer solitary pursuits such as reading and listening to music. These observations of extreme introversion were also found by this author (Bartol & Holanchock, in press) for sex offenders in general.

Sadistic murderers, according to Brittain, are most dangerous when they have suffered a loss of self-esteem, such as being laughed at by a woman, mocked by acquaintances, or demoted or discharged from employment. More often than not they have no prior criminal record. They are drawn to semi-skilled employment, but show a poor work record. They are usually fascinated by the occult, black magic, werewolves, vampires, and horror portrayals in films, magazines, and television. Apparently, they demonstrate strong attraction for objects which have sexual meaning for them—women's shoes, purses, stockings, and underwear, but as we shall see in Chapter 9, it would be wrong to assume that all fetishists are potentially sadistic murderers.

The murders of the sexual sadist are normally carefully planned, perhaps weeks in advance. These murderers do not seem at all concerned about the moral implications of their brutal acts and treat their victims as objects. According to Brittain, the sight of suffering and the helplessness of the victims increasingly excites sadistic murderers. They *usually* kill by strangulation, because of the control over the victim this method offers them. Shooting is too sudden, and a quick death is anticlimactic. Following death, victim mutilation is common. After the macabre murder, the sexual sadist returns calmly home and exhibits very few indicators of tension or guilt.

Upon arrest, not only are there few signs of guilt, but the murderer may even enjoy talking about or describing the incident in detail. He appears to bask in the attention he receives from criminal justice officials and from the news media. What was once a mundane existence turns into an exciting period of his life, and he feels he has made his mark on history.

Brittain makes no attempt to formulate his observations into a theory about causation. His purpose is to "give a factual description for practical use." He does emphasize, as does Lunde, that given the opportunity the sadistic murderer is likely to murder again.

Because of the rarity of mass murderers, empirical and objective data are difficult to obtain. We must at present rely on the subjective observations, inferences, and interpretations of the few clinicians who have had the opportunity to work with mass murderers. There are also relatively few professional studies published in scientific journals to provide us with data from reasonably large samples which we could use for comparison purposes. We may speculate, for example, that the sadistic murderer is an extremely introverted creature who has failed to emerge from the preconventional stage of moral development (no empathy for victims). It is also interesting to note that most clinical accounts of sadistic murderers have found them to be deeply intrigued with horror films and photos in "torture" magazines. In fact, Brittain claims that many mothers of sexual sadists are found to bring books and magazines dealing with sadistic, criminal, or pornographic material to their incarcerated sons. This observation suggests that there is a strong modeling or imitative influence exerted by the entertainment media on the sexual sadist, and that this modeling acquisition is condoned or accepted by at least one parent. However, if we consider the popularity of horror films and torture magazines in society in general, we would have to admit that there is an extremely large number of individuals who follow many of the clinical descriptions of the sexual sadist. The problem is, what variables distinguish the murderer from the nonmurderer? The answer is likely to lie in a number of factors, the combination of which will be unique to that particular individual. The sadistic murderer as a personality type is extremely rare.

While the clinical observations of Lunde and Brittain provide valuable clinical data toward the understanding of the mass murderer, there are probably many maximum security facilities that have at least one so-called "mass murderer" who is black, extraverted, and undercontrolled, and who shows very few features of either paranoid schizophrenia or sexual sadism. In fact, "F," whose case history was presented in the previous section, was one of a number of mass murderers in that institution at that time. The label "paranoid schizophrenia" may be all too readily attached to individuals who do not correspond to our frame of reference and value system.

PRISON HOMICIDE

An area which has received little attention in traditional homicide research is that of killings within prisons. According to Toch (1977), violence rates in most prisons are increasing much more quickly than those in the rest of society. A comparison of the similarities and differences in homicides in and out of prison might help us understand some of the factors that promote homicide.

Sylvester, Reed, and Nelson (1977) analyzed homicides in state and federal prisons housing 200 or more adult male felons during the year

1973. The study was concerned with homicides within or directly contiguous to penal facilities and included killings of correctional personnel as well as inmates. The researchers analyzed the homicide event itself along with the demographic, medical, psychological, and criminal traits of the victims and assailants. Information on 128 prison homicides was obtained; 78 of the 128 were between inmates, ten involved inmate killing staff, three staff killing inmates, and one incident involved one prison staff member killing another staff member. Thirty-five incidents involved an unidentified assailant killing an inmate, and in one case one staff member was killed by an unidentified assailant.

Guards were more likely to be killed by groups of assailants, whereas inmates were more likely to be murdered by a single assailant. Stabbing was the method most frequently used to inflict death; the Sylvester project reported that three-quarters of all victims died in this manner. Eight percent of the victims died of strangulation, 5 percent were beaten to death, 5 percent were killed by firearms, and about 4 percent were victims of arson. A notable feature of prison homicide is the severe degree of the beatings or stabbings administered—often considerably exceeding that necessary to inflict death. Half the victims died instantly or within an hour of the assault, and another 20 percent died within two hours of the assault.

In reference to apparent motive, fifteen of the homicides were primarily a result of homosexuality, while in six additional instances homosexuality was judged to be a secondary motive. The frequency of prison homosexuality as a motivating factor in prison violence has also been noted by Toch (1977). By all indications, homosexuality inspires violent behavior in much the same way as does heterosexuality. Jealousy, feelings of rejection, and refusals to accept the end of a relationship are motivating circumstances which seem to play a significant role in generating violent episodes.

Informing on others, "snitching," was involved in sixteen cases, arguments resulted in fifteen, and quarrels over money, property, or drugs accounted for another twenty-five killings. Racial tension precipitated only seven cases. In about a quarter of the cases, no apparent motive could be ascertained.

The homicides occurred in proportion to the racial composition of the prison, suggesting that racial conflicts and tensions are not as dramatic statistically as has been suggested. Intraracial homicides with Blacks killing Blacks and Whites killing Whites were more frequent than interracial ones, a finding which is consistently reported in the general homicide literature. The Sylvester project did find, however, some evidence to suggest that black assailants were more likely than white assailants to be administered prison discipline, referred for prosecution, and indicted for homicide. In the cases brought to court, however, the chances for conviction were about equal for both groups.

The study reported some interesting differences between single-assailant and multiple-assailant events. The three leading motives for the former were homosexuality, arguments, and debts; the leading motives for multiple-assailant crimes were "snitching," gang phenomena, drug quarrels, and homosexuality. The authors of the project observed that single-assailant events appeared to stem from personal involvements, while multiple-assailant murders were precipitated by maintenance of "inmate social order." More than half of the single-assailant situations appeared to have been victim precipitated. In a majority of the multiple-assailant events, the victim appeared to play a more passive role. Multiple assailants were more likely to kill in the victim's cell, while single assailants tended to kill in a number of other prison locations. Finally, single assailants, compared to multiple, used a wider variety of weapons in killing their victims. Multiple assailants relied heavily on stabbing. These data suggest that in prison multiple-assailant homicides are planned, purposeful acts, while single-assailant events are more spontaneous quick-decision actions prompted by interpersonal conflict.

Unfortunately, psychiatric or personality variables on the participants were not included in the analysis, apparently because of a number of deficiencies, including unwieldy terminology used by clinicians in their assessments. Of considerable interest, however, is the past assault and criminal history of the assailants. About one-half were serving time for other serious crimes against persons at the time of the prison homicide; one-quarter of these violent prisoners were imprisoned for killing another person. Once in prison, the assailants continued to be violent. Sixty percent of the assailants had received prison disciplinary action for assault prior to the prison homicide. This finding underscores again the importance of considering the past behavioral history of an individual in determining the likelihood of subsequent violence. The fact that individuals who commit homicide in the free world may be just as likely to commit homicide in prison emphasizes the importance of studying the characteristics of the individual. The violence-prone person is as likely to react with a favorite response pattern in prison as in the outside world. Individuals who killed guards were especially likely to have a previous record of serious crimes against persons, Sylvester and colleagues found. Ninety-one percent of these assailants were serving sentences for serious crimes against the person, and 80 percent had been cited for acts of assaultive behavior while in prison.

MOB VIOLENCE

The powerful effects of crowds on individual behavior has been a subject of interest for social scientists since the early 1900s. Crowd influence is usually studied under the rubric "collective behavior," which includes riots, fads, gang rapes, panics, lynches, demonstrations, and revolutions. For our purposes we are concerned with collective behavior only as it affects the instigation and maintenance of violence.

One of the first theorists of collective behavior was Gustave LeBon, whose 1896 book *The Crowd* is regarded as the classic study of groups. Because his views were colored by the French Revolution, LeBon was not very kind in his perception of individual behavior swayed by the crowd. Individuals who normally are nonviolent and law abiding are capable of the kind of violence, intolerance, and general cruelty found in the most "primitive savages," he believed. The person enmeshed in the mob loses sensibility and the ability to reason. Somehow, the individual forfeits his or her own mind to the crowd, and the crowd or collective mind is dangerously brutal and destructive to people and property. Even educated people become simple minded and irrational under the influence of the collective mind. Essentially, LeBon claims, each person comes under the control of the "spinal cord" rather than the brain.

Most everyone is familiar with illustrations and dramatizations of a "berserk" mob clamoring for the destruction of some political, social, or physical institution or for swift "justice" for some individual or group. Descriptions of mob actions often liken them to brush fires which grow in intensity and are quickly out of control. However, since mob actions are usually "natural events" and difficult to put under the scrutiny of scientific, laboratory precision and quantification, the processes and causes involved in mob action are still not well understood.

Recently, the social psychologist Philip Zimbardo (1970) and others (Diener et al., 1973; Diener et al., 1976) attempted to create crowd-like situations in the laboratory in an effort to get a better handle on the process of deindividuation, a phenomenon discussed in Chapter 4. It is Zimbardo's contention that the process of deindividuation can account in large measure for the tendency of otherwise "tame" individuals to engage in antisocial, violent forms of behavior. The reader will recall that deindividuation is characterized by the reduction in feelings of personal distinctiveness, identifiability, personal responsibility, and the lowered threshold of normally restrained behavior when in a crowd. Such conditions, according to Zimbardo, encourage antisocial behavior characterized by selfishness, greed, hostility, lust, cruelty, and destruction. It is this writer's view that the process of deindividuation is an

234

extremely important contributor to mob violence. The search for an explanation of group violence perpetrated by habitually nonviolent individuals will be based heavily on the available research and theory related to that process.

A description of one of Zimbardo's experiments should clarify the phenomenon of deindividuation and help explain how it can be generated. In one extensively quoted experiment, Zimbardo manipulated two variables: feelings of anonymity in female college students and characteristics of the victim. He randomly assigned coeds to either a deindividuation group or an identifiable group. Subjects in the deindividuation group wore very large white lab coats, hoods over their heads, worked in dimly-lit conditions, and avoided using names. In contrast, conditions for the identifiable group were designed to ensure that subjects felt anything but anonymous. These subjects wore large name tags, were greeted by name, worked under fully illuminated conditions, and did not wear lab coats or hoods.

The experiment was ostensibly set up to study empathy, but the real purpose was to determine the effects of deindividuation on aggressive behavior. Aggressive behavior was measured by the length of time a painful electric shock was administered by members of each group to a "victim," who in actuality was a confederate of the experimenter. This

FIGURE 8-1. Three subjects used in Zimbardo's experiment on deindividuation listen to the tapes of their soon-to-become "victims." Note the similarities of these hooded costumes to traditional Ku Klux Klan dress.

"victim" was trained to writhe, twist, and grimace as though she was receiving painful electric shock; of course, she never did.

Zimbardo manipulated characteristics of the target stimulus (victim) by having the groups shock two different victims. The groups listened to a five-minute tape-recorded interview between one of the future victims and the experimenter. In this interview, one victim was portrayed as a warm, sincere, honest person while the second was obnoxious, self-centered, conceited, and critical. After each interview, subjects were allowed to administer electric shock, in a group, while the victim was allegedly participating in a conditioning experiment in an adjacent room with a one-way mirror—a condition which permitted subjects to observe the victim's performance and reactions to the shock.

Zimbardo reasoned that, compared to the identifiable group, members of the deindividuation group would administer shocks of longer duration to the helpless victim because of the diffusion of responsibility, contagion effects, and loss of personal identity. He also hypothesized that it would not matter whether the victim was nice or not so nice, because the heightened arousal experienced under the deindividualized conditions would interfere with discrimination of differences in target stimulus. Put another way, the excitement and resulting arousal engendered by shocking someone without the threat of any repercussions would prevent discernment of the target (the person receiving the shock).

One further hypothesis was formed. Because the act of administering shock without responsibility would be so exciting and reinforcing for its own sake (what he called affective-proprioceptive feedback!) Zimbardo predicted that members of the deindividuation group would increase the duration of electric shock administered to the victim as the experiment progressed. In brief, the person finds that doing the antisocial behavior feels so good each time she does it that the behavior builds upon itself in intensity (vigor) and frequency.

Results of the experiment supported all three hypotheses. The total duration of shocking was twice as long for the deindividuation group as for the identifiable group. Second, the deindividuation group administered the same amount of shock regardless of whether the victim was depicted as nice or obnoxious. And third, the length of shock given to both victims was increased by the deindividuation group as the experiment progressed. Zimbardo concluded: "Under conditions specified as deindividuating, these sweet, normally mild-mannered college girls shocked another girl almost every time they had an opportunity to do so, sometimes for as long as they were allowed, and it did not matter whether or not that fellow student was a nice girl who didn't deserve to be hurt" (1970, p. 270).

The above hypotheses explain, at least in part, the observation that once a mob becomes violent or destructive it is extremely difficult to terminate the collective behavior, no matter what the victims (or the police) do. Although a victim may plead, beg, scream, or fight back, and although the victim may be completely innocent, the crowd will continue to hit, rape, or abuse the target stimulus. These hypotheses also help explain why some violent offenders repeatedly stab, hit, or shoot a victim. Almost everyone has heard of an incident where an offender has emptied a gun into the victim's body or stabbed the victim perhaps 40, 50, or more times. The offender possibly became so absorbed in the response and its reinforcing qualities that the behavior built upon itself and escalated.

Among the conditions which terminate this escalating, violent behavior are: 1. a marked change in the state of the victim; 2. change in the state of the person or persons performing the act, such as fatigue, exhaustion, or loss of consciousness; or 3. a total change in the state of the instrument being used, such as the knife breaking or the gun running out of bullets. Once the mob action is triggered and increases in intensity, even a prestigious powerful authority figure may be unable to stop the violence.

Another factor involved in mob behavior is that the noise, excitement, and arousal of the crowd serve as catalysts to individual members, because of the contagion effect, which is so powerful that independent thinking processes may be temporarily suspended. The effects of alcohol and certain drugs also appear to encourage the alteration of consciousness, gradually obliterating independent thought and normal social behavior.

The effects of deindividuation observed in the laboratory raise the question of how the process may affect real-life situations where individuals either wear deindividualizing uniforms (e.g., military personnel and police), observe "everyone else is doing it," or feel chronically insignificant among the human masses. Under long-term deindividualizing conditions, it is not surprising for a person to want to gain control of a situation. Many of the early skyjackers in this country during the 1960s were often described as desperate, ineffectual people trying to be significant and in control of their predicament. Feelings of insignificance and of being dehumanized may force an individual to resort to violence to gain control and significance. Holding a gun at someone's head or a knife at a victim's throat compels the victim to take the desperate individual seriously and to acknowledge the power and control that the person has. As Zimbardo suggests, ". . . violence and destruction transform a passive, controlled object into an active, controlling person" (1970, p. 304).

Dehumanization, a process that helps us cope with extremely stressful situations, is similar to deindividualization and deserves some attention. By dehumanizing someone, we deny that person human characteristics such as feelings, thoughts, families, kindness. We see the person as an object or as something less than human. When we dehumanize people, it makes it much easier to kill them. Thus, airmen dropping bombs on a village must dehumanize the victims in order to tolerate the stress and arousal generated on these deadly missions. Military men often refer to the enemy in dehumanizing terms such as "gooks" or "krauts," thus denying them a personal identity.

The process of dehumanization is likely a significant contributor to mob violence, mass murders, and planned murder schemes such as those found in terrorist attacks, political kidnappings, and political bombings. Dehumanizing the victims makes the "mission" much more tolerable, "ethical," and patriotic, and one can still argue that the actions are directed toward achieving a better and just world.

If the dehumanization hypothesis is accurate, then the more kidnappers, terrorists, skyjackers, or others get to know their intended victims, the less likely they may be to kill them. Thus, the waiting game may indeed be a good method to use in promoting the safety of the victims, since the assailants or offenders become more personally acquainted with their targets with the passage of time.

SUMMARY

Homicide should not be viewed simply as an impulsive act which suddenly springs out of the psyche. It is a form of behavior that the perpetrators believe will change the present predicament they find themselves in. Violent behavior is *learned*, usually through imitation and practice.

Sociological data indicate that violence occurs in certain people, under certain conditions and situations, more often than in others. For example, black young males appear especially prone toward violence. We also learned that victims often play a significant role in precipitating the attacks.

Homicide has drawn a disproportionate amount of the research literature, while aggravated assault is generally neglected. Some authorities argue that the two are inseparable. Homicide, they say, is often the result of an assault which went beyond the expectations of the offender. This is a questionable position which must await further research focusing on the two forms of violence.

Psychiatric theories and interpretations of murder have been permeated with psychoanalytic concepts that are not amenable to experimental verification. Moreover, they do not seem to have advanced our understanding of homicide and violence to any great extent.

Several theories concerning the relationship between personality or behavioral patterns and violence were presented. All emphasized to varying degrees the concepts of control over one's environment and learning how to gain that control.

Studies of mass murderers have thus far been limited to clinical observation and interpretation. Clinical descriptions indicate that they tend to be white males, who were not drinking at the time of the offense, and who usually selected victims on the basis of some specific attribute. It has been proposed that mass murderers be placed into two classifications: paranoid schizophrenics or sexual sadists. The former are severely disturbed "mentally ill" offenders who would require extensive psychiatric or psychological treatment. Sexual sadists appear to be highly introverted people who have not emerged from the preconventional stage of moral development. They appear to imitate sadistic and violent events which are communicated through mass media and which they find exciting.

There has been little empirical confirmation of clinical descriptions of the mass murderer, particularly the two kinds described by Lunde. It appears that there are numerous mass murderers presently housed in various correctional facilities who do not dovetail with clinically-based theories. Therefore, the area of mass or serial murder needs to be subjected to much more well-designed research before we can begin to make accurate statements about psychological characteristics.

Prison homicide is a neglected phenomenon to which we paid some attention. It was pointed out that people who are persistently violent outside prison are often violent inside prison as well.

Finally, mob violence and the processes of deindividuation and dehumanization were discussed. It seems that deindividuation is a concept which can account for collective violence in an important and scientifically verifiable way. Among other things, deindividuation enables one to copy the behavior of the group without the normal constraints and concerns of accountability for one's own behavior. Dehumanization, which can occur in both individual and group crime, allows the person to deny the humanity of his or her victim and thus helps justify the violent act.

KEY CONCEPTS FOR REVIEW

Homicide
Race and homicide
Sex and homicide
Victim-offender relationship
Weapons and homicide

Aggravated assault
Psychoanalytic perspectives of homicide
Undercontrolled offenders
Overcontrolled offenders
Internal control
External control
Type A and Type B
Environmental control
Mass murderers
Sexual sadism
Sadistic murderers
Prison homicide
Mob violence
Deindividuation
Dehumanization

MAJOR THEORISTS AND RESEARCHERS

Block
Wolfgang
MacDonald
Bromberg
Guttmacher
Abrahamsen
Toch
Megargee
Glass
Lunde
Brittain
Sylvester, Reed, and Nelson
LeBon
Zimbardo

SUGGESTED READINGS

Lunde, D.T. *Murder and madness.* San Francisco: San Francisco Book Co., 1976.
A very well-written psychiatric viewpoint of mass murderers and the judicial process.

Palmer, S. *Psychology of murder.* New York: Thomas Y. Crowell, 1960.
A detailed, biographic research project on convicted murderers in New England.

Toch, H. *Violent men: An inquiry into the psychology of violence.* Chicago: Aldine Publishing Co., 1969.

A careful examination of the life patterns of convicted men who are prone to violence.

Wolfgang, M.E. *Patterns in criminal homicide.* Philadelphia: Univ. of Pennsylvania Press, 1958.
The landmark, extensively quoted original study of Wolfgang on the characteristics of Philadelphia homicides.

SEXUAL OFFENSES

NINE

Sex offenders are most likely to commit a deviant act when oppression increases and alternative adaptations are unavailable. Thus many sexual offenses take place shortly after a rejection by a significant person, a vocational failure or a humiliation which leads to some lowering of status.

Halleck, 1967, p. 195

All societies regulate sexual behavior, although regulations vary widely from culture to culture. Sexual behavior is a subject fraught with religious injunctions, moral codes, taboos, norm expectations, myths, and unscientific conclusions. The daring venture of Albert Kinsey and his colleagues in publishing scientific evidence gathered at the Institute for Sexual Research was influential in mitigating some of the misunderstandings and fallacies about sex. However, many myths and misconceptions still linger, especially those pertaining to the sex offender. The public usually reacts with disgust, anger, and fear upon hearing about "degenerates" who molest young children, show their genitals, or watch unsuspecting women undressing. Moreover, the community very often clamors for the strict, maximum prosecution of the offender. Some people are convinced that the sex offender is a fundamentally deranged or evil person who is driven by some inner sinister force. The popular notion about sexual offenses locates the problem within the individual and assumes that society should protect its citizens from such a warped personality.

In addition to the many misconceptions, we have numerous antiquated sexual laws based on unfounded logic which dictate harsh punishments for certain sexual deviances. A majority of criminal laws directed at sexual offenses are not based on scientific evidence but on moral and social philosophies about the harmful effects any sexual deviance allegedly has on the fabric of society.

Clinical and research studies reveal that, with the exception of most rapists, the average sex offender is not different from anyone else in general behavior, feelings, or beliefs. Rather than being prone to violence and cruelty, most sex offenders are timid, shy, harmless, and socially inhibited individuals. Furthermore, carefully executed scientific investigations have consistently indicated that, although sex is a strong biological drive dependent upon complex physiological factors, the various ways of satisfying that drive are *learned*. The learning comes in part from the beliefs, behavior, and feelings expressed by significant models in the social environment such as parents, peers, and siblings, and it is readily conveyed by the entertainment media in the form of films, television, and reading material. The learning process is further influenced by one's subculture, socioeconomic class, religion, and geographical area. These social variables affect the processes involved in observational learning, moral development, and patterns of reinforcement.

However, a very important determinant in the acquisition of deviant sexual behavior is the classical or Pavlovian conditioning discussed in Chapter 2. We have focused on conditioning as a process whereby people avoid certain behavior because they associate it with fear or pain. Furthermore, we used this associative link as a partial explanation for the avoidance of criminal behavior in most people. However, the associative link may also occur between *pleasurable* feelings or arousal and a certain behavioral pattern. Thus, conditioning may be used to explain not only why many people avoid illegal behavior, but also why some people are drawn to illegal or deviant behavior. It is easier to explain this phenomenon if we pay close attention to the *stimuli* linked to pleasurable arousal.

Through the process of conditioning, virtually any stimulus or set of stimuli can assume sexually arousing properties for an individual: hubcaps, Holiday Inn signs, shapely legs, paper clips, slurping one's soup. Stimuli which repeatedly appear in the presence of sexual excitement can take on sexually arousing properties by themselves. Recall the classic example of Pavlovian conditioning, where a bell paired with food eventually becomes associated with food. The same process appears to hold for the acquisition of numerous forms of sexual behavior. A particular stimulus repeatedly paired and associated with sexual arousal will be capable of inducing sexual arousal when the individual sees, feels, smells, or even thinks about the object or behavior—whatever it may be. Notice that the stimulus may be an object, a behavior, or a thought, as well as a person.

A particularly frequent and apparently powerful event which facilitates the bonding of stimuli to sexual arousal is masturbation. The intrinsically physiological pleasure and arousal generated by masturbation can serve as a strong bonding agent, particularly if paired repeatedly with some object, behavior, or fantasy. Also, it is important to realize that we have two powerfully reinforcing events in masturbatory activity: sexual arousal and the reduction of that arousal (orgasm). On the basis of clinical studies, it appears that masturbatory conditioning plays an integral part in the acquisition of both normal and deviant sexual behavior.

Research has indicated that males are more susceptible to sexual conditioning than females are (Akers, 1977), and as pointed out in Chapter 2, introverts are more readily conditioned than extraverts are. Hence, a majority of sexual deviations should be demonstrated by males, especially introverted males. This prediction is well supported by scientific evidence which will be reviewed later in the chapter.

Conditioning dictates that forms of sexual behavior or the attachment of sexual significance to stimuli may occur by chance or accident. By chance, a stimulus may be present during an intensely pleasurable experience, or the individual may hit upon a behavior or pattern of behaviors which turns out to be particularly exciting and rewarding.

Therefore, learning and conditioning are both involved in the acquisition of every sexual behavior, whether members of a given society call it deviant or normal. The association between a stimulus and pleasurable arousal (conditioning) prompts the behavior, and the performance of the behavior is reinforced by the pleasure derived (instrumental learning). In this sense, sexual deviances are socially learned habits. If past and present rewards associated with a sexual act prevail over punishments and aversive consequences also associated with the act, and if the rewards also override the expectancies attached to alternate forms of behavior in that context, then that act is the one most likely to be manifested when the proper opportunity arises.

This chapter will be concerned with sexual offenses which are considered by law as having an unwilling victim. Sexual practices such as prostitution and homosexuality will not be covered, except for some forms of predatory homosexuality which will be included in the section on pedophilia.

RAPE

Because rape features both aggressive and sexual elements, it was difficult to decide whether to cover the offense in the chapter on violence and aggression or in this one, with other sexual offenses. Rape is nearly always a brutal, demeaning, and cruel act with little concern or empathy for the victim, but it is also motivated in many cases by a drive for sexual excitement or stimulation. It appears under the heading of sexual offenses because it serves as a good connector between violence, which we discussed earlier, and other sexual offenses. However, because prostitution is illegal in most states, it will be included in the chapter on female crime.

Definitions and Classifications

According to the *Uniform Crime Reports, forcible rape* is "the carnal knowledge of a female, forcibly and against her will" and includes rape by force, assault to rape, and attempted rape. The definition excludes statutory rape, male rape, and rape by fraud. In *statutory rape,* the critical factor is the age of the girl, whether she provides consent or not. The age limitation is an arbitrary legal cutoff point considered to be the age at which the girl has the maturity to give her meaningful consent and understand the consequences. Although limits vary from state to state, most legal age limitations are either sixteen or eighteen. Thus, if it can be proved to the satisfaction of the court that an adult male has engaged in sexual relations with a female who was under the legal age at the time, he can be convicted of statutory rape. *Rape by fraud* refers to the act of having sexual relations with a consenting adult female under fraudulent conditions, such as a physician or psychotherapist having sexual intercourse with a patient under the guise of effective treatment. The legal scope of forcible rape is usually confined to imposed sexual contact or assault with adolescent and adult females who are not related to the offender. Thus, the definition precludes rape of a wife by her husband, although a few states have considered or actually have included that under the term. Rape of a daughter by a father is classified as *incest* rather than rape in most states. Rape of males is also included in some state statutes.

One of the major problems in classifying and studying rape is that many police agencies and jurisdictions do not adhere to the UCR instructions and vary widely in their classification systems. In an extensive survey by Chappell (1977a), most police agencies reported that vaginal penetration was the *minimum* requirement for an alleged offense to qualify as rape. Additionally, over one-half of the police agencies surveyed required, as a minimum, evidence of both penetration and force, while another one-third required evidence of penetration, force, and a weapon, and/or resistance by the victim. As might be expected, the average number of rapes reported to the latter police agencies were significantly fewer than the average number reported to other police agencies requiring less demanding proofs.

Prosecutors, as you might expect, appeared to be more stringent about minimum requirements than the police agencies. A majority of 150 prosecutors across the country polled in the Chappell survey felt that the minimum requirements for filing a complaint of forcible rape were: 1. evidence of penetration, 2. lack of victim consent, 3. threat of force, and 4. female sex of the victim. It is intriguing to note, however, that 92 percent of the prosecuting agencies sampled did not have *formal* guidelines available for filing a charge for forcible rape. Therefore, the response from the prosecutors' offices did not necessarily reflect legal statutes or guidelines, but more probably the prosecutors' own judgments about what elements were necessary before rape charges could be filed.

In addition to different requirements for defining rape, some police agencies make distinctions between attempted rape and forcible rape, while the UCR practice is to include both under the heading forcible rape. Although some police agencies follow the UCR guidelines for classifying rape, about one-third have more stringent requirements, and about one-fifth have less stringent requirements. Moreover, many jurisdictions, especially the larger ones, have different degrees of forcible rape (e.g., first and second degree). In cases involving multiple offenses (i.e., rape plus burglary, homicide, or robbery), the offense considered more "serious" takes precedence and is more likely to be tabulated in the offense statistics, while lesser crimes committed at the same time are not included. For instance, since homicide is considered to be a more serious crime than forcible rape, homicide-rapes traditionally are tabulated under homicide and not under rape. Hence, we have very little data on homicide rapes.

Therefore, because of the wide variation among criminal justice agencies in classifying and defining rape, statistical comparisons and information pertaining to the "average" rape offense must be viewed cautiously. Until relatively standardized, national guidelines and legal definitions of what constitutes forcible rape are developed, national comparisons of rape characteristics should be considered as approximate overall patterns with some distortion in their accuracy.

Forcible Rape

According to UCR (Kelley, 1977) there were 56,730 forcible rapes reported to the police in this country in 1976. Although the incidence of rape may be grossly underreported because of the victims' fear and embarrassment, this statistic indicates that every year 52 out of every 100,000 inhabitants in the United States report having been raped. Rape reports for females living in metropolitan areas are three times greater than for females living in rural areas. Susan Brownmiller (1975) speculates that the actual rape rate may be 20 times greater than the reported rate, although this statistic is conjecture and not based on any empirical data. A more empirical survey concerned with victimization rates and based on randomly selected households shows that only one out of every four forcible or attempted rapes is reported to police agencies (Hindelang et al., 1976).

Rates of reported forcible rape have more than doubled in this country since 1965 (Chappell, 1977a). This dramatic increase in reporting probably reflects a higher level of community awareness about forcible rape in recent years, combined with the women's movement, increased training of law enforcement officers, and the gradual revision of statutes making courtroom testimony less stressful for the victim. In the national survey of 150 prosecutors' offices conducted by the National Institute of Law Enforcement and Criminal Justice (Chappell, 1977b), 61 percent of the respondents believed that the increased rape rate reflected a change in public attitude toward the crime. Another third of the prosecutors felt that the increase was a result of heightened "sensitivity" of the criminal justice system. It is interesting to note, however, that a vast majority of the prosecutors felt that the increased rape rate mainly reflected a "general pattern of increased violence" in America, even though nothing in the statistic justifies the assumption that more rapes are actually occurring.

Although the statistical incidences of forcible rape amount to less than 1 percent of the total crime index and only 6 percent of the total violent crime rate (Kelley, 1977), the psychological effects on the victim both during and after the incident are often severe and incalculable. Since rape cases usually require a thorough investigation and attention to detail (Chappell, 1977a), the rape victim, upon reporting the assault to police agencies, is expected to recall and describe personal, stressful sexual events in vivid detail for law enforcement personnel who too often are men. Following this ordeal, she is required to undergo an intimate medical examination to obtain evidence of penetration and use of physical force.

If the victim is able to withstand these immediate embarrassing and stressful conditions combined with the reactions of parents, husband, and friends, along with possible threats from the assailant, the next step in the process requires the preparation and successful prosecution of the case in court, usually before a jury and often accompanied by media coverage. This preparation may also require a polygraph to establish the victim's credibility. Since corroborating witnesses are generally difficult to come by, the bulk of the prosecuting evidence rests with the victim herself. In the Chappell survey (1977b) cited above, 92 percent of the prosecutors sampled asserted that the credibility of the victim was one of the most important elements in convincing juries to convict for forcible rape.

Therefore, although rape is an infrequent crime, it is not only often violent physically but also highly traumatizing psychologically to the victim. Below we will look at the situational variables common to rape incidences and the psychosocial characteristics of the offender.

Situational Characteristics

The very recent and extensive national surveys undertaken by the National Institute of Law Enforcement and Criminal Justice and directed by Duncan Chappell (1977a, 1977b) will be the main authoritative source for many of the statistics cited in this section. As noted earlier, we should be cautious about making authoritative assertions on the basis of these data, because of the high variability among police agencies in classifying and defining rape. However, these data represent one of the first national surveys on forcible rape undertaken and suggest some trends and intriguing results regarding forcible rape, information generally held to be only hypothetical in the past.

The Chappell surveys found that rapes in large cities are most likely to occur in the victim's residence or outdoors. But in small cities (less than 100,000) and especially in rural areas, they are most likely to occur in motor vehicles, which probably reflects the higher frequency of hitchhiking in smaller communities. In fact, hitchhiking accompanied 20 percent of all rapes reported in the small cities, compared to 10 percent in large metropolitan areas.

The victim and the offender are strangers about 50 to 60 percent of the time, while reported rapes between relatives occur about 5 percent of the time, friends about 10 percent of the time, and "acquaintances" in about 25 percent of the total offenses (Chappell, 1977a; Brodsky, 1976). The higher incidence of rapes between strangers might partly reflect the greater tendency of victims to report being raped by strangers than by friends or relatives. Since injured victims are also more likely to report the assault, the discrepancy in this statistic might also point out that a rapist is more apt to inflict physical injury on a victim who is a stranger—a point we shall return to in the next section.

Rape offenses generally occur during the late evening and early morning hours (i.e., 8 p.m. to 2 a.m.) and almost always in darkness. There are several possible explanations for this, the most obvious being that the assailant chooses a time and a place where potential witnesses are less readily available and detection is remote. However, the rapist might also feel more "deindividualized" and more able to regard the victim as an object. Speculating still further, if we analyze the situational characteristics in conjunction with the personality of the rapist, we might discover a breed of "night rapist" who depersonalizes his victims as objects and another type of "day rapist" who perceives the victim as a woman representing her sex and to be humiliated.

Another plausible explanation is that alcohol and drugs are more readily used during the evening hours, and alcohol and other drugs seem to be involved in about half of the reported rape cases (Chappell, 1977a; Brodsky, 1976; Queen's Bench Foundation, 1978). In approximately 25 percent of the incidences, only the offender was considered to be under the influence of drugs, while in another 18 percent both the offender and the victim were. The accuracy of these statistics must remain questionable unless the assailant was arrested immediately after the rape and given a blood test. It is very difficult for a frightened, traumatized victim to determine whether her assailant was actually drugged or simply behaving unusually. It is also highly unlikely that the victim would report to a police agency that she herself was in an altered state of consciousness, since this might undermine her credibility. Another possible explanation for nighttime rapes, which also might serve for hitchhiking assaults, is that the rapist interprets a woman out late at night in a bar or hitchhiking by herself as "asking for it."

The fears of women about being attacked and harmed by strangers are not unfounded. Physical assault is commonly reported in rapes, occurring in about one-half of those incidents reported to the police and two-thirds of those reported to the prosecutor. The discrepancy probably reflects the prosecutor's need to establish legally that the assault was a forcible rape. Weapons are used in half of the assaults reported, with firearms and knives being by far the most frequent. About one-fourth of the rape victims sustain an injury serious enough to warrant medical treatment or hospitalization. Furthermore, and contrary to popular advice and the statutory requirement in some states that a woman should resist her assailant to the utmost, there appears to be a direct relationship between the tendency to resist rape and the physical injury sustained. On the average, the greater the victim's resistance, the greater the physical injury she receives. Interestingly, victims from smaller cities offer more resistance (both verbal and physical) than do victims from larger cities. Thus, they are more likely to receive some degree of personal injury than are victims from larger cities. We shall return to the resistance-injury phenomenon when we discuss types of rapists, since it is important to realize that resistance can be very effective in warding off some assailants, whereas it antagonizes and incites others to more violence.

Rapists often expect more than vaginal intercourse. In approximately 25 percent of the rapes Chappell studied, the assailant also demanded oral sexual acts; about 10 percent demanded both oral and anal sexual acts; about 6 percent anal sexual acts only; and 4 percent "other" sexual acts. The pattern of seeking other than vaginal intercourse appears to be especially characteristic of large city rapists. Similar findings have been reported by Amir (1971) for Philadelphia rapists.

Gang rapes are surprisingly common, occuring in about one out of every four reported rapes in this country. Amir (1971) found that in Philadelphia during 1958 and 1960, 43 percent of the about 1,000 reported rapes were committed by multiple assailants; but in the Chappell survey, pair rapes (two assailants) were reported about 15 percent of the time and gang rapes (more than two assailants) about 11 percent of the time. This phenomenon seems to be primarily a result of group contagion, deindividuation, and feeling part of the gang (Brownmiller, 1975), and it will receive more attention in Chapter 10.

The discrepancy between the national data and Amir's Philadephia study regarding incidents of multiple rape may be a result of the very high percentage (80 percent) of Blacks in Amir's sample; that is, multiple rapes may be more characteristic of the Black than of the general population. Nationally, about half of the individuals arrested for rape are white (Kelley, 1977). In addition, in jurisdictions of all sizes, rape is overwhelmingly an intraracial affair, with Blacks raping Blacks and Whites raping Whites (Chappell, 1977a).

Offender Characteristics

What kind of a person rapes? How did he get that way? Why does he do it? Can the "rapist personality" be easily identified? Are they "sick animals?" Unfortunately, and surprisingly, well-executed research directed at those questions has been very sparse. Most of the clinical reports and studies directed at rapists' characteristics have come in the form of case studies or anecdotal accounts which make generalizations tentative.

One of the most consistent findings in the literature and in national statistical surveys is that rapists tend to be young. The FBI reports that over half of those arrested for forcible rape in 1976 were under age twenty-five, and 80 percent were under age thirty (Kelley, 1977). Henn et al. (1976a) report that 75 percent of those accused of rape and referred to a mental health evaluation team in St. Louis between the years 1952 and 1973 were under age thirty. The Queen's Bench Foundation (1978) found that 70 percent of their sample of 73 convicted rapists were under twenty-five.

Another consistent discovery about men who have been arrested for rape is that, in general, they have been in conflict with society prior to the rape incident. About one-fourth of those arrested for forcible rape have raped previously, and about one-third have a prior arrest history for violent offenses other than rape (Chappell, 1977a).

Occupationally, people arrested for rape tend to come from the blue-collar working class (about 50 percent) and another sizeable portion (approximately 30 percent) are unemployed. Very few individuals from the professional and "white-collar" occupational fields are arrested for rape. Interestingly, the number of professional people that are accused drops precipitously when the rape charge gets to the prosecutor's office, while the other occupational groups either stay the same or increase. At face value, these data suggest that the more affluent or privileged offender is less likely to be charged with rape. They also suggest that individuals lacking occupational and/or social skills are more likely to be arrested for rape.

According to prosecutors, about one-fourth of those accused of rape admitted that the incident was planned and premeditated (Chappell, 1977b). The problem with this statistic, however, is that most suspects are unwilling to admit premeditation, since it makes the case against them that much tighter. Therefore, it is highly probable that the number of premeditated rapes is substantially higher than those reported by prosecutors. Amir (1971) claims that, on the basis of his analysis of the reported rapes in Philadelphia, 71 percent were planned. The Queen's Bench Foundation study (1978) found that over two-thirds of the convicted rapists interviewed admitted that their intention was rape prior to the attack.

Generally, criminal behavior is a response pattern the offender believes will gain him some kind of personal reinforcement. The rapist rapes because he expects certain personal gain from the incident in that particular context. The word "planning" is rather vague for our purposes, implying as it does that the offender thought about how he was going to rape several hours, days, or even weeks prior to the attack. It is extremely difficult to determine what the temporal cutoff point should be to constitute premeditation. On the other hand, it would be inaccurate to consider the "average" rapist as reacting to *spontaneous* urges of sexual energy and passion which have welled up in his psyche suddenly, unpredictably, and without warning.

We learn from most accounts of rapists themselves that there may be a number of things they "desire" from the incident. For instance, one particular assailant may habitually obtain personal satisfaction and rewards from violently raping seventy-five-year-old women in their apartments on carpeted floors during daylight conditions. Taking this example one step further, let's assume that he has a rug-cleaning job which periodically takes him into the apartments of elderly women. Fortuitously, he occasionally encounters older women under specific conditions which trigger his sexual assault pattern. Do we consider his sexual assaults "spontaneous" or "planned"?

Although the majority of offenders were thinking of *forcible* rape at the time of their offense, one study reports that close to two-thirds chose their victim because she was simply available and/or defenseless (Queen's Bench Foundation, 1978). Less than half of the rapists saw their victims as sexy or physically attractive. However, a quarter of the rapists also said that another determining factor for their selection of the victim was that she appeared to be a "loose" woman. Examples of loose women given by the rapists were hitchhikers who looked like hippies, women who worked as waitresses, and women who were said to be having sexual relationships with more than one man.

The notion of the "crazy rapist" or the "sick rapist" appears unfounded. Individuals charged with rape are rarely found to be psychotic or insane. In fact, rapists appear to demonstrate fewer psychotic or insane behaviors than the general population (Henn et al., 1976). The most frequent diagnostic label assigned to rapists is "antisocial personality disorder" (Henn et al., 1976; McCaldon, 1967; Kopp, 1962), which is not surprising when we consider that label's meaning. The "antisocial personality disorder" diagnosis is reserved for individuals who are "undersocialized" and repeatedly in conflict with society. As we have discovered, rapists tend to have a track record of antisocial behavior and crimes against society. The diagnostic label simply summarizes the behavioral history and probably does not reflect inhibiting or severe emotional problems *per se*. The evidence available to date indicates that the great majority of men who commit rape appear to be "sane," mentally competent young men who are fully aware of their actions.

Types

Some attempts have been made to categorize the personalities of rapists. A group of researchers at the Bridgewater Treatment Center in Bridgewater, Massachusetts (Cohen, Seghorn, & Calmas, 1969; Cohen et al., 1971) recognized that the act of rape involves both sexual and aggressive features, and they tried to formulate a classification system of personality types based on the specific aggressive and sexual elements demonstrated by the assailants.

For example, Cohen and his colleagues saw one group of rapists as being primarily violent and aggressive in their attack, with a minimum or total absence of sexual feeling. These men use the act of rape to harm, humiliate, and degrade the female. The victim is brutally assaulted and subjected to sadistic acts such as biting, cutting, or tearing of breasts and genitals. Almost always the victim is a complete stranger to the rapist and only serves as the best available object or stimulus for his aggression. The assault is not very sexually arousing for the assailant, and he often must begin masturbation to become tumescent. Resisting this type of rapist only makes him more violent.

Despite the fact that many of these rapists are married, there is considerable evidence of ambivalence toward the women in their lives (Cohen et al., 1971), and their relationships with women are often characterized by periodic irritation and violence. They generally see women as hostile, demanding, and unfaithful creatures. In addition, they often select as their targets for sexual assault women whom they consider active, assertive, and independent. The occupational history of these assailants is stable and often shows some level of success. Normally, the work is "masculine," such as truck driving, carpentry, mechanics, plumbing, etc. Attack typically follows some incident which has made the rapist angry about women and their behavior. Because the victim of the assault rarely has played any direct role in generating the aggression, this assailant is called a *displaced aggression* rapist.

A second group of rapists is drawn to rape because of an intense sexual arousal initiated by stimuli in the environment which are often quite specific. Aggression is not the significant feature in the attack; the basic motivation is the desire to prove sexual prowess and adequacy. These individuals tend to be extremely passive, withdrawn, and socially inept. This type of rapist lives in a world of fantasy centering on images of how the victim will yield eagerly under attack, submit to pleasurable intercourse, and find his skill and performance so outstanding that she will plead for a return engagement. Under these conditions, he will be able at last to prove his masculinity.

In his daily activities this rapist is often described by others as a quiet, shy, submissive, and lonely "nice man." Although he is a reliable worker, his withdrawn, introverted behavior, lack of self-esteem, and low levels of need for achievement prevent him from succeeding in either educational or occupational areas. Because his rapes—or attempts at rape—are an effort to compensate for his overwhelming feelings of inadequacy, this offender is referred to as the *compensatory rapist.*

Although his victim is usually a stranger, he has probably seen her around, watched her, or followed her. Specific stimuli about the victim probably excite him. For example, he may be especially drawn to wealthy college women, but because of his inadequacy feels they would probably have nothing to do with him under normal circumstances. However, if he can prove his "loving" ability without the asking and the expected rejection, the victim will want him again. If the victim resists him with vigor, he is likely to flee. However, if she is so frightened that she passively submits, he will go through with the rape without much force or violence. This sexually aroused passive assailant will often ejaculate spontaneously, even upon mere physical contact with the victim. Generally this type of rapist only engages in periodic attempts at uninvited intercourse and does not demonstrate other kinds of antisocial behavior.

A third type of rapist is, according to Cohen, the one in whom sexual and aggressive features seem to coexist at equal or near equal levels. In order for him to experience sexual arousal, it must be associated with violence and pain, which excite him. He rapes because of the combination of violence and sexual features he finds in the assault. This rapist is convinced that women enjoy being roughed up, being forcefully raped, and in general being dominated and controlled by men. In this sense he perceives the victim's resistance and struggle as a game, a form of protesting too much, when she really wants to be sexually assaulted and raped. These offenders are frequently married, but because they display little commitment, they also sometimes have a history of a series of marriages and divorces. Their background is very often full of various antisocial behaviors beginning during adolescence or before and ranging from truancy to rape-murder. In the extreme, this type engages in sexual sadism much like the displaced aggression rapist, where the woman is viciously violated and murdered. This rapist is classified as *sexual-aggressive.*

An illustrative case of the sexual-aggressive rapist is found in the autobiography of Kenneth P. Rogers (1974), a convicted rapist-murderer. At an early age Rogers began associating sex with violence, although it is unclear as to why. In his autobiography he tries to make a connection between parental physical punishment which was administered with a "slight bit of affection and love" and his confusion about sex and aggression. He regarded his mother as overprotective and overcontrolling, and he presented his father only in terms of "muscles and hair, anger, despair."

Rogers displays a long history of numerous rapes followed by imprisonment and a career which finally culminated in the rape and murder of three young women. His first rape occurred when he was fourteen, when he assaulted a girl of his age who was waiting for her mother after swimming. He was not arrested for this initial offense. From this point on, Rogers sexually assaulted women over a period of fifteen years, often followed by convictions and imprisonment. On several occasions his rapes occurred within days of his prison release.

Although Rogers' book is tinged with sensationalism and detail, the felon-author makes important observations about his own behavior. He found himself chronically haunted by "an overpowering desire to be the accepted male of the species," and consumed by intense thoughts and fantasies about the female anatomy. Despite being attractive and intelligent, he lacked social skills and had considerable difficulty in developing relationships with women. Most of his attacks were preceded by feelings of low self-esteem, depression, and helplessness about his predicament. These feelings combined with sexual cues (e.g., breasts, buttocks, and thighs) generated sexual arousal and precipitated assault. Once the context excited his arousal, he felt powerless to alter his course of action.

The *modus operandi* of his offenses usually followed a specific sequence, apparently designed to maintain complete control over his victim. He disrobed the victim, performed cunnilingus, demanded fellatio, and then forced vaginal intercourse. If the victim resisted, he would become angry and physically assault her. If the victim displayed attempts at sexually controlling the situation, he would also become angered. Rogers required omnipotence over the female. By his own admission his rewards in rape were "instant pleasure" and to bend people to his will. He asserted that he felt like "a man" following the rape. Rogers rarely expressed empathy or concern for his victim until after he raped her. He believed the victim enjoyed the assault, particularly after he spent time performing cunnilingus during the initial stage of the assault.

After each imprisonment, the rapes became progressively more violent. Rogers felt that prison failed to deter him and only increased his bitterness and anger. No one seemed to give a damn. Prison officials at one point diagnosed him a "psychopath," a label he failed to understand but that he felt gave him some status.

After fifteen years punctuated by rape, arrest, and imprisonment, his sexual-aggressive motivation built to the point where at age twenty-nine he raped and murdered a thirteen-year-old girl. A few weeks later, on Christmas eve, he strangled his wife of three months (whom he had raped earlier in their relationship) and raped and strangled her best friend. On December 29, 1969, he was sentenced to two concurrent 75- to 100-year terms for two counts of murder and was sent to Menard Penitentiary. On July 6, 1970, Rogers was also sentenced to 75 to 100 years for the rape-murder of the thirteen-year-old.

A fourth type of rapist demonstrates neither strong sexual nor aggressive features, but engages in spontaneous rape when the opportunity presents itself. The act of rape is usually carried out in the context of some other antisocial act, such as robbery or burglary. The victims simply happen to be available, and they are sexually assaulted with little aggressive or sexual feeling. Generally, this type of offender has a history of antisocial behavior. These individuals qualify as *impulsive rapists*.

Coleman (1976) suggests that a fifth rape category be added: the *psychopathic rapist*. Cold, selfish, and unfeeling, the rapist takes sexual satisfaction when the mood moves him: "I wanted it so I took it." He finds nothing wrong with this behavior. He assaults, robs, and rapes in response to the needs of the moment. It is debatable, however, whether this type really differs substantially from the impulsive rapist who has many characteristics of the psychopath.

Case studies and empirical evidence tend to support the first four descriptive categories presented above. But, as we have continually pointed out, personalities rarely fit neatly into typologies, which are only very rough devices for conceptualizing and simplifying behavior. In addition to formulating personality types, research should concentrate on the developmental processes and situations which predispose the rape-prone personality toward sexual assaults upon women.

Generally speaking, sexual socialization appears to play a crucial role in the rapist's perception of what rape accomplishes and his conceptions of what constitutes being "masculine." It is important to realize that sexual socialization (or learning about sex) is rarely acquired entirely from the home or school; much of it comes from peers, friends, mass media, and experimentation. Stop for a moment and think about how you learned about sex. Recall the strange things you first heard—the misconceptions, the taboos. Males likely learned it is "manly" to take the sexual initiative with females, even if they resist. Relating details of the sexual conquest to friends represented the badge of manhood or masculinity. On the other hand, if attempts to conquer turned out to be awkward, fumbling disasters, it was unlikely that a full report would be offered. Moreover, these aborted attempts were seen as personal failure and a sign of immaturity or personal and sexual inadequacy. In relation to our topic here, many people (both men and women) learn that a woman cannot be raped unless she wants to be, a canard sometimes known as the "pencil-in-the-moving-bottle" hypothesis. Others hear that women want to be dominated and controlled and that successful lovers demonstrate the "who-is-boss" syndrome. It is interesting to note in this context that some victims of rape actually receive marriage proposals from their assailant (Russell, 1975). Other rapists ask their victims to evaluate their performance during the act.

In other words, rapists are not born rapists, they learn to be rapists, and much of the sexual teaching has been done by peers, social models, and the entertainment media, however misguided these models are. The typologies suggested by Cohen and his colleagues basically reflect the unique learning experiences and processes an individual has been exposed to during his formative years. Fortunately, from the array of learning experiences and developmental opportunities they have, most people eventually acquire a close approximation of sexual sophistication and some understanding of the needs of others. Rapists, on the other hand, have remained sexually and, in some ways, socially immature. For example, they seem to be still at the adolescent conceptions of believing men are supposed to do it *to* women, not *with* them.

Recent evidence supports the immaturity hypothesis. Michael Goldstein (1977) found that convicted sex offenders (who were mostly rapists) continue in adulthood to derive most of their sexual pleasure from fantasizing sexual stimuli they had derived from the media, while average males (controls) drew much of their sexual pleasure from real-life sexual encounters. Goldstein also discovered that rapists have pervasive and obsessive preoccupations with sexual matters to the point where the sexual preoccupation permeates a considerable segment of their lives, and where normally nonerotic material becomes vividly incorporated into sexual fantasies. "For example, one rapist reported becoming very sexually excited and desirous of carrying out a sexual assault after reading a report of rape by a rape victim—the more the victim described the terror, the more excited he became. Incidentally, the potent erotic stimulus appeared in the *Ladies Home Journal!*" (Goldstein, 1977, p. 14).

Goldstein found that rapists, unlike the average male, relied substantially more on masturbation during adulthood, and that those masturbatory practices were frequently accompanied by erotic material obtained from the entertainment media. Furthermore, sexual offenders had *fewer* contacts with erotica during formative years than did the normally developing male. If you combine a limited exposure to erotica with a highly repressive and punitive attitude regarding sexual curiosity—as the research consistently indicates is true in the case of rapists—you have very rich soil for sexual misconceptions and ignorance to grow in. Eysenck (1972) reports that by the time the average male is fourteen years old he has seen at least one picture of a couple engaged in intercourse, but the *typical* sex offender does not see a similar depiction under age eighteen.

Although we should remain skeptical about generalizations based on limited data, Goldstein's investigations fit with an immaturity hypothesis which presumes that rapists, as a group, are sexually naive. Not only does the background of rapists display abnormally limited exposure to sexual materials, but it also appears that they continue to live in a world of fantasy combined with frequent, self-induced arousal through masturbation. Sex for many rapists appears limited, veiled in misinformation and ignorance.

Goldstein saw the erotica as beneficial to human sexual development, but it should be mentioned that his erotica referred to sexual acts between consenting partners and were without antisocial elements. The effects of antisocial sexual depictions on film or in photographs remains very much an open question and must await further investigation. Abel *et al.* (1975) used audiodescriptions of various rape and nonrape sexual scenes while they measured changes in penile circumference of rapists and nonrapists. The findings revealed that the rapist group was sexually aroused by both rape and mutually enjoyable intercourse scenes, while nonrapists only responded to the mutually enjoyable descriptions, suggesting that rapists are not able to differentiate sexual arousal on the basis of the victims' reactions.

Statistical investigations in Denmark have focused on the relationship between availability of erotic materials and the rates of sex crimes. Increased availability of explicit sexual materials in that country has been accompanied by a decrease in the incidence of all sex crimes (Committee on Obscenity and Pornography, 1970). Similarly, the Danish researcher Berl Kutchinsky (1973) found that child molestation dropped from an annual rate of 220 cases to 87 per year after the introduction of hard-core pornography.

PEDOPHILIA

Pedophilia, commonly known as child molestation, refers to the use of prepubertal children (under age thirteen) by adults for sexual gratification. Occasionally, researchers will extend the definition to include ages thirteen through fifteen, but the literature usually reserves the label "hebephilia" for sexual contact with young adolescents. In most definitions, the pedophilial act occurs between an adult and child (or children) who are not closely related. Sexual acts between members of a family when at least one participant is a minor are usually referred to as incest.

The offender, or pedophiliac, is almost always male, but the victim may be either female (heterosexual pedophilia) or male (homosexual pedophilila). Heterosexual pedophilia appears to be the more common, and rough estimates suggest that there are two heterosexual offenses for every homosexual one (Revitch & Weiss, 1962). The behavior of the pedophiliac or child molester is usually limited to caressing the child's body, fondling the child's genitals, and/or inducing the child to manipulate his genitals. Heterosexual penetration is rare.

Statistics on child molestation are difficult to obtain, since there are no central or national recording systems for sexual offenses against children, and since there has been no nationwide study undertaken and published in this country. Also, offenders may be prosecuted under a variety of statutes, such as sodomy, incest, indecent exposure, or lewd and lascivious behavior. Although the UCR lists sex offenses, it does not differentiate child molestation from the mixture of other possible sexual offenses. One California study (Frisbie, 1965), based on nearly 2,000 males referred to Atascadero State Hospital for evaluation for sex offenses, estimated that five out of every 1,000 adult males in the general population were arrested and referred for pedophilia. Schultz (1975) cites statistics which suggest that there are between 200,000 and 500,000 cases of "sexual assaults" on female children ages four to fourteen every year. Estimates on male child victimization are largely unavailable.

Situational Characteristics

The child molester rarely harms the child physically, and rarely is there evidence of coercion or force (Schultz, 1975). An investigation by McCaghy (1967) found that in three-fourths of the child molestation cases examined, there was no evidence of any kind of coercion, verbal or physical. Although there are exceptions, depending on the particular situation and numerous other variables, the evidence to date suggests that child molesters generally cause neither physical injury nor permanent psychological "damage" to the child. In fact, the extent of psychological trauma appears to depend primarily on how society reacts to the incident, not how the child initially views it. The child is particularly affected by the parents' reaction. If the parents view the incident as "dirty," "vile," and "disgusting," and are convinced that the "highly negative" incident is going to leave permanent psychological scars on the child's personality, the child may very well learn to interpret the incident in a similar fashion. Upon learning of the incident, some adults become agitated and hysterical, and they overreact and physically attack the offender—or they may even berate, belittle, and punish the victim. The criminal justice system often perceives the child molester as sinister and prescribes some of its most severe penalties for these offenders.

In most instances the offender and the victim know one another, often very well (McCaghy, 1967; Virkkunen, 1975; Schultz, 1975). Many victims were actively seeking affection from their offenders at the time of the incident. Some victims feel kindly and lovingly toward the offender. Others may engage in seductive behavior without realizing its potential consequences. It is also not uncommon for the sexual behavior between the offender and the victim to have gone on for a sustained period of time.

The form of the sexual contact depends upon the degree to which the offender has had previous nonsexual interactions with children, the nature of the relationship between the child and the offender, and the age of the offender and the victim. Offenders who have had only limited or minimal interactions with children are substantially more likely to perform or expect genital-genital and/or oral-genital contact, rather than to indulge only in caressing or fondling. Furthermore, the more familiar the offender and the victim are with one another, the greater the tendency for genital-genital or oral-genital contact.

Offender Characteristics

Although there is considerable variability in the age of child molesters, the average age is forty. While approximately 75 percent of the rapists are under thirty, about 75 percent of the child molesters are over that age (Henn et al., 1976b). However, despite the statistical finding that child molesters tend to be older than most other sexual offenders, there tends to be a pattern of victim preference as a function of age. That is, older pedophiliacs (over fifty) seek out immature children (ten or younger); younger pedophiliacs (under forty) prefer girls between the ages of twelve and fifteen (Revitch & Weiss, 1962).

About two-thirds of those arrested and convicted for child molestation come from the unskilled or semiskilled occupational groups (McCaghy, 1967; Gebhard et al., 1965). However, it is difficult to determine the representation of other occupational groups because members of the higher occupational and socioeconomic classes may handle the incident quite differently to prevent embarrassment for their families or additional trauma for the victim during the criminal justice process.

Because of the extremely negative attitude society exhibits toward child molesters, pedophiliacs usually resist accepting full responsibility for their offenses (McCaghy, 1967). Many claim that they went blank, were too drunk to know what they were doing, or do not know what came over them. They assign the cause of their behavior to external forces or motivating factors which were beyond their personal control. A general observation which can be made about criminal behavior is that the more heinous the crime in the view of society, the less likely the offender is to be willing to take direct personal responsibility for it. Some offenders claim that they were another person, were hypnotized, or were taken hold of by some strange force. Apparently the incident is so condemned by society and so foreign to the person's self-image that he finds it difficult to accept as part of his personal response repertoire.

Those charged with child molestation rarely exhibit any serious or pronounced behavioral problems other than the pedophilia (Henn et al., 1976b). Among the most frequent clinical diagnoses made—when they are made—are organic brain syndrome or mental retardation. Since pedophilia and exhibitionism are the most common sexual offenses committed by senile and arteriosclerotic men (Coleman, 1976), the organic brain syndrome classification is not really surprising.

If pedophiliacs are not usually found to have "psychiatric" or behavioral problems, what prompts them toward this particular behavioral pattern? A common clinical observation is that pedophiliacs select children for sex objects because they are haunted by feelings of masculine and sexual inadequacy in adult relationships. They feel, according to the hypothesis, uncomfortable and terrified of being ridiculed about their sexual and social behavior by the adult world. By returning to the world of the child, they can be safely curious, awkward, and inexperienced. This observation might help explain in part why pedophiliacs rarely engage in heterosexual intercourse. There is also evidence to suggest that homosexual pedophiliacs feel particularly insecure about themselves sexually (Fisher & Howell, 1970).

Although the inadequacy hypothesis appears to have some validity, it fails to explain why the individual chooses children as sex objects compared to other innocuous objects which would provide neither embarrassment nor ridicule. Moreover, many men feel sexually inadequate. Why do some choose rape and others pedophilia, while still others avoid both altogether?

There is every reason to believe that pedophilia is a *learned habit*. It probably represents a process of early learning that failed to be replaced by more rewarding later experiences. The background of most people reveals that it is not an uncommon experience to have engaged in sexual play with playmates as a child. For the pedophiliac, the childhood sexual play may have been particularly vivid, rewarding, and stimulating, and very possibly the most sexually arousing experience he has ever had. When he entered adulthood, at least chronologically, sexual play with adults perhaps was found less arousing, satisfying, and rewarding. For instance, he might have been unable to make sexual contacts because he was shy and socially withdrawn, or perhaps he was ridiculed for sexual inadequacy, or perhaps he was unable to find the adult opportunity. Under these conditions, he probably sought the most available sexual avenue, masturbation. As mentioned earlier, clinical studies continually indicate that masturbation is one of the most powerful initial reinforcers found in most sexual offenses. During masturbation, the pedophiliac's fantasies may focus on the few satisfying sexual experiences or activities he has engaged in with his childhood playmates. Repetitive masturbatory activity of this kind would reinforce the immature level of sexual behavior previously associated with childhood. Also, remembering that introverts condition more readily than other personalities, it is not surprising that many pedophiliacs are found to be introverted and socially withdrawn. Continual association between the pleasurable masturbatory activities and fantasies about positive childhood sexual experiences results in a strong bond between sexual arousal and children. Eventually, children become sexual stimuli to the individual, capable of arousing sexual excitation. However, one should realize that masturbation by itself does not increase feelings of adequacy and competence; the realistic effects one has on others are the most effective modality for achieving this.

Types

Cohen and his colleagues (1969) have proposed an interesting and widely quoted typology of child molester personalities, similar to the rape typology presented earlier. The child molester in one descriptive category desires to touch, fondle, caress, taste, and smell the child. He has never been able to develop a mature relationship with his peers, male or female, and he feels most comfortable when he is relating to children. He seeks them out as companions and tries to be around them as much as possible. The sexual contact comes only after a period of a relationship with the child. Socially, this immature individual is described as passive and dependent. Such pedophiliacs are called *pedophile fixated*, or what this author prefers to call *immature child offenders*.

A second group, the *regressed child offender*, had a fairly normal adolescence and good peer relationships and heterosexual experiences, but later developed feelings of masculine inadequacy and self-doubt. As these feelings increased, occupational, social, and sexual adjustments became marginal, frequently resulting in alcoholism, divorce, and poor social and occupational performance. The pedophiliac acts are almost always precipitated by significant jolts to the offender's sexual adequacy by female and male peers. Often, the precipitating condition is the discovery that his wife or woman friend is having an affair with another man. Unlike the immature child offender, the regressed child offender normally prefers victims he does not know and who live outside his neighborhood. Furthermore, the victim is almost always female.

The third type of child offender attaches both sexual and aggressive components to the child. Individuals in this group are apt to have a history of antisocial behavior. The majority prefer boy to girl victims (homosexual pedophilia), and they are often sexually sadistic in order to satisfy their need for stimulation and thrills. Since the primary aim is to obtain stimulation without consideration for the victim, this group attacks the child with cruel and vicious assaults to the genitals or introduces the penis or elongated objects into the victim orally and anally. The more harm and pain that is inflicted, the more this offender becomes sexually excited. This type of child molester is called the *aggressive child offender* and is the one most often responsible for the kidnapping of children for sexual abuse and murder. Coleman (1976) suggests that this offender closely resembles the psychopath and might be better labeled psychopathic offender.

The first two categories, the immature and the regressed child offenders, follow the theoretical explanation of pedophilia discussed above quite well. In each case the individuals cling to earlier, more rewarding experiences they had with childhood playmates. These earlier experiences may have become intensely connected to sexual arousal induced by masturbation or other sexual activities and pleasurable thoughts related to them.

The aggressive or psychopathic child molester, on the other hand, may represent at least two personality types. One is illustrated by the psychopath who failed to learn adequate societal roles and whose behavior is directed strictly by his own self-interest and need for stimulation. The second personality belongs to the individual who has, through the processes of learning, conditioning, and modeling, come to associate sex with violence. Like the immature and regressed offender, he feels most comfortable with children because of earlier learning experiences and poor adult experiences. It is possible that he began associating childhood sex and violence at an early age and may have a history of engaging in sadistic sexual play with childhood playmates.

An example of an aggressive child molester who combined violence and sex was Albert Fish (1870–1936), whose background is cited in Nash (1975). Fish, who was called the "moon maniac," admitted molesting more than 400 children over a span of about twenty years. In addition, he confessed to murdering six children and made vague reference to numerous other killings. He was tried and convicted of murdering a twelve-year-old girl and was executed in the electric chair in 1936.

Fish thought the conditions of his childhood led to a "perverted" life and to crimes. He was abandoned at an early age and placed in an orphanage where he first witnessed and experienced brutal acts of sadism. Fish was quoted as saying, "Misery leads to crime. I saw so many boys whipped it ruined my mind." He apparently began his career of child molesting in earnest when his wife ran off and left him for another man. This event suggests that his child molesting corresponded with a breakdown of relationships with adults, at least with his wife.

Despite numerous attempts by his defense attorneys to prove him insane, psychiatrists continued to evaluate him sane, although—according to one psychiatrist—he appeared to live in a world of "unparalleled perversity." Eager to discover what it was like to die in the electric chair, he marched to his execution unassisted, jumped into the seat, and helped the executioner fix the electrodes on his legs.

Groth and Burgess (1977) proposed another clinical typology, one based on the manner in which the pedophiliac regards and treats the child. Using information gathered on 137 convicted child molesters and 74 victims, the authors were able to subdivide the offenses into major categories: 1. the *sex-pressure* offense, where no physical force was used, and 2. the *sex-force* offense, using threats, physical force, or both. According to Groth and Burgess, the sex-pressure offender may employ the *enticement* method, characterized by attempts to seduce the child through persuasion or cajolement, or he may use the *entrapment* method, where he places the child in the position of feeling indebted or obligated in some way to the offender. These offenders not only feel more comfortable with children, but actually feel affection for the child. The sexual involvement may be long term and the contact frequent.

The sex-force offender may use one of two methods for assaulting the child. In the *exploitive* assault, the offender forces himself on the child and uses just enough force or threat to subdue the victim for the sexual act. Basically, this offender uses the child as an object for sexual gratification and has little or no concern for the victim. In *sadistic assault*, the offender derives stimulation and sexual arousal from psychologically and physically hurting the child. That is, aggressive behavior is "eroticized." The child is often beaten, choked, tortured, and sexually abused. According to Groth and Burgess (1977, p. 261), "the assault has been planned out, thought about, and fantasized for some time prior to its actual commission." Fortunately, according to Groth and Burgess, this offender is relatively rare.

Certainly the Groth-Burgess typology has some commonalities with the Cohen typology. The immature and the regressed child offenders display features which are seen in the sex-pressure offense, and the aggressive child offender shows strong similarities to the sex-force offender. It may be more appropriate—or at least more realistic—to classify the child offender according to the degree of coercion or force he uses in the offense rather than attempt to formulate strict categories.

If pedophilia is a learned habit, we would expect a fairly high incidence of repeated pedophiliacs. Like the national incidence rate, however, pedophiliac recidivism rates are difficult to find. In the California study by Frisbie (1965), recidivism rates over a five-year period for California offenders were reported to be 18.2 percent for heterosexual pedophiliacs and 34.5 for homosexual pedophiliacs. However, as Schultz (1975) noted, most pedophiliac offenses go unreported. Additionally, the second time around the pedophiliac is undoubtedly more careful. Although it employed a very select sample of arrested and unarrested pedophiliacs, a Dutch study (Bernard, 1975) reported that at least half of its respondents claimed to have had sexual contacts with at least ten or more children. Fourteen percent indicated they had had sexual contacts with more than 50, and 6 percent said between 100 and 300 children. Fifty-six percent of this sample indicated they had one or more "regular" sexual contacts with children. Moreover, fully 90 percent asserted that they did not want to get rid of their pedophilia, presumably because of its reinforcement value.

EXHIBITIONISM

Exhibitionism refers to the deliberate exposure of the genitals to another person for the purpose of sexual rewards. Several authors have reported that exhibitionism (indecent exposure) is the most frequent sexual offense known to the police (e.g., Wincze, 1977; Coleman, 1976). In Canada and the United States, exhibitionism accounts for about one-third of all sex crimes (Evans, 1970; Rooth, 1974) and in the United Kingdom it accounts for one-fourth (Feldman, 1977). From all indications the practice of exposing oneself is principally a "Western" world phenomenon. In India, for instance, extensive surveys have failed to uncover a single case (Rooth, 1974). The incidence in Japan for one year was 59 convicted cases, compared to 2,767 in England and Wales during that same year. Of course, the actual frequency is very likely to be considerably higher than that found in official statistics, since most offenses are not reported.

The exhibitionist is almost always male. Female strippers are usually "exposed" for economic gain and not for the purpose of sexual arousal on their own part. Moreover, persons watching strippers do so voluntarily, and frequent their places of work with that intention in mind. Exhibitionists, by contrast, often delight in surprising and shocking their audiences, with either a flaccid or erect penis. Although masturbation sometimes accompanies the exposure, a majority of exhibitionists prefer to masturbate immediately following the exposure.

Situational Characteristics

If the offender is not particularly brazen about his exposure procedure he may habitually hide behind the curtain of a window in his home at about the time school lets out and, as young girls walk by, tap on the window, quickly show himself, and make a fast retreat behind the curtain. Another favorite procedure is to use a car, drive slowly by a female or a group of females, open the car door, show himself, and quickly drive away. The bolder exhibitionist is often the "street flasher" who opens his coat to a selected victim, makes certain the impression registers, and then runs or walks off.

Favorite locations for exposure vary, but most exhibitionists prefer public places such as parks, theaters, stores, or relatively uncrowded streets. A Toronto study (Mohr et al., 1964) reports that 74 percent of a sample studied preferred open places, and most displayed themselves from a parked car. The remainder of the sample generally preferred their own home and often exhibited themselves through windows or doorways.

The overwhelming majority of exhibitionists prefer strangers for victims and rarely expose more than once to the same female. Although the preferred victim is usually female, an exhibitionist will occasionally expose himself to adult males and male children, and this probably is a result of victim availability rather than homosexual tendencies. If their preference is adult women, exhibitionists will usually expose to them individually, while those who prefer female children will generally prefer them in small groups of two or three (Evans, 1970; Mohr et al., 1964). Most adult female victims are in their late teens or early twenties, usually unmarried.

A majority of exhibitionists look for a specific stimulus or set of stimuli in their victims. For example, an exhibitionist may have a definite preference for exhibiting to young girls between the ages of nine and eleven who look "naive." Some look for a pretty face, dark hair, low socioeconomic class, shapely legs, or various other characteristics. Exhibitionists also tend to be consistent in the setting and time of day they choose for exposure. In fact, many are so predictable that once reported, they are easily detected and arrested.

Offender Characteristics

The onset of exhibitionism occurs for most males at puberty, and the peak period occurs between ages fifteen and thirty (Evans, 1970). Contrary to popular belief, onset after that age is extremely rare except in the case of mental impairment due to organic factors or senility. Exhibitionists usually have at least average intelligence, although they often underachieve both educationally and occupationally. The majority appear to have a reliable work record (Mohr et al., 1964).

Psychosis and severe emotional problems are found no more frequently in exhibitionists than in the general population. Interestingly, a number of authors have commented on a positive correlation between voyeurism ("Peeping Toms") and exhibitionism (e.g. Mohr et al., 1964; Smukler & Schiebel, 1975). That is, voyeurs tend to be exhibitionists and vice versa. Although there does appear to be a moderate relationship between exhibitionism and voyeurism, there is no evidence that exhibitionists become involved in other sexual deviations or antisocial behavior.

Exhibitionists very rarely assault their audience physically, nor are they interested in heterosexual intercourse with them. It is highly probable that if the victims expressed interest in heterosexual activity, most exhibitionists would be frightened and confused and would flee. The major reason for exhibitionism is, in most cases, the sexual excitation (reward) the offender gets from shocking, surprising, frightening, or interesting his chosen audience. Observing the reactions in his victim's face and eyes generates considerable sexual arousal. Later, he will probably masturbate to that image. On the other hand, if his exposure fails to engender the anticipated frightened or surprised response from his victim, it often results in disappointment and lowered self-esteem.

Although many exhibitionists are married, the majority are considered socially and sexually inadequate both by themselves and their spouses. Many are introverted, shy, socially reserved individuals who feel uncomfortable in most social situations. Generally, they are described by others as unassertive, self-effacing, timid, and passive. A majority of exhibitionists feel the urge to expose following a blow to their fragile self-esteem, which prompts heightened feelings of inadequacy and stress. The urge to engage in sexually deviant behavior as a response to feelings of inadequacy and stress stems, in part, from 1. the feelings of adequacy they experience in controlling the exposure incident, 2. the attention they obtain from their symbol of masculinity, and 3. the contravening effect highly pleasurable and rewarding sexual activities provide for nonsexual stress. Once the urge for exposure is initiated, it is further triggered by the availability or anticipated availability of females who possess certain physical characteristics that the exhibitionist has endowed with high sexual valence.

Therefore, like other sexual offenses, exhibitionism is a learned behavioral pattern reinforced by sexual excitement and tension reduction. Many exhibitionists indicate that their behavior was initially acquired through some preadolescent sexual play or nonsexual accident. The history of a majority of exhibitionists includes a vivid memory of some young female expressing amazement or fear at their penis, particularly with regard to its size and shape, when viewed either accidentally or during sexual play. Characteristically, this attention brought sexual excitement and masturbation, accompanied by the imagery of the incident. The incident by itself is usually not sufficient enough to establish deviant behavior; rather, later, repetitive pairing of the memory of the event with the sexual arousal derived from masturbation leads to exhibitionism. Pleasurable, repetitive masturbatory activities in the presence of this mental imagery strongly encourage eventual exposure of the penis to victims who are perceived as similar to the initial observer. The intense sexual arousal experienced during real-life exposure, followed soon after by arousal reduction achieved through masturbatory orgasms, is a strongly reinforcing sequence of events. Each time the exhibitionist exposes and receives this sequence of rewards, the behavior pattern becomes that much more strongly entrenched.

When subsequent periods of stress and inadequacy crop up, exposure is one increasingly effective way of dealing with uncomfortable emotions, especially when the preferred victims are available. Therefore, because exhibitionism is a learned habit, it continues to be repetitive and relatively resistant to extinction. Exhibitionists this author has worked with had exposed many thousands of times without detection or complaint from their victims. Irritated parents of children who have seen an exhibitionist in action are the usual complainants to the police.

VOYEURISM AND FETISHISM

Voyeurism, also known as scotophilia or inspectionalism, refers to the tendency to gain sexual excitement and gratification from the observation of others in a sexual context. Voyeurs, who are almost always male, watch unsuspecting females undressing or a couple engaging in sexual relations. Fetishism, not to be confused with partialism (an exaggerated sexual interest in some part of the female anatomy), refers to a sexual attraction to objects rather than to people. For example, the individual may become sexually aroused at the sight of boots, purses, nylons, panties, fur, or even tail pipes on motor vehicles. The fetish object may be kissed, fondled, tasted, smelled, or just looked at.

Both voyeurism and fetishism are no more than minor sexual offenses, since they usually do not result in harmful consequences for members of the community. However, they may precipitate harassment, trespassing, burglary, damage, or theft of objects, and therefore require police involvement. To look out a window and see someone staring in at you can be an unnerving experience.

Recall that the voyeur is sometimes an exhibitionist, and vice versa. However, the voyeur, like the exhibitionist, does not usually become involved in other forms of antisocial behavior. Nor is there danger of a progression from minor sexual offenses to more serious ones such as forcible rape. The voyeur does not harm his victims physically, and in fact is often and accurately described as a very passive, shy, introverted, submissive, and harmless person. Clinical studies reveal that he suffers from strong heterosexual anxieties and immaturity.

However, one observation made in the Queen's Bench Foundation study (1978) demands attention. About 10 percent of the convicted rapists interviewed stated that they had watched their victim through a window or other place of observation before the rape. The authors suggested that, in view of this finding, some "Peeping Toms" should be further examined for possible rape tendencies. However, some distinguishing aspects about the voyeur-rapists should be noted. All but one had intentions of forcible rape while observing. The one rapist who indicated he did not have the intention of raping at the time admitted he did intend to "have sex." In addition, all but one of these offenders had weapons in their possession at the time (knives, guns, meat forks), even though they ordinarily did not carry them. Also, forceful entry into the victim's apartment was the common approach, and the victim was raped with extreme violence.

It is a mistake to equate these rapists with the typical voyeur. Their intention from the beginning was to attack their victim, usually with violence. Moreover, these offenders appeared to have watched the victim to determine whether anyone else was at home, the best way to get in, and the habits of the victim. The usual voyeur gets his "kicks" by watching, imagining, and masturbating with no intention of assaulting the victim.

It should be emphasized that voyeurism is considered deviant in our culture when the behavior becomes the person's exclusive and dominating outlet. Voyeurism, like other forms of sexual deviation, is a learned behavior. Although each individual acquires the tendency to view in a unique way, many report the preadolescent experience of becoming sexually aroused while watching some unsuspecting woman undress. A common theme running through clinical studies is that the mental imagery of that scene is later coupled with sexual arousal, again usually achieved through masturbation. Eventually, the masturbatory conditioning produces a desire to observe different, realistic sexual scenes. Keep in mind that an important component in the sexual thrills experienced by the voyeur is the requirement that his "victim" be unaware of his presence.

Fetishism is principally a male phenomenon in which the individual carries on his activity in the privacy of his home without interfering with others. Through classical conditioning, a variety of objects may assume sexual significance. A majority of fetish objects, however, are those worn by the female, such as undergarments, shoes, boots, or hosiery.

In an excellent demonstration of fetish conditioning, Rachman (1966) showed male subjects a slide of a pair of women's black boots, followed immediately by slides of attractive, naked women (sexual arousal). After a number of such trials, the subjects became sexually excited, as measured by erections, in response to the boots slide itself. There were also indications that the subjects not only became aroused by the particular boots, but also by slides of other boots and shoes as well.

The person with a strong attachment to a fetish might come into conflict with the law, because one of the major avenues for obtaining used fetishes is to steal—or belong to a fetish exchange club. Since clothes dryers are more in vogue in modern society than clotheslines, the fetishist's traditional method of stealing from the backyard clothesline during the evening has been replaced by more daring techniques. One is burglary. In this sense, it is conceivable that an indeterminate number of unexplained burglaries are a result of an impatient quest for fetishes! Some fetish burglars find sexual excitement just being in someone's house without their knowledge and presence. It is also not unusual for the fetish burglar to take some other object along with his fetish, either to throw off suspicion or to be able to give the police a "reasonable" explanation for the burglary if apprehended.

SUMMARY

Sexual offenders, who are usually male, are often seen by the public as sinister degenerates who prey on society, and some of its most punitive measures are reserved for them. Research evidence shows, however, that except for rapists and other sadistic offenders, who make up a small percentage of the sex offender statistics, sex offenders are actually harmless and timid and not much different from anyone else in behavior, feelings, or beliefs.

We have seen in this chapter that sexual "aberrations" such as voyeurism, fetishism, exhibitionism, and pedophilia are learned behaviors, primarily through conditioning. The individual has become conditioned to be sexually aroused by the object of his interest—be it a woman's stocking, a blond-haired child, or the shocked reaction on the face of a victim. Many of the behaviors date back to childhood. Events and stimuli which were found pleasurable and arousing in childhood are imagined in conjunction with sexual excitement, usually achieved through masturbation. Eventually, these events or stimuli become intensely linked to pleasurable experiences to the point where they are actively sought out. Sometimes, behavior directed at obtaining the events or stimuli which generate the sexual excitement runs counter to the law or to social mores.

Fetishism, exhibitionism, voyeurism, and nonviolent pedophilia are problems chiefly because of the effect they have on society and on the victims. Sex offenders do not generally progress from the "milder" offenses to the more serious rape and sadistic sexual assaults. There is no evidence to indicate that the negative effect of these behaviors is long-lasting; children, in fact, are more adversely affected by the reactions of other adults and of parents than by the exhibitionist or the nonviolent pedophiliac.

Rape, by contrast, is a violent crime which presents serious concerns in terms of prevention and treatment. We saw that there are different categories of rapists, but that all have acquired the desire to rape through socialization in some form—the media, their conceptions of what is "masculine," or their belief that women really want to be raped. The displaced aggression rapist is characterized by a need to harm and humiliate women and thus attacks his victim with violence. Compensatory rapists are passive, withdrawn, and socially inept men who desire to demonstrate their sexual competence without violence. The sexual-aggressive rapist follows many of the features of the psychopath and is basically interested in fulfilling his need for excitement and stimulation. A fourth type, the impulsive rapist, sexually assaults because the victim happens to be in a situation which offers the opportunity.

Some evidence indicates that exposure to nonviolent erotica has a positive effect on sexual adjustment; that is, sexual offenders of all types appear to have had limited, late-in-their-development exposure to sexually explicit material.

KEY CONCEPTS FOR REVIEW

    Rape
    Displaced aggression rapist
    Compensatory rapist
    Sexual-aggressive rapist

Impulsive rapist
Pedophilia
Immature child offenders
Regressed child offenders
Aggressive child offenders
Sex-pressure offender
Sex-force offender
Exhibitionism
Voyeurism
Fetishism
Partialism

MAJOR THEORISTS AND RESEARCHERS

Amir
M. Cohen
Mohr

SUGGESTED READINGS

Amir, M. *Patterns in forcible rape.* Chicago: Univ. of Chicago Press, 1971.
The classical study of the many characteristics of rape.

Cohen, M., Seghorn, T., and Calmas, W. "Sociometric study of the sex offender."
Journal of Abnormal Psychology, 1969, 74, 249–255.
A well written, psychological perspective of the personality patterns of
rapists.

Mohr, J. W., Turner, R. E., and Jerry, N.B. *Pedophilia and exhibitionism.* Toronto: Univ. of Toronto Press, 1964.
One of the most comprehensive examinations of pedophilia and exhibitionism available.

Wincze, J.P. "Sexual deviance and dysfunction," in D.C. Rimm and J. Somervill
(eds.), *Abnormal psychology.* New York: Academic Press, 1977.
A balanced, well-integrated psychological presentation of deviant sexual
behavior.

FEMALE
CRIMINALITY

TEN

The traditional studies of female criminality have remained unchallenged for too long, their ideologically informed, culturally specific explanations of the behaviour and nature of women, influencing both social research and policy, require critical reappraisal and analysis.

Smart, 1977, p. xv

Until recently, criminology has been a traditionally male enterprise, with male scientists studying predominantly male offenders. One of the most apparent reasons for this focus is that a majority of the crimes, especially the violent ones, have been and continue to be committed by males. Some contemporary feminist-criminologists (e.g., Carol Smart, 1976; Laura Crites, 1976; Freda Adler, 1975) have asserted that the lack of proper attention to female criminality reflects the general lack of scientific interest in female activities by the male-dominated criminal justice system. Judging from the theories and conclusions made in the very few documents written over the past 70 years, this allegation appears fully justified. Sexism and discriminatory attitudes permeate virtually every theoretical and empirical publication focusing on the female offender. The historical literature testifies that it was commonly believed that women are socially, psychologically, and biologically inferior creatures. Because of this inferiority and passivity, women's criminal behavior is not only rare, but also considerably easier to understand and explain. The following brief summaries will serve to illustrate this general orientation toward the female criminal.

In a classical work on the relationship between women and crime, Cesare Lombroso and his son-in-law G. Ferrero (1895) argued that women are nearer their savage origins than men and that their primitive, "natural role" is to lead inactive, domestic lives. Fulfilling this natural role has resulted in a lack of genius, poorly developed socially desirable skills, and inferior social position. Staying home by hearth and children has essentially retarded the intellectual, social, and psychological development of women. Therefore, woman's general development has lagged substantially behind the more competitive, bread-winning male, and in this sense, the theory goes, women are in most respects inferior to men. Moreover, women are generally similar to the passive ovum which awaits penetration by the sperm. They are inherently psychologically passive and unassertive, physiologically immobile, and sexually submissive.

According to Lombroso and Ferrero, women's biological and psychological natures essentially restrain them from engaging in criminal activity, and therein lies the fundamental reason for the infrequent occurrence of female crime. The few women who do become criminals are more "masculine" than noncriminal women, and because they possess the worst features of both sexes, they are considerably more ferocious and cruel than a majority of male criminals. The criminal woman, being psychologically and biologically more like the average male, also lacks a "maternal sense." Since she still possesses her natural, primitive female traits, however, she lacks a "sense of property" and thus has no compunctions about stealing or shoplifting. Presumably, this lack of property sense accounts for the high ratio of females detected in shoplifting offenses.

Otto Pollak's The Criminality of Women (1950) made a major impact on post-war perspectives on female criminality (Klein, 1973). Although he recognized the importance of social determinants, Pollak contended that the basic biological and physiological nature of women accounts for a vast majority of female crime. Specifically, in order to ensure domestic tranquillity and the propagation of the human species, females have been biologically programmed to conceal their lack of sexual arousal and enjoyment. Woman is a good actress when it comes to sexual intercourse, particularly in cleverly feigning excitement. Pollak argues that this "natural" deceit enables women to transfer deceitfulness and dishonesty to all phases of their life, including criminal pursuits. Thus, to Pollak all women are master liars and deceivers, skills which are biological by-products of concealing lack of sexual excitement. Economic factors play a minor role in female criminal behavior, while sexual-psychological factors play major roles. The kinds of crimes committed by women are largely dictated by concealment, misrepresentation, and behind-the-scenes ploys and treachery. Shoplifting and prostitution, both common female crimes, lend themselves well to object and sexual-arousal concealment. And because of the inherently deceitful nature of these crimes, along with the male-dominated criminal justice lenience toward female criminals in general, crime rates for women are markedly underreported.

The views of Lombroso and Pollak exemplify the somewhat extreme but pervasive viewpoints of many criminologists over the past 75 years or so. Although the female offender is beginning to receive increased attention from social and behavioral scientists, information concerning the relationships between women and crime is still scant. Recently the debate has focused on whether the women's movement has influenced the increased crime rate for women or whether the crime rate has indeed actually increased in relation to previously reported rates. Recent authors have delved into FBI statistics, pulled out what appears to be evidence of alarming increases in crime rates, and commented on them. Some have pointed to Manson followers Sandra Good and Lynette Fromme, to the militant female members of the Symbionese Liberation Army, the female bomb throwers of the Weathermen, or the female terrorists of West Germany. We will find, however, that these examples of middle-class, politically motivated young women differ in a number of important elements from the "average" female offender. Also, most of these female offenders responded violently through male leadership, encouragement, and power.

Some authors have asserted that any notion of psychological or physiological differences in the sexes in explaining crime rates is misguided, while others take an opposite near-Lombrosian stance. When criminologist Armand Mergen was asked by *Newsweek* magazine precisely why so many young women became violent terrorists, he responded that it was due to the "typical emotional fervor of females" (*Newsweek*, August 15, 1977, p. 30). We have a long way to go before we get a valid handle on the female offender, despite the recent interest in the area.

INCIDENCE AND TRENDS

The FBI *Uniform Crime Reports* reveal what appears to be an alarming increase in female crime in recent years. Arrest statistics show that between the years 1967 and 1976, male arrests increased 15 percent, while female arrests increased 64 percent (Kelley, 1977). The number of female arrests increased 93 percent for violent crimes—including a whopping 187 percent increase in arrests for females under eighteen for violence—and 147 percent for property crime (see Table 10–1). The specific offense of larceny-theft (which includes theft of bicycles, automobile accessories, shoplifting, pocket-picking, and other stealing without force or fraud) showed particularly large increases during the ten-year period. Among the FBI nonindex crimes, fraud, possession of stolen property, narcotic-related offenses, and driving under the influence showed substantial gain in the number of females arrested between 1967 and 1976.

As impressive as these national arrest statistics are, they are also misleading. Closer examination of the FBI arrest data shows that females accounted for about 17 percent of all the arrests for all criminal offenses and about 11 percent of all arrests for violent crimes in 1976. When we

TABLE 10–1
Arrest Trends for Female Offenders
Between 1967 and 1976, by Age

Offense	Total			Under 18		
	1967	1976	% Change	1967	1976	% Change
Criminal homicide[1]	937	1,214	29.6	53	85	60.4
Robbery	1,940	5,491	183.0	526	1,740	230.8
Aggravated assault	7,986	14,248	78.4	1,114	3,021	171.2
Burglary	6,095	12,461	104.4	3,008	6,358	111.4
Larceny-theft	73,722	188,349	155.5	34,665	73,135	111.0
Motor vehicle theft	3,341	4,697	40.6	2,243	2,735	21.8
Violent crime[2]	10,763	20,953	94.6	1,693	4,846	186.2
Property crime[3]	83,158	205,507	147.1	39,916	82,225	106.0
Other assaults	18,100	31,079	71.7	4,266	9,342	119.0
Arson	370	955	158.1	156	428	174.4
Forgery, counterfeiting	4,384	9,762	122.7	480	1,233	156.9
Fraud	9,093	31,729	248.9	317	729	130.0
Embezzlement	820	2,061	151.3	19	65	242.1
Vandalism	4,515	8,877	96.6	2,976	4,954	66.5
Prostitution	16,396	31,157	90.0	434	1,485	242.2
Narcotic drug laws	6,969	42,860	515.0	1,653	12,141	634.5
Offenses against family and children	3,870	3,500	−9.6	267	907	239.7
Curfew violations	11,482	12,824	11.7	11,482	12,824	11.7
Runaways	39,814	58,687	47.4	39,814	58,687	47.4

[1]Homicide in this table excludes manslaughter by negligence.
[2]Violent crime includes offenses of murder, robbery, and aggravated assault.
[3]Property crime includes offenses of burglary, larceny-theft, and motor vehicle theft.
SOURCE: FBI *Uniform Crime Reports*, 1977, p. 176.

look at the 1967 data, we see that females accounted for 12 percent of arrests for all criminal offenses and about 10 percent of the violent crime arrests, indicating that the female crime increase is really not all that substantial. The 5 percent increase in arrests for *all* female crimes during the ten-year period is largely due to moderately significant increments in the number of female property offenses. Specifically, females accounted for 16 percent of the arrests for property crimes in 1967, but they increased to 23 percent of the total property arrests in 1976. Overall, the most frequent crimes for which females were arrested are distinctly nonviolent and nonaggressive, and for the past three decades national statistics indicate that female *violent* crime has remained constant.

An additional factor in the apparently dramatic increases in female crime is the very relatively low base rates for many of these crimes to begin with. That is, prior to the late 1960s, reported crimes for females were so low that any relatively small increase in reported arrests would show a substantially large increase if expressed in percentages. For example, if two offenses occurred in a given year, and six additional offenses occurred in a subsequent year, the total increase in that offense would amount to 200 percent!

Despite the relatively low female increases when compared to the total crime increments for both sexes and population growth, many social scientists (e.g., Adler, 1975) claim that the so-called dramatic increases in female crime are primarily due to the women's liberation movement. Presumably, the movement has made women more aggressive and competitive and more likely to engage in violent crime as a result of re-socialization of gender roles. These contentions are simply not supported by the data. As noted by Laura Crites (1976), the women's rights movement has by and large neglected the subgroups consisting of poor, minority women, the groups that are clearly overrepresented in female offenses. "These women, rather than being recipients of expanded rights and opportunities gained by the women's movement, are, instead, witnessing declining survival options" (Crites, 1976, p. 37). Moreover, most women at the lower socioeconomic end of the scale either vocally oppose the movement or do not understand it; nor do they consider themselves a part of it. From all indications, the women's movement has been a white, middle-class phenomenon, although significantly positive steps have been made to embrace all subgroups (e.g., 1978 Women's Year Conference, Houston). On the other hand, a vast majority of female offenders come from low status occupational groups and racial minorities. About 50 percent of women in prison are black and 15 percent Hispanic, and they are drawn almost entirely from the lowest socioeconomic level (*The New York Times*, March 14, 1976). They tend to be undereducated, unemployed, and with children. Given these facts, it is difficult to justify the contention that the women's movement has directly contributed to the overall increase in female crime rates.

It is probable, however, that as women obtain more responsible, better-paying, and more professional employment as a result of the movement, certain kinds of white-collar criminal offenses such as fraud and embezzlement will increase among women. So far, the indicators have not strongly shown the emergence of this phenomenon. Embezzlement for males increased from an incidence of 3,105 cases in 1967 to 3,853 in 1976, while female embezzlement went from 820 to 2,061 incidents, which is certainly not an overwhelming increase during the ten-year interval. Female fraud arrests, however, increased from about 9,000 in 1967 to about 32,000 in 1976, while the male rate went from 30,000 to 53,000. While appearing as some support for the influence of women's liberation, the increases in fraud rates are believed to be due principally to irregularities in dealing with welfare checks and other government payments (The New York Times, March 14, 1976).

One possible spin-off from the women's movement is the way criminal justice personnel handle female offenders in general. Traditionally, police have treated female offenders leniently and paternalistically (Simon, 1975; Crites, 1976), but the rhetoric and activities of the movement may have prompted more strict handling by the criminal justice system. This change in perspective toward female offenders may account for some of the slight increases in reported arrests, although it will still mainly affect the minority, poor offender.

Now that we have discussed some of the problems with female offender national statistics and the conflicts with interpreting these crime rate data, let us address the question: have female crimes increased? The answer is yes, but proportionately no faster than the male crime rates. For example, while female property crimes have increased by approximately 122,000 arrests between 1967 and 1976, male property crimes have increased by about 226,000 during that same period of time. Considering that 51 percent of the population in this country is female, we can see that male property arrests are increasing at a faster rate than female property arrests. Except for fraud, embezzlement, and runaways, males had similar or greater increases in all criminal arrests than did females in the ten-year period. The runaways, of course, refer specifically to juvenile offenders and not to adult offenders.

FEMALE DELINQUENCY

The research on female delinquency, like that on adult female offenders, is sparse. There is little reason to believe that the *basic* learning principles involved in the development of criminal behavior are any different for girls than for boys. The socialization emphasis, however, is quite different. In spite of the influence of the women's movement, most little girls are taught to do things in a different way from most little boys; girls are expected to imitate female models, boys male models.

Statistics on total arrests of delinquents show clear sex differences. Most delinquent boys are arrested for burglary, auto theft, vandalism, and assault, whereas delinquent girls are often arrested for running away, incorrigibility, and "sex delinquency." It is difficult to ascertain precisely what these statistics mean. Certainly they reflect, in part, social and judicial biases. Research shows, for example, that boys are involved in running away, incorrigibility, and sexual acting out at least as frequently as girls are, but they are rarely reported (Gold, 1970). It should also be noted that boy delinquents are most often apprehended by the police, while girl delinquents are most often reported to the court by the parents, usually the mother (Conger, 1977).

The available research on the personality characteristics of female delinquents finds that they tend to be analogous to personality characteristics among boy delinquents (Achenbach, 1974). That is, the undersocialized, the disturbed, and the socialized delinquent are also the three common categories found among girl delinquents. The distribution among girls is different, however. The most prominent feature of girl delinquents is the manner in which they express antisocial behavior. While most boys express aggression and antisocial actions directly, most girls express aggression indirectly. The most common complaint about girl delinquents is their general antagonism and rebelliousness toward parents and others in authority. The antagonism is often expressed by stubbornness, moodiness, running away from home, sexual delinquency, and not responding well to orders. All these are relatively indirect approaches to discontent and conflict, at least compared to assaults, vandalism, arson, auto theft, and so forth displayed by male delinquents. Closer examination of the socialization processes will reveal that girls are taught not to lash out, not to fight physically, but rather to deal with anger and frustration indirectly or verbally.

Research evidence has been contradictory with reference to the effects of broken homes, absent fathers, cold mothers, or alcoholic parents on female delinquency in comparison to male delinquency. Female delinquents have found their parents wholly inadequate as conduct models, but so have male delinquents. In summary, while official statistics report clear sexual differences, the rates are probably influenced by cultural discrimination and the socialization process. It is unlikely that the learning process for girl delinquents is any different than that for boy delinquents. The manner in which aggression and antisocial behavior are expressed, however, appears to be strongly influenced by socialization. Specifically, girls act out indirectly while boys do so directly.

Types of Female Offenders

Since few attempts have been made to classify female offenders into personality types, Cathy Widom (1978) conducted a study to determine whether the more outstanding behavior characteristics of female offenders correspond to those of male offenders. She collected responses on a number of self-report personality inventories completed by 66 female offenders who were in the Awaiting Trial Unit at Massachusetts Correctional Institution (Framingham). She learned that 93.5 percent of the women had been convicted of offenses prior to their current arrest. Widom then analyzed the response data by statistical methods designed to group them into clusters which could be more easily interpreted.

Although the results are only suggestive because of the small sample, Widom found that about 6 percent of the sample had the characteristics of poor socialization, high hostility, impulsivity, low anxiety, and aggression in common. She felt that this group could fulfill the behavioral features of the psychopath described in Chapter 3. A second group, 18 percent of the sample, was found to have in common the features of impulsivity, undersocialization, high anxiety, depression, and guilt-proneness, which appear to correlate with behaviors demonstrated by the emotionally disturbed offender. Widom identified a third group which had no indications of emotional problems but did have several personality characteristics resembling the overcontrolled personality described by Megargee (1966). This group included 26 percent of the sample. Widom notes that up to now the overcontrolled personality has been neglected in the literature on female criminality. A fourth group, 26 percent of the total, had many features of the "normal criminal" in that there were no indications of unusual response patterns in the personality inventories. In many respects, this group corresponded to the socialized offender.

The psychopathic group had the most previous convictions, while the overcontrolled group had the least. Convictions for the former group included theft or larceny, prostitution, narcotic violations, forgery and check offenses, armed robbery, and homicide. Other background variables between the four groups were not notable.

The four groups resembled those reported by Blackburn (1970) with male criminals. The psychopathic group was the smallest in both the Blackburn and Widom studies. However, unlike the Blackburn offenders, Widom's females could not be distinguished on the basis of extraversion. This discrepancy might be a result of cultural differences between the American and British samples. In any event, the Widom data suggest that female offenders show personality characteristics similar to those of males.

In the rest of this chapter we shall examine the female offender in relation to the criminal behaviors of violence, prostitution, and the so-called sex-related property crime of shoplifting.

WOMEN AND CRIMES OF VIOLENCE

Socialization Factors

Crime statistics and numerous scientific papers attest to the observation and common belief that men are generally more violent and aggressive than women. Because cross-cultural studies reveal that this violence pattern holds for almost all societies, some theorists have advanced the hypothesis that violence is an innate trait in human males just as it is in subhuman males. On the other hand, they hypothesize, the female member of the animal species is innately passive, nonaggressive, and nonlethal. What the innate theorists appear to neglect is the immense cognitive capacity and learning potential of humans, which subhuman species simply do not have.

The trend today is for behavioral and social scientists to hypothesize that sex differences in human violence are a result of differences in socialization, social control, and opportunity. Contemporary theory asserts that males are taught that aggression—in some cases violence—is a mark of masculinity. Males are rewarded for assertive, competitive, and active mastery of the physical and social environment. Games and sports featuring physical prowess and competitive spirit are a hallmark, but are chiefly masculine domains. In geographical areas in which hunting is possible, the boy is often taught and encouraged to handle firearms in preparation for the hunt and participation in his gender role. He is also continually exposed to aggressive male models, both real and imaginary, such as cowboys, soldiers, football players, and gun-toting detectives.

Traditionally, the social training of the girl has been quite different. Until very recently, aggressive behavior has been considered "unladylike" and has been actively discouraged, and it still continues to be in much of the population. In most countries, girls have been more closely supervised and more strictly disciplined. An active interest in conventionally masculine sports and games still marks the "tomboy" in many social circles, often causing parental worry. Girls have been trained to handle anger-provoking situations and injustices in non-physical ways, such as dealing with them verbally, reporting them to authorities, or withdrawing. Even the female models supplied by the media still fail to measure up in aggression to male models (but, as we shall see, this is very likely to the good). Wonder Woman, Isis, and the Bionic Woman are relatively unaggressive characters compared to Superman, Batman, and other male models. The female prototype of justice-for-all exerts just enough "passive" force (repelling bullets) to terminate attacks on herself and others she protects, without appearing overly aggressive.

We have already seen that guilt, defined as expectation of social disapproval or punishment, appears to be a powerful inhibitor of aggression. A review of the contemporary research literature reveals that women express more guilt feelings (self-criticism, self-blame, and self-remorse) about aggressive behavior than men do (Frodi, Macaulay, & Thome, 1977). The greater tendency of females to feel guilty about displaying aggression strongly suggests that they receive a larger amount of conditioning opposing direct aggressive expression than do males, and that this conditioning results from some form of punishment, social control, and social disapproval from parents and peers. This socialization or conditioning process, designed to engender guilt feelings about female aggressive behavior, may account in part for the large sex differences reported for violent crime.

Although the evidence is not clear, empathy or the ability to feel with the victim is assumed to inhibit the expression of aggressive and violent behavior. Repeatedly, the evidence has favored the view that females demonstrate significantly more empathy than males (Hoffman, 1977). However, the exact relationship between feelings of empathy and aggression has not yet been adequately determined, nor have the reasons for greater female empathy been empirically sifted out. Despite the paucity of research on this relationship, it would seem that the ability to empathize with the victim is highly likely to inhibit aggression and violence directed at that victim, and that the greater tendency of females to empathize accounts for some portion of the sex differences found in violent crimes. However, the issue of why women are more empathetic than men remains unclear. Theoretical explanations range from socialization differences to innate predispositions. For example, there is evidence that newborn females are more apt to cry in response to the sound of another infant's cry than are newborn males, a finding which suggests the possibility of a constitutional precursor at birth (Hoffman, 1977). It is possible, therefore, that females are biologically preprogrammed to react empathetically to the plight of others, and that this predisposition is either attenuated or accentuated by the social environment during childhood development. There is also evidence that the socialization of boys not to cry may play a significant part in their relative lack of empathetic feeling (Hoffman, 1977). That is, there is evidence that children who openly express their own distress by crying are more apt to respond empathetically to others in distress than are children who are discouraged from crying. Boys are also taught to act rather than feel, even in situations that call for feeling.

In addition to the evidence that females show greater guilt about aggressive acts and express more empathy for the victim, there are a number of findings suggesting that males and females perceive and interpret aggressive situations differently (Frodi, Macaulay, & Thome, 1977). For example, it appears that women, compared to men, are less likely to perceive aggressive content in ambiguous material and are also less prone to interpret various kinds of behavior by others as aggressive. Also, there is evidence that females have a higher "boiling point" than males when it comes to the overt expressions of aggression (Baron, 1977). That is, males can be provoked at lower levels of insult than females. However, there is also evidence that under strong provocation the sex differences in susceptibility to react aggressively vanish.

Overall, when we examine the available aggressive models, the reinforcement patterns, and the conditioning attitudes of the American culture, we see that the opportunities to acquire aggressive and violent behavior are clearly in favor of males. Furthermore, this socialization process begins early. Aggressive behavioral patterns established at age eight appear to be by far the best predictor of aggressive behavior in later life (Lefkowitz et al., 1977). As early as age three, there appears to be a strong tendency for boys to engage in more vigorous, destructive, and aggressive play than girls (Moyer, 1973).

Researchers frequently observe that a high proportion of female as well as male delinquents come from unstable homes where parents provided poor models and offered only haphazard discipline, random reinforcement, and unsystematical, illogical conditioning regimens. In these situations, "socialization" is usually gained from peers who themselves often come from similar home situations. Of course, much of the female delinquency is not violence oriented; it is largely sexual promiscuity, running away from home, and other more passive behavioral patterns reflecting misdirected socialization from parents and peers, at least as far as society is concerned.

Biological Factors

Despite claims that socialization accounts for the sex differences in violent crime rates, there is still a substantial number of well-designed studies which continue to suggest that biological-physiological factors are also influential in producing sex differences in crime rates. As much as many social scientists play down the importance of biological variables, the relationship between biological and even genetic factors and aggression cannot be overlooked.

There is little doubt that a majority of men are larger in physical size than a majority of women, and that genes are powerful determinants of this size potential. Furthermore, large individuals are more likely than smaller ones to use their size in gaining rewards and successes by aggressive means in our society. We have seen, for instance, that mesomorphs are overrepresented in criminal and delinquency statistics, presumably because of their more muscular, rigorous stature. Although some may argue that a finger on the trigger does not take much brute strength, a life style of habitually aggressive solutions to problems and social conflicts normally does require a certain physical status. Someone of small physical stature is not likely to rely heavily on physical aggression to obtain goods, services, and social rewards, although there are exceptions.

But the research points to something beyond the genetic determination of physical size or the socialization process that may influence the tendency to aggress. We have already reviewed briefly the physiological components and systems which show a relationship with aggression, but perhaps one of the more outstanding relationships is that found between aggression and hormones. After a careful review of the existing research on aggression, Stonner concludes, in reference to human aggression: "Although the exact contribution of hormonal effects to aggressive behavior may prove extremely elusive (due to the different socialization pressures exerted on high-testosterone females or low-testosterone males), there is fairly strong evidence that male hormones do affect aggression in some manner" (1976, p. 246).

Since the bulk of the research on the effects of hormones on aggression has been conducted on subhumans, extrapolation from animal studies to humans must remain tentative. However, an overwhelming number of animal studies have shown that the male hormones of androgen and testosterone are powerful instigators of aggression (Moyer, 1971; 1973; Johnson, 1972), and their potential contribution to sex differences in human aggression must be reckoned with. It is highly likely that hormones (and other biological factors, such as nervous system characteristics) interact with social and environmental factors to produce aggression and violence.

At this point it is relevant to return to the "premenstrual syndrome" discussed in Chapter 7. As you may recall, the premenstrual syndrome refers to the cyclic physiological and psychological changes which occur prior to the onset of menstruation (usually four to seven days before). These changes may include increases in tension, irritability, depression, emotional lability, anxiety, swelling of the extremities and breasts, fatigue, and headaches. Difficulties associated with menstruation rather than premenstruation are generally referred to as dysmenorrhea. Many of the difficulties related to premenstruation and menstruation are believed to be largely due to changes in the hormonal balance between estrogen and progesterone (Tasto & Insel, 1977). During the preovulatory phase (menstrual onset to day fourteen) estrogen dominates over progesterone, and this dominance increases to a peak at day fourteen (ovulation) when the progesterone level increases and eventually dominates estrogen. Progesterone dominance appears to have the strongest association with high risks of suicide, especially violent suicide (Wetzel & McClure, 1972), hospital admissions due to depression and schizophrenia (Tasto & Insel, 1977), and crime (Dalton, 1964; Moyer, 1971). Unfortunately, the relationship between the premenstrual syndrome, or between dysmenorrhea, and violent crime has yet to be convincingly documented. The most heavily quoted study on the subject was that of Morton and colleagues (1953), and it appears to have a number of serious methodological flaws (Parlee, 1973). Morton used a sample of female prisoners and reported that 62 percent of the violent crimes committed by these women occurred during the premenstrual week and another 17 percent during menstruation itself. This study has often been cited as evidence for the existence of a significant relationship between the premenstrual syndrome and violent crime. To my knowledge, however, the Morton investigation has not been replicated.

In another relevant study, Dalton (1961) interviewed 156 newly convicted women on the first weekend after their sentencing. She reported that 22 percent of the women committed crimes during the premenstrual period (four days prior to menstrual onset), and another 26 percent committed crimes during the menstrual period. However, "crime" in the Dalton study did not refer to violent crime, but rather to shoplifting, burglary, embezzlement, forgery, and prostitution. While the increased tension, irritability, and moodiness sometimes accompanying the menstrual cycle may be related to a propensity toward violent crime or crime in general, considerable well-designed research is still needed in order to make valid judgments.

Victims and Situations

A consistent finding is that women who do murder usually choose as a victim (or victims) a member of the family, especially a child or husband, or an intimate acquaintance or lover (e.g., Hoffman-Bustamante, 1973; Ward et al., 1969). In most instances the victim is unable to defend himself or herself. Adult victims tend to be ill, drunk, or asleep, or they are caught off guard. The realization that the victim is unable to defend himself or herself strongly suggests that the act was premeditated, with expectations of success and little chance for any reprisal. Although Wolfgang (1958) found that the most commonly used weapon for female murderers was the knife, it is not entirely clear whether this pattern still exists. In any event the female's preference for the knife as a murder weapon has been taken as evidence that in her daily domestic duties this is the lethal instrument she is most familiar with and that it is the most symbolic of her gender role. It may also be simply a matter of the most available weapon in the vicinity under the circumstances.

A sizeable proportion of the murders committed by women involve their children, an act known as infanticide. In a Canadian study (Rosenblatt & Greenland, 1974), it was found that 50 percent of the women convicted of murder had killed their children, a finding which is supported elsewhere (Horoszowski, 1975; Resnick, 1970). Harder (1967) found that children are the victims of almost half the total murders in Denmark, while in England and Wales, Scott (1973) reports that about one-third of total murders were of children. In both Denmark and England-Wales, the majority were killed by the child's parents, particularly the mother.

Resnick (1970) suggests that infanticide be divided into two separate categories: 1. neonaticide, which refers to the killing of the newborn during the first day after its birth; and 2. filicide, the murder of a son or daughter older than 24 hours. According to Resnick, two-thirds of the mothers who commit filicide are psychotic, compared to only 17 percent of the women of the neonaticide group. A vast majority of the filicide group are suffering from serious depression, while very few women in the neonaticide group exhibit this feature. Furthermore, suicide attempts accompany one-third of the filicides, but rarely accompany neonaticide. Maternal depression and suicide are common characteristics reported in other studies. The Canadian study by Rosenblatt and Greenland (1974) discovered that over one-third of the mothers attempted suicide after attacking their children and that serious depression was a common diagnosis. Corroborative evidence to this effect was also reported in the Danish study by Harder (1967). One further important observation was made by the Canadian group. Prior to actually killing their children, 41 percent of the mothers expressed fear or the intention of killing to friends, physicians, or helping agencies.

A large number of the mothers indicated that their reasons for killing the children were basically altruistic. That is, the mother was convinced that she acted in the best interest of her victim and that the death would allow the child to escape from what she considered a cruel and miserable world. Apparently, the depression plaguing many of these women clouded their perspective of the world, and they desired to spare their children further unhappiness. Resnick (1970) elaborates that while altruism was the basic motive for the killing in a majority of felicide cases, neonaticide was largely the result of a desire simply to get rid of the child. The suicide in the felicide cases, therefore, may be an attempt on the part of the distraught mother to escape with her child to something better.

In a majority of the maternal child-abuse cases, the motivations are quite different. The instigating circumstances of child abuse frequently have strong indications of frustration, social and economic setbacks, marital disenchantment, and blows to self-esteem. Abusive mothers often account for the assault by explaining that the child was making excessive demands or refused to do something when the mother was under considerable frustration and stress (Bennie & Sclare, 1969). The beating of the child was intended to get him or her to mind, to stop demanding things, or to stop some kind of annoying behavior. Supporting a social learning and modeling viewpoint, a large number of studies have found that the abusive parent has often been subjected to abuse in his or her own childhood (Steele & Pollack, 1968; Spinetta & Rigler, 1972; Lascari, 1972). This finding suggests that abusive parents learn to cope with frustration compounded by what they perceive as unmanageable, demanding children by "teaching" them to mind their elders and be less demanding. A parent raised by parents who often used physical force to discipline and who grows up in a violent home environment is likely, on the basis of his or her own models, to use physical force and violence in attempting to solve family problems.

PROSTITUTION

Often called "the world's oldest profession," prostitution has held a dominant place in female criminality. In the United States, prostitution in some form is illegal in all states except Nevada (Bell, 1976). The question of whether it should be regarded as a criminal behavior has constantly been shrouded in controversy and highlighted by myths and misconceptions. Since it is presently a crime and predominantly a female one, some consideration of the relevant parameters is necessary.

Prostitution may be broadly defined as the offering, agreement to offer, or provision of sexual relations in return for money or special favors; it may involve either a heterosexual or a homosexual pairing.

More commonly, however, prostitution is restricted to the procurement of sexual intercourse with a woman by a man in return for money.

The prostitute is known under a variety of euphemistic names, including the generic "hooker" and "whore," and her turf may be referred to as the "red-light district." Hooker is believed to have derived from the band of young women who followed the encampments of troops assigned to General Joseph Hooker during the Civil War (Adler, 1975). Prostitute comes from the Latin "to stand in a place," and whore is a derivative of the Indo-European term "dear" or "friend." Specific terms are also sometimes used to classify prostitutes. For example, "streetwalker" is usually reserved for lower-level prostitutes who literally walk the streets, while "call girl" refers to high-class women who make appointments with selected clientele. Other status layers found in the subculture of the prostitute include the bar girl, the masseuse, escort, stag party worker, hotel girl, convention girl, and circuit traveler. The term red-light district is believed to be a carryover from the western railroad construction camp days, when railroad men would hang their red signal lanterns outside the tents of women with whom they were spending the night (Winick & Kinsie, 1971).

It is estimated that the number of full-time prostitutes in this country range from 250,000 to 500,000, and it is believed that their primary clientele are white, middle-class men between the ages of thirty and sixty (Haft, 1976). The fact that, nationally, only an estimated 31,000 arrests for prostitution were made in 1976 suggests that police agencies interpret the criminality of the behavior with wide and subjective latitude, depending on social and political pressures and the context within which the arrest is made. Although statistics are lacking, it is highly probable that the arrests are used as a procedural harassment with some purpose in mind other than an idealized goal to eliminate prostitution.

Theorists and researchers have long postulated many biased, subjective generalizations about the prostitute. They have variously asserted that she is feeble-minded, emotionally disturbed, a latent or manifest homosexual, oversexed, sexually deprived, a primitive creature, or someone who is rigidly fixated at her Oedipal (or Electra) stage of psychosexual development. From all indications, none of these assertions adequately describe the prostitute. The evidence shows that women who become prostitutes come from many different walks of life, possess varied educational and family backgrounds, demonstrate a wide range of personalities, and express a wide variety of motivations for prostitution involvement. Coleman (1976) finds that, as we go up the social-class structure to high-class call girls, the majority are physically attractive, intelligent, well-educated, and sophisticated young women who are convinced that they are involved in a perfectly acceptable, lucrative business.

Most prostitutes, especially at the lower-status prostitution levels, seem to come from lower-class or lower-middle-class homes. In addition, a frequent observation about their family backgrounds is that a majority come from unstable families where there was only one parent and where there was a definite alienation of the girl from her parent or parents. The mean age at which women who engage in prostitution leave home, usually because of a family dispute, is sixteen (James, 1976). In addition to their unsatisfactory home life during preadolescence, many prostitutes reported having had a very negative sexual experience in the home during their preadolescent or adolescent years. Forty-one percent said they had incestuous sexual experiences, usually with their father (James, 1976). Forty-seven percent reported they had been raped, and 17 percent had been raped more than once—most before they were sixteen years old.

On the average, prostitutes first became aware of prostitution at about age fourteen, and began prostituting with regularity at age eighteen (James, 1976). The important sources of information about prostitution were girl friends, relatives, and the neighborhood. The assumption that a majority of women are lured into prostitution under false pretenses, drugs, or force by organized crime or some brutal pimp is unsubstantiated. Available evidence reveals that only a small portion (less than 20 percent) were actively recruited by pimps, madames, or organized crime. Freda Adler (1975) points out that the contemporary prostitute is, in many instances, socially and culturally indistinguishable from women in general. "The flashy and distinctive styles of dress have either disappeared altogether or have faded into the commonplace as they have been adopted as fashion by the rest of society. It is often no longer possible to distinguish the prostitute from the matrons, college girls, or debutantes who might congregate at any public gathering" (Adler, 1975, pp. 73–74). Also, since contemporary women are no longer willing to accept sexual activity as a measure of female morality, Adler contends that a wide variety of women are pursuing prostitution as a career. She even suggests that the time may be ripe to recruit prostitutes as social workers to specialize in the treatment of sexual problems of men.

What motivates women to engage in prostitution? One of the most common answers, although perhaps an overly simple one, centers around economic considerations. Many women go into prostitution for the money. For example, James found in her revealing survey of 134 prostitutes (1976) that 85 percent said "easy money" was the primary motivation behind their commitment to prostitution. They saw it as an extremely lucrative business which enabled them to live in a way that would otherwise be unobtainable. In addition to material rewards, prostitution offers attractive social rewards—parties, dancing, restaurants, increased subcultural status, and the opportunity to know different kinds of people. Interestingly, and contrary to popular belief, only 1 percent of the prostitutes in the James study mentioned sexual gratification as either the primary or the secondary reason for entering prostitution.

The finding that sexual motivation is not an outstanding reason for entering the business damages the theory that it is a method of satisfying an inherent craving for sex or an abnormal sex drive. Furthermore, the opposite myth, which posits that prostitutes as a group are sexually frigid women, is also unsupported by the available data. In fact, data suggest that prostitutes may be more sexually responsive in their personal lives than women in general (e.g., Pomeroy, 1965; James, 1976).

A theory advanced by Gibbens (1957) that the prostitute has a burning desire to turn men into swine and treat them as dirt and with hostility (a desire which he called the "Circe complex") is also unsupported by the James data. She found that only 1 percent of her sample felt that prostitution afforded a significant outlet for hostility toward men.

The theory formulated by Greenwald (1958) and others that prostitution is a way of combating fear of homosexuality and an opportunity to prove "normality" also appears to be on shaky ground. James reports that 35 percent of the prostitutes she polled had experienced a lesbian relationship, another 7 percent had "frequent" homosexual activity, and an additional 7 percent considered themselves exclusively lesbian. Compared to the general female population, these figures appear high, but it should be emphasized that the prostitution sample was drawn from a group of individuals who felt comfortable about so-called deviant sexual behavior. Also, the prostitute's frequent economically driven encounters with men who generally regard her as a sexual robot, combined with her frequent contacts with prostitutes with similar interests and needs, may be strong prompters for homosexual contacts.

There is also little hard evidence to support the Freudian theory that prostitution is a manifestation of the Electra (or Oedipal) complex. This theory posits that prostitution is a result of early sexual love for the opposite-sex parent, and that subsequent sexual partners only represent insufficient surrogates. Presumably, the bulk of the sexual energy and attraction remains attached to the initial love object and, because later partners only serve as substitutes, complete satisfaction is unobtainable. Remaining unsatisfied, the sexually promiscuous female endlessly but subconsciously searches for the most treasured first love object—the father. Therefore, according to the Freudian perspective, prostitution is viewed as an individual psychopathology rather than as a social phenomenon. A rather consistent finding reported in the research literature, however, is that more than half of all prostitutes did not have an available father figure in the home while growing up and thus were unlikely to develop an unconscious, imagined incestuous relationship with their fathers.

To conclude this section by affirming that the reason women go into prostitution is financial, however, is premature and an oversimplification of human behavior. There is little doubt that financial gain and improved status offer extremely powerful reinforcements, but we should wonder why several million more women do not pursue the lucrative business. It would appear that other significant factors are operating besides money. Obviously, some women cannot become gainfully employed prostitutes because of restrictive marriages, moral values, geographical location, opportunity, or physical appeal. But prostitution is very likely to involve more than these parameters.

Human behavior is an infinite array of learned response patterns, and prostitution as a complex behavior should be no exception. A frequent observation is that most prostitutes "find out" about prostitution through the friends and people they know and interact with, and that they get started through the efforts and encouragement of friends. These personal contacts provide significant models and influential opportunities for imitative learning. In addition, the sex-for-sale behaviors (which also include the arts of luring and contacting "johns" or customers) must offer greater reinforcement possibilities (money, excitement, adventure) than their previous life's predicament. If the home situation is bad and the individual feels alienated from parents or parental surrogates, prostitution offers a more positive and potentially exciting alternative. Furthermore, perhaps the relationship with a pimp (or madame) who often serves as husband, boyfriend, father, lover, agent, and protector (James, 1976) is considerably more rewarding than the relationship with family.

Once these expectations and potentially rewarding behaviors concerning prostitution are acquired, continued involvement in the business will depend upon the actual rewards obtained. Do the positives of prostitution outweigh the negatives? It is hypothesized here that not all personalities are suited for long-term prostitution. Some women are better able (or better prepared) to handle different kinds of sexual contacts than others. To be habitually used solely as a sexual object would appear to require, among other things, a learned method of detachment and the availability of other sources of self-esteem, such as what might be gained from a pimp or an understanding friend. This author does not agree, for example, with the observation by Bell (1976) that prostitution is very similar to other occupations; despite the "easy" monetary gains, prostitution is a relatively emotionally stressful and psychologically draining occupation. One prostitute interviewed by Kate Millett (1974) explained: "The worst part about prostitution is that you're obliged not to sell sex only, but your humanity. That's the worst part of it: that what you're selling is your human dignity. Not really so much in bed, but in accepting the agreement—in becoming a bought person" (p. 140).

In the Jennifer James study, at least 50 percent of the prostitutes surveyed thought that emotional stress, worries about physical harm at the hands of customers, or lowered self-esteem were the primary disadvantages of their work. Stress from worrying about venereal disease, reactions of society and family, personal vulnerability, and feelings of helplessness were listed as primary disadvantages for another 20 percent.

The adaptation to a new self-concept and value system is likely to present problems for many. While recognizing that prostitution draws a wide variety of personalities, it is also highly probable that certain personalities gravitate to certain methods of soliciting. For example, there is good reason to believe that extraverted women make better candidates than introverted women because of their social skills and ability to detach or anesthetize themselves from continual sexual encounters with a variety of men. Velarde (1975) reports that primary criteria always considered by prostitution recruiters or establishments are an outgoing, charming personality and an attractive body.

SHOPLIFTING

A criminal offense closely associated with female criminality is amateur and "professional" shoplifting. Although it is estimated that between 70 and 85 percent of adult shoplifters are women (Russell, 1973), firm data to verify these estimates are unavailable. Updated studies of shoplifters, including demographic and psychological variables, are scarce. Perhaps the most heavily quoted source on the subject is Mary Owen Cameron's *The Booster and the Snitch: Department Store Shoplifting,* which examines shoplifting during the late 1940s and early 1950s in one store in Chicago. Other, more recent authoritative sources are virtually non-existent.

In addition, department stores and other businesses vary widely in their procedures concerning referral of apprehended shoplifters to the police, making comparable data acquisition even more difficult. A study by Hindelang (1974) found that whether charges were filed depended upon the retail value of the stolen object, what was stolen, and how it was stolen, and not the demographic and personality characteristics of the shoplifter. More specifically, it did not appear to matter whether the offender was male or female, black or white, poor or middle class; what determined referral for arrest was whether the item was expensive, whether it had considerable re-sale value (liquor and cigarettes), and whether the item was stolen in a professional, skillful way. These discretionary practices help mask the numerous, complex parameters involved in shoplifting. With these limitations in mind, let's examine what is known about shoplifting, particularly as it relates to the female offender.

Cameron (1964) divided shoplifters into one major dichotomy—the commercial shoplifter, which she called the "booster," and the amateur pilferer, or "snitch." Boosters are similar to other professional thieves in that they steal for substantial financial gain by skillfully taking re-sale items from prechosen locations, and they are an accepted part of the criminal subculture. The booster uses a wide range of techniques which may include a "booster box"—a package designed for concealing items inserted through hidden slots or hinged openings—or a "stall" which could be a container such as a shopping bag, a coat with hidden compartments, or an oversized purse. Some women boosters have developed the art of "crotch-walking," which is the technique of being able to walk normally while holding between the thighs stolen items, such as a large ham or a small television set.

Snitches, on the other hand, are, according to Cameron, "respectable" persons who rarely have a criminal record. They do not consider themselves criminals or thieves, and the idea that they may actually be arrested and prosecuted rarely crosses their minds. Very often, once apprehended they claim they stole the item on impulse, don't know what came over them, and find it difficult to believe what is happening. They often offer to pay for the item and promise that it will not happen again.

Boosters, however, fully understand the consequences of their actions and rarely make a fuss if apprehended. Female snitches typically take inexpensive items they can use personally, and the stolen objects are often found in a special sale or in the bargain basement. Male snitches apparently prefer more expensive items, such as books, stereo equipment, records, and jewelry. Some social scientists have suggested that these sex differences in preferred objects reflect basic differences in gender roles, with women more drawn to clothes, cosmetics, and food—all items tied to the traditional, female domestic role.

The motivations behind amateur shoplifting remain obscure. Theories concerning the intentions of snitches run from primarily economic ones or attempts to stretch the family budget (e.g., Cameron, 1964), to an attempt to satisfy unmet emotional needs centering around matrimonial stress, loneliness, and depression (Russell, 1973). The notion of shoplifting as a means to alleviate unmet emotional needs fails to hold up under logical scrutiny. The behavior gains attention, but it also becomes aversive in many cases. The belief that stealing represents an unconscious (or conscious) attempt to find a love object has not been substantiated. On the other hand, the contention that shoplifting has primarily an economic motivation appears to be an oversimplification. Shoplifting is pursued by different people for different reasons.

One thing appears clear. *Kleptomania,* or the neurotic compulsion to steal, has been reported as very rare, both by clinicians and researchers. Some have even questioned its existence as a meaningful behavioral pattern. Perhaps one of the strongest bits of evidence against a compulsion to steal is the exceedingly low recidivism rate. The amateur shoplifter rarely shoplifts again once apprehended (Cameron, 1964; Russell, 1973). If kleptomania were an important ingredient in shoplifting, we would expect the neurotically driven snitch to steal repeatedly, regardless of the number of times apprehended, and recidivism rates would reflect this.

In summary, the study of shoplifters is one of the most neglected areas of criminal research. Beliefs that shoplifting is predominantly a female endeavor, or an act pursued by the menopausal woman or the kleptomaniac have not been strongly supported by the research that is available. Although there are assertions that women far outnumber men, two recent studies refute this. Carol Smart (1976) reviewed the official statistics for England and Wales and discovered that since 1972 proportionately more men than women have been convicted of the offense. Russell (1973) notes that in his experience preadolescent and adolescent shoplifters are predominantly male.

SUMMARY

Women criminals have received short shrift in the criminological literature. Until recently, they were dismissed by theorists as either inferior creatures (Lombroso) or passive and deceitful (Pollak). Contemporary studies of the woman criminal have been more promising, but we have far to go before we approach an understanding of female crime.

Contrary to assertions by some feminist authors, there is no evidence that crimes by women are increasing any more rapidly than crimes by men. Crime in general is on the upswing, and women are entering it more rapidly than before, but proportionately crimes by women make up a steady percentage of all crimes.

The women's movement, which has been blamed (and sometimes

lauded) for an alleged increase, undoubtedly has had the effect of changing the way criminal justice personnel respond to women criminals.
However, the movement does not appear to have had an appreciable
effect on women in the lower socioeconomic classes where most female
crimes occur. With the expansion of job possibilities, the movement may
indirectly effect an increase in white-collar crime, but to date no trend in
this direction is evident.

Differences in the incidence of female compared to male delinquency
and crime appear to be largely due to the socialization process, especially the way girls are taught to deal with frustration and conflict.
Society continues to indoctrinate girls to cope with conflict by indirect,
relatively passive action, while boys are encouraged to be more aggressive and direct. Redefinition of male and female "roles," already in
progress, may bring about considerable change in the socialization
process. What effect this new awareness will have on female criminality
remains to be seen.

Personality characteristics of female offenders need much more study,
but some of the research to date illustrates few personality differences
between men and women criminals. That is, the woman offender is as
likely to be psychopathic, or as frustrated or emotionally disturbed as the
male.

Crimes of violence by women appear as rare today as they did in
earlier times. Part of the reason for the lack of violence is due to the
socialization process, but there are also physiological differences between men and women which cannot be ignored in the studies of causal
factors of crime. Hormonal differences between males and females may
play an important role, although socialization appears to be the predominant factor.

When women are arrested for violent crimes, the victims are most
often their children, husbands, lovers, or other close acquaintances. We
saw, too, that the methods and weapons of women murderers are significantly different from those usually used by male murderers. Motivations for child abuse also differ considerably from those for infanticide.

Prostitution, often viewed as a victimless crime, accounts for a good
percentage of the statistics on women and crime. The myths of the
oversexed, the undersexed, the latent homosexual, or the intellectually
inferior woman have been laid to rest, with current research suggesting
that a prime factor for women's entering into prostitution is economic. It
is, of course, far from the only factor.

More research is needed regarding specific crimes committed by
women. Shoplifting, for example, has been believed to be predominantly a female offense, but research has brought this belief into question. The theory that shoplifting is often a behavior engaged in to satisfy

unmet emotional needs, or a form of kleptomania, has also not been supported by the few studies thus far conducted.

KEY CONCEPTS FOR REVIEW

Women's liberation and crime
Female criminal personalities
Sex socialization
Premenstrual syndrome
Neonaticide
Filicide
Prostitution
Shoplifting
Booster
Snitch

MAJOR THEORISTS AND RESEARCHERS

Pollak
Crites
Widom
Adler
James
Cameron

SUGGESTED READINGS

Adler, F. *Sisters in crime.* New York: McGraw-Hill, 1975.
The classic work on female criminality written in a clear, easy, flowing style.

Crites, L. (ed.). *The female offender.* Lexington, Mass.: Lexington Books, 1976.
A collection of articles dealing with the judicial process and how it affects female criminality.

Simon, R. *Women and crime.* Lexington, Mass.: Lexington Books, 1975.
A well-documented, comprehensive presentation on the female offender.

Smart, C. *Women, crime and criminology: A feminist's critique.* London: Routledge & Kegan Paul, 1976.
A well-documented and contemporary overview of female criminality from a British perspective.

SPECIAL OFFENSES

ELEVEN

Because the criminal is more the 'master of his own fate,' he is less likely to feel himself directed by strange and uncontrollable forces.

Halleck, 1967, p. 76

We shall examine in this chapter the violent offenses of hostage-taking, arson, robbery, and the property offense of burglary which, because of their uniqueness and overlap with other offenses, did not quite qualify as appropriate topics within earlier chapters. As in other types of crime, however, the perpetrators of these special offenses perceive their act as a means of gaining something personally and subjectively meaningful. Many of the offenders involved in hostage-taking, for example, primarily desire recognition, significance, and change and control over their lives. People who participate in robbery and burglary seem to be motivated by economic reasons; arsonists may demonstrate a combination of motives, such as revenge and money.

The concept of psychological control is an extremely important one which appears to play a major role in the motivations of many special offenders, especially hostage-takers. It is also a relatively new concept in the field of psychology and is in the process of being revised and reformulated. Because of the significance of control to special offenses, we will begin this chapter by becoming familiar with some of its features.

CONTROL

A rapidly growing body of psychological research is demonstrating that one of the most ubiquitous of all human motives is to gain control over one's environment (Harvey & Smith, 1977). Apparently, people must feel that they have an effect on events and have control over what happens to them; if they feel they have lost control, or that their behavior has little effect, they become helpless and depressed or adopt other maladaptive patterns (Seligman, 1975). When the sense of helplessness becomes widespread and intense, people may become profoundly depressed and apathetic and may entertain thoughts of suicide. They may feel so hopeless that even their motor behavior slows down. Depressed people believe that their actions have very little influence on changing things, and they make little effort toward producing change. Depressed persons may "mope" and fail to find interest in any activity. If, however, an event occurs where they again feel that their behavior does make a difference, the depression may begin to dissipate. This is why therapists advocate that depressed persons "get out and do something." Increasing the responding rate increases the probability of response success in controlling events. In some therapies, the clinician will even encourage anger, because at least the person is doing something and may begin to feel more effective.

If persons determine that the events which happen to them are independent of their responses (helplessness), they then make an attribution about the cause (Abramson *et al.*, 1978). Is the lack of influence due to their own inability or is it due to the environment?

Let's suppose you are taking a course that is crucial for you to pass. You find you like the course content, but regardless of how hard you study, you consistently fail exams. Eventually, you begin to feel helpless about improving your grade. When the grades are posted you find each time that out of 50 students you are the only one flunking the course. Under these conditions you are likely to attribute the cause of your helplessness to your own inability and may conclude that you are simply stupid. However, if everyone else is also flunking the course following intensive study, you are less likely to attribute the cause of your helplessness to yourself—it's the fault of the professor, the exams are too difficult, you may even begin to think that the professor is the stupid one. When you attribute the cause of your helplessness to people or events outside yourself, you are participating in *external attribution*; *internal attribution* is attributing the cause to yourself. Realize that there are two related events here: first, feeling the helplessness, and second, locating the cause.

Living under dire poverty conditions where the opportunity to get out of one's plight is limited is conducive to feelings of helplessness. However, how a person copes under these conditions depends upon his or her attribution of cause. Research has shown (e.g., Abramson et al., 1978) that people who attribute the source of their helplessness to themselves are more apt to have lower levels of self-esteem than those who attribute the cause to external agents. It appears much easier to deal with uncontrollable events when everyone else is in the same situation, as might happen, for instance, in an extensive natural disaster such as a flood. Conversely, when one is personally responsible for his or her own helplessness, this produces not only lowered self-esteem but also depression and feelings of wanting to give up.

Individuals have adapted to a sense to helplessness under poverty or limiting situations by attributing the cause of these problems to the system, to government, to politicians, or to other external agents. External attribution provides some relief from helplessness and helps one deal with depression and cope with the environment.

Before discussing the helplessness-crime relationship, we should also distinguish between *general* and *specific* feelings of helplessness (Abramson et al., 1978), terms which refer to how widespread or generalized attributions are. *General helplessness* is attributing the source of helplessness to a broad range of circumstances; *specific* is attributing the source to a certain situation (see Table 11–1). Under conditions of specific helplessness a person feels that, while things are hopeless in this situation, things are not so hopeless in others. Young criminals may be operating under specific helplessness situations, while older crimi-

TABLE 11-1
Examples of Control as a Function of Internal-External Attribution and Generality of Attribution

Range of Attribution	Internal (Self)	External (Others)
General	I lack intelligence and social competence.	Society does not care. There is a lack of opportunity in American society.
Specific	I hang around with the wrong people.	New York City discriminates.

nals may be functioning under the general type, especially following experiences with the criminal justice system and incarceration. This phenomenon might account for the relationship consistently reported between age and crime; the higher rates for the young might reflect their retaining some hope of changing their predicament.

Research on control and feelings of helplessness to date has focused on the clinical problem of depression and its treatment and has not yet been directed at criminal behavior. It would appear, however, that one of the most important psychological components in understanding criminal behavior is control and personal attribution of cause. Crimes involving hostage-taking, arson, and bombing seem especially closely related to attempts at mastery and control over fate. For example, hostage-taking incidents, when not specifically for economic gain, often include offenders' alternating suicidal threats with controlling behaviors. Many hostage-taking incidents appear to be desperate attempts on the part of the hostage-taker to become competent and have mastery over the environment.

Why one person skyjacks an aircraft full of hostages, another resorts to moping and inactivity, and another to suicide under feelings of helplessness depends upon expectations and attribution of cause. Terrorists may skyjack because they attribute the cause to a government or social system which engenders helplessness, while the lone, depressed skyjacker may be attributing the feeling of helplessness to his or her own incompetence. Very often, a hostage-taking incident by an individual is precipitated by a series of blows to his or her feeling of control and competence. It appears to be very important to understand this psychological motive when dealing with hostage-takers who are not principally motivated by economic gain.

The more generalized the feelings of helplessness across situations, the less convinced one is that behavior will change things for the better. A suicidal skyjacker may still feel that he or she can affect the environment in some way; otherwise the skyjacking would be completely meaningless from his or her perspective. A skyjacker who does not contemplate suicide probably has feelings of helplessness which are less generalized and more specific; that person would probably be more convinced about the effectiveness of his or her behavior for gaining some control.

The discussion above must remain hypothetical until research is conducted on helplessness as it is related to criminal behavior. However, the reader should keep in mind that the issue of psychological control may enter into some of the following offenses in a crucial, but as yet poorly understood way.

HOSTAGE-TAKING OFFENSES

The hostage-taker holds victims against their will and uses them as objects for material gain or personal advantage. Typically, this offender threatens the lives of the victims if certain demands are not met within a specified time interval. Hostage-taking includes skyjacking, kidnapping, and terrorism.

FIGURE 11-1. Law enforcement authorities unearth a buried moving van in which 26 children and their school bus driver had been held captive after their July, 1976, abduction in California.

Murray Miron and Arnold Goldstein (1978) divide hostage-taking offenses into major categories based upon the offender's primary motivation: *instrumental behavior* and *expressive behavior*. Instrumental acts involve some recognizable, material gain for the offense, such as when a kidnapper abducts a child to obtain a ransom. Expressive hostage-taking is done not so much for material gain but more for the psychological gain of significance and control. Very often, the expres-

301

sive offender feels that he or she has little control over what happens and would like to change this. The offender wants to become important and believes that media coverage will achieve this. To the observer, the acts of the expressive offender often seem senseless and even suicidal. A skyjacker who demands that a pilot fly an aircraft full of passengers from one continent to another is an example.

Offenses sometimes begin as instrumental acts but develop into expressive ones. A perpetrator who originally takes a hostage for material gain may find that his or her demands are unrealistic and beyond the power of the authorities; in this case, the person may decide to play out the scenario for the attention, significance, and control it provides over others. Sometimes both instrumental and expressive motives are clearly involved in the hostage-taking from the beginning. That is, the perpetrator expects both material and psychological gain from the abduction.

We will focus on terrorism and skyjacking as two contemporary offenses that illustrate hostage-taking. The processes in noneconomic kidnapping, however, are the same as those found in these offenses.

Terrorism

Miron and Goldstein tell us that a large percentage of the acts by terrorists are in the form of expressive suicide. Specifically, the sole purpose of the terrorists is to establish the significance and importance of themselves as heroes and martyrs through heavy media coverage. Very often, the motives of self-importance are masked by lofty proclamations of some political cause.

An illustration of control and self-aggrandizement appears in the following terrorist incident, which also happens to be a skyjacking. On October 13, 1977, a Lufthansa Boeing 737 twin jet bound for Frankfurt and carrying 82 passengers was commandeered by four terrorists (two men and two women). During the 110-hour ordeal, the terrorists ordered the pilot to fly from Palma on to Rome, Cyprus, Bahrain, Dubai, Aden, and finally to Mogadishu. Soon after the airliner was diverted from its original destination, the leader (who called himself Captain Mahmoud) declared that he was in control by screaming into the open radio that the aircraft was under his "supervision and control" (Time, October 31, 1977). The terrorists repeatedly threatened to blow up the plane if anyone refused to do what was demanded. One passenger later explained that Mahmoud constantly threatened to execute anyone who questioned his control (Newsweek, October 31, 1977). The terrorists did not seem to have clearly specified plans or objectives, and several times they appeared indecisive and unsure of themselves. At one point, only

40 minutes before the first of the terrorists' several deadlines for blowing up the plane, they demanded that it take off for an unknown destination. Ostensibly the terrorists were demanding the release of eleven other terrorists imprisoned in West Germany; however, their plans were not well constructed and they had no solid method of determining whether the eleven prisoners were actually released.

FIGURE 11-3. Terrorists bombed the TWA terminal at La Guardia Airport in December 1975. The blast caused 11 deaths and 53 injuries.

Passengers found the terrorists, especially Mahmoud, unpredictable and frantic throughout the incident. Mahmoud at one point shouted, "I am going to kill them all" into the open radio (*Newsweek*, October 31, 1977, p. 53). At another point he dragged three suspected-Jewish girls from their seats and told them that they would be executed the next day; he then changed his mind, proclaiming himself a "freedom fighter," not a "terrorist." At another point Mahmoud caught a passenger's eye, leveled a pistol at him, and sneered, "I don't like your face."

After an emergency landing, the Lufthansa pilot asked to check the landing gear. He was permitted to do so, but this so enraged the leader that he accused the pilot of trying to escape, forced him to kneel in the aisle and beg for mercy, then shot him in the face in full view of the terrified passengers.

After a number of missed deadlines, the terrorists brought matters to a head by dousing the passengers with liquor, tying them, fixing plastic charges inside the plane, and demanding that the eleven prisoners be released immediately. Informed that this had been done, the terrorists extended the deadline seven hours, the time it would take for the prisoners to be flown to meet them. Jubilant, Mahmoud told the hostages not to take personally what happened to them. It was, he told them, just part of the struggle against "imperialism and Zionism" (*Newsweek*, October 31, 1977, p. 54).

Whether the hostages would have been executed is anyone's guess. Before the final deadline expired, a crack team of West German commandos boarded the plane and quickly killed three of the confused terrorists, and critically wounded the fourth, Mahmoud's woman friend. As she was carried out of the aircraft on a stretcher, she flashed the "V" sign for victory. Unless we consider the significance and attention the incident received, it is difficult to determine precisely where the "victory" lies.

An hour after hearing of the unsuccessful mission of his comrades, Andreas Baader (the co-founder of the Baader-Meinhof gang) committed suicide along with two fellow terrorists in their prison cells. A fourth gang member stabbed herself in the chest and throat with a prison breadknife, but she survived.

Throughout the incident it was difficult to discern what the instrumental goals of the terrorists were. They jumped from one ambiguous cause to another—Jews, society, government, and authority. By all indications, Miron and Goldstein may be correct in their contention that the work of terrorists is primarily expressive suicide. In a *New York Times* editorial (October 30, 1977, p. 17) shortly after the event, Henry Brandon concluded ". . . among the adherents of Andreas Baader and Ubrike Meinhof no apparent aim or ideology can be found except hatred of political stability, of economic affluence and of middle-class aspirations." He called their motives "politics of hatred."

The Lufthansa incident demonstrates a situation where the hostage-takers had little chance of success or personal safety and where events continually included threats of death for the hostages and suicide for the offenders. The terrorists' primary aim appeared to be to frighten and dominate the hostages and all those who observed. The events represented in large part an array of histrionics designed to gain maximum media coverage to show the importance and power of the group. If anyone threatened this perspective of power, the terrorists generated events which showed observers who was really in control. For example, unexpected take-offs and landings, shooting the pilot, and not allowing anyone, including children, to deplane at any point were all control maneuvers. Despite this display of power and control, the terrorists manifested a remarkable inadequacy for problem solving throughout the ordeal, a characteristic that Miron and Goldstein emphasize in discussing expressive hostage-taking.

There were 239 separate terrorist attacks in 1976 ranging from bombings to kidnappings to assassinations (including 61 attacks on U.S. citizens or property); this compares to only 37 in 1968 (Newsweek, November 14, 1977). Between the years 1967 and 1975, terrorists the world over took 800 lives and wounded 1,700 persons (Time, October 31, 1977, p. 41).

In 1977 it was estimated that there were 140 terrorist organizations throughout the world (Time, October 31, 1977, p. 45), 50 of which were well organized (Kupperman, 1977). Many, like West Germany's Baader-Meinhof, Red Army Faction, or Italy's Red Brigades, seem to seek to destroy the society they live in and give little coherent thought to ultimate goals. In most terrorist groups a definitive ideology is nonexistent.

The lack of clearly established purposes or goals characteristic of most terrorist groups implies that their motives may be predominantly expressive or based on needs for excitement. Possibly, they may also represent desperate attempts at gaining control over their fate and social environment. In fact, in most cases of terrorist attacks, the behavior suggests more a reaction to helplessness than any concerted effort toward governmental or ideological reform.

The intense fear terrorists try to establish in the public and hostages, and the lives they sometimes take indiscriminately, certainly signify that many are not at high levels of moral development. People at high levels of moral development are unlikely to endanger or take innocent lives, regardless of how lofty the ideology may be. Many investigators have also noted that terrorists are often educated, middle-class youths, many of whom are women (Kupperman, 1977), who have become disenchanted and depressed with their way of life. The middle-class disenchantment may be a result of feeling powerless in a society they believe to be misguided.

Skyjacking

Although the Baader-Meinhof incident described above happened to be a skyjacking, it had features primarily reflective of terrorism. In this section, we shall consider skyjackings which are perpetrated primarily out of the offender's wish to gain individual significance and control rather than out of ideological motives.

The first recorded skyjacking took place in 1930 when a group of political activists in Peru seized a plane and used it to shower sections of Peru with propaganda pamphlets (Arey, 1972). Following the Peruvian skyjacking and up to 1961, there were a total of 32 skyjackings throughout the world, although none of them involved American aircraft. On May 5, 1961, shortly after the Bay of Pigs invasion, the first American aircraft was skyjacked when Antilio Ortez, armed with knife and revolver, demanded that the pilot of a National Airlines Convair 440 fly him to Cuba. His expressed intention was to warn Castro of an assassination attempt, information he apparently thought would gain him special recognition in the leader's eyes. The plane landed successfully in Cuba, Ortez left it, and he was never heard from again; after a couple of hours the airliner was allowed to return to Florida. On July 24 of that same year, Wilfredo Oquendo took over an Eastern Airlines Electra with 38 aboard and diverted it from its Tampa destination to Havana.

These first two American skyjackings appear to be primarily instrumental in that each offender desired transportation to Cuba. For the next incident the intentions were not quite so clear, however. Without a ticket, Bruce Britt boarded a Pacific Air DC-3 bound from Chicago to San Francisco on July 31, 1961. Armed, he demanded that the airliner change its flight plan to Arkansas so that he could see his wife. He then shot a passenger agent who attempted to pursue him, and he shot the pilot, who had refused to take off. Fortunately, Britt was disarmed by the co-pilot and a number of passengers before any further incidents.

A trickle of skyjacking continued until the epidemic years between 1968 and 1978. In 1968, there were 36 skyjackings, 20 of these involving American aircraft, with most diverted to Cuba (Arey, 1972). The contagion effect became even more apparent in 1969 with 71 skyjackings, 58 of which were diverted to Cuba from the United States and other parts of the world. Some skyjackers were homesick Cubans, some claimed to be political activists, but most apparently wanted to be someone significant and newsworthy. Sixty-nine skyjackings occurred in 1970, and similar frequencies continued until the United States began to clamp down on airport security. During the years 1973 and 1974, for example, only four American aircraft were involved in skyjackings, none of which turned out to be successful in terms of getting the skyjacker flown to the desired destination (Civil Aeronautics Board, 1975).

Because of the rash of skyjackings in the late sixties and early seventies, Federal Aviation Agency psychologist John T. Daily began to develop a "behavioral profile" to help identify the potential skyjacker before he or she boarded the plane. Daily and Pickrel (1975) found that, in general, skyjackers were different from the usual air traveler in such aspects as socioeconomic class and mannerisms in the airport terminal. They found that the "typical" skyjacker was generally an unsuccessful member of society, inadequate socially and occupationally, lacking in resourcefulness, and appeared to have substantial feelings of helplessness. Apparently, the skyjacking was a way of improving his or her situation and gaining some control and significance in the world.

Specific characteristics are not disclosed to the general public, since to do so would compromise the usefulness of the profile. However, the basis of the profile lies in the differences between the potential skyjacker and the *usual* air traveler. We would expect the usual traveler to be rather blase about the routine of waiting to board the plane, unless it was a first-time trip. The potential skyjacker, depending upon his or her motives for the incident, is apt to be different in mannerisms, arousal, and dress.

Comments

Miron and Goldstein issue some thoughtful considerations and suggestions for handling the hostage-taker. First, offenders should be denied the excitement and stimulation they hope to initiate; this requires that a potentially chaotic situation should be made calm and orderly as much as possible. Moreover, high arousal and excitement tend to disorganize people's response patterns (Broen, 1968), rendering them anything but level-headed. Therefore, highly aroused captors are apt to do things they normally would not do under less stressful conditions. Miron and Goldstein advocate that the police not overreact to hostage-takers, but only utilize as much personnel as absolutely necessary. In addition, the media should be careful about accelerating the incident by adding excitement and importance with lights, cameras, and commentators.

Second, the offenders must *feel* that they are in some control of the situation. One of the things that has been pointed out about hostage-takers is their feeling of helplessness and powerlessness, which probably stimulated the hostage-taking to begin with. If captors do not feel that they are gaining control, they may show onlookers they can do so. For example, they might shoot one of the hostages and throw the body out to be seen.

Third, in hostage situations time can be a good ally. Once the early minutes of a crisis are passed and some stability and calm have been brought to the incident, the passage of time can play a positive role. Time does a number of things. Following the initial high levels of excitement and stress, the body winds down, eventually to a point where the person feels tired, sluggish, and depressed. Under these conditions the event takes on some aversive properties which the person would like to escape from. Time also affects the relationships between the persons involved in the situation. Social psychological research has shown that the more familiar one is with an object or person, the more one tends to become attracted to it (e.g., Freedman et al., 1978). Of course, this relationship continues up to a point where excessive long-term familiarity may breed contempt. In most hostage situations, however, the more the victim and the captor get to know one another, the more they tend to like one another. This phenomenon indicates that after a period of time the offender is less likely to harm the hostage.

The attraction between victim and captor is called the Stockholm effect, after an incident in Sweden where one of the female hostages fell in love with and married one of her abductors. Police negotiators have noted that on occasion the hostages will side with their captors in working out demands. It is possible that the Patricia Hearst kidnapping on February 4, 1974 resulted in a similar process. Rather than being "brainwashed," she might have developed an attraction for her captors and temporarily identified with their values and goals.

How can a hostage-taking incident, which by its very nature is stressful, generate attraction? There is evidence to indicate that, besides the effects of mere exposure increasing attraction for an object or person, unpleasant emotion may also intensify attraction (Middlebrook, 1974). Research by Stanley Schachter (1971) has suggested that when a person is physiologically aroused he or she may have difficulty labeling the emotion, because a number of different labels might be appropriate. It does not seem to matter whether the arousal is from a negative set of circumstances or from positive ones. For example, sexual deprivation may lead to physiological arousal that is labeled love. The same procedure may operate in a highly arousing hostage-taking incident, where the familiarity of the people combined with high arousal leads to attraction on the part of the hostage-taker and the victim.

Of course, if the victims or the kidnapper are deindividualized by hoods or masks, then the incident is less likely to develop into mutual attraction. Also, ideals and purpose may override any notion to see the victims as people, as in the case of some acts of terrorism.

ARSON

Arson is the "willful and malicious burning of another's property or the burning of one's own property for some improper purpose such as defrauding an insurer" (Boudreau et al., 1977). Arson has become the nation's fastest growing crime (Newsweek, January 24, 1977). The number of deliberately set fires in 1976 exceeded 100,000 a year—triple the rate of ten years earlier—and caused more property losses ($1.4 billion) than any of the major property crimes (Boudreau et al., 1977). Arson is a violent crime as well as a property crime. Intentionally set fires killed 1,000 persons in 1975, including 45 firefighters, and injured about 10,000 (Teague, 1976).

Arson losses do not include buildings alone, but also motor vehicles, forests, and watershed areas. In 1975, $80 million were lost to motor vehicle arson and about $60 million to incendiary forest fires.

There is a wide variety of motives for arson, including profit, revenge, spite, jealousy, crime concealment, intimidation, vandalism, and excitement. Most of the fires set by juveniles appear to be for the same motives as those found in vandalism: getting back at authority, the dare, status-seeking, and general excitement. The predominant motive for adult arsonists appears to be revenge. John Boudreau and his colleagues (1977) list six important motives for arson and also try to estimate their relative frequencies:

1. The first is revenge, spite, or jealousy. Arsonists in this category include jilted lovers, feuding neighbors, disenchanted employees, and people who want to get back at someone who they feel cheated or abused them. Alcohol is frequently associated with this motive; that is, the arson was committed while the offender was drinking heavily (Inciardi, 1970). Robbins and Robbins (1964) found that revenge accounted for 47 percent of the fires set by adults compared to only 5 percent of those set by juveniles. Inciardi found that 58 percent of his adult arsonists set fires for revenge.

The case of Caesar, who is serving time in a maximum security prison, illustrates the revengeful arsonist quite well.

He is an eighteen-year-old Puerto Rican, small in stature, but highly aggressive in his approach to people. Friends described him as always having a chip on his shoulder and always wanting "to be somebody." He dropped out of school in the sixth grade and can neither read nor write. He was born in Puerto Rico, the tenth of sixteen children, and his parents migrated to Harlem when he was five. His family remained intact, but lived under extremely crowded and poor conditions.

Caesar was arrested and convicted at age fourteen for armed robbery of a pawn shop and was placed on probation. Later that year he was arrested for assault with a deadly weapon (a knife) but the case was dismissed because the victim dropped the charges. At age fifteen he was again arrested for assault, and again the charges were dismissed for the same reason. Several other arrests followed: trespassing, breaking and entering, all of which were dismissed.

At age seventeen Caesar was refused entry into a night club on the basis of his being a member of a violent gang. He had a scuffle with the doorman, who quickly won out. Caesar then found three empty quart beer bottles in a nearby alley and filled them with gasoline he siphoned from a car. He stuffed tightly twisted newspaper into the top of each bottle, carefully lit one at a time, and threw them through three separate windows of the nightclub. Twenty-five customers were burned to death in the ensuing inferno, and another ten were critically hurt. Caesar was apprehended at the scene and eventually convicted on 25 counts of murder, arson, and assault.

Caesar admitted in an interview that his primary aim was to close the place down. He did say that he did not care whether the owner died in the fire (he in fact escaped). He said he was angry at the time, had been drinking, and really did not stop to think about the distant consequences of his actions. He only wanted instant revenge. Caesar felt that the next time he would be more direct in getting to those responsible rather than "killing all those people." Prison records have him diagnosed as "dyssocial, with features of pyromania."

2. Vandalism or malicious mischief are also motives expressed or otherwise uncovered in arson. Incendiary fires protesting authority or relieving boredom are by far the most common for juveniles. The Robbins study reported that 80 percent of the fires set by juveniles stemmed from this class of motives.

3. Crime concealment or diversionary tactics. At least 7 to 9 percent of convicted arsonists are believed to be trying to obliterate the evidence of burglaries, larcenies, and murders (Robbins & Robbins, 1964; Inciardi, 1970). The offenders in this category expect that the fire will destroy any evidence that a crime has been committed. The intent may be to destroy paper which contains evidence of embezzlement, forgery, or fraud. Arson has also been used to divert attention while the perpetrator burglarizes another building.

4. Profit, insurance fraud: Studies show that this category constitutes one of the smallest motives expressed by convicted arsonists.

However, since the profits gained from this activity are large and the probability of detection small, the actual incidence rate is believed to be much larger than the reported statistics. Arsonist offender characteristics consistently reported in the literature include below-average intelligence and a tendency to be socially and vocationally unskilled. In addition, heavy alcohol consumption and high arousal (revenge), which disorganizes response patterns, most often accompanied fire setting by convicted arsonists. It is reasonable to assume, however, that arson for profit is usually performed with intelligence, knowledge, and careful planning, and thus has very low probability of detection.

The Boudreau et al. review noted that there were a surprising number of ways to profit from arson. If the property is insured for more than its fair market value, burning it for financial gain from the insurance company is a powerfully reinforcing alternative. Another frequent plan is to destroy property of a company that has an overstock of goods and which is floundering financially or handicapped by poor management, obsolete merchandise, or the need to renovate to meet fire and safety standards. In some instances, a professional "torch" is hired to carry out the job while the insured is conveniently out of town.

5. *Intimidation, extortion, sabotage:* This category refers to fires set by striking workers or employers to intimidate the other side, by others who wish to intimidate witnesses, or by extortionists. By most accounts, the frequency of this motive is extremely low.

6. *Pyromania and other psychological motives:* Pyromania is a psychiatric term for an "irresistible urge" or passion to set fires. Although the term is out of vogue in much of psychiatry, having been replaced by "impulsive firesetting," it continues to be used with frequency in the criminal justice system. Still, the existence of the "compulsive firesetting syndrome" as a distinct entity remains very much an open question.

Pyromania was originally coined in the early nineteenth century to designate a form of insanity identified by the impulse to set fires without apparent motive (Schmideberg, 1953). Around the mid-1800s clinicians noted a relationship between firesetting and sexual disturbances, a practice which is still very evident in the psychoanalytic literature. For instance, Gold (1962, p. 416) contends that the roots of arson are "deep within the personality and have some relationship to sexual disturbance and urinary malfunction." Abrahamsen (1960, p. 129) writes: "Firesetting is a substitute for a sexual thrill, and the devastating and destructive powers of fire reflect the intensity of the pyromaniac's sexual desires, as well as his sadism."

The more orthodox psychoanalytic thinking specifies a connection between pleasurable urination (urethral eroticism) and firesetting. For example, Otto Fenichel (1945, p. 371) concluded: "Regularly deep-seated relationship to urethral eroticism is to be found. . . . In the same way that there are coprophilic perversions based on urethral eroticism, perversions may also be developed based on the derivative of urethral eroticism, pleasure in fire." This theory is based in part upon the observation that many firesetters are or have been enuretic (bedwetters) (Halleck, 1967). This does not mean that all enuretic people are firesetters, only that firesetters appear to have more than their share of bedwetters. Precisely what the fire-enuresis relationship means and how strong it is must await further research. Most of the evidence to date is based on anecdotal case summaries of three or four "pyromaniacs" interviewed by clinicians with theoretical biases.

The relationship between sexual arousal and firesetting is plausible, especially when we consider that through the process of classical conditioning virtually any object or event can become associated with sexual arousal and gratification. The fact that some arsonists have been found to have fetishes or previous arrests for sex offenses (MacDonald, 1977) lends some support to this possibility. Thus, individuals who are sexually aroused by fire are most likely highly conditionable introverts. We would also expect them to be sexually, socially, and vocationally inadequate (an observation which has already been made by Levin, 1976), since the offender perceives firesetting as a way of becoming significant and resolving conflicts.

One of the problems with clinical research thus far has been the prejudicial tendency to interpret statements made by firesetters. A vast majority of so-called pyromaniacs have said that the fire and the commotion following it were "thrilling," "stimulating," and "exciting." The psychoanalytic clinician far too often interprets these statements as unconscious expressions of sexual arousal and gratification when they may be nothing more than what the offender says they are—"thrilling." Depending on the theoretical orientation of the investigator, some research reports have as many as 30 percent of firesetters reported as pyromaniacs (e.g., Robbins & Robbins, 1964), while others (e.g., Inciardi, 1970) find no pyromaniacs, simply a sizeable number of excitement seekers.

While some firesetters may obtain sexual arousal and gratification from some specific aspect of the fire, there is very little evidence that a significant number do. For example, in an extensive analysis of 68 convicted arsonists in institutions in Florida, South Carolina and North Carolina, there was no evidence of more sexual abnormality than in a comparable group of controls (Wolford, 1972). Certainly, a fire attracts many people: a building in flames draws large crowds that often hamper fire fighting operations. There have been some instances where volunteer firemen or even police officers have started fires to become heroic, breach the boredom, or try out new fire-fighting equipment (Inciardi, 1970; MacDonald, 1977). However, whether people are drawn to fire because of sexual needs is very much an open question.

In addition to the excitement and general arousal fires generate, fires may provide a means of control and power over the environment. Seeing a raging fire and the equipment it necessitates is likely to promote feelings of power for an individual who feels inadequate and powerless. While the firesetter desires to see the event he or she generated, the fire often spreads more quickly and extensively than the person had intended. In some instances, unintended injury or death occurs.

BOMBING

"During the early morning of January 24, a high-order explosive detonated in a restaurant in New York City. Fifty-three persons were injured and four persons were killed. Monetary damage was estimated at $300,000. After the incident, a group advocating independence for Puerto Rico claimed credit for the bombing" (U.S. Department of Justice, 1976, p. 18).

"Six persons were killed as the result of a firebombing in Baltimore on July 17. One subject allegedly threw three Molotov cocktails at his girlfriend's residence after an argument over the theft of money. Approximately $15,000 in property damage occurred at the residence. The subject was arrested by the Baltimore Police Department ten minutes after the fire and charged with six counts of homicide, six counts of burning with intent to murder, and one count of discharging a Molotov Cocktail and arson" (U.S. Department of Justice, 1976, p. 28).

"On December 7, a subject was killed by a dynamite explosion after he had been responsible for six bombing incidents in the Youngstown area. During a two-day period, December 6 and 7, the subject is believed to have detonated dynamite bombs at four private residences and two commercial establishments. Damage as a result of the six incidents has been estimated at $106,000. When authorities attempted to contact the subject for an interview concerning the attacks, he ran into a wooded area and an explosion was heard. A search of the area revealed the subject's body. Death by suicide was the ruling of the county coroner" (U.S. Department of Justice, 1976, p. 36).

Each of the above events describes a bombing incident where someone was killed for different motives and under different circumstances. The first was the act of a terrorist group; the second was related to anger, frustration, and high states of arousal; in the third incident, it is difficult to determine motives. Many of the motives for bombing are believed to resemble those for arson. However, it would appear that bombers are more intent on destruction and injury than arsonists are, and they do not wish to cover up the cause of the destruction. Moreover, bombing generally requires more technical know-how than arson and it is also a more dangerous offense. The planning, construction, safe transportation, placing, and activating of an explosive device requires more skill than dropping a match onto gasoline-soaked rags under a stairwell.

The apparent motives for bombings seem to change with the times. Between the years 1968 and 1971, nearly half of the bombings in the U.S. were a result of "social protest" (Moll, 1974), while in 1975 over a third of the bombings were due to "personal animosity" and another third to "malicious destruction" (U.S. Department of Justice, 1976). In 1975 only 10 percent of the bombings were related to social protest. Over half the deaths due to bombing reported in 1975 were due to personal animosity, whereas none were attributed to malicious destruction. Targets for bombings are most frequently residences (28 percent) or commerical buildings (23 percent). About 8 percent of the incidences were directed at school facilities and another 10 percent at automobiles. California led all states in the number of incidents, accounting for over a quarter of the total bombings in the United States.

While there is certainly no single bomber-type personality, MacDonald (1977) contends that there is a personality pattern drawn to bombing which demonstrates most of the characteristics of the "compulsive fire-setter"; he calls it the compulsive bomber. "Compulsive" means that the individual is drawn to the activity again and again. Learning theory, by the way, accounts for compulsive behavior extremely well. A person feels "compelled" to do something because he or she has received reinforcement for that activity in the past. The reward might be in the form of tension or arousal reduction or psychological gain. Eventually, with at least periodic reinforcement, the behavior develops into a habit, the learning term for compulsion. Thus, if there is a compulsive bomber, there is some aspect about making and exploding bombs that provides rewards for that particular individual to the point where he or she is strongly and repeatedly drawn to that activity.

MacDonald reports that the compulsive bombers he has known exhibited a fascination with bombs from childhood. In addition, he finds them keenly interested in discussing explosive devices and various techniques of detonating. Large segments of their life appear devoted to the study, development, and experience of bombing. More importantly, they derive excitement from their actions and are aroused by only one aspect of the explosion: the power, the fire or the noise. One bomber confessed, "I want to become more than what I am" (MacDonald, 1977, p. 40).

In line with the psychoanalytic tradition, however, MacDonald links sexual gratification with bombing, claiming that one in six compulsive bombers obtain sexual pleasure from their explosions. This is apparently based on his observation that sexual deviation is prominent in some bombers. We learned in Chapter 9 that persons plagued by sexual deviations also tend to be highly conditionable and quickly and easily associate events, objects, and people to other events, objects, and people. It may be that the individual associates bomb explosions with pleasurable or positive events, possibly even sexual ones. Furthermore, men who feel sexually inadequate tend to have a low opinion of themselves, and bombing may provide a buttress for their self-image. They may feel more powerful and effective after creating an explosion. If this is the case, we would expect that compulsive bombers would be more likely to plant a bomb following a significant blow to self-esteem and loss of control.

George Metesky, a fifty-six-year-old bachelor, was the so-called "Mad Bomber of New York," planting 32 pipe bombs between 1940 and 1956, all supposedly designed to draw attention to the unfair labor practices of a major utility. Metesky was working for United Electric (now known as Consolidated Edison, or Con Ed) in 1931 when a gush of hot gas from a boiler knocked him down. At the time he got up and walked away without apparent injury, but he later claimed illness from the accident, inability to work, and expected compensation. When the company repeatedly denied his requests, Metesky undertook an intense campaign designed to bring attention to Con Ed's "dastardly deeds." He planted bombs in locations which would receive heavy press coverage (Macy's Department Store, the New York Public Library, Grand Central Station), but he claims he did not intend to harm anyone. Fortunately, no one was killed during his bombing missions, but some 22 were injured. Although his first bombing attempt failed, he subsequently became more sophisticated, technically competent, and successful.

Metesky at one point wrote a letter to the editor of a New York newspaper:

> Have you noticed the bombs in your city, if you are worried, I am sorry, and also if anyone is injured. But it cannot be helped, for justice will be served, I am not well and for this I will make the Con Edison sorry. Yes, they will regret their dastardly deeds. I will bring them before the bar of justice, public opinion will condemn them, for beware, I will place more units under theater seats in the near future. F.P. (MacDonald, 1977, p. 47).

The phrase "dastardly deeds" eventually spelled his downfall. Investigators searching files of Con Ed for evidence of disgruntled employees uncovered it in the file folder of Metesky, who had used it in a letter to the company many years before.

Brussel (1968), the consulting psychiatrist in the Mad Bomber case, writes a detailed account of the events surrounding the search for the bomber and the arrest, when over a half-dozen law enforcement officers closed in on Metesky's home. He greeted them cordially and immediately guessed their purpose. He smiled frequently and appeared to be in a state of high self-satisfaction. He dressed in a pin-striped, double-breasted suit, wore freshly shined shoes, and carefully brushed his short hair.

Throughout the judicial proceeding and court trial, Metesky beamed and seemed to be enjoying the excitement he had created and the attention he was gaining. In 1957 the court found him "insane" (Brussel contends he was suffering from "paranoia"), and he was committed to Matteawan State Hospital. Metesky was released in 1973.

Although he was considered insane, he displayed a life-long design to draw attention to his plight and the injustice done to him. It was Metesky's way of coping with his feelings of helplessness. Very possibly, another principal reason for his bombings was to add excitement to his life or to become "famous" as the Mad Bomber. Overall, it appears that Metesky was successful in creating some significance for himself.

BURGLARY

Burglary, referring to the unlawful entry of a structure to commit a felony or theft (Kelley, 1977), is another crime on the increase, according to statistics. Approximately 3 million burglaries were reported in 1976; during the five-year-period 1972 to 1976, burglary increased 30 percent.

Like other criminal offenses, burglary seems to be a youth crime, as over eight out of every ten persons arrested in 1976 were under twenty-five. To some extent this arrest ratio may also reflect the lack of sophistication and motives found in younger burglars who, because of their inexperience, are more likely to be detected. Burglary is also a male enterprise, with only 5 percent of those arrested being female. Although the arrest ratio is slightly in favor of Whites, non-Whites are over-represented in proportion to their numbers in the general population (Pope, 1977a).

Burglaries of residential homes most frequently occur during the daytime and weekdays, whereas nonresidential businesses are usually burglarized late at night and on weekends (Pope, 1977b). This is not surprising, since burglarly is a "passive crime" in that the offender selects times and places that minimize encounters with victims on the property. Burglary also offers the greatest probability of success with the least amount of risk. Not only is it a crime without victim contact and identification, but it also does not require weapons, and the penalties are less severe than those for robbery. Juvenile offenders are more likely than their older counterparts to burglarize during daytime hours (Pope, 1977c). In fact, a prime time for many juvenile burglaries is at the end of the school day, approximately between 3 p.m. and 6 p.m.

Research data indicate that a large proportion of arrested burglars commit the offense near their own residence, and this seems especially true for juvenile offenders (Pope, 1977a). The Santa Clara Criminal Justice Pilot Program (1972) found that over one-half of the apprehended offenders traveled no more than a mile from their place of residence to commit the offense. It is difficult to generalize from this statistic, however, because it refers to *apprehended* burglars, who are ostensibly less skilled and thus more detectable than those more competent.

Over half the apprehended burglars worked with an accomplice (Chimbos, 1973; Pope, 1977a). Very few worked with more than three accomplices. Younger offenders and females are more likely to use accomplices than older males (Pope, 1977a). However, this pattern also depends upon the sophistication of the offender. Experienced, competent offenders who realize the formidable challenge presented by protection agents (alarms, safes, police) may also be more likely to take on assistants (Shover, 1972). Also, if the Santa Clara project sample is representative of burglaries in general, it appears burglars are rarely under the influence of alcohol and other drugs *at the time of their crime.* Less than 1 percent of those apprehended were under the influence of those substances.

Like for other criminal offenses, the best predictor of future occurrences for burglary is the track record of the offender. A California analysis found that 80 percent of the offenders studied had a prior record (Pope, 1977c). Of these, 58 percent had a prior burglary arrest and 47 percent had prior drug arrests. Males were far more likely to have a previous criminal arrest record than females.

Amateur burglars usually take money or personal items that they need, whereas the professionals take items which have excellent re-sale value, such as stereos, cameras, television sets, jewelry, and furs (Vetter & Silverman, 1978). The main reason for this is that the professional usually has access to a "fence," whereas the amateur rarely has that contact. A *fence* is a person who knowingly buys stolen merchandise for the purpose of re-sale and is an integral component in the burglary cycle.

As you might expect, the motives for burglary are varied, but the majority are for monetary gain. When done competently, burglarly is a lucrative business, with the monetary rewards far surpassing those the professional burglar would get in the "straight world." David (1974) found that a husband and wife team he interviewed made, on the average, $400 to $500 a day, while a solitary offender in his sample made about $500 per week. Not only is it a lucrative business with low risks, but many of the professionals also conceive of their profession as a challenging art and skill to be continually developed and refined. In this sense, it is also highly adaptive and represents an instrumental behavior supported by strong reinforcement.

Shover (1972) discusses some of the outstanding features of the competent professional burglar, whom he calls the "good burglar." He demonstrates technical competence, maintains a good reputation for personal integrity, specializes in burglary for income, and has been at least relatively successful at the crime, according to Shover. A good reputation in this sense means he or she is close-mouthed, stands up to the police, and is sympathetic toward the criminal way of life—the reputation, of course, is "good" among colleagues in the criminal subculture. Success is normally measured by rate of detection and conviction in relation to the income gained through burglary. Also, since the probabilities always exist for detection, and since incarceration means financial loss, another hallmark of the "good burglar" is his or her ability to recruit competent lawyers and bondsmen and to manipulate the criminal justice system. These skills and techniques are not openly available to anyone for the asking. Shover finds that, with rare exceptions, one becomes a good burglar by stealing with and being tutored by another good burglar.

Scarr (1973) identified another factor operating in both casual and professional burglaries, along with desire for financial and material rewards: the challenge of successful, skillful burglarizing in and of itself. Some burglars want to be known as the "best around" in their specialty, independently of the material rewards. These needs for social rewards such as status, recognition, and increases in self-esteem appear to be especially powerful motives in juveniles.

A significant number of burglars steal to support an expensive drug habit. However, the exact frequency to which addicts are responsible for property crimes is unknown and awaits more empirical study (Scarr, 1973). There are also a number of breaking and entering incidents into private homes where nothing seems to have been stolen at first glance; later, the homeowners realize that one or more articles of clothing are missing. These incidents are likely the work of burglars seeking fetishes for sexual gratification, as we noted in Chapter 9. On some occasions, they take a valuable item to distract the victims and the police from their real intention.

A number of clinicians (e.g., MacDonald, 1975) have noted that some people break into a residence just for the sexual excitement and stimulation the act itself generates. This behavioral pattern resembles that of the voyeur in that the offender finds excitement looking at or going through the personal items of other persons without their knowledge.

In summary, most burglars anticipate material rewards for their behavior and, to a lesser extent, social rewards for a job well done. In addition, most competent burglars see the reinforcements they get as far outdistancing the risks of punishment. While there may be some persons who burglarize for the purpose of obtaining sexual fetishes or for the excitement of the act itself, we must assume that the number of such incidents is small until further research has been conducted.

ROBBERY

Robbery accounts for nearly half of the violent crimes reported to the FBI (Kelley, 1977) and is among the most feared crimes among the American population (Garofalo, 1977). It is one of the few crimes where there exists a high probability of threat of physical harm from a stranger, and it can happen to anyone. Yet, it is among the least studied criminal offenses. One reason for this is that robbery seems so obvious, so straightforward: people rob (and burglarize) to obtain money. The returns are substantial, the process is quick, and one avoids working for a living. While much of this may be true, there are numerous shortcomings to oversimplifying human behavior, as we have seen. The motives of offenders are as varied as the offenders themselves. People behave in a certain way because they feel that is the way that works best for them, even if the behavior happens to be suicidal; at a particular moment in time, suicide was the best approach to take. Robbery is no different. Because the scientific literature on the subject is sparse, much of our discussion will be based on combining what we do know about robbers with speculation along the lines of the perspective of this book.

To be robbery, an offense must include the threat or the use of force and the taking of property. Specifically, "robbery is the stealing or taking of anything of value from the care, custody, or control of a person, in his presence, by force or by threat of force" (Kelley, 1977). Thus, one of the distinctions between robbery and burglary is the contact between the offender and the victim. Furthermore, the threat or use of force means

FIGURE 11-2. Cache of weapons and ammunition recovered in San Francisco, California, following the arrest by local police and FBI Agents of several members of an urban guerrilla group active in the Bay area.

that the offender threatens bodily harm to the victim if he or she resists or impedes the offender's progress; usually, this threat is backed up by a weapon. Nationally, about half of all robberies in 1976 were committed with the use of firearms, while another third were "strong-arm" robberies where no instrument other than physical force was used (Kelley, 1977).

The combination of taking property and threatening physical harm to a victim creates some problems in classification for statisticians and criminologists. Should the offense be considered a "property crime" or a "violent crime?" Wolfgang and Ferracuti (1967) argue that robbery—like homicide, rape, and aggravated assault—develops within a subculture of violence and, thus, should be classified as a violent crime. On the other hand, Normandeau (1968) contends that robbers are generally not violent and come more from a subculture of theft than one of violence. Normandeau based his judgment on a study of Philadelphia robberies, in which he discovered that 44 percent of the cases involved no physical injury to the victim. While the other 56 percent did sustain some injury, only 5 percent needed to be hospitalized.

If robbery is a crime of violence as reasoned by Wolfgang, springing from violence as a way of life, we should find some support for this in the backgrounds of the offenders. We would expect criminal records and a social history peppered with violent incidents. In a study of Boston robberies in 1964 and again in 1968, Conklin (1972) found no "excessive amount" of prior criminal violence in the backgrounds of robbery offenders when they were compared with the "general criminal populations of the country." In addition, less than one-third of the robbery victims during those years sustained injuries in the incidents. A similar finding was reported by Normandeau (1968) and Spencer (1966), neither of whom found robbers with high conviction records for violence. What is suggested in the research, however, is that robbers who relied on violence in the past are more likely to use it in the future, whether in robbery or in some other crime.

The problem of how to classify robbery can partly be solved by classifying it as both a property crime and a violent crime. In fact, Vetter and Silverman (1978) suggest that it is most accurately catalogued as a violent property offense. Most robbers, they point out, try to intimidate and frighten victims through threats of violence. The perpetrator rationalizes that the more fear that can be induced (without panic) the less resistance will be encountered. As in skyjacking, the more the victim expresses fear and compliance, the greater the feelings of control experienced by the perpetrator. If the perpetrator feels the control threatened, he or she may either flee or exert greater force. If the offender chooses the latter course and elects to remain at the scene, there continues to be the high probability that resistance or interference by the victim will result in personal injury. We saw in an earlier chapter that blocking someone's progress toward a goal often produces frustration, which in turn increases the chances for violence. It is not unusual, for example, for a robber to beat up a victim because the victim was not carrying enough money (MacDonald, 1975).

Strong-arm robbery (without instrument or weapon) is more likely to result in injury to the victim than is robbery with firearms. This surprising discovery can be partially explained by the fact that victims are less fearful when robbed by someone not ostensibly armed. In the absence of a gun or other weapon, their resistance to losing personal property is stronger, and they are more apt to hamper the progress of the strong-arm offender. The tendency to resist, therefore, probably accounts for some of the higher rates of victim injury in these situations. Furthermore, the offender is likely to feel more confident, powerful, and in greater control of the incident when he or she has a weapon. Because of this increase in confidence, the robber is more likely to be less anxious and disorganized in response patterns. Under these conditions, the offender is more able to think clearly and make less lethal decisions.

Assessing skilled bank robbery, Peter Letkemann (1973) makes some pertinent remarks about the successful robber's confidence and victim management. First, he analogizes between the burglar and the technical skills of the mechanic, and between the professional bank robber and the trade skills of the clinician. Burglars do not have to be concerned with people, but professional robbers must be able to maintain control and handle their victims at all times. Bank robbers assert that the key to successful robberies is confidence and the ability to control people under stress. Confidence, they believe, is reflected in the tone of voice and the general behaviors of the robber. High levels of self-confidence are crucial in the amount of control they are able to wield. In addition, successful robbers note that the posture and physical location of the victims are designed to enhance the offender's control over them.

Letkemann also makes the interesting observation that professional bank robbers express dismay over the the media's treatment of the subject. Television and movies generally downplay the seriousness of bank robbery, they believe, and they now have to work harder to convince their victims that they mean business. Also, the media encourage the development of "heroes" among the victims, and robbers consider heroes "irrational and extremely dangerous."

Similar to many other crimes, robbery in general is primarily an offense of the young, black male. Over half of those arrested for robbery in 1976 were under twenty-one, and three out of four arrested were under twenty-five. About two out of every three were Blacks, and 93 percent were male. *Bank robbery* has increased 74 percent between the years 1972 and 1976. This national increase reflects in part the proliferation of small, out-of-the-way, peripheral banks established for customer convenience. Employees of banks are also instructed not to resist; the owner of a local liquor store or "mom and pop" store is more likely to cause problems for the offenders. Also, compared to other business establishments, the cash flow in banks is apt to be more substantial, at least in the eyes of the offender.

The FBI's Annual Report for fiscal year 1977 states: "Recent FBI experience indicates a rising trend of bank robbers motivated by the need to support an expensive narcotics habit. . . . More than one-third of the total persons identified under the Federal Bank Robbery Statutes during Fiscal Year 1977 were reported to be drug users." The relationship between drug users and bank robbers was also noted by Conklin (1972), who developed a four-group typology of robbers, one of which

FIGURE 11-4. Bank surveillance camera records robbery in progress in Norfolk, Virginia.

was labeled the *addict robber*. Conklin subdivided addict robbers into those addicted to opiates, particularly heroin, and those who regularly used other drugs, such as amphetamines. In both cases the robbery was related to the use of drugs. However, the level of commitment to robbery among addict robbers is relatively low, although their commitment to theft is high. The addict regards robbery as more dangerous than shoplifting, burglary, or larceny; however, it offers fast, tangible cash to support the drug habit. Conklin contends that the addict robber chooses victims who are vulnerable but who are also probably carrying reasonable sums of money. As a rule, the robber does not select large and secure commercial businesses because of the necessary planning involved. Also, many addict robbers do not carry firearms for fear they will have to use them.

Conklin also describes the *professional robber*, the *opportunist robber*, and the *alcoholic robber*. The first is rather self-explanatory: he carefully plans a big heist, often with colleagues, executes the plan, and, if successful, lives off the proceeds until they run out. Conklin sees this fellow as being hedonistic and fun-loving. He finds the rewards for his work direct, fast, and often very profitable. In this sense robbery is a heavily rewarded, instrumental behavior.

Most professionals are skilled in the use of firearms, and many will not hesitate to use them to escape. They are also often experienced in bank robbery to the point of avoiding the unnecessary hitches the less experienced robbers may encounter. For example, one group of professionals made it a point never to rob customers in the establishment they were robbing, because the customers were more apt to offer resistance over their own personal money and valuables than over those of the establishment.

The opportunist robber, as described by Conklin, is probably the most common of the four types. He selects targets which are accessible and vulnerable and robs when the opportunity presents itself. Favorite targets include elderly women, inebriated individuals, cabdrivers, and people alone on dark streets. This type is also the youngest and least experienced of the robber typology. He tends to be black, young, male, and from a lower socioeconomic family, and simply desires cash in his pocket.

Although opportunists explain their crime as "just happening," they recognize what a specific behavior can bring them under optimal conditions. In general, they commit their crime on the street and rarely carry firearms. More often than not, they rob in groups and run from the scene rather than plan routes or use get-away cars.

The alcoholic robber has no commitment to robbery as a life style and rarely has a commitment to theft as a way of getting money. According to Conklin, alcohol impairs his judgment and loosens his inhibitions. In many cases, robbery is an afterthought following a fight or a scuffle with someone or at a place of business.

As is true for almost all typologies, finding individuals to fit into Conklin's can be troublesome. Where do we place the person who robs the establishment as a means of social protest? What about the person who robs for attention or excitement or as a form of suicide? It is feasible, too, that some persons rob to gain control over the dire straits which restrict, such as their lack of social status among peers. Regardless of how we classify them, persons who rob are employing deviant behavior to change their life condition for the better, in their own eyes. While the decision to rob may be quick, the behavior does not evolve out of some psychological void. The offender expected some gain, materially, socially or psychologically, under that particular set of circumstances.

SUMMARY

Offenses which do not fit well into specific categories already presented in previous chapters have now been introduced. Hostage-taking, arson, bombing, burglary, and robbery are also offenses which have received little attention in the psychological and psychiatric research literature.

The theory of helplessness was offered as having excellent potential for explaining hostage-taking offenses which lack apparent rationale and concrete purpose. It was suggested that a primary motive of many of these offenders is an attempt to gain some control over their environment and establish some degree of personal significance in their lives. Examples of terrorist and skyjacker behavior were used to illustrate this desire for control.

Arson and bombing offenses have drawn more psychiatric attention than hostage-taking, but much of the theory is permeated with the alleged connection between sexual needs and firesetting or bomb throwing. While it is possible for a person to make this connection through conditioning, the sex-firesetting relationship for most offenders must remain highly suspect until further research is conducted.

Burglary and robbery have drawn little research from any discipline, probably because they appear to be so transparent and easy to explain. This may be more the case for burglary than for robbery. In the latter, the motives seem more complicated: the risks are high and successful robbers must be able to handle people under stress. Motives have been suggested ranging from suicide to excitement.

KEY CONCEPTS FOR REVIEW

Control
External attribution and internal attribution
General helplessness
Specific helplessness
Instrumental hostage-taking
Expressive hostage-taking
Terrorism
Skyjacking
Stockholm effect
Arson
Pyromania
Bombers
Burglary

Robbery
Professional robber
Opportunist robber
Alcoholic robber
Addict robber

MAJOR THEORISTS AND RESEARCHERS

Miron and Goldstein
Conklin
Boudreau
MacDonald

SUGGESTED READINGS

Conklin, J.E. *Robbery and the criminal justice system.* Philadelphia: Lippincott, 1972.
The classic work on robbery, this book offers one of the most comprehensive treatments ever done of this violent property crime.
MacDonald, J. *Bombers and firesetters.* Springfield, Ill.: Charles P. Thomas, 1977.
One of the very few books on bombers and firesetters available, this presents theory and numerous case histories from the perspective of a psychiatrist.
Miron, M.S., and Goldstein, A.P. *Hostage.* Kalamazoo, Mich.: Behaviordelia, 1978.
A readable, how-to book in handling hostage situations.
Seligman, M.E. *Helplessness: On depression, development, and death.* San Franciso: W.H. Freeman, 1975.
Although the book emphasizes clinical depression, it is an extremely well-written and comprehensive account of the research on helplessness and control.

DRUGS AND CRIME

TWELVE

The reasons for taking altering drugs, whether to relieve unbearable tensions or frustrations, 'get high,' or improve performance, are all related to attempts to adjust (improve one's temporary state) or cope (improve the outcome of some longer-range goal). However, drug abuse of whatever kind represents an inadvertent failure in coping (or even in adjusting), just as much reactive violence does.

Tinklenberg & Stillman, 1970, p. 328

The relationship between drugs and crime may be viewed from two perspectives: 1. drug possession, use, and sale are criminal activities; 2. drugs have some effect on criminal behavior. Concentrating on drug possession and consumption would require sifting through varied regulations and statistics, many of which are ambiguous and confusing and differ from state to state. For our purposes, we are most concerned with the effect various types of drugs have on the criminal behaviors we have discussed throughout this book. Is a person more likely to be violent while under the influence of drugs? And if so, which ones? Are some drugs so addictive that persons will resort to criminal activity to obtain them? Are people more sexually aroused under the influence of certain drugs and thus more likely to rape or otherwise sexually assault?

Four major drug categories will be covered, with special emphasis directed at the drug within each group that is most often associated with crime. *The hallucinogens* (or psychedelics), which include LSD (lysergic acid diethylamine), mescaline, psilocybin, phencyclidine, ketamine, marihuana, and hashish, will be our first focus. Hallucinogens, so called because they sometimes generate hallucinations, refer to chemicals which lead to a change in the consciousness involving an alteration of reality. In some respects they replace the present world with an alternative one, although the person using them can generally attend to the drug world and the nondrug world at the same time (Ray, 1972). Marihuana is usually classified as a hallucinogen, although it is certainly a mild one. Because of its widespread use and the popular tendency to associate it with crime and bizarre behavior, it will be our main topic of discussion under the hallucinogens category.

We will also explore the *stimulants,* so called because they appear to stimulate brain functions and the central nervous system. They include the amphetamines, clinical antidepressants, cocaine, caffeine, and nicotine. Because of their significant relationship with crime, the amphetamines and cocaine will be the principal subjects of discussion representing this drug cluster.

The third group will be the *opiate narcotics,* which generally have a sedative (sleep-inducing) and an analgesic (pain-relieving) action. Heroin will be the major topic in this section.

Finally, alcohol will represent a group of chemicals known as *sedative-hypnotics,* which depress central nervous system functions. In most instances the sedative-hypnotics are all capable of inducing degrees of behavioral depression and reducing anxiety and stress.

The association between drugs and crime is complicated by a threefold interaction: the pharmacological effects of the drug (the chemical effects of the drugs on the body), the psychological characteristics of the individual using the drug, and the psychosocial conditions under which the drug is taken. The pharmacological effects include features of the nervous system, such as the amount of transmitter substances within nerve cells, body weight, blood stream composition, and other physiological features which significantly influence the chemical effects of the drug. The psychological variables include the mood of the person at the time the drug is consumed, previous experience with the drug, and the person's expectancies about the drug's effects. Psychosocial variables include the social atmosphere under which the drug is consumed. That is, the people present and their expectations, moods, and actions are all very important components of an individual's reactions to the drug.

In order to gain an understanding of the effects of any drug, the pharmacological, psychological, and psychosocial variables all must be taken into account. When we are dealing with the complex topic of crime, deciphering the crime-drug connection is doubly difficult, and the conclusions are necessarily that much more complicated and tentative.

Before we proceed, the reader must become familiar with two terms that are heavily used in the drug literature: *tolerance* and *dependence*. Drug tolerance refers to the "state of progressively decreased responsiveness to a drug" (Julien, 1975, p. 29). Specifically, tolerance is indicated if the individual requires a larger dose of the drug to reach the same effects previously experienced while taking the drug. In other words, the person becomes psychologically and physiologically "used to" the drug.

Dependence is usually looked at from two perspectives: physical and psychological. In simple terms, physical dependence refers to the physiological distress and physical pain a person suffers if he or she goes without the drug for any length of time. Psychological dependence is difficult to distinguish from physical dependence, but it is characterized by an overwhelming desire to use the drug for a favorable effect. The person is convinced that he or she needs the drug to maintain an optimal sense of wellbeing. The degree of psychological dependence varies widely from person to person and drug to drug (Hofmann, 1975). In its extreme form, the person's life is permeated with thoughts of procurement and administration of the drug, and he or she will do anything to obtain it, including resorting to robbery or prostitution.

Secondary psychological dependence may also develop. While primary psychological dependence is associated with the reward of the drug experience (positive reinforcement), secondary dependence refers to expectancies about the aversive withdrawal or the painful effects of going off the drug. Thus, to avoid the anticipated pain and discomfort associated with withdrawal, the individual continues to take the drug (negative reinforcement).

CANNABIS

Marihuana, which apparently originated in Asia, is among human beings' oldest and most frequently used intoxicants. The earliest reference to it was found in a pharmacy book written in 2737 B.C. by the Chinese emperor Shen Nung (Ray, 1972), who called it the "Liberator of Sin" and recommended it for such ailments as "female weakness," constipation, and absent-mindedness. The origin of the word marihuana is unknown, but it is commonly believed that it either came from the Mexican slang for cheap tobacco called "mary jane," or the Portuguese word *"mariguano,"* meaning "intoxicant."

The drug is crudely prepared from the Indian hemp plant *cannabis saliva*, an annual which is cultivated or grows freely as a weed in both tropical and temperate climates. The psychoactive (intoxicating) properties of the plant reside principally in the chemical tetrahydrocannabinol (THC), found mainly in the resin of the hemp plant. Thus, the concentration of THC within parts of the plant determines the potency or psychoactive power of the drug.

THC content varies from one preparation to another. Part of this stems from the plant quality itself, since the THC content depends on the strain of the plant, the climate, and the soil conditions. For example, the resin is believed to retard the dehydration of the flowering elements and thus is produced in higher quantities in hot, tropical climates than in temperate zones (Hofmann, 1975). Consequently, cannabis grown in the tropical zone (Mexico, Columbia, Jamaica, and North Africa) possesses greater psychoactive potential than American-grown hemp, a product which is not highly prized by experienced cannabis users.

The types of cannabis extracts used most commonly in the United States are marihuana and hashish. Marihuana is usually prepared by cutting the stem beneath the lowest branches, air drying, and stripping seeds, bracts, flowers, leaves, and small stems from the plant (National Commission on Marihuana and Drug Abuse, 1973). There is no evidence that the female cannabis plant contains more THC than the male. Hashish, the arabic word for "dry grass," is produced by scraping or in some other way extracting the resin secreted by the flowers. Therefore hashish, which is usually sold in this country in small cubes, has more THC content than marihuana. Hofmann (1975) reports that in equal amounts (measured by weight) the THC content in hashish ranges from 5 to 12 percent, while the more potent forms of marihuana (e.g., ganja from Jamaica) contain about 4 to 8 percent THC. Mexican marihuana contains less than 1 percent of THC, and American marihuana often less than 0.2 percent.

When exposed to air over a period of time, marihuana appears to lose its psychoactive potency due to the conversion of THC to cannabinol and other inactive compounds (Mechoulam, 1970). Cannabis extracts with higher levels of resin deteriorate more rapidly than with lower levels.

In the United States, marihuana and hashish are usually smoked, most often in hand-rolled cigarettes. A common practice in other countries, however, is to consume cannabis as "tea" or mixed with food or beverages.

Psychological Effects

The psychological effects of cannabis extracts are so subjective and depend on such a wide range of variables that generalizations must be accompanied by the warning that there are numerous exceptions. Reactions to cannabis, like all psychoactive compounds, are dependent upon the complex interaction of both pharmacological and extra-pharmacological factors, which would include the mood of the user, the user's expectations about the drug, the social context in which it is used, and the user's past experience with the drug. All of these elements contribute significantly to how the individual will react. The substantial influence of extra-pharmacological factors combined with the widespread variation in THC content in any sample of cannabis make comparable research data on humans exceedingly difficult to obtain.

It is commonly reported (e.g., Hofmann, 1975; Ray, 1972; Tinklenberg & Stillman, 1970; National Commission, 1972) that low doses of THC (five to ten mg.) generally produce the following experiences:

1. Well-being, relaxation, and tranquillity. These effects seem to be experienced by most users, usually two to three minutes after inhalation of smoke from a marihuana cigarette. On the other hand, the person who is apprehensive, depressed, or upset at something may become more so following a "joint."

2. Swings of humor. Periodic spells of hilarity and laughter may be followed by a contemplative silence. For some, experiences and thoughts may become more tragic and strangely more significant.

3. Altered perceptions of sounds, colors, objects, and events. Sounds may become clearer, colors more vivid and shimmering, and objects more distinct. Social relationships may take on more meaning and importance, and lost friendships may become more tragic.

4. Disorders of time perception. Estimates of time passage may be altered, often in the direction of underestimating how long an event was. In some cases, there emerges an inability to separate the past, the present, and the future (Snyder, 1971).

5. Rapid intrusion of thoughts. Some users have impressions that their thought processes have speeded up, sometimes to an excessive degree. Some find their thoughts "moving faster than expression." With the rapid intrusion of thoughts cross-firing to other thoughts, the subject finds it difficult to focus upon any one task, and inexperienced users may find this a frightening experience.

6. Short-term memory impairment. Often there is difficulty remembering events which took place minutes or even seconds before. Memory becomes disordered and jumbled, a phenomenon which may be reflected by disjointed speech patterns, incomplete sentences, and sudden conversational tangents.

These phenomena are not experienced in a continuous, predictable fashion but are episodic and come and go, sometimes at will. To repeat an earlier statement, psychoactive drug experiences are unique for each individual. Except for increases in heart rate, increases in peripheral blood flow, and reddening of the membranes around the eyes, there have been few *consistent* physiological changes reported for all persons (Hofmann, 1975; National Commission, 1972; Canadian Government Commission of Inquiry, 1971). Moreover, there is no record of a fatality directly attributable to cannabis extracts, nor of irreparable injury to organs or tissue (Hofmann, 1975).

Although a number of reports have asserted that there is no substantive evidence to support the contention that cannabis stimulates sexual arousal or improves sexual performance, subjective ratings of sexual feelings are most difficult to prove or disprove scientifically. Many users claim heightened sexual enjoyment when using the drug, and it is entirely possible this is the case for some. However, there is no evidence that criminal sex offenders are under the influence of cannabis when offending (National Commission, 1973).

There is good reason to believe that a significant number of larcenies, robberies, or burglaries are committed by individuals who desire to support a drug habit. However, the American experience has been that cannabis is not habit-forming to the point where the offender needs a "fix" to prevent withdrawal, physiologically or psychologically (Hofmann, 1975; National Commission, 1973). Therefore, it appears that very few individuals participate in criminal activity for the specific purpose of supporting a cannabis "habit."

There are possible adverse reactions to cannabis. In very rare instances, psychotic episodes have been reported after the individual has taken the drug. However, the available evidence strongly suggests that the individual was psychotic prior to cannabis intake (National Commission, 1973) and that the cannabis does not generate psychotic behavior in an emotionally balanced individual. There have also been some instances of "acute brain syndrome," a disorder which resembles those found in patients with exceptionally high fever (Weil, 1970). In the few cases reported, this syndrome normally follows heavy cannabis intake. The subject is disoriented, confused, and has visual and auditory hallucinations, but the symptoms disappear as soon as the THC is metabolized by the body and eliminated.

Another syndrome often cited in the medical literature is the so-called "amotivational syndrome." According to the research, some individuals who use cannabis regularly over a long period of time begin to exhibit reduced motivation and ambition, apathy, low frustration tolerance, and general loss of effectiveness as contributing members of society

(McGlothlin & West, 1968). The individual's life is seemingly preoccupied with cannabis, a pattern somewhat similar to the skid row alcoholic's state. The adolescent who has used cannabis regularly for at least a year appears to be particularly susceptible (Kornhaber, 1971). However, a number of other researchers have reported they could find no evidence for the amotivational syndrome. In one study using college students, no significant motivational differences were found between regular cannabis users and nonusers (Hochman & Brill, 1973). Rubin and Comitas (1976) found that subjects who smoked 7 to 25 cigarettes a day for 10 to 25 years showed no signs of the amotivational syndrome. Because of the conflicting information at this point, conclusions as to the existence of the amotivational syndrome cannot be made.

Cannabis and Crime

Although cannabis is widely used, public concern about the connection between the drug and crime was stimulated by a number of articles printed in a New Orleans newspaper as far back as 1926 (Ray, 1972). In 1931 Fossier published an article which contended that one out of every four persons arrested in New Orleans was addicted to cannabis. With public interest activated, a further drive to get the "dangerous" drug outlawed was spearheaded by the then Commissioner of Narcotics, Harry Anslinger, who was instrumental in convincing states and Congress that marihuana often led to serious crime and was a threat to the moral fabric of American society. During this time (the 1930s), various articles and speeches associated marihuana use with both violent and perverted crime.

In 1937 Congress passed the Marihuana Tax Act, a bill intended to insert further muscle into the anti-marihuana laws which already existed in 46 states. The Tax Act did not actually outlaw cannabis, but it taxed the grower, distributor, seller, and buyer prohibitively and established so much bureaucratic hassle that it was nearly impossible to have anything to do with any form of cannabis (Ray, 1972). Thirty-two years later (in 1969) the United States Supreme Court declared the Marihuana Tax Act unconstitutional. What is amazing about the attitudes that existed during this time, however, was that none were supported by a comprehensive scientific investigation. The information communicated was anecdotal and was based upon "documentation" of the "I know a case where" or "I heard about a case where" variety.

In 1939 Bromberg published the results of a study conducted in New York between the years 1932 and 1937. Out of a total of 16,854 prisoners, only 67 were admitted cannabis users, and only six of those were indicted for a violent crime. Bromberg concluded that the relationship between marihuana use and crime was not substantiated, but staunch believers of the marihuana-crime connection were not impressed.

During the early 1940s, New York's Mayor LaGuardia asked the New York Academy of Medicine to investigate the effects of marihuana to try to establish some conclusions. Similar to the Bromberg findings, the LaGuardia report did not find evidence to support the contention that marihuana use led to crime (see Mayor's Committee on Marihuana Report, 1944).

Numerous research projects directed at cannabis were launched during the 1950s, 1960s, and early 1970s. Many of these studies suffered methodological shortcomings and lacked reasonable parity for dosage level, means of administering the drug, and THC content in the drug itself. Personality factors of the subjects were not considered enough, and experimental settings and instructions were haphazard. At first, some of the research suggested a relationship between cannabis usage and criminal behavior. However, with more modern standards of analysis which controlled for demographic and criminal background variables, the earlier results were found to be spurious (National Commission, 1972). To date, no investigation directed at the connection between the use of cannabis and criminal activity has established a *causal* link. Of course, this assertion excludes the illegal acts of selling or obtaining the drug and subsequent conviction based on its possession.

Research carried out in recent years along with the reviews conducted by government-sponsored commissions have strongly indicated that marihuana does not directly contribute to criminal behavior. The National Commission on Marihuana and Drug Abuse (1972, p. 470), based on an extensive literature review and study, came to this conclusion: "There is no systematic empirical evidence, at least that is drawn from the American experience, to support the thesis that the use of marihuana either inevitably or generally causes, leads to or precipitates criminal, violent, aggressive or delinquent behavior of a sexual or nonsexual nature." The National Commission's Report (p. 470) adds: "If anything, the effects observed suggest that marihuana may be more likely to neutralize criminal behavior and to militate against the commission of aggressive acts."

One of the predominant effects of THC is relaxation and a marked decrease in physical activity (Tinklenberg & Stillman, 1970). THC induces muscular weakness and inability to sustain physical efforts so that the user desires nothing more strenuous than to stay relatively motionless. As Tinklenberg and Stillman (1970, p. 341) point out, ". . .

'being stoned' summarizes these sensations of demobilizing lethargy."
It is difficult to imagine how "stoned" users would be prompted to
engage in assaultive or violent activity. If anything, and as noted by the
National Commission, we would expect THC to reduce criminal activity. There is good evidence to support this observation.

Tinklenberg and Woodrow (1974) found that drug users who use
mainly marijuana seem less inclined toward violence or aggression than
their counterparts who prefer other drugs, such as alcohol or amphetamines. After examining drug usage among lower-class minority
youth, Blumer and his associates (1967) made the same observation. In
fact, they found that marijuana users deliberately shunned aggression
and violence; in order to maintain group status it was important to
remain "cool" and nonaggressive, regardless of the provocation.

Although the empirical findings indicate that cannabis does not, as a
rule, stimulate aggressive behavior or other criminal actions, any time
we are dealing with human behavior there will be exceptions. Individuals familiar with the effects of cannabis have heard of the occasional
negative experiences produced by THC, known in drug parlance as the
"bummer." Although the phenomenon is rare, some people do have
experiences which make them bizarre, panicky, hypersensitive, and out
of contact with time. For example, some individuals experience rapid,
disorganized intrusions of irrelevant thoughts which might prompt
them to feel that they are losing control of their mind. It is possible that
under these conditions they will interpret the actions of persons around
them as preventing them from escaping their dilemma. Hypersensitive,
they might regard others as purposely trapping them or adding harder
drugs to the grass. Under such conditions it is plausible these panicky
individuals might attack those surrounding them.

Investigators of cannabis effects often agree that individuals who act
violently under the influence of the drug are most likely predisposed to
act that way to begin with, with or without the drug (National Commission, 1972). Much of the evidence indicates that violent marihuana users
were violent prior to using cannabis. In other words, they learned the
behavioral pattern independently of cannabis.

In summary, there is no solid evidence to indicate that cannabis
contributes to or encourages crime. Negative attitudes and beliefs about
the relationship appear to be based on myth and misinformation and are
probably partially a carry over from the 1930s. In fact, there is some
evidence to suggest that cannabis users are less criminally prone than
users of other drugs, such as alcohol and amphetamines. There are also
no supportive data that cannabis is habit forming, at least to the extent
where the user must get a "fix" and will steal, burglarize, or rob to obtain
the necessary funds to purchase the drug.

AMPHETAMINES AND COCAINE

Amphetamines and cocaine are classified as central nervous system stimulants because they have highly similar effects. Amphetamines are part of a group of synthetic drugs known collectively as amines. Amines produce effects in the sympathetic nervous system (which is a subdivision of the autonomic nervous system) which arouses the person for emergent action that might include fighting or fleeing from a frightening situation.

Amphetamines are traditionally classified into three major categories: 1. amphetamine (Benzedrine), 2. dextroamphetamine (Dexedrine), and 3. methamphetamine (Methedrine or Desoxyn). Of the three, Benzedrine is the least potent. All may be taken orally, inhaled, or injected, and all act directly on the central nervous system, particularly the reticular activating system (Bloomquist, 1970). Once the drug is taken, it is rapidly assimilated into the bloodstream, but it is metabolized and eliminated from the body relatively slowly. Both psychological and physiological reactions to these drugs vary dramatically with the dose, and the effects of massive quantities intravenously injected differ substantially from low doses administered orally. The reactions to the drugs also vary widely among individuals. For our purposes here we will refer to "amphetamines" in the broad sense, and therefore the term will include all three categories.

Common slang terms for amphetamines include: bennies, dexies, co-pilots, meth, speed, white cross, uppers, "A," pep pills, diet pills, jolly beans, black bombers, truck drivers, eye openers, wakeups, hearts, footballs, bombitas, crossroads, cartwheels, coasts-to-coasts, splash, and purple hearts. The slang names are derived from the various effects, the purposes to which the drug is put, the shape and color of the drug, or the trade names of the manufacturers.

The American pharmaceutical industry has produced an estimated 8 to 10 billion doses of these drugs annually (Hofmann, 1975), which is believed to be considerably more than the estimated number of prescriptions for amphetamines written for the same period of time. It has been suggested that a sizeable portion of these compounds end up in the black market for distribution. Unlike cannabis or cocaine, the drug is a synthetic compound and can be easily produced by self-appointed "chemists" for illegal distribution on a large scale. Some investigators estimate that the illicit manufacture of amphetamines now exceeds by three to ten times the amount of drugs produced legally in North America (Solursh & Clement, 1968).

Cocaine (coke, snow, candy) is a chemical obtained by extraction from the coca plant (*Erythroxylon coca*) native to Peru. The coca seems to thrive at elevations of 2,000 to 8,000 feet with heavy rainfall (100 inches per year), and has long been used by Peruvians living in the Andes. Mountain natives chew coca leaves almost continually and commonly keep a ball of them tucked in their cheek (Ray, 1972). Coca leaves are also used as tea. Cocaine is much more expensive than amphetamines, partly because of its restriction by the Harrison Narcotic Act of 1914, which also inhibits opium and its derivatives.

Cocaine in the United States is usually administered nasally (sniffing) or intravenously by injection. Cocaine taken orally is poorly absorbed because it is hydrolyzed by gastrointestinal secretions. Light users normally sniff the drug to obtain their "high," but chronic sniffing can result in nasal irritation and inflammation. The common unit in the black market is the "spoon" which approximates one gram of the diluted drug. In most cases cocaine is diluted 20 to 30 times its weight (Hofmann, 1975).

Psychological Effects

In small doses, both amphetamines and cocaine increase wakefulness, alertness, and vigilance, and improve concentration and produce a feeling of clear thinking. There is generally an elevation of mood, mild euphoria, increased feelings of sociability, and a belief that one can do just about anything. In large doses, the effects often produce hypersensitivity, delirium, panic, aggression, psychosis, hallucinations, and irritability. If these drugs are injected at chronically high doses, "toxic psychosis" may be precipitated, a syndrome with many of the psychotic features of paranoid schizophrenia. With the metabolization and elimination of the drug, the psychotic episode usually dissipates. There is some evidence that about 5 to 15 percent of the individuals experiencing an amphetamine-induced toxic psychosis do not recover completely for several years (Hofmann, 1975).

Our concern in this section is the heavy user of amphetamines and the so-called "speed freak," since the relationship between the amphetamines and crime is believed to exist principally among this group. If there were a strong relationship between general amphetamine use and crime, this country would have been in shambles long ago.

The heavy user or speed freak often engages in "runs" where for several days he or she repeatedly injects amphetamines, gradually increasing the magnitude and frequency of the injections. Some users may "shoot" or "crank up" to several thousand milligrams in a single day. The user may inject both amphetamines and metamphetamines, but usually prefers shooting the latter. Crystalline metamphetamine ("crystal") is normally used for this purpose and is dissolved sparingly in water before the injection. In the beginning stages of the run, the user usually feels energetic, talkative, enthusiastic, confident, and powerful. He or she does not sleep and usually eats very little. After the first few days, however, some unpleasant symptoms set in. For example, the person often becomes confused and disorganized and manifests bizarre patterns of thought and behavior. The person may participate in compulsive, repetitive acts that appear meaningless, or may formulate elaborate paranoid delusional systems about being watched. He or she may become irritable and hostile, and may demonstrate violent behaviors as "protection" against the wrath and disloyalty of others, including closest friends.

Tolerance to amphetamine builds rapidly; beyond the fifth day of a run, no quantity of drug may produce the desired effect (Hofmann, 1975). Toward the end of the run, the toxic symptoms begin to dominate, fatigue sets in, the drug is discontinued, and a deep, prolonged sleep generally follows. Sometimes this period is called the "crash" or "fall out." Following the sleep period, which may even last several days, the user is usually lethargic, ravenously hungry, and often deeply depressed. It is not unusual for suicidal thoughts to dart in and out of his or her mind or for actual attempts at self-destruction to take place. The user may at this time begin another run, but runs are most often separated by days or weeks.

One of the more pleasurable and reinforcing aspects about the run is the "flash," the immediate effect of the intravenous injection itself. Some users describe the flash as a sudden, overwhelming pleasurable "rush" similar to ice water in the veins or to an instant total body orgasm, although others strongly disagree with these descriptions. Some users even assert that the pleasure of the injection is the main motivation for the run, while the other effects remain secondary.

The "spree" is the term reserved for short runs and is usually accomplished through injections of cocaine. The effects of cocaine are not as long-lasting as amphetamines, and thus a heavy user may go through a supply in an evening (Hofmann, 1975). The other effects of cocaine are the same as those reported for speed, particularly methamphetamine. Because "coke" is more expensive, the supply usually more difficult to obtain, and the effects shorter in duration, speed is the preferred drug. Hofmann questions why cocaine is even purchased when it is so clearly inferior to the more effective amphetamines. He suggests that the power of word-of-mouth advertising in the drug world has perhaps oversold it.

Amphetamines, Cocaine, and Crime

It is difficult to determine what kinds of people participate in runs or sprees. Some believe that speed freaks are essentially hedonistic people whose only desire is to experience the effects of speed as intensely and continuously as possible (Hofmann, 1975). There is evidence that the rewarding effects of speed can be so reinforcing to certain individuals that they can become hooked on the drug psychologically as solidly and completely as heroin. The life style of speed freaks often resembles that of a narcotics addict. The pattern of abuse rarely leaves time for other activities, such as steady employment, and unless they are independently wealthy, it may be necessary for the drug users to obtain financial support through illegal avenues (Connell, 1968; Hofmann, 1975). This pattern may involve prostitution, larceny, burglary, or robbery.

In addition, the paranoid phase of the run is often characterized by threats and shows of aggression and violence (Tinklenberg & Stillman, 1970; Hofmann, 1975; National Commission on Marihuana and Drug Abuse, 1973). Ellinwood (1971) studied the case histories of thirteen persons who committed homicide under amphetamine intoxication and found in most cases that the homicidal act was directly related to the psychotic-paranoid stage of intoxication. Bell (1967) found in a two-month study of 60 convicted murderers in Japan that 31 had a history of amphetamine abuse. Reports from law enforcement officials and drug users themselves have corroborated the potential violence demonstrated during amphetamine intoxication. Due to the possibility of violent episodes, heavy abusers often "crank up" at "splash houses" where violence can be relatively contained and hidden.

Despite the indicators that there may be a significant relationship between amphetamine abuse and violent crime, we lack reasonable estimates of how widespread the violence rate may be, or even whether it is a significant problem. Many such crimes, such as those which occur at splash houses, probably go unreported. Even if we had statistics regarding the relationship, the establishment of cause-and-effect connections would be difficult.

No physical dependence on the effects of amphetamines or cocaine is said to develop (Hofmann, 1975). On the other hand, there is reason to believe that a psychological dependence develops in heavy users who often engage in runs and sprees. Runs and sprees are also likely to raise havoc with employment unless one is involved in self-determined hours of working such as may be found in some forms of pushing, prostitution, or burglary. It seems probable that heavy users gain financial support through illegal means not only to support their drug habit (which is relatively inexpensive) but also for daily living necessities. As noted earlier, the FBI has reported that one-third of those apprehended for robbery are regular drug users; the types of drugs referred to in this statistic as well as the nature of their consumption are unknown, however. Without further specification, the statistic cannot be evaluated.

The National Institute on Drug Abuse (1978) communicates obvious skepticism about any possibility of amphetamine abuse being related to crime. However, this is one area in which we have very little knowledge. The medical and pharmacological literature consistently supports the existence of toxic psychosis characterized, in part, by aggressive and violent behaviors. How much actual violence occurs, and to what extent the habitual "runner" engages in illegal activity (besides the illegal drug consumption itself) are unknown. Research directed at causal relationships rather than simply at correlations between past use of the drug and criminal offenses is needed.

NARCOTIC DRUGS

The word "narcotics" provokes negative reactions in many people and very often is quickly associated with crime. Like the word "dope," it has been widely misused to denote all illegal drugs. In this chapter, narcotic drugs will refer only to derivatives of, or products pharmacologically similar to products of the opium or poppy plant, *papaver somniferum*.

The opium plant is an annual which grows about three to five feet high. It is believed to have originated in Asia Minor and is still grown there in large quantities, especially in Turkey. That country and others in the Far East are the primary and constant sources of both legal and illegal derivatives of the opium plant, generally referred to as opiates. One of the reasons that these areas remain the trade center for opiates is the availability of cheap labor. It is estimated that for the collection of one kg. of opium it typically requires 280 hours of labor (Hofmann, 1975). The opium must be gathered at just the right time after the poppy's petals fall. A seed pod forms several days after the petals drop, and it is this pod which contains the opium. A small cut is skillfully made in the pod and a milky liquid gradually seeps out. The liquid (which is opium) coagulates upon exposure to the air and is then scraped off into a container.

Narcotic drugs can be divided into three major categories on the basis of the amount of preparation they require: 1. natural narcotics: this category contains opium and the two naturally occurring narcotics it possesses, morphine and codeine; 2. semi-synthetic narcotics: this group includes the derivative of morphine and codeine chemically prepared—heroin, dehydromorphinine exymorphone, metopon, and others; and 3. synthetic narcotics: these narcotics are wholly prepared chemically but are highly similar pharmacologically to the chemical structure of the opium derivatives. These compounds include meperidine, methadone, and phenazocine.

All are narcotics because they produce similar effects: relief of pain, relaxation, peacefulness, and sleep (*Narco* is of Greek origin meaning "to sleep"). The major medical uses of the narcotics, or opiates, include relief of pain, treatment of diarrhea, and relief of coughs (Julien, 1975). While the opiates have relieved human suffering considerably, they have also generated problems for society. The opiates are highly addictive for some individuals, to the point where they develop a relentless and unmanageable craving for the drug. It should be realized, however, that many heavy users of opiates lead successful, productive lives, without significant interference in their daily lives. There is no single type of opiate user.

Heroin

The most heavily used illegal narcotic in this country is heroin (also known as "H," scrag, smack, junk, and horse), which is usually prepared illegally in laboratories in southern France (Hofmann, 1975). Elsewhere (e.g., Singapore, Philippines, Afghanistan), morphine is preferred to heroin. Why heroin is preferred in this country is not completely understood, since the effects of the two drugs are highly similar (Hofmann, 1975). It is known that heroin is faster acting and more potent per unit weight. Levitt (1977) states that heroin actually has little pharmacological activity of its own and must be first converted in the brain to morphine. In other words, it is really morphine rather than heroin which produces the narcotic properties. Apparently, the slower activity property of morphine is due to the "blood-brain barrier": morphine has considerably more difficulty entering the brain than heroin and consequently is less potent and slower acting.

Heroin normally looks like a white, crystalline material characterized by the bitter taste of alkaloid. The appearance is largely dictated by the diluents it is sold with, which in most cases make up about 95 to 98 percent of the total weight. A good "bag" of heroin contains about 300 mg. of diluents and only 15 mg. of heroin (Hofmann, 1975). Recent estimates indicate that the "average" bag contains much less heroin, probably around five to six mg. per 300 mg. The bitter taste is also not always a good index of the purity of the heroin, since many diluents are produced to taste bitter also.

Effects

Heroin is rarely taken orally, because the absorption rate is slow and incomplete. It may be administered by intramuscular, subcutaneous ("skin popping"), or intravenous ("mainlining") injection, or it may be inhaled ("snorted"). The experienced heroin user strongly prefers mainlining because of the sensational thrill, splash, rush, or kick he or she receives by this route. The sensation, which is usually abdominal, is almost instantaneous, with maximal intensity. As in amphetamine injections, a large number of opiate addicts regard the "rush" as one of the primary motivations for using heroin, and many regard the sensation as very similar to sexual orgasm.

The effects of heroin depend upon the quantity taken, the method of administration, the interval between administrations, the tolerance and dependence of the user, the setting, and the user's expectations. The effects of the initial injection or intake of heroin vary widely from individual to individual. Levitt (1977) estimates that only about 10 percent find initial injections of opiates pleasant, 50 percent find them neutral, and 40 percent unpleasant. In most cases, those who find the experience unpleasant do not continue using the drug unless peer pressure offsets the negative aspects. The effects of the injections usually wear off in from five to eight hours, depending on the tolerance of the user and numerous other variables.

Heroin, like all the narcotics, is a central nervous system depressant. For users who find the effects positive, it promotes mental clouding, dream-like states, light sleep punctuated by vivid dreams, and a general feeling of "sublime contentment" (Hofmann, 1975). The body may become permeated with a feeling of warmth and the extremities may feel heavy. There is little inclination toward physical activity; the user prefers to sit motionless and in a fog. Time becomes of no concern or interest.

If heroin is used regularly a tolerance develops rapidly, but not as completely as that found for the amphetamines during the end of a run. The user will find that larger doses are necessary to reach the intensity of the rush and the contentment which follows. Because heroin is an expensive drug, the habit can become difficult to maintain without outside or illegal funds.

The degree of physical dependence is related to the amount injected and how often. Generally speaking, the longer and more frequent the use, the more difficult the withdrawal. Whether the dependence is primarily psychological or physiological is a matter for debate; for a majority of heroin addicts, it appears to be both. The heavy user is generally sick upon waking, and the withdrawal symptoms slowly increase in intensity, reaching a peak at between 36 and 72 hours. Withdrawal symptoms include nausea, severe abdominal cramps, uncontrollable diarrhea, vomiting, chills, "goose bumps," profuse sweating, hostility and anger, restlessness, lack of appetite, and some involuntary twitching and kicking movements. It should be emphasized that many heroin addicts do not demonstrate these characteristics upon withdrawal, however. Unfortunately, a very large number of heroin addicts return to the habit following detoxification, regardless of whether or not they experienced the symptoms.

Heroin and Crime

No other drug group is as closely associated with crime as the opiates, particularly heroin. The image of the "junkie" as a desperado looking for a fix is familiar to everyone. It is assumed that, because of the adverse effects of the drug, the heroin user is bizarre, unpredictable, and therefore dangerous. Recalling, however, the twilight state opiates initiate, it is difficult to envision the addict harming or attacking anyone. Unlike the amphetamines, high doses of opiates produce sleep rather than psychotic or panic states. The research evidence strongly indicates that opiate addicts do not, as a general rule, participate in violent crimes such as assault, rape, or homicide (National Institute on Drug Abuse, 1976; Canadian Government's Commission of Inquiry, 1971; National Commission on Marihuana and Drug Abuse, 1973; Tinklenberg & Stillman, 1970). However, many heroin addicts do not have the legitimate income to maintain the costly enterprise of opiate consumption and must turn to criminal activities for support. The criminal activities are income-generating offenses such as burglary, robbery, shoplifting, and prostitution. It is estimated that between 66 and 80 percent of heroin addicts have committed at least one income-generating crime (National Institute on Drug Abuse, 1978). Most (60 percent) of these crimes were clearly nonviolent property offenses, but about another 25 percent involved robbery. The offense proportions vary widely from one city or geographical area to another.

The data we now have cannot supply us with information about what proportion of all crime opiate users commit. Police administrators have estimated that between 30 and 70 percent of all crime is committed by opiate users (Pomeroy, 1974). However, these estimates are not based on hard data or valid analyses and must remain speculative. There is considerable evidence that drug-using criminals are involved in crime prior to beginning the regular use of opiates (National Institute on Drug Abuse, 1978). There is also evidence to show that criminal involvement (especially property crime) increases after opiate use.

The most consistent and overwhelming finding between opiate addiction and *income-generating crime* is that the two are highly correlated. That is, income-generating offenses are often perpetrated by opiate addicts, and opiate addicts are frequently involved in income-generating offenses. What, precisely, this relationship means is another story. It could mean that certain types of people are more likely to shoot heroin and engage in criminal activity. Or, that heroin addiction prompts otherwise law-abiding citizens to support their habit by illegal means. Or, that criminals are also drug addicts. Or, that heroin addiction causes people to become criminal because the drug "messes up their minds." No matter how many correlational studies are undertaken, we are still without a clear understanding of the connection between opiate addiction and crime. What is desperately needed in the drug field are a number of well-designed longitudinal studies designed to follow both the user and the nonuser from an early age up through their careers.

A number of investigations have examined the primary means of support among drug patients who were being treated. In a 1971 study of 125 addicts in Chicago, 38 percent said that their major occupation was "hustling," including shoplifting and burglary (Hughes et al., 1971). Another 34 percent were primarily involved in "dealing" or drug distribution. In another study involving 259 users, it was learned that thievery, burglary, or "hustling" stolen goods were the primary means of support for 39 percent; another 21 percent were engaged in "dealing." Five percent supported themselves either through pimping or prostitution (Eckerman et al., 1971; also in National Institute on Drug Abuse, 1978). Other studies have shown that female addicts not engaged in prostitution relied heavily on drug sales and shoplifting as primary means of support (National Institute on Drug Abuse, 1978).

ALCOHOL

Despite the social concern over heroin, grass, and speed, alcohol (ethanol, ethyl alcohol, grain alcohol) has been and remains the number one drug of abuse. It is estimated that there are 15 million alcoholics in this country (Coleman, 1976), and that two out of every three American adults report drinking behavior at least once a year (Albrecht, 1973). Alcohol is responsible for more deaths and violence (it is the third major cause of death) than the other drugs combined. Twenty-five thousand individuals are killed per year in traffic accidents where an individual was driving under the influence of alcohol (Glaser, 1978).

Psychological Effects

Alcoholism as an addiction can be just as devastating to a person, emotionally, as heroin addiction. Like the heroin addict, the alcoholic may have an overpowering compulsion to use the drug and may demonstrate a strong psychological and physical dependence. Compared to the other drugs of abuse, however, attitudes of society toward alcohol use are dramatically different. In virtually every part of the United States it is socially acceptable to consume the drug, and it is legal. Drinking behavior that does not lead to heavy intoxication in public is entirely unregulated. In private, you can get as drunk as you wish, a privilege traditionally disallowed for other drugs.

The effects of alcohol are complex. At low doses (two to four ounces of whiskey) alcohol appears to act as a stimulant on the central nervous system. The person may feel "high," euphoric, full of good cheer, and be socially and physically warm. At moderate and high quantities, however, alcohol becomes a central nervous system depressant. There is a reduction in neuromuscular coordination, visual acuity, and perception of pain and fatigue. The ability to concentrate is impaired, and the ordinary restraints on speech and behavior are weakened. Very often, self-confidence is increased and the person becomes more daring, sometimes foolishly so. In general, alcohol at moderate levels begins to numb the higher brain centers which integrate information with judgment. It should be emphasized at this point that the levels of intoxication are not necessarily dependent upon the intake of alcohol, but like other drugs, they depend on the interplay of a number of variables. One important variable appears to be the amount of alcohol found in the blood stream (see Table 12–1).

Alcohol and Crime

James Coleman (1976) refers to alcohol as a "catalyst for violence" and points out that about one out of three arrests in the United States results from the abuse of alcohol. A survey of all state prisons in 1974 found that 43 percent of the inmates had been drinking when they committed the crime they were serving time for (Law Enforcement Assistance Administration, 1976). Daniel Glaser (1978, p. 275) estimates that ". . . about half the people arrested on any charge in the United States either are under the influence of alcohol when taken into custody, or are held for acts committed when drunk, or both." Some of the offenses are probably misdemeanors, such as public drunkenness. But alcohol also plays a large part in violent crimes.

The relationship between alcohol and violence has always been suspected and feared. While it was believed to exist as a matter of common sense, however, a landmark study by Wolfgang (1958) on 588 Philadelphia homicides brought it into clearer focus and stamped it with scientific confirmation. The Wolfgang survey reported that in 9 percent of the cases, alcohol was present in the victims at the time of the offense; it was present in the offender 11 percent of the time. More importantly, however, alcohol was present in *both* the offender and the victim in 44

TABLE 12-1

Alcohol Levels in Blood for the Average Male and Female, Following Alcohol Consumption on an Empty Stomach

Alcohol consumed	Approximate Alcohol Concentration (in %)	
	155-lb. male	110-lb. female
1 oz. whiskey (86 proof) 12 oz. beer	.018	.025
2 oz. whiskey 24 oz. beer	.040	.050
3 oz. whiskey 36 oz. beer	.053	.074
4 oz. whiskey 48 oz. beer	.070	.100
6 oz. whiskey 60 oz. beer	.105	.148
8 oz. whiskey 72 oz. beer	.140	.200
10 oz. whiskey 84 oz. beer	.175	.248

Usual Reported Effects of Alcohol Consumption

Blood concentration	Effects
.010-.030	Slight change in feelings.
.030-.070	Feelings of warmth, relaxation, friendship.
.070-.150	Talkative, noisy, rowdy; impaired performance in complex tasks such as driving. (.10-15 usually defines "legally drunk.")
.150-.300	Confusion, slurred speech, staggering. Almost everyone at this level acts drunk.
.300-.400	Severe intoxication; individual may pass out.
.400 or above	May cause coma or death from respiratory paralysis.

percent of the homicides. Not only did the Wolfgang study point out that alcohol was a factor in nearly two-thirds of the homicides in Philadelphia during those years, but also that in nearly half the incidents both parties were drinking. The Wolfgang findings indicate that alcohol becomes most volatile when at least two persons are drinking; the data also suggested that alcohol appeared to make the victim as belligerent as the offender in at least one-third of the Philadelphia killings. Subsequent research has continued to support this finding. A high percentage (approximately 50 percent) of heavy drinking in homicide *victims* has been reported by Cleveland (1955), Fisher (1951), Bowden et al., (1958), Verkko (1951), Wilentz (1953), Bensing & Schroeder (1960), and Spain et al. (1951).

Even more studies have found that a large portion of *offenders* (also approximately 50 percent) had been drinking when they committed a violent crime. Cole and his colleagues (1968) report that 51 percent of a sample of California women arrested for homicide had been drinking at the time of the offense. Fifty-five percent of British murderers (Gillies, 1965) and 51 percent of French murderers (Derville et al., 1961) were drinking at the time. Nichol et al. (1973) found that the more severe the drinking problem, the more serious the violent offense. This pattern was also found in Wolfgang's original study, in that alcohol was involved significantly more often in violent homicides than in nonviolent ones. Mayfield (1976) reports that 57 percent of a sample of convicted murderers were drinking when they killed. Rada (1975) cites evidence that 50 percent of a sample of rapists were drinking at the time of the offense. Shupe (1954) obtained urine and blood samples from persons arrested immediately after committing a felony. He found that two-thirds of those arrested for murder (20 out of 30) and nearly half of those arrested for rape (19 out of 32) had at least .10 percent alcohol content in their body fluids. Not only is there evidence for the relationship between alcohol and violent crime in adults, but that association appears to exist in youthful offenders as well. Tinklenberg (1973) found that 53 percent of a sample of California youth under age nineteen convicted of murder, manslaughter, or assault were under the influence of alcohol at the time of their crime.

The relationship between alcohol and violence is well supported, but why does it exist? Several theories have been proposed to explain the correlation. One popular theory hypothesizes that alcohol influences some physiological mechanism within the brain which is responsible for aggression. Some theorists also believe that alcohol energizes a portion of the brain which is responsible for general activity levels (e.g., Barry, Koepfer, & Lutch, 1965) or feelings of power (McClelland et al., 1972). Others contend that alcohol reduces feelings of guilt and anxiety toward aggressive behavior, thereby facilitating its expression (e.g., Kastl, 1969; Tamerin & Mendelson, 1969). These theories predict that the more alcohol is consumed, the greater the stimulation, or the more extensive the lack of inhibition to aggress.

More recent evidence, however, suggests that the relationship is not that clearcut. A series of studies by Stuart Taylor and his associates (Taylor & Gammon, 1975; Taylor et al., 1976a, 1976b) have found that small doses of alcohol (0.5 ounces of vodka or bourbon per 40 pounds of body weight) tend to inhibit aggression, while larger doses (1.5 ounces per 40 pounds) tend to facilitate aggression. Therefore, depending on the amount, alcohol may either inhibit or facilitate expressions of aggression and violence.

The Taylor experiments are in agreement with the known pharmacological effect of alcohol. At small amounts, alcohol appears to stimulate ("energize") the central nervous system, generating mild euphoria and a sense of wellbeing. This "good cheer" becomes readily apparent at a party when, after a couple of drinks, people tend to take on a happy frame of mind. As the alcoholic intake increases, however, it begins to depress the integrating functions of the cortex, causing some disorganization in the appropriate response sequences in the social setting. At moderate levels of alcoholic intoxication, threats and altercations increase, and the party may become unpleasant with gestures and threats of belligerence. At high levels, motor coordination and self-control begin to disintegrate, giving way eventually to stupor. Under high intoxication levels, of course, alcohol-induced violence becomes a remote possibility. From what we understand about the effects of alcohol so far, the relationship between it and violence appears to be curvilinear, as illustrated in Figure 12–1.

The Taylor studies also emphasize another important point: aggression and violence do not generally occur unless the persons involved are

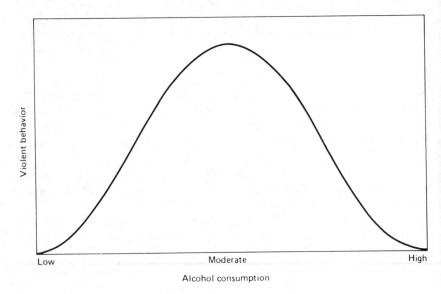

FIGURE 12-1. Hypothesized relationship between the tendency to be violent and the amount of alcohol consumed.

threatened or provoked in some manner. This finding supports well the victim-precipitated violence observed by Wolfgang and others. It seems that in many cases of homicide and aggravated assault, the victim is also partially at fault.

The complexities of the violence-alcohol relationship do not end here. Alan Lang and his colleagues (1975) found that the alcohol consumed by a person may not be as important as what the person expects from it. Some people expect certain effects, independent of the pharmacological effects. Some anticipate acting more aggressively "under the influence" because alcohol is supposed to have that effect. If a person expects alcohol to influence behavior in a preconceived way, it probably will, according to Lang. Moreover, the person avoids blame for his or her actions, because society tends to accept the "I-was-drunk" explanation. In fact, Sobell and Sobell (1973) have suggested that one of the rewarding aspects of heavy drinking is that it provides a socially acceptable excuse for engaging in inappropriate behavior.

In the Lang et al. (1975) experiment, half of the subjects were led to believe that they would be drinking alcohol, which actually was either vodka or tonic water. The other half were told they would be drinking tonic water, not alcohol. However, half the members of this second group were actually given vodka, and the other half received the tonic water they expected. The study's results indicated that "the only significant determinant of aggression was the expectation factor; subjects who believed they had consumed alcohol were more aggressive than subjects who believed they had consumed a nonalcoholic beverage, regardless of the actual alcohol content of the drinks administered" (p. 508).

This experiment underscores one of the central themes embedded in this book. Expectancies largely dictate what a person will do in a given situation. It is possible that some people become belligerent while drinking because they expect that alcohol should prompt that kind of behavior. This expectancy is learned, primarily through social learning. If people expect to be peaceful and relaxed under the influence of alcohol, then it is highly likely that they will feel precisely that way.

One of the more viable theories advanced on why people drink alcohol to excess is the tension-reducing hypothesis, which states that alcohol, because it is a depressant drug, reduces tension and that this relief of tension reinforces the drinking response (Marlatt, 1976). Therefore, when a person is anxious and tense, one way to reduce this tension is to consume alcohol. Marlatt also brings in the expectancy factor, however, by commenting: "There is ample reason to believe that many drinkers, both alcoholics and nonalcoholics, have learned to expect that taking a drink or two will make them feel more relaxed" (1976, p. 277).

Others may drink because they expect alcohol to act as a "social lubricant." Shy, introverted persons may, after a couple of drinks, become the life of the party because they believe in the power of alcohol. McClelland and his colleagues observed that alcohol leads to feelings of "social power" and "personal power." ". . . men drink primarily to feel stronger. Those for whom personalized power is a particular concern drink more heavily" (McClelland et al., 1972, p. 334). In this case, some people may drink because they expect alcohol will provide the courage to influence what happens to them; we are again discussing control over one's environment.

The pharmacological effects of alcohol are obviously important. For example, a number of researchers (e.g., Shuntick & Taylor, 1972; Teger et al., 1969) have suggested that different types of alcohol influence behavior differently. Presumably, alcoholic beverages which contain more congeners are more likely to prompt aggressive behavior. The term "congeners" is used to refer to a group of chemicals found in commercial alcoholic beverages. Bourbon contains the most congeners, while vodka contains the least (Carroll, 1970). In general, the brown-colored liquors (whiskey, scotch) contain more congeners than clear liquors do (light rum, vodka, gin). If congeners are instrumental in the alcohol-violence correlation, then we would expect that bourbon would be more likely to be related to aggressive behavior than vodka. So far, the evidence remains unclear, and the relationship appears more complicated than originally believed. Taylor and Gammon (1975) report data that while bourbon may have more potency for aggressive behavior than vodka, vodka appears to be absorbed into the blood stream more quickly. Thus, during a 90-minute period, subjects who drank equal amounts of bourbon and vodka had greater amounts of vodka than the more slowly-absorbed bourbon in their blood stream.

The expectancy factor also comes into play here. That is, liquors like bourbon, whiskey, rye, and scotch are traditionally regarded as more masculine than the lighter-colored liquors. Those individuals who regard themselves as more masculine (and more aggressive) are more apt to order scotch on the rocks (or beer) than a daiquiri or a gimlet. This "macho" factor must also be examined more carefully in research designs.

In summary, there is a significant relationship between alcohol and the violent crimes of assault, rape, and homicide. In fact, the alcohol-violent crime relationship is stronger than reported for any of the other drugs reviewed in this chapter. At the same time, we need to temper that statement by acknowledging that the relationship is complex and that we do not yet know precisely what it means. The nature of the alcohol-violent crime correlation is predicated on a large matrix of interacting pharmacological, psychological, and social variables. More experimental studies designed to ease out the *causal* links will be the only way of providing the final answers.

SUMMARY

This chapter evaluated the relationship between crime and a number of drugs commonly associated with criminal behavior. Four major drug categories were identified: the hallucinogens, the stimulants, the opiate narcotics, and the sedative-hypnotics. Rather than discuss all the drugs in each category we considered only those commonly believed to be associated with criminal behavior.

Cannabis extracts, which include marihuana and hashish, are very mild hallucinogens with few psychological side effects. No significant relationship between cannabis use and crime has been consistently reported in the research literature. Much of the present day hullabaloo concerning marihuana and crime appears to be a carryover from attitudes developed during the pre-1950 era.

Amphetamines and cocaine represented the stimulant group. Most illegal users of these amphetamines do not participate in crime other than possession or sale of regulated drugs. However, there are numerous documented cases in which heavy users of amphetamines entered psychological states which predisposed them toward violence and paranoid features. In addition, correlational studies have found that many violent offenders have a history of amphetamine abuse, but as in all correlations, it is difficult to determine what contributes to what. Research evidence suggests that most violent offenders who are also heavy users of amphetamines were violent prior to, or independent of, amphetamine abuse.

Heroin was the representative narcotic drug considered. Heroin and most other narcotics appear to be strongly addictive, particularly relating to psychological dependency. Evidence also indicates that the drug is addictive enough, and also expensive enough, to require substantial funds for its use. There is a high correlation between opiate and heroin addiction and *income-generating* crimes. This correlation strongly suggests that many opiate users burglarize, shoplift, and generally "hustle" to support their drug habit.

Alcohol represented the sedative-hypnotic group. Of all the drugs reviewed, alcohol shows the strongest relationship with violent offenses such as rape, homicide, and aggravated assault.

However, the relationships between crime and all the drugs discussed in this chapter are complex, involving poorly understood interactions between numerous pharmacological, social, and psychological variables. Research is beginning to ease some data out of the complicated crime-drug relationship, but much more needs to be done before any solid understanding of the relationship can occur.

KEY CONCEPTS FOR REVIEW

Hallucinogens
Stimulants
Opiate narcotics
Sedative-hypnotics
Tolerance
Dependence
Cannabis
Amphetamines
Cocaine
Narcotics
Heroin
Alcohol
Congeners

SUGGESTED READINGS

Canadian Government's Commission of Inquiry. The non-medical use of drugs: Interim report. London: Penguin Books, 1971.
Concise, readable presentation of the relationship between major drugs and crime.

Hofmann, F.G. *A handbook on drug and alcohol abuse: The biomedical aspects.* New York: Oxford Univ. Press, 1975.
An outstanding and comprehensive treatment on all aspects of drug abuse, especially as it relates to crime.

Julien, R.M. *A primer of drug action.* San Francisco: Freeman, 1975.
An excellent review of the effects of the major drugs, written for the undergraduate without a background in the sciences.

National Commission on Marihuana and Drug Abuse. *Drug use in America: Problems in perspective,* 2nd report. Washington, D.C.: U.S. Government Printing Office, 1973.
An objective, research-based report on the empirical findings concerning the relationship between drugs and crime.

TREATMENT OF CRIMINAL BEHAVIOR

THIRTEEN

The idea that nothing works is mental depression rather than communication.

Morris, 1977, p. 155

In the previous chapters we examined criminal behavior from a psychological perspective. Learning principles were used to help explain how deviant behavior is acquired as well as how and why it is evoked and maintained. In this chapter we shall see what empirical evidence tells us about the effectiveness of procedures for suppressing, treating, and preventing criminal behavior. It is not the intention here to provide a comprehensive discussion of the many kinds of treatment methods employed in the correctional system. Rather, only some of the more widespread problems, philosophies, and treatment procedures will be discussed and, in some cases, merely touched upon. To do justice to the area of correctional psychology would require an extensive book in its own right.

Three points should be stressed at the outset. First, the position taken in this book is that criminal behavior represents a variety of response patterns that an individual feels are effective in dealing with the world, but which society or the powerful in-group considers illegal or against its best interest. The individual comes to think that the behavioral patterns are effective because he or she has seen them work for someone else or has discovered that they help in attaining something positive or avoiding something negative. Moreover, if the behaviors are learned, it stands to reason that they can be altered through learning principles. Behaviors that no longer prove effective in obtaining certain goals are replaced by more effective ones.

Second, because people learn different behaviors in different ways and for different reasons, deviant or antisocial behaviors will always exist in situations where people with different capacities are interacting with the social and physical environment. Because of the vast complexities in behavior, no matter how regimented and controlling the environment, there are always a few individuals who deviate. In this sense, criminal behavior is inevitable and probably will always exist—unless of course social regulations and criminal laws are abolished or laws are passed which are "impossible" to violate. This does not mean, however, that criminal behavior cannot be controlled, reduced, and modified to a large extent.

Third, the areas of correctional rehabilitation, prisoner treatment programs, deterrence, punishment, and crime prevention are permeated with disenchantment, controversy, and mythology. There are cries from all sides that "it just doesn't work" or "it can't work," whatever the approach. The intention of this chapter is not to dwell upon or analyze the criminal justice or correctional system. Rather, we will look at those areas in which psychology has been applied to corrections, and where the procedures used have not been understood, have been researched insufficiently, or have been incorrectly implemented.

SOCIETAL RATIONALE FOR IMPRISONMENT OF OFFENDERS

Four fundamental considerations are usually in operation when offenders are sentenced: 1. protection of other members of society, 2. rehabilitation or behavioral correction, 3. punishment, and 4. deterrence. The first consideration is the most straightforward for the justification of legal punishment. If the criminal is believed dangerous to society, it is obvious that society must be protected from future injustices and injury. Put the criminal away and throw away the key. Since the notions and determinations of "dangerousness" were presented earlier in the book, they will not be covered in any detail here.

The question of the usefulness of rehabilitation and treatment often creates heated debate. Recently, a tidal wave of discontent about the effectiveness of rehabilitation on criminal conduct has swept through the correctional system. Riding the crest was the provocative article by R.M. Martinson (1974) which argued that the concept of rehabilitation through any form of treatment presently being used does not work. Correctional managers were put on notice that rehabilitation programs were not efficacious (Adams, 1977). Although the disenchantment has subsided somewhat, the concept of rehabilitation has yet to gain a comfortable foothold in the correctional system. In this chapter we will review and critically examine the concepts of rehabilitation and treatment, especially with reference to behavior modification.

Punishment and deterrence are closely linked. Presumably, the threat of punishment deters people from doing things society regards as illegal or immoral. Society has for a very long time assumed that some form of punishment is an effective method of behavior control and suppression. Even the insect world relies on aversive or painful stimuli to discourage behavior. Think of a bee sting and how rapidly you condition to stimuli associated with bees and hives.

The basic justification for the use of punishment as a deterrent is twofold. First, it is believed that punishment and its public disclosure reveal to the members of a society what the consequence of legal transgression will be. The rationale is: this is what will happen to you if you violate the law. The underpinning of the rationale is that the threat and the fear of punishment should act as a potent deterrent. Second, punishment applied directly to the offender should deter him or her personally from future violations. In fact, it is traditionally assumed that direct application of aversive circumstances should be more effective than the observation or knowledge of punishing consequences. In other words, if a shoplifter is not deterred from a first offense by the presence of signs that he or she will be prosecuted, then the embarrassment at having his or her name published and the pain of paying a fine should prevent future infractions.

Theoretical discussions on the effects of deterrence often revolve around the dichotomy expressed above, with the term general deterrence used for the threat of punishment on the public at large and special deterrence for the actual experience of punishment (see Andenaes, 1968). The long-debated question of how effective general and special deterrence are on criminal conduct has never been satisfactorily answered, and because of the complexities involved, it may never be. It is reasonable to assume, however, that general deterrence or the threat of punishment does prevent a significant number of people from violating the law. Indirect evidence for this is provided when law enforcement agencies go on strike.

In October, 1969, 1,600 Montreal police officers and 600 administrators out of a total of 3,833 went on strike, an event which lessened the threat of punishment and decreased substantially the chances of criminal detection. The work stoppage lasted for sixteen hours, during which there were nine bank holdups and seventeen robberies of commercial establishments (Law Reform Commission of Canada, 1976). Overall, there was a dramatic increase in criminal behavior (estimates as high as 300 percent were reported in some localities), although property offenses declined because homeowners and storeowners increased their surveillance.

In August 1971, another police strike took place, this one in Sydney, Nova Scotia, and a similar wave of violence and vandalism occurred before heavy rains cooled things down. The 1977 blackouts in New York City stimulated a rash of looting and vandalism and appeared to be partly due to the effects of deindividuation, which, you will recall, lowers the sense of responsibility and the threat of punishment.

There are numerous other examples where threat of punishment is decreased in some way and a certain segment of the population engages in criminal conduct. Due to the threat of punishment established through socialization and moral development, however, it is reasonable to assume that a large segment of the population will not engage in "serious" criminal activity, even if there is no police officer at the elbow. For some people, fear of social or parental disapproval and even self-disapproval operate as sufficient deterrents. More in keeping with the complexities of human behavior, it is probable that some combination of the above internal and external checks are operating for most people.

Let's now examine the concepts of punishment and deterrence, particularly what is known from the psychological research concerning their effects on human behavior. We will look at punishment as a deterrent and also as a potential modifier of behavior.

THE EFFECTS OF PUNISHMENT

One deeply ingrained, widespread belief is that punishment—or the threat of it—will deter a person from committing additional wrong or illegal acts. Put simply, the notion that you will get punished for something should prevent you from engaging in that act in the future. In this context, it is not unusual to hear people clamor that the high crime rate exists because society is too soft on the criminal. If capital punishment could be brought back, the logic goes, the homicide rates would decrease. Variations on this theme include the assertion that what the juvenile delinquent needs is a good whipping and that parents are not strict enough and should use the belt more "like my ole man did to me." Spare the rod and spoil the child is a maxim which has guided many parents in the socialization of their children.

On the other side of the ledger are the people who assert that punishment is a very ineffective way of socializing children or controlling crime. Clinicians and psychologists have been particularly vocal in advocating the elimination of punishment and the encouragement of more humane, less brutal methods of socialization. Freud and most of his followers agreed that any form of punishment can permanently scar the normal development of the child. Discipline should be accomplished through reasoning with the child and not through physical beatings or threats of withdrawal of love or approval. An early psychologist whose views have strongly influenced education, Edward Lee Thorndike, believed that punishment was a poor method of eliminating or suppressing behavior. Later work by the learning psychologists B.F. Skinner and William Estes supported the Thorndike contention and the antipunishment banner was carried up through the 1950s.

What is amazing is that during these years conclusions about punishment were based on so little experimentation and empirical data. Fortunately, during the late 1950s N.H. Azrin and his colleagues re-examined punishment under laboratory conditions. It was discovered that punishment was not only a more complex phenomenon than originally believed, but also it could be a highly effective method for response suppression under certain conditions. Azrin's experiments stimulated further research by numerous other investigators and for the first time the literature on punishment began to build on a solid, empirical foundation.

Before we review this research, it is essential that we define our term. "Punishment" is typically described in two ways: 1. presentation of an aversive or painful stimulus when a certain behavior occurs, and 2. presentation of any event that reduces the probability of responding (Walters & Grusec, 1977). The administration of an electric shock, a slap, or a verbal reprimand are examples of the first definition. Thus, no distinction is made as to whether the punishing stimulus is physical, psychological (withdrawal of love), or social (embarrassment in front of relevant others). The second definition is more functional in that any situation or event which reduces the occurrence of a behavior is by definition "punishing." Although there are several situations in which one definition fits better than the other, most researchers prefer the first because it includes an aversive connotation.

Severity of Punishment

The effectiveness of punishment in controlling or suppressing antisocial or illegal behavior is determined by a number of factors. There is a large body of evidence based on experiments with animals that the more severe the punishment the greater the suppression of behavior—at least temporarily. Because of the complexities inherent in human cognitive ability and the ethical problems relating to punishing human subjects to a severe degree, the effects of punishment intensity on humans appears less clear. Meaningful *threats* of severe punishment seem to be effective as general deterrents of disapproved behavior for most people (Baron, 1977). This may be a different story for psychopaths and undersocialized offenders, however.

Experimental studies which have applied severe punishments for the suppression of specific behavior in humans are, for obvious ethical reasons, rare. Therefore, the effect of severe punishment as a specific deterrent on humans is largely unknown. However, administration of relatively mild punishment (time out in a room away from others, mild verbal reprimand) has been shown to be a highly effective procedure with children, if done with a clear understanding of the principles involved (e.g., Brown & Tyler, 1968; Brown & Elliott, 1965).

The effectiveness of severe punishment—either threatened or applied—would seem to depend upon a number of important variables; when, how often, how, and why are crucial factors. If a person feels that the punishment is legitimate and fair, it is likely to affect his or her behavior differently than it would if it was interpreted as being unfair and unjust. In the latter case, the subject may seek brutal revenge toward the punisher. We shall spend more time later looking at these variables.

One thing needs to be emphasized before proceeding. The research literature continually points out that, regardless of the severity of the punishment, the punished response will emerge again if a satisfactory alternative response pattern does not exist in the person's repertoire. That is, punishment by itself is not effective in the long run. If an alternative response pattern does exist, and if it has achieved rewards for the individual in the past, the person will not only discard the punished pattern more rapidly but will be more likely to keep it suppressed for longer periods of time. Note that this point assumed that the gains from the alternative behavior subjectively outweigh the gains of the punished behavior. On the other hand, if the punished behavior has been frequently and strongly reinforced in the past and the alternative response pattern has not been frequently or attractively rewarded, then the individual will probably suppress the punished behavior in the presence of the punishing agent, but then resume the behavior in the absence of that agent or punishing situation.

Let's say seven-year-old Benjamin tends to be light-fingered around the family's supply of petty cash. Father institutes various punishment and deterrence mechanisms. A mild verbal rebuke and a lecture on ethical conduct have a temporary effect, but the temptation to supplement his supply of baseball cards is too overwhelming, and Benjamin soon dips into the till again. Father removes the cash, administers a few belts with the meter stick, and withdraws the privilege of staying up to watch Spider Man. Benjamin will probably not hit the money jar again for a while, but he might surreptitiously dig into mother's sweater pockets, because those baseball cards are important to him. If, however, his parents provide opportunities for Benjamin to earn his own cash—alternative forms of behavior—along with the knowledge of punishment and proper moral development, the plan is far more likely to work.

Andenaes also illustrates this point when he remarks, "A professional criminal may be so strongly involved in his profession that he feels there are no real alternatives regardless of the penalties" (1969, p. 88). Andenaes elaborates by offering the example of an eighty-seven-year-old

FIGURE 13–1. Exterior of small state prison.

Greek pickpocket who had 50 previous convictions and had spent as many years behind prison walls. The old man had not developed an alternate way of making it in the world, and, once released from prison, he quickly reverted to his habitual response pattern.

This is an important point for the field of corrections. One of the reasons that punishment and the threat of it has failed to act as an effective deterrent is that offenders often lack alternatives, with payoffs equivalent to the illegal or antisocial behavior. Their most deeply ingrained, early formed habitual behaviors for getting the things they want are the behaviors they have been incarcerated for. Attempt at rehabilitation must carefully take this into consideration. Inmates must be trained to develop alternative behaviors that are attractive and effective in acquiring material, social, and psychological rewards. If an inmate is trained to be a sheet-metal worker, then that person must gain at least some of the rewards provided by the preferred criminal behavior. It is also important for the "convict" to be able to get a job following incarceration and to be accepted by that particular employment community.

Therefore, punishment or nonreward for criminal behavior, if delivered under optimal conditions and coupled with the acquisition or strengthening of socially approved alternative behavior, theoretically would be an excellent procedure to follow in eliminating and controlling criminal behavior. Realistically, however, it is difficult to achieve for a number of reasons. Below we will discuss some additional variables that are important in the delivery of punishment.

Consistency and Immediacy of Punishment

Two other principles formulated from the learning laboratory are important to consider if the threat or application of punishment is to be effective in suppressing behavior: *consistency* and *immediacy*. One of the conclusions established from the learning experimental data is that in order for punishment to be most effective it must be administered with consistency, rather than occasionally or haphazardly. Consistency means that a specific event must be administered each time a specific behavior occurs. For example, if punishment occurs at random across a wide variety of behaviors, the individual begins to believe that punishment is not contingent upon anything that he or she is doing, but rather is due to chance or fate. On the other hand, if a person receives an immediate punishing event contingent upon the performance of an act, the act is quickly suppressed, or at least an association between the act and an aversive event is established.

As we saw in Chapter 5, a very common observation from the family backgrounds of delinquents is that discipline was administered inconsistently and often without apparent rhyme or reason. Under these conditions the individual begins to develop the belief that whatever happens is a matter of chance or luck; events are really beyond his or her control. Detection and arrest for illegal or delinquent behaviors are due to an unlucky break, and the court disposition is based on whim and fate. This finding indicates that parents who have decided to punish a child for behaving in a specific way should be consistent in their practices; if society has elected to employ punishment as a deterrent, it should also adhere to the same principle.

In actuality, we know that punishment for antisocial or criminal behavior is dished out inconsistently and periodically by society and the judicial system. Very few property and few less serious crimes are detected, and when they are it is often due to chance or an accident on the part of law enforcement or the offender. Punishment is administered with discrimination and often depends upon what judge one gets. Under these conditions, crime pays—particularly property crime. In the long run, the number and value of the rewards gained through many forms of criminal behavior far outnumber the sporadic negative events of punishment administered by society. Moreover, the general deterrence of threat of punishment is undermined because the public also realizes the remote chance of detection and eventual punishment. It is interesting to note, also, that the more severe penalties (incarceration) are reserved for crimes ordinarily not repeated by the offender (e.g., homicide), while the lighter sentences are directed at crimes where high property and material gain are often the rule.

Immediacy, the second principle, refers to the duration of time between the target behavior and the delivery of punishment. Research on subhumans repeatedly demonstrates that in order for either reward or punishment to be maximally effective, it must be administered as soon after the onset of the act as possible. Delayed reinforcement or punishment is an inefficient way of modifying or suppressing behavior. A clear example of this principle can be found in the experience of housebreaking puppies. Punishment and reprimand should follow as soon after the beginning of the act as possible if housebreaking is to occur within a reasonable period of time. If you punish the pup sometime after the act, he not only does not understand the reason for it, but probably begins to feel that punishment occurs in your presence but is not directed at any specific behavior. Through conditioning he learns to fear you but does not become housebroken.

The optimal time delay for punishment to produce maximum results is obviously more complicated in humans, but the research directed at this question is sparse and incomplete. Humans can store in memory the contingencies between behavior and punishment more efficiently than can lower animals and can also be reasoned with verbally. It would appear, however, that regardless of the superior human brain, deviant behaviors would be most intensely associated with aversive conditions if the aversive agents were delivered as soon after the beginning of the act as possible. This is because the act is still vividly in a person's mind, and conditioning is most potent when features of the event and stimuli are linked to the physiological discomfort accompanying the event.

In our society punishment for a criminal act is often delayed for months or years after the offense was committed, because of the overcrowded court dockets and the overworked judicial system. Case preparation also takes time. On occasion, the offender is detected and arrested while the offense is in progress and is immediately incarcerated while awaiting trial. In general, however, the various forms of punishment for criminal offenses are so far removed as to make their effectiveness minimal or nonexistent.

Other Considerations

Punishment seems to be more effective if the socializing agent is respected and liked, presumably because the positive agent increases the subjective discomfort experienced (Walters & Grusec, 1977). Peers and friends as punishing agents would be more productive in suppressing undesirable behavior than unknown, disliked, or impersonal agents. If your friends and loved ones think less highly of you because of your actions, it hurts much more than if a stranger does.

Also, some professionals resist punishment, assuming it produces psychological side effects and emotional scars. Walters and Grusec consider this part of the "punishment mythology," and they conclude after an extensive and critical review of the general punishment literature that, "There is no reason to believe, on the basis of the existing experimental evidence, that punishment is necessarily accompanied by undesirable emotional disturbances" (1977, p. 165). We have seen earlier, however, that forms of *physical* punishment may have the side effect of training individuals, through the process of modeling, to behave aggressively under certain conditions.

One common belief is that an effective way to inhibit criminal behavior is to have others watch via public or media displays what happens to people who perform that behavior. This notion has some research support. Seeing someone getting punished for a deviant behavior appears to be effective in temporarily suppressing that behavior, even though the consequences for deviation are never directly experienced by the observer (Bandura, 1965). This finding is very much in line with the social learning perspective. Since much learning and response acquisition are accomplished through imitation, it would also appear to hold that response suppression may be developed through the same process. That is, witnessing a relevant, significant model being punished for a certain response would tend to reduce or suppress a similar response in the observer. However, these inhibition effects of modeling should also depend upon the extent to which the person can identify with the model and situation. In other words, can the observer imagine him- or herself in that set of circumstances and believe "this could happen to me"? While these suggestions seem consistent with the findings, they must remain hypothetical. Again, there needs to be considerably more empirical study before a clearer understanding of the effects of vicarious punishment on deviant behavior is achieved.

In summary, punishment is an effective technique for suppressing behavior under certain conditions. The timing, the method, the intensity, and the perceived purpose are all important considerations in threatening and applying punishment. Unless optimal conditions can be achieved, however, punishment may prove to be an extremely unproductive, ineffective procedure. Moreover, alternative behaviors, with pay-offs, must be made available if the undesired behavior is to be suppressed for long periods of time. If recidivism rates are any indication, the present social system for punishment of criminal behavior is extremely ineffective as a specific deterrent. Although its effectiveness as a general deterrent is difficult to gauge, it does seem to deter some segments of the population from serious criminal activity under most conditions.

DEVELOPMENT OF ALTERNATIVE BEHAVIORS

The fundamental goal of rehabilitation and treatment for the offender is to suppress unlawful, antisocial behavior and to develop lawful alternative behavior which will generalize to the world beyond the confines of an institution, or at least the treatment situation. Under the constraints of political, social, and economic pressures, this goal is difficult even to approach. For example, the positive, alternative behavior to be developed must be both meaningful and capable of bringing significant social, psychological, and material rewards. This goal, for many reasons, is a very tall order. It would mean educating the general public and many professionals about the long-term benefits and the probabilities of success, and there would be many failures, especially in the beginning. It would also require staggering financial investments in facilities, well-trained staff, job placement, and long-term, carefully executed research. The prison as it now stands is a poor setting in which to try to implement this approach. It would have to be replaced by a progression of educational and employment steps complemented with counseling by well-trained personnel and strong commitment from administration. On the other hand, unlawful behavior would have to be made less attractive than alternative behavior, perhaps by burdening it with the threat of heavy material and social costs, such as financial restitution and public exposure.

These proposals probably sound like an idealized package that has been heard in some form several times before. Also, correctional personnel who have been exposed to wide varieties of "hard-core" criminals daily and under adverse conditions are apt to view a large segment of the prison population as totally incorrigible and to suspect and resist any notion of rehabilitation. Under the stress and fight for survival (patterns

FIGURE 13–2. Still-in-use cell-block in an unidentified prison.

that are found in prisons) daily exposure to this negative side of human behavior is enough to make anyone pessimistic and suspicious about do-gooders who fail to understand the realistic side of prison life or the life patterns of habitual offenders.

It must be admitted that many convicted individuals are unlikely to benefit from any such program and should remain in prison for society's protection. For those individuals, an institution serves as society's protector, but let's not fool ourselves by calling it a "correctional facility." There is also little doubt that the threat of imprisonment serves as a deterrent for some potential offenders. Moreover, prison in many ways is an easy, simple solution which powerful members of society use to placate the public about the "crime problem," and this latter approach would be the most difficult to change.

Despite these realities, evidence from psychological research strongly suggests that the "suppression-alternative behavior" model provides us with the most powerful technique we presently have available for altering a significant portion of the criminal behavior patterns. The model still requires extensive refinement and carefully monitored applications across numerous conditions. Critics rightly point out that the track record of rehabilitation is a dismal failure, but they wrongly assert that rehabilitation cannot work. Present debate focuses on the poor success of rehabilitation and treatment, but not enough on alternative methods. In the next section, we examine more closely whether the rehabilitation concept has indeed failed and the reasons why or why not.

Rehabilitation and Treatment

According to Rick Carlson, "Rehabilitation is out of fashion today. It is not dead yet, but the literature is littered with death warrants" (1976, p. 32). He implies that the behavioral science profession (psychologists, psychiatrists, and social workers) are responsible for overselling a worthless bunch of goods to the correctional system.

Numerous other practitioners, administrators, and academicians have come to the same or similar conclusions, but the most visible have been those of Robert Martinson (1974). Martinson reviewed 231 studies of prison rehabilitative programs and concluded: "With few and isolated exceptions, the rehabilitative efforts that have been reported so far have had no appreciable effect on recidivism" (p. 25). His conclusion that "nothing works" has had a powerful effect on criminal justice administrators. For a while, there was an avid shift away from rehabilitation and toward other models of corrections, such as strict punishment without any rehabilitation. Now that the dust has settled somewhat and the eagerness to discard rehabilitation programs in their entirety has subsided, even Martinson (Lipton, Martinson, & Wilks, 1975) has reduced his onslaught to *"almost* nothing works."

One of the first to criticize Martinson's "nothing works" doctrine was Ted Palmer (1975), who pointed out that Martinson tended to reject any type of rehabilitative treatment which was not *highly* successful. It seems that Martinson was seeking a cure-all approach that would work for everyone, all or almost all of the time. Martinson was not interested in partial success, and he appeared indifferent to the fact that about one-half (48 percent) of his 231 sample studies showed success with at least part of their subjects.

Stuart Adams (1976) pointed out that correctional treatments appear to be as effective as the partial success rate achieved thus far by traditional psychotherapy with the general population. Adams also noted that many of the projects which Martinson considered failures demonstrated behavioral improvement during treatment, but that there was a regression to original behavior upon return to the original environment (Adams, 1977). In some cases the return to criminal behavior occurred years after improved behavior during treatment. Martinson's tendency to regard only the long-term signs of cure masks the short-term effect of correctional treatment. Unless the individual has sufficient alternative behavior patterns and skills for pay-offs in the outside world, an eventual return to original ways is not surprising. Recall our earlier discussion about the effectiveness of punishment along with the need to provide alternative, satisfying behaviors. Adams posits: "Careful examination of Martinson's methods and conclusions suggests that he has given us a mixture of science, rhetoric, and legerdemain, and it is difficult to say which predominates" (1977, p. 325).

Seymour Halleck (Halleck & Witte, 1977) notes that Martinson's critique spanned the years 1945 to 1967, when evaluation and research methodology relating to corrections was in its infancy. "Evaluations since 1967 have, in general, been more thorough and more reliable statistically than those before that date" (Halleck & Witte, 1977, p. 376). Halleck believes that the more recent evaluations are more promising and cites, as examples, two work-release programs in California which significantly reduced the recidivism rate.

One of the most cogent arguments against eagerly accepting the ineffectiveness of correctional treatment was voiced by Herbert Quay (1977). Quay noted that evaluations of correctional treatment programs have concentrated more on the adequacy of the research designs and measurement of outcomes than on the integrity of the program being evaluated. Evaluations of programs must include the rationale and goals of the treatment used and how that treatment was delivered. Does what actually happens meet the requirements spelled out for that particular form of treatment? Simply labeling a program "treatment" or "counseling" does not tell us very much about what happened in the program. For example, were the counseling sessions actually held? How well were they attended? Were the inmates coerced into participating in the program, or were they able to volunteer freely without implicit threat?

Quay also advocates scrutinizing the delivery of the treatment. Were the "counselors" untrained prison guards or naive psychologists? Quay suggests that some evidence of competence to deliver treatment might be measured by the counselors' past educational experience, academic degrees, or similar qualifications. In evaluating rehabilitation programs, we should also examine the nature of the training and orientation given to the counselors. Was the training provided in two one-hour lectures by disinterested instructors? Or was the training given intensively over a period of weeks by stimulating personnel? What kind of supervision did the treatment personnel receive?

Finally, how generalizable is the treatment approach to all inmates? To be most effective, any treatment-rehabilitative program should be formulated in relation to the needs and potentialities of a given individual, a consideration sometimes called *differential treatment.*

In his review of the literature, Quay finds that studies evaluating correctional treatment have provided little information concerning the above considerations. In one of the two studies which did describe in some detail the treatment procedures, goals, and personnel (Kassebaum et al., 1971), it was quite evident that the planning, goals, and implementation of the program were poorly done.

Before people jump on the bandwagon to proclaim the ineffectiveness and worthlessness of correctional treatment, therefore, it must be given a chance to perform under sophisticated planning, careful and dedicated execution, and well-designed methods of evaluation. It would be a mistake to discard a potentially useful concept because of misunderstanding and poorly conceived evaluation methods, and wait for the rehabilitative treatment pendulum to swing back a decade or two later.

Psychotherapy

Despite all the problems in evaluating rehabilitative programs, are there any forms of psychological treatment which are effective, or at least potentially effective, in suppressing unlawful behavior and which also develop alternative behaviors that generalize from the treatment situation to other situations? Before we can answer this difficult question adequately, we must describe briefly what is meant by psychological treatment or psychotherapy.

Psychotherapy refers to a set of procedures or techniques used to help individuals or groups alter their maladaptive behavior, develop adaptive behavior, or both. The behavior may be considered maladaptive by the individual or by society. "Psychotherapy," "therapy," and "treatment" are often used interchangeably in the professional field. Psychotherapy can be divided into five very broad categories: psychoanalytic therapy, behavior therapy, humanistic-existential therapies, interpersonal therapy, and group therapy. Each has been tried to some extent within the correctional system under wide variations in method, purpose, and commitment. In recent years, various forms of group therapy, reality therapy (a form of humanistic-existential therapy), and behavior therapy have been the most popular in correctional institutions.

Behavior therapy (also called behavior modification) has drawn the greatest amount of attention and controversy, for a number of reasons. For one thing, it carries with it the stamp of scientific approval and has been shown to be highly effective in changing and developing specific behaviors under controlled, experimental conditions. Another strong selling point is its apparent simplicity and the ease with which it can be applied by paraprofessionals with minimal training. Probably its strongest appeal for administrators lies in the fact that it is economical because it does not require a legion of high-level professionals, and it can be immediately beneficial for controlling unmanageable behavior in the institution. Because of its precision and quantification of observable behaviors, it also lends itself very well to evaluation and research.

By contrast, despite the fact that hundreds of thousands of persons go through some form of psychotherapy each year, we have little scientific information to show how often other forms of treatment are successful: ". . . the wide variation among therapists, patients, goals, procedures and definitions of success have made it virtually impossible to reach any valid conclusions" (Coleman, 1976, p. 716). Behavior therapy has provided us with the data to determine success and failure rates and what is meant by those rates. Therefore, it would be useful to examine some of the programs utilizing this treatment method on adult and juvenile offenders. This is not to say that other forms of therapy are not as effective or as useful.

Treatment procedures using a more humanistic approach offer some excellent possibilities in the correctional system, particularly when it comes to establishing some personal control over the environment. Institutionalized humans often must fight for some control over their personal lives or else they would succumb to hopelessness, depression, and despair. If the treatment does not allow considerable freedom of choice and enable the individual to live more satisfactorily, then the treatment methods will be resisted. Humanistic-oriented therapy offers this possibility. In fact, one of the major problems with behavior therapy in corrections is that its methods are interpreted by many inmates as just one more procedure used by society to usurp personal freedom and increase environmental control.

To go over the therapies utilized in correctional facilities in adequate detail would require another volume. However, behavior therapy will be discussed in the remainder of this chapter, not only because of the widespread attention it has received, but also because it is one of the few psychological treatment methods which lends itself to critical evaluation and empirical scrutiny.

Behavior Therapy

We referred above to the controversy surrounding behavior therapy, or behavior modification. What has happened is that the public and the media have too often associated it with brain control, brainwashing, or with radical surgical procedures on portions of the brain. This conception has been further distorted by prisoner complaints directed at some poorly planned behavioral programs which have drawn the attention and the indignation of civil rights groups, followed by lawsuits and congressional hearings (Kennedy, 1976). Apparently because of political and public pressure, the Federal Bureau of Prisons decided to discontinue its behavioral-based project START in February 1974. This decision was followed within a week by an announcement by the Law Enforcement Assistance Agency (LEAA) that it was discontinuing its funding of prison programs involving behavior modification.

Some of the intense criticism was justified, because some of the modifiers and researchers misused the program. Most of the criticism, however, mistakenly saw various medical procedures and forms of drug control as synonymous with behavior modification. Although a wide assortment of techniques "modify" behavior, they are not all considered members of the official behavior modification club. Qualifying requires the systematic application of learning and/or conditioning principles to change behavior. This still includes a large, heterogeneous club membership, but at least it eliminates the drug-psychosurgical approaches.

One way to distinguish the behavioral modifier from the traditional psychotherapist is to realize that the latter usually discusses changing the internal characteristics of the person, while behaviorists focus more on the person's external environment, both physical and social. Instead of homing in on unobservable inner conflicts or employing models which depict the "inner life" forces of a person, behaviorists are interested in observable behavior and the environmental events which maintain and significantly influence it. A behavior which is chosen to be changed is a *target behavior*. The basic technique for changing it is to weaken (or, in some instances, enhance) the associative or reinforcement link between it and an environmental event.

Behavioral techniques assume that the vast majority of both normal and deviant behaviors are acquired through learning and conditioning principles. Since they are acquired this way, it is to be expected that they can also be changed this way. Developing desirable behaviors through reinforcement and suppressing undesirable ones through the absence of reinforcement or punishment is a major characteristic of behavior therapy.

Behavior therapy was developed on learning-conditioning principles derived from well-controlled, precise laboratory environments or small-scale, well-designed demonstration projects, and this is one of its problems. Because of the clarity and careful language surrounding the principles, they appear deceptively simple. However, applying the behavioral principles gained through controlled experimentation to complex, natural environments has been difficult and frustrating (Reppucci & Saunders, 1974). This is an important point and one we will return to after reviewing some of the behavior treatment programs in the correctional setting.

The social and physical environment is a crucial consideration in planning any behavior therapy program. Before the treatment program can be effectively implemented, the target behaviors and the environmental events which accompany them must be accurately described and carefully evaluated as to how, when, and where they occur for a particular individual. This information is normally gathered through direct observation of the individual in a situation where he or she typically exhibits the target behavior, and through interviews with the individual and others who are acquainted with the behavior. In the planning stage, these initial data concerning the target behavior (such as frequency) provide baseline or pretreatment information which is useful for later determining how effective the treatment plan has been. Once the target behaviors and the conditions under which they occur are determined, the next step usually involves establishing a two-fold plan: 1. the associative or reinforcement bond between the target behavior and the environmental event must be weakened; 2. more desirable behavior must be instituted through reinforcement. When the plan has been implemented, comparing treatment data with baseline data helps to determine whether or not it is working. If the original treatment does not work, the conditions will be reassessed and a modified plan will be introduced.

The above description oversimplifies the procedure steps, but it provides the reader with a rudimentary image of the basic process. Behavior therapy encompasses a wide variety of techniques, with each giving different emphasis to conditioning, instrumental learning, or social learning in their procedures. At this point, the reader will get a better grasp of the different kinds of methods and their effectiveness if we look at examples of behavior therapy in the correctional setting.

Behavior Therapy in Corrections

Most of the large-scale projects using behavior therapy in corrections have involved delinquents and, in a few cases, "predelinquents." Only a few behavioral programs have focused on adult offenders. Some of the projects have been tried in a correctional institution, others in a community-based residential facility, and still others in a community-based home as a means of prevention. Examples of institution-based programs include the CASE project at the National Training School for Boys in Washington, D.C., the Intensive Training Program at Murdock Center in North Carolina, and the Youth Center Research Project in California. Institution-based projects involving adult offenders include the Patuxent Institute in Maryland, the Special Treatment and Rehabilitative Training Program (START) in Springfield, Missouri, and the Rehabilitation Research Foundation (RRF) at Draper Correctional Center in Elmore, Alabama.

One of the best-known, illustrative community-based residential programs is Achievement Place, which began in Lawrence, Kansas. Other community-based prevention programs include the Social Learning Project developed at the Oregon Research Institute by Gerald Patterson, the Family and School Consultation Project developed by Richard Stuart in Michigan, the PICA/PREP program in Silver Springs, Maryland, and the Hunt School Project developed by John Burchard in Burlington, Vermont. We will go over a few of these projects to try to provide a flavor for the problems, failures, and successes that are possible.

The CASE Project. One of the pioneering efforts to deal with delinquent boys whose criminal records included rape, auto theft, and homicide was designed by Harold Cohen and his colleagues (1967) in Washington, D.C. The project was called CASE I (Contingencies Application for Special Education—Phrase I), and it involved sixteen residents of the National Training School who volunteered for the eight-month demonstration experiment. The basic goal of CASE I was to increase the educational achievement level of the boys and to improve their attitudes toward school in general. In this sense, the program was designed to develop alternative behaviors. Cohen realized that the typical academic reinforcers, such as grades, promotion, and diplomas, were insufficient to motivate delinquent boys. Instead, for a specified performance on academic subjects, they received daily points which could be exchanged for edibles, items from the Sears catalog, time in the lounge with a juke box, television privileges, and so forth.

In many behavioral programs, objects like points, coins, tickets, stars, poker chips, or check marks are used as *tokens* which are earned by meeting specific performance standards for desirable behavior, and which can be exchanged for various rewards and privileges. In some programs these tokens may also be taken away as punishment for undesirable behaviors. A behavioral system using tokens is referred to as a *token economy* and has been used frequently in institutional settings for retarded, emotionally disturbed, and criminal-delinquent populations.

The CASE I program showed such promise in academic gains, as reflected in standardized tests and in a marked change in attitude toward school, that Cohen and his associates (Cohen & Filipczak, 1971) developed another program—CASE II. This model involved 25 boys from the National Training School ranging in age from fourteen to eighteen. Forty-four percent were at the school because of auto theft and 10 percent because of housebreaking. The primary aim of CASE II was to strengthen academic behaviors in the boys to the point where they would be able to re-enter the public schools within one year.

The rationale for improving academic skills relates to the treatment objectives discussed earlier. If the delinquent can be taught alternative, more desirable skills in place of the undesirable, he or she may have more adaptive ways of dealing with the environment. However, these newly acquired skills must also offer the same social and material pay-offs as the original behaviors. Considering the long delay and remote pay-off gained from education, it is questionable whether this alternative behavior is really all that satisfactory.

The subjects in CASE II could earn tokens by studying and by obtaining a 90 percent performance on individualized educational material. Near the end of the program, the student could earn extra points by participating in group academic settings that were analogous to the traditional classroom environment.

The results showed substantial gains in academic performance during the three months in the program as measured by standardized tests. However, the change in antisocial behavior upon release from the program was much less impressive. Although the CASE students stayed out of trouble longer than a similar group processed through the National Training School, there were few differences in recidivism rates between the two groups three years after release from the program and institution.

The START Program. The Special Treatment and Rehabilitation

Training program in Springfield, Missouri was established in a federal security facility to deal with a particularly problematic portion of the adult prison population. As it turned out, it also became one of the most publicized and controversial attempts at behavior therapy (Johnson, 1977). The population in the program was unusually assaultive, abusive, and generally recalcitrant in the institution. Therefore, the objective of the program was to train the inmates to behave in a conventional prison environment.

The unmanageable inmates were transferred involuntarily to START from various institutions within the Federal Bureau of Prison's system at the recommendation of an institution supervisor and approval from the central office. The START program consisted of three basic systems: the progressive level system, the point system, and the individual contract system (Kennedy, 1976).

The level system referred to different privileges that an inmate could win on the basis of desirable behavior. The system began by confining the inmate for a two-week period in his cell without privileges—the "orientation" level. In order to progress from this level to other more pleasant levels the inmate had to earn "good days" by receiving acceptable ratings on a twelve-item behavior check list. At each level the inmate received more tangible rewards, increased his time out of the cell, earned more money, and gained opportunities for self-improvement courses. However, because the objective was to return the subjects to a regular prison, the earned privileges could not exceed those normally allowed in the federal prison system.

In the point system, inmates could earn points (tokens) which could be exchanged for commissary items or used for renting equipment or ordering books. Similar to the level system, the twelve specified behaviors for points pertained to work habits, social behavior toward others, and personal hygiene. In the contract system, inmates could earn points by completing certain tasks that had been mutually agreed upon by the inmate and his treatment team.

Inmates were punished for rule infractions by being placed in their rooms without privileges and without opportunity to gain points or good days. This separation procedure was maintained until the inmate demonstrated a willingness to cooperate.

About half of those inmates who began the program completed the requirements, and of those, approximately 50 percent are no longer in segregation units (Johnson, 1977), the places where they were at the time of their transfer to START. However, the program was plagued by several serious problems at its inception. First, START was a highly coercive treatment program—the inmates had no say as to whether or not they wanted "treatment." From all indications, behavior programs must have inmate cooperation and a reasonable amount of their input into the planning if they are to be successful (Kennedy, 1976). Prisoners interpreted the program as a form of punishment, and some even went on a 65-day hunger strike to protest their treatment. Others sued, charging that their Constitutional rights were being violated. With inmate and public opposition and judicial pressure beginning to mount, the Federal Bureau of Prisons finally ordered the program terminated for "economic reasons."

Another major flaw in the program related to the lack of individualization allowed the inmates. No attempt was made to provide a wide variety of reinforcers that were meaningful to the individual inmate. Still another flaw was the explicit goal of the program, which was to produce submissive, conforming inmates. No attempts were made to develop new, alternative, social, personal, vocational, or academic skills, which may have made the program more attractive. Moreover, the intent to make prisoners submissive apparently was sometimes accompanied by unnecessary punishment and physical abuse (Kennedy, 1976).

We could review other projects within institutions using behavioral principles, but the results would be similar—demonstrated effectiveness within the institutional setting, but questionable generalizability to the natural environment. Even within the institution, however, behavioral programs have encountered problems in addition to those referred to above. On the surface, behavior therapy seems to offer a simple, straightforward method of alleviating certain pressing behavioral problems, but this simple method requires a high amount of environmental control and a high degree of cooperation and commitment from those even remotely involved in the program. Transferring the techniques from the controlled psychological laboratory to the numerous constraints and attitudes of the correctional facility is a burdensome and delicate task. After struggling with the discouraging problems they encountered in implementing their program in a correctional institution, Reppucci and Saunders concluded: "The usefulness of behavior modification techniques in natural settings is often quite limited because even minimal conditions necessary for behavior change are difficult to obtain" (1974, p. 659). For example, prison personnel failed to cooperate or hindered the program by not delivering points for appropriate behaviors. Sometimes, bureaucratic red tape delayed the exchange of tokens for rewards.

In summary, while the literature consistently shows that such programs are somewhat effective in changing undesirable, institutional behaviors to desirable ones while the person is in the institution, there is little information about their effects on behavior *outside* the treatment environment (Burchard & Harig, 1976; Johnson, 1977; Reppucci & Saunders, 1974). Almost all the behavior programs have concentrated on ameliorating undesirable or unmanageable behaviors in order to facilitate the smooth operation of the institution or correctional facility. Bed making, room cleaning, personal hygiene, social appropriateness, eye-contact when spoken to, washing hands before eating—all were behaviors that rapidly and impressively improved after behavior therapy, but whether these behaviors continue in their natural environment remains very much an open question.

In an excellent review and analysis of the pertinent literature, Burchard and Harig assert: ". . . we know of no instance where there was a systematic effort to determine what behaviors are the most critical (either positive or negative) with respect to an individual's ability to adapt to his or her own natural environment . . . it may be that a disproportionate emphasis on decreasing profanity and increasing academics and cleanliness, may not be all that adaptive" (1976, p. 416).

Community-based Residential Homes. One of the most exemplary applications of behavior therapy has been made in a community-based residential home project called *Achievement Place,* a home-style treatment facility for predelinquent youths. *Predelinquent* was a term used by the court and juvenile officials to refer to youths who had committed only minor offenses, but who were in danger of becoming habitual lawbreakers.

Achievement Place is based on a social learning explanation of delinquent behavior. That is, it is assumed that the past learning environment of the predelinquents failed to provide adequate models, instructions, and the feedback necessary to develop appropriate behavioral patterns. The program was designed to correct those deficits by developing appropriate behaviors through modeling, practice, and instruction supervised by "teaching parents"—two adults who lived with the seven or eight boys in the project. The residents, it was expected, would be motivated to acquire the desirable social, academic, and personal skills through the awarding of points upon the manifestation of specified, desirable behaviors.

The points (in the form of tokens) could be exchanged for a variety of privileges normally found in most homes. O'Leary and Wilson (1975, p. 210) classified the Achievement Place privileges according to the following general headings: 1. Basics—use of tools, games, recreation area, going outside; 2. Snacks—after school and before bedtime; 3. Away time—permission to leave Achievement Place to go home, downtown, or to a sports event; 4. Allowance—points exchangeable for $1 to $2 per week; 5. Bonds—Savings for gifts and special clothing; 6. Special privileges—point-price negotiables.

The token economy is set up in such a way that the resident can gain points for appropriate behavior and lose points for inappropriate behavior. However, the system is flexible enough to allow a resident to earn additional points without necessarily losing privileges at any time. Appropriate behaviors include social and academic skills and the development of self-help habits, all of which are clearly spelled out in the Achievement Place manual.

When youths are first placed in Achievement Place they are put on a daily point system, where the points are accumulated one day for privileges the next day. If the resident earns points consistently under this system, he or she is advanced to the weekly point system where the points are accumulated over a week; this buys privileges for the following week. If the resident performs well under the weekly system for four straight weeks, then he or she may advance to the merit system. Here the resident receives privileges free and is evaluated carefully to determine whether desirable behaviors can be maintained only by social reinforcers, such as the praise and affection of the teaching parents and peers, rather than by tangible tokens.

Youths who demonstrate success on the merit system may advance to the final stage, called the homeward bound system, which means that they can go home for five or six nights a week. While in this phase of the program, youths return to Achievement Place for one or two nights a week to discuss any problems they are having in the home. After several weeks and if things are going well, they may remain at home during the full week if they so choose.

If, during any phase of the program, youths exhibit undesirable behavior which is considered critical to eventual success in the community, they may be placed back to an earlier stage and will have to re-earn the right to move up into a more advanced system. Throughout the stages, the teaching parents maintain contact with juvenile officials, teachers, and youths' parents. Eventually, while the child is in the homeward bound program, the meetings with parents and other involved parties fade from weekly to monthly occurrence, and eventually to no meetings at all, unless there is a problem.

Since the first Achievement Place opened in 1967, a number of similar homes have been established throughout the country (O'Leary & Wilson, 1975; Trotter, 1973). Trotter also did a follow-up of the Achievement Place youths in comparison to those released from an institution (Kansas Boys School) and boys placed on formal probation. The recidivism rate for Achievement Place youths was 6 percent during the first year, compared to 13 percent for institutionalized youths, and 31 percent for those placed on probation. During the second year, Achievement Place recidivism was 19 percent, compared to 53 and 54 percent for institutionalized and probation youths, respectively. Although the samples are by no means comparable, the data do suggest that Achievement Place was reasonably successful in eliminating potentially delinquent behaviors. However, even community-based treatment programs seem to have problems with generalizability to the natural environment.

Comments

Where do we go from here? Although behavioral treatment is useful for controlling institutional behavior and can help in promoting the acquisition of social and academic skills, it has yet to demonstrate outstanding effectiveness in reducing criminal behavior in the natural environment. Other forms of psychological treatment or psychotherapy have fared no better. If traditional psychotherapy has not produced an impressive track record for members of the general population who actively seek help (Rachman, 1972), we cannot expect miracles with incarcerated offenders, many of whom do not wish to change their deviant behavior unless something better comes their way. Also, the forms of therapy offered by the correctional system are usually directed at ameliorating the stresses of prison life—and keeping inmates "in line"—and not at stresses they will eventually encounter in their natural environment upon release (Maier, 1976).

It should be emphasized in all fairness, however, that behavioral programs within the institution are often handicapped by inadequate facilities, staff, programs, and financial support. Adding to these restraints are legal, political, and social pressures. If these restrictions were reduced, the scientific community might be able to design and formulate programs which would be more effective and generalizable, and would involve more personal commitment and freedom of choice by the inmate.

The aim of traditional psychotherapy is to correct the internal conflicts of the individual which are causing him or her to be emotionally distressed. However, when used with the criminal, it fails to take into consideration that his or her behavior is in most instances a learned way of dealing with and adapting to the environment. Emphasizing internal conflicts while neglecting environmental forces is a poor approach to use with the offender. As we have stressed throughout this book, most criminal behavior is not a psychologically abnormal or "sick" pattern, but a learned adaptation (not approved by the powers in society) to a particular environment. Trying to transfer psychotherapy from those psychologically disturbed individuals who normally seek it to a correctional institution simply does not wash.

A fact in the prison which makes treatment and rehabilitation difficult is that there are two systems at work—the formal system dictated by the authorities and an informal system run by the inmates. In the informal system we have two processes at work: *criminalization* and *prisonization*. In criminalization, inmates teach one another the skills and attitudes of deviant careers (Feldman, 1977). It is a criminal subculture where common goals, attitudes, skills, and feelings are exchanged, and often it is a close-knit club.

Prisonization is the process whereby the criminal learns the rules, general culture, and expectation of the prison community. With these two learning processes at work, which are often in conflict with society's learning expectations, it seems that the longer one spends in prison the more likely one will pursue the career he or she has learned better. Research has continually indicated that the longer a person spends in prison the more likely that person is to re-offend. We would also expect that offenders will fine-tune their methods to the point where detection would be more difficult, and this might account in part for statistics that crimes are committed by the young. The older offender in some cases has developed more sophisticated methods, which are less likely to be detected. Also, the longer one spends in prison or in a correctional facility the less likely one is to improve or develop social and vocational skills necessary to "make it" outside the criminal culture. Generally, the only skills which are developed and strengthened are those that enhance survival in the deviant environment.

Most would agree that there is a strong relationship between personally meaningful employment and recidivism, particularly for economically motivated crimes (Halleck & Witte, 1977; Kennedy, 1976; Jenkins & Barton, 1973). If the individual is engaged in rewarding employment and manages through appropriate social and job-related skills to keep the job, he or she will be less apt to be involved in antisocial behavior. It may be no accident that many members of the unemployed groups and the criminally prone are young, black males from low socioeconomic classes with poor educational attainment and vocational skills. For example, Daniel Glaser writes "unemployment may be among the principal causal factors involved in the recidivism of adult male offenders" (1964, p. 329). Moreover, it is estimated that the unemployment rates for ex-offenders is three times the rate for the general public, and that most who received "vocational training" are not able to use it (Dale, 1976).

Additionally, the recidivism rate for the unemployed or underemployed ex-offender is four times that of the fully employed ex-offender. Of course this relationship does not necessarily prove that these are causal factors in the tendency to re-offend. It might just as well read that offenders who are particularly prone toward antisocial behavior are also less likely to find and maintain suitable employment. However, it is difficult to ignore statements like the one made by Mitchell Dale: "An opportunity to live a normal, noncriminal productive life is denied the ex-offender immediately upon his release from the penal institution. We effectively preclude his rehabilitation by failing to train and educate him, by refusing to hire him, by allowing the private bonding industry to intimidate employers, and by enacting restrictive occupational licensing requirements at the behest of self-serving economic groups" (1976, p. 336).

It would appear that meaningful, committed vocational and social training combined with appropriate employment placement is one step in the right direction. This does not mean that vocational-rehabilitation counseling and training in social skills would prevent many from returning to their old deviant habits once they get back to their natural environment, but it is a good bet that it would prevent a significant portion from doing so.

Another problem relates to the Constitutional rights of inmates. To coerce or force an inmate to participate in a treatment or rehabilitative program violates ethics and, in the long run, the effectiveness of any program is threatened. Not only must the Constitutional rights of the incarcerated be scrupulously protected, but they must also be informed of the realistic benefits for voluntarily participating in any treatment-rehabilitation program. Although the boundaries between what is coercive and what is not are unclear (Warren, 1977), the inmate should be able to decide for him- or herself not only whether he or she wants treatment or rehabilitation, but also what specific kind. Possibly, the lack of differential features in package programs in present day vogue may be one explanation why particular kinds of treatment are successful for some individuals and unbeneficial for others. It is also possible that rehabilitative treatment may not be the best prescription for some offenders at all (Adams, 1977).

TREATMENT AND REHABILITATION CONSIDERATIONS

The general treatment or rehabilitative scheme emphasized in this chapter is to develop alternative behaviors which are more socially desirable while eliminating, or at least suppressing, less desirable ones. There is nothing new or surprising about this proposal; it has been suggested many times before. The major problem, however, is how this can be accomplished.

First, we must realize that the most effective program for treatment and rehabilitation requires that it be specifically tailored to each offender's needs, experiential background, ability, and personality. Second, it must also be sound ethically, by providing the offender with the opportunity to decide whether he or she wants rehabilitation or treatment. In view of the success rates of criminal behavior and the length of time the offender has been reinforced for this behavior, it should come as no suprise that many will not want either. One of the major flaws of behavior modification described in this chapter has been the tendency of clinicians to bring a treatment package of generalized treatment for *all* offenders without their active participation or commitment to the program. This point must be emphasized again because it is extremely crucial to the success of any rehabilitation or treatment program instituted in a correctional facility. The rehabilitation or treatment must be *differential,* and the offender must be convinced that it will be a useful and meaningful alternative to present behavioral patterns.

If the offender observes or discovers that alternatives work for other offenders, then he or she may be more inclined to try developing more of his or her own. Of course, the so-called "hard-core" criminal would probably be less inclined than the delinquent, because the criminal behavior of the former has such a long record of proven effectiveness. Why change what works well? This suggests that the younger the offender, the more effective a rehabilitative program. However, the older offender can be worked with effectively if we understand we are dealing, in many cases, with a long-standing way of life which has proved useful over a period of many years. When people who in many cases have never had to live under certain subcultural conditions equivalent to the offender propose a training program which is going to provide "adaptive" skills, many types of offenders will suspect a "con job."

Of course, all this presupposes that we have methods which are reasonably productive in developing alternative behavioral patterns. Behavior therapy applied to behavioral problems in the general population has proved extremely effective, particularly for clients who come voluntarily to the therapist for help in alleviating behaviors which cause them social embarrassment or personal discomfort. It could prove equally effective to an incarcerated offender who actively seeks help for a problem which could be dealt with within the institution. But in many cases, perhaps most, the therapist or counselor who works on vocational or therapy programs is an agent for the administration or the society, implementing a program for them, and not at the request of the offender.

In a recent study by Abrams and Siegel (1978), a treatment program which used transcendental meditation (TM) was found effective in helping prisoners deal with prison life. Of the 200 maximum security inmates who participated in the program, 90 percent indicated that they were "very satisfied" with the program and could see positive changes in themselves. The researchers found that inmates signed up for the program in numbers which far exceeded their ability to handle them. One very important fact should be noted. The program, while approved by the institution, was not designed, initiated, or conducted by the institution. It was strictly voluntary and was supervised by persons not employed by the prison. The inmates apparently volunteered because they wanted to, not because there was institutional coercion to do so. In part, the "success" of the program may be due to the offenders' commitment to it. The offenders felt it was *their* choice to participate.

Also, the TM procedure provided the inmates with some techniques for control and some skills for dealing adequately with a prison environment, an environment which takes away many aspects of control from inmates. The whole matter of control is an essential one in the design and execution of any program. Techniques and procedures which do not allow the subject to perceive that he or she has some control over fate are bound to be resisted and resented.

While this chapter has advocated differential treatment and differential rehabilitation, there are some very general features regarding offender types in relation to rehabilitation and treatment, which we will now consider. It would be foolhardy to believe that a generalized prescription will be productive in working with all humans. However, the features of some of the offender categories lend themselves better than others to formulating general objectives in designing and conducting treatment or rehabilitation. The points to follow have been communicated to some extent in earlier chapters, but it is useful to see them in summarized form as they relate to treatment suggestions.

The Psychopath

Unfortunately, the psychopath remains a therapeutic enigma. After over three decades working with psychopaths, Cleckley (1976) concludes that there are two major difficulties hampering effective treatment of them: 1. their apparent immunity from control by the law, and 2. their lack of response to psychotherapy of any kind.

With reference to the first issue, it is only under very unusual circumstances that psychopaths get convicted of any of their criminal offenses, primarily because they have extraordinary talent in demonstrating innocence, rationale, and penitence for their behavior. If by some quirk of fate a psychopath is convicted and incarcerated, he or she typically assumes the role of the model prisoner, providing visible indications of moral rebirth, salvation, rehabilitation, and absolute reform with an apparent potential for becoming a conscientious, law-abiding citizen. If the pscyhopath is committed to a mental institution, he or she is just as skillful at convincing the hospital officials and the psychotherapists, even capable and highly experienced ones, that the therapy and rehabilitation have proceeded according to textbook principles. In addition, the psychopath usually has friends and relatives so baffled that they avidly support a move for his or her immediate release, convinced that the person will change his or her ways. It is important to realize that the psychopath is extremely effective at gaining early parole. Despite indications to the contrary, research and clinical experience warn us that the psychopath who exhibits a pattern of violence is likely to continue this pattern after prison release.

On the more positive side, it has been found that psychopaths show a gradual reduction in the severity of antisocial behavior with age, and that by the time they reach approximately age forty, much of their asocial, acting-out behavior has dissipated. This has been credited to the combination of a maturation of the nervous system and the cumulative effects of socialization.

However, clinicians have yet to devise an effective treatment approach for the criminal psychopath. After his 30 years of clinical experience, Cleckley dejectedly stated, "Over a period of many years I have remained discouraged about the effect of treatment on the psychopath. . . . I am no longer hopeful that any methods available today would be successful with typical psychopaths" (Cleckley, 1976, pp. 438–439). Hare (1970) concurs with Cleckley's observations. Psychopaths see nothing wrong with their behavior and, in addition, find it rewarding. Moreover, because of lack of anxiety or rapid adaptation to stress, they do not condition well to society's expectations and rules under threat of social censure, punishment, embarrassment, or imprisonment.

We simply do not know enough about the causes of psychopathic behavior to modify and change it. Only carefully designed, meaningful research will provide sound, testable answers. Present evidence strongly indicates that the emotional arousal (anxiety) level must be increased to the same level as that of nonpsychopaths. Hare (1970) suggests that behavior therapy, which is usually effectively employed to reduce anxiety as an underpinning for behavior disorders, might be implemented to *induce sufficient* anxiety in the psychopath. Schachter and Latané's (1964) findings indicate that drug therapy might be useful in pharmacologically generating sufficient arousal. Once the arousal level is increased, it is assumed that the psychopath would then be susceptible to conditioning, and thereby learn socially acceptable behavior as normals do. One problem with this approach noted by Coleman (1976) is that the antisocial behavior is a lifestyle and not any isolated, specific maladaptive behavior. Behavior therapy has proved its worth on specific behaviors, but as yet not on a habitual, general behavior pattern such as that illustrated by the psychopath.

One other important point concerning the treatment of the psychopath should be mentioned. Psychopaths appear to have considerable mastery and control over their environments in most situations. The absence of anxiety or depression might well be a result of this sense of personal control and competence. Treatments are most often designed to re-establish personal control and mitigate environmental control over events. Possibly, the very premise upon which most forms of pscyhological treatment are based is completely inappropriate for the already competent-feeling psychopath.

The Sex Offender

As we have learned, sex offenders display a wide range of behaviors and include several distinct types. However, when conditioning has promoted an association between events or objects and sexual arousal, behavior therapy has offered very effective procedures for breaking the link (e.g., Wolpe, 1973). For example, many sex offenders, such as pedophiliacs and exhibitionists, have benefited substantially from desensitization methods directed at a particular set of associations. The associative link between sexual arousal and some object (or event) can be skillfully broken by developing a response or reaction which is incompatible with the original response connected to the object. For example, a person can be taught to be relaxed in the presence of stimuli which previously activated sexual excitement. When the stimuli appear in future encounters, the person will experience relaxation rather than excitement.

Many rapists appear to need an accurate re-education about sexual attitudes and values. They also need to develop empathy and understanding for the feelings of others, particularly women, along with social skills for interacting with both men and women. Of course, if accurate information about sexual attitudes and feelings had been communicated early in life by parents and peers, a large percentage of rape incidents probably would never have occurred. Since rape is most often a violent offense, the points covered in the following section would also apply to it.

Violent Offenders

Violent offenders, in general, have a history of resolving their conflicts through aggressive, violent patterns. They have learned that the most productive way available to them for dealing with conflict under certain conditions is to be aggressive. Subjectively, they anticipate that aggressive action will improve their situation. Many times the victim of the aggression feels the same way. Teaching the offender to solve problems through methods that are nonviolent and are both effective and socially desirable, is a tall order. It is also only part of the solution. The social environment of the offender must also learn to deal with conflict differently.

Researchers (e.g., Baron, 1977; Bandura, 1973) have for some time advocated the elimination, or at least the reduction, of aggressive models so prevalent in many cultures. Violence seen on TV and in movies and read about in magazines—combined with real-life aggressive models such as parents and peers—offers an environment where everyone seems to use aggressive means to resolve conflicts. Not only is the social environment full of aggressive models to imitate, but aggressive models (such as toy guns for children and hand guns for adults) permeate American society. Aggression as a means of adaptation and, in some cases, survival, is heavily relied on in many sectors of American society. Thus, the reduction of violence will not only require working with the offender, but with society as well.

The Disturbed Offender

The disturbed offender, examples of whom are found in all types of crime, often seems to be trying to gain some sense of control over his or her life and add significance to existence. In many cases this offender lacks social skills and productive ways of dealing with the environment. In an effort to regain significance and control, he or she may resort to antisocial behavior. An understanding of these motives and a plan to institute feelings of control and self-worth would seem to be basic requirements for treatment.

SUMMARY

While the rehabilitation-treatment approach has gained some attention and commitment from corrections in recent years, it has also been greeted with much opposition and with the belief that it simply does not work. Some authorities feel that the entire idea has been oversold. Opponents point to the high recidivism rates following rehabilitation or treatment as objective indicators of the concept's unproductivity. By most measures, the rehabilitation-treatment approach has not been impressive in reducing crime over the long term. Major reasons for this ineffectiveness seem to be faulty implementation of an alternative-suppressive model of behavior change, or general resistance from the legal, political, social, and correctional forces operating within the institution.

Punishment can be an effective suppressor of undesirable behavior under certain conditions. However, the criminal justice system is generally not set up to offer these conditions. This seems to be especially true for specific deterrence, although our present system should not be underestimated in its effectiveness as a general deterrent. Punishment, we saw, is a very complex procedure which must be applied with a good understanding of its principles. However, even when applied with the knowledge of how to produce effective results for suppression of undesirable behavior, it *still* must be supplemented with alternative response building, if desirable behavior is to predominate.

Alternative response building (which is the ultimate goal of rehabilitation and treatment) is no more the forte of the correctional system than is punishment. Successful rehabilitation or treatment requires genuine commitment from all levels of correctional personnel, a clear focus on the objectives, a solid understanding of the principles, well-trained staff, and understanding and commitment from the community. This combination of optimal conditions remains elusive to the correctional system.

Rehabilitative or treatment programs that have been instituted are often so ill-defined, political, and permeated with ethical issues that they are destined to fail. They are often not tailored to the individual and are usually designed to suppress undesirable behaviors (or build alternative ones) relative to the facility's smooth operations. They are seldom able to be generalized to the offender's post-prison or natural environment.

Various forms of behavior therapy hold the greatest promise for accomplishing behavioral change in offenders. However, while behavioral principles have strong empirical support from the laboratory, they have many problems when applied to human beings in a complicated natural environment. The present packaging of behavioral methods needs considerable refinement in its application in the correctional system.

Ethical issues and the offender's rights have to be carefully considered in any approach using punishment, rehabilitation, or treatment. The offender must also be committed to the goals and purposes of the program, an aspect often overlooked. Otherwise, upon removal from the situation, the offender will probably revert quickly back to his or her old successful response patterns.

Rehabilitation and treatment as effective approaches to reducing crime are not dead; it simply seems that they have yet to be correctly instituted. We should remain optimistic about changing criminal behavior in a humanistic way, as long as we understand the complexities involved and as long as we can live with slow progress when delving into unknown areas where there are limitless combinations of variables.

> *Science is a solver of problems, but it is dealing with the limitless, just as, in a cruder way, were the Romans. Solutions to problems create problems; their solutions, in turn, multiply into additional problems that escape out of scientific hands like noxious insects into the interstices of the social fabric (Eiseley, 1969, p. 43).*

KEY CONCEPTS FOR REVIEW

General deterrence
Specific deterrence
Severity of punishment
Consistency of punishment
Immediacy of punishment
Suppression-alternative behavior model
Rehabilitation
Differential treatment
Psychotherapy
Behavior therapy
CASE
START
Token economy
Achievement Place
Criminalization
Prisonization

SUGGESTED READINGS

Burchard, J., and Harig, P.T. "Behavior modification and juvenile delinquency," in H. Leitenberg (ed.), *Handbook of behavior modification and behavior therapy.* Englewood Cliffs, N.J.: Prentice-Hall, 1976.
A critical review of the applications of behavior modification to juveniles.

Walters, G.C. and Grusec, J.E. *Punishment.* San Francisco: W.H. Freeman, 1977.
A comprehensive and easy to read book on the contemporary viewpoints and research on punishment.

Wicks, R.J. *Correctional psychology.* San Francisco: Canfield Press, 1974.
Written for the undergraduate student with little background in psychology, this book presents a clear overview of the various psychotherapies used in corrections.

Wolpe, J. *The practice of behavior therapy,* 2nd ed. New York: Pergamon Press, 1973.
An outstanding presentation of the basic theories and practice of behavior therapy.

REFERENCES

Abel, G., Madden, D., & Christopher, R. The components of rapists' sexual arousal. *Panel at the American Psychiatric Association*, New York: May, 1975.

Abrahamsen, D. *Who are the guilty?* Westport, Conn.: Greenwood Press, 1952.

Abrahamsen, D. *The psychology of crime.* New York: Columbia Univ. Press, 1960.

Abrams, A. E., & Siegel, L. M. The transcendental meditation program and rehabilitation at Folsom State Prison. *Criminal Justice and Behavior*, 1958, 5, 3–20.

Abramson, L. Y., Seligman, M. E. P., & Teasdale, J. D. Learned helplessness in humans: Critique and reformulation. *Journal of Abnormal Psychology*, 1978, 87, 49–74.

Achenbach, T. M. *Developmental psychopathology.* New York: Ronald Press, 1974.

Adams, S. S. Evaluating correctional treatments. *Criminal Justice and Behavior*, 1977, 4, 323–340.

Adler, F. *Sisters in crime.* New York: McGraw-Hill, 1975.

Akers, R. L. *Deviant behavior: A social learning approach* (2nd ed.). Belmont, Calif.: Wadsworth, 1977.

Albrecht, G. L. The alcoholism process: A social learning viewpoint. In P. G. Bourne (Ed.), *Alcoholism: Progress in research and treatment.* New York: Academic Press, 1973.

Allsopp, J. F., Criminality and delinquency. In H. J. Eysenck & G. D. Wilson (Eds.), *A textbook of human psychology.* Baltimore: University Park Press, 1976.

Allsopp, J. F., & Feldman, M. P. Extraversion, neuroticism and psychoticism and anti-social behaviour in school girls. *Social Behaviour and Personality*, 1975, 2, 184–188.

Allsopp, J. F., & Feldman, M. P. Personality and anti-social behaviour in school-boys. *British Journal of Criminology*, 1976, 16, 337–351.

Amir, M. *Patterns in forcible rape.* Chicago: Univ. of Chicago Press, 1971.

Amsel, A. The role of frustrative nonreward in noncontinuous reward situations. *Psychological Bulletin*, 1958, 55, 102–119.

Anastasi, A. *Psychological testing* (4th ed.). New York: Macmillan, 1976.

Andenaes, J. Does punishment deter crime? *The Criminal Law Quarterly*, 1968, 11, 76–93.

Andenaes, J. The general preventive effects of punishment. In I. Radzinowicz & M. E. Wolfgang (Eds.), *Crime and justice* (Vol. 2). *The criminal in the arms of the law.* New York: Basic Books, 1969.

Anderson, D. C., & Lupo, J. V. Non-human aggressive behavior: Trends and issues. In D. J. Madden & J. R. Lion (Eds.), *Rage • hate • assault and other forms of violence.* New York: Spectrum Publications, 1976.

Ardrey, R. *The territorial imperative.* New York: Atheneum, 1966.

Arey, J. A. *The sky pirates.* New York: Charles Scribner's Sons, 1972.

Aronfreed, J. Moral development from the standpoint of a general psychological theory. In T. Lickona (Ed.), *Moral development and behavior.* New York: Holt, Rinehart & Winston, 1976.

Arthur, R. G., & Cahoon, E. B. A clinical and electroencephalographic survey of psychopathic personality. *American Journal of Psychiatry*, 1964, 120, 875–882.

Bandura, A. Influence of models' reinforcement contingencies on the acquisition of imitative responses. *Journal of Personality and Social Psychology*, 1965, 1, 589–595.

Bandura, A. *Aggression: A social learning analysis.* Englewood Cliffs, N. J.: Prentice-Hall, 1973a.

Bandura, A. Social learning theory of aggression. In J. F. Knutson (Ed.), *The control of aggression.* Chicago: Aldine, 1973b.

Bandura, A. *Social learning theory.* Englewood Cliffs, N. J.: Prentice-Hall, 1977.

Bandura, A., & Huston, A. Identification as a process of incidental learning. *Journal of Abnormal and Social Psychology*, 1961, 63, 311–318.

Bandura, A., Ross, D., & Ross, S. Vicarious reinforcement and imitative learning. *Journal of Abnormal and Social Psychology*, 1963, 67, 601–607.

Bandura, A., & Walters, R. H. *Adolescent aggression.* New York: Ronald Press, 1959.

Bandura, A., & Walters, R. H. Social learning and personality development. New York: Holt, Rinehart & Winston, 1963.

Baron, R. A. Human aggression. New York: Plenum Press, 1977.

Baron, R. A., & Bell, P. A. Aggression and heat: Mediating effects of prior provocation and exposure to an aggressive model. Journal of Personality and Social Psychology, 1975, 31, 825–832.

Baron, R., & Byrne, D. Social Psychology (2nd ed.). Boston: Allyn & Bacon, 1977.

Baron, R. A., and Lawton, S. F. Environmental influences on aggression: The facilitation of modeling effects by high ambient temperatures. Psychonomic Science, 1972, 26, 80–83.

Baron, R. A., & Ransberger, V. M. Ambient temperature and the occurrence of collective violence: The "long, hot summer" revisited. Journal of Personality and Social Psychology, 1978, 36, 361–366.

Barry, H., Koepfer, E., & Lutch, J. Learning to discriminate between alcohol and nondrug conditions. Psychological Reports, 1965, 16, 1072.

Barthol, R. P., & Ku, N.D. Regression under stress to first learned behavior. Journal of Abnormal and Social Psychology, 1959, 59, 134–136.

Bartholomew, A. A. Extraversion-introversion and neuroticism in first offenders and recidivists. British Journal of Delinquency, 1959, 10, 120–129.

Bartholomew, A. A. Some comparative Australian data for the Maudsley Personality Inventory. Australian Journal of Psychology, 1963, 15, 46–51.

Bartol, C. R. The effects of chlorpromazine and detroamphetamine sulfate on the visual stimulation preferences of extraverts and introverts. Psychophysiology, 1975, 12, 22–31.

Bartol, C. R., & Holanchock, H. A. A test of Eysenck's theory of criminality on an American prisoner population. Criminal Justice and Behavior, in press.

Baxstrom v. Herold. U.S. Reports, 1965, 383, 107–114.

Bayer, R. Heroin addiction, criminal culpability, and the penal sanction: The liberal response to repressive social policy. Crime and Delinquency, 1978, 24, 221–232.

Bazelon, D. L. Psychiatrists and the adversary process. Scientific American, 1974, 230, 18–23.

Bell, D. S. Addiction to stimulants. Medical Journal of Australia, 1967, 1, 41–45.

Bell, P. A., & Baron, R. A. Aggression and heat: The mediating role of negative affect. Journal of Applied Social Psychology, 1976, 6, 18–30.

Bell, P. A., & Baron, R. A. Aggression and ambient temperature: The inhibiting and facilitating effects of hot and cold environments. Bulletin of the Psychonomic Society, 1977, 6, 240–242.

Bell, R. R. Social deviance: A substantive analysis. Homewood, Ill.: Dorsey Press, 1976.

Bennie, E. H., & Sclare, A. B. The battered child syndrome. American Journal of Psychiatry, 1969, 125, 975–979.

Bensing, R. C. & Schroeder, O. Homicide in an urban community. Springfield, Ill.: Charles C Thomas, 1960.

Berger, H. Uber das Electrenkephalogram des Menschen. Archiv fur Psychiatrie und Nervenkrank-heiten, 1929, 87, 527–570.

Berkowitz, L. *Aggression: A social-psychological analysis.* New York: McGraw-Hill, 1962.

Berkowitz, L. The frustration-aggression hypothesis revisited. In L. Berkowitz (Ed.), *Roots of aggression.* New York: Atherton Press, 1969.

Berkowitz, L. The contagion of violence: An S-R mediational analysis of some effects of observed aggression. In W. J. Arnold & M. M. Page (Eds.), *Nebraska Symposium on Motivation.* Lincoln, Neb.: Univ. of Nebraska Press, 1970.

Berkowitz, L. Words and symbols as stimuli to aggressive responses. In J. F. Knutson (Ed.), *The control of aggression.* Chicago: Aldine, 1973.

Berkowitz, L., & LePage, A. Weapons as aggression-eliciting stimuli. *Journal of Personality and Social Psychology,* 1967, *7,* 202–207.

Berlyne, D. E. *Conflict, arousal, and curiosity.* New York: McGraw-Hill, 1960.

Bernard, F. An inquiry among a group of pedophiles. *Journal of Sex Research,* 1975, *11,* 242–255.

Beyer, M., Holts, S., Reid, T., & Quinlan, D. Runaway youths: Families in conflict. Paper presented at the meeting of the Eastern Psychological Association, Washington, D.C., May 4, 1973.

Blackburn, N., Weiss, J., & Lamberti, J. The sudden murderer. *Archives of General Psychiatry,* 1960, *2,* 670–678.

Blackburn, R. Personality in relation to extreme aggression in psychiatric offenders. *British Journal of Psychiatry,* 1968, *114,* 821–828.

Blackburn, R. Personality types among abnormal homicides (Research Report #1). London, England: Special Hospitals Research Unit, 1970.

Blackburn, R. Personality types among abnormal homicides. *British Journal of Criminology,* 1971, *11,* 14–31.

Block, R. *Violent crime.* Lexington, Mass.: Lexington Books, 1977.

Bloomquist, E. R. The use and abuse of stimulants. In W. G. Clark & J. del Giudice (Eds.), *Principles of psychopharmacology.* New York: Academic Press, 1970.

Blumer, D. Epilepsy and violence. In D. J. Madden & J. R. Lion (Eds.), *Rage • hate • assault and other forms of violence.* New York: Spectrum Publishing, 1976.

Blumer, H., Sutter, A., Ahmed, S., & Smith, R. *ADD center project final report: The world of youthful drug use.* Berkeley, Cal.: Univ. of California Press, 1967.

Borgstrom, C. A. Eine Serie von Kriminellen Zwillingen. *Archiv fur Rassenbiologie,* 1939.

Boudreau, J., Kwan, Q., Faragher, W., & Denault, G. *Arson and arson investigation.* Washington, D.C.: U.S. Government Printing Office, 1977.

Bourne, L. E., & Ekstrand, B. R. *Psychology: Its principles and meanings* (2nd ed.). New York: Holt, Rinehart & Winston, 1976.

Bowden, K. M., Wilson, D. W., & Turner, L. K. A survey of blood alcohol testing in Victoria (1951–56). *Medical Journal of Australia,* 1958, *45,* 13–15.

Brittain, R. P. The sadistic murderer. *Medicine, Science and the Law,* 1970, *10,* 198–207.

Brodsky, C. M. Rape at work. In M. J. Walker & S. L. Brodsky (Eds.), *Sexual Assault: The victims and the rapist.* Lexington, Mass.: Lexington Books, 1976.

Brodsky, S. L. (Ed.). *Psychologists in the criminal justice system.* Urbana, Ill.: Univ. of Illinois Press, 1973.

Brodsky, S. L. Criminal and dangerous behavior. In D. Rimm & J. Somervill (Eds.). *Abnormal psychology.* New York: Academic Press, 1977.

Broen, W. E. *Schizophrenia: Research and theory.* New York: Academic Press, 1968.

Bromberg, W. Marihuana: A psychiatric study. *Journal of the American Medical Association,* 1939, *113,* 4–12.

Bromberg, W. *The mold of murder: A psychiatric study of homicide.* New York: Grune & Stratton, 1961.

Brown, B. S., & Courtless, T. F. Fantasy and force: A study of the dynamics of the mentally retarded offender. *Journal of Criminal Law, Criminology, and Police Science.* 1970, *61,* 71–77.

Brown, D. G., & Tyler, V. O. Time out from reinforcement: A technique for dethroning the "duke" of an institutionalized group. *Journal of Child Psychology and Psychiatry and Allied Disciplines,* 1968, *9,* 203–211.

Brown, J. S., & Farber, I. E. Emotions conceptualized as intervening variables—with suggestions toward a theory of frustration. *Psychological Bulletin,* 1951, *48,* 465–495.

Brown, P., & Elliott, R. Control of aggression in nursery school class. *Journal of Experimental Child Psychology,* 1965, *2,* 103–107.

Brown, R. *Social Psychology.* New York: Free Press, 1965.

Brown, R. Schizophrenia, language, and reality. *American Psychologist,* 1973, *28,* 395–403.

Brownmiller, S. *Against our will: Men, women and rape.* New York: Simon & Schuster, 1975.

Brussel, J. A. *Casebook of a crime psychiatrist.* New York: Bernard Geis Associates, 1968.

Buikhuisen, W., & Hemmel, J. J. Crime and conditioning. *British Journal of Criminology,* 1972, *17,* 147–157.

Bullock, H. A. Urban homicide in theory and fact. *Journal of Criminal Law, Criminology and Police Science,* 1955, *45,* 565–575.

Burchard, J., & Harig, P. T. Behavior modification and juvenile delinquency. In H. Leitenberg (Ed.), *Handbook of behavior modification and behavior therapy.* Englewood Cliffs, N.J.: Prentice-Hall, 1976.

Burgess, P. K. Eysenck's theory of criminality: A test of some objectives of disconfirmatory evidence. *British Journal of Social and Clinical Psychology,* 1972, *11,* 248–256.

Burton, R. V. Generality of honesty reconsidered. *Psychological Review,* 1963, *70,* 481–499.

Burton, R. V. Honesty and dishonesty. In T. Lickona (Ed.), *Moral development and behavior.* New York: Holt, Rinehart & Winston, 1976.

Buss, A. H. *Psychopathology.* New York: Wiley, 1966.

Buss, A. H. Aggression pays. In J. L. Singer (Ed.), *The control of aggression and violence.* New York: Academic Press, 1971.

Butler, D., Riener, J., & Treanor, B. *Runaway house: A youth-run service project.* (Prepared for the Center for Studies of Child and Family Mental Health). Washington, D.C.: U.S. Government Printing Office, 1974.

Butler, R. A. Curiosity in monkeys. *Scientific American* (reprint #426). San Francisco: W. H. Freeman, 1954.

Button, A. Some antecedents of felonious and delinquent behavior. *Journal of Child Clinical Psychology*, 1973, 2, 35–37.

Byrne, D. An introduction to personality: Research, theory and applications. (2nd ed.), Englewood Cliffs, N.J.: Prentice-Hall, 1974.

Calhoun, J. B. Phenomena associated with population density. *Proceedings of the National Academy of Sciences*, 1961, 47, 428–429.

Calhoun, J. B. Population density and social pathology. *Scientific American*, 1962, 206, 139–148.

Cameron, M. O. *The booster and the snitch.* New York: Free Press, 1964.

Canadian Government's Commission of Inquiry. *The Non-medical use of drugs: Interim report.* London: Penguin Books, 1971.

Canter, S. Personality traits in twins. In G. Claridge, S. Canter, & W. I. Hume (Eds.), *Personality differences and biological variations: A study of twins.* Oxford: Pergamon Press, 1973.

Cantwell, D. P. A medical model for research and clinical use with hyperactive children. In D. P. Cantwell (Ed.), *The hyperactive child.* New York: Spectrum Publishing, 1975.

Capute, A. J., Niedermeyer, E. F. L., & Richardson, I. The electroencephalogram in children with minimal cerebral dysfunction. *Pediatrics*, 1968, 41, 1104.

Carlson, R. J. *The dilemmas of corrections.* Lexington, Mass.: Lexington Books, 1976.

Carroll, R. B. Analysis of alcoholic beverages by gas-liquid chromatography. *Quarterly Journal of Studies on Alcohol*, 1970, Supplement 5, 6–19.

Carver, C. S., Coleman, A. E., & Glass, D. C. The coronary-prone behavior pattern and the suppression of fatigue on a treadmill test. *Journal of Personality and Social Psychology*, 1976, 33, 460–466.

Carver, C. S., & Glass, D. C. Coronary-prone behavior pattern and interpersonal aggression. *Journal of Personality and Social Psychology*, 1978, 36, 361–366.

Cavan, R. S., & Ferdinand, T. N. *Juvenile delinquency.* Philadelphia: Lippincott, 1975.

Cavior, N., & Howard, L. R. Facial attractiveness and juvenile delinquency among black offenders and white offenders. *Journal of Abnormal Child Psychology*, 1973, 1, 202–213.

Chaffee, S. H., & McLeod, J. M. Adolescents, parents, and television violence. Paper presented at the meeting of the American Psychological Association, Washington, D.C., September, 1971.

Chappell, D. *Forcible rape: A national survey of the response by police* (LEAA). Washington, D.C.: U.S. Government Printing Office, 1977a.

Chappell, D. *Forcible rape: A national survey of the response by prosecutors* (LEAA). Washington, D.C.: U.S. Government Printing Office, 1977b.

Chesno, F. A., & Kilmann, P. R. Effects of stimulation intensity on sociopathic avoidance learning. *Journal of Abnormal Psychology*, 1975, 84, 144–150.

Chimbos, P. D. A study of breaking and entering offenses in "Northern City," Ontario. *Canadian Journal of Criminology and Corrections*, 1973, 15, 316–325.

Christiansen, K. O. A review of studies of criminality among twins. In S.

Mednick & K. O. Christiansen (Eds.), *Biosocial bases of criminal behavior.* New York: Gardiner Press, 1977a.

Christiansen, K. O. A preliminary study of criminality among twins. In S. Mednick & K. O. Christiansen (Eds.), *Biosocial bases of criminal behavior.* New York: Gardiner Press, 1977b.

Civil Aeronautics Board. *Supplement to the handbook of airline statistics.* Springfield, Va.: National Information Service, 1975.

Claridge, G. Final remarks. In G. Claridge, S. Canter, & W. I. Hume (Eds.), *Personality differences and biological variations.* Oxford: Pergamon Press, 1973.

Clarizio, H. F., & McCoy, G. F. *Behavior disorders in children* (2nd ed.). New York: Thomas Crowell, 1976.

Clark, K. B. The pathos of power: A psychological perspective. *American Psychologist,* 1971, *26,* 1047–1057.

Cleckley, H. *The mask of sanity.* (5th ed.). St. Louis: Mosby, 1976.

Cleveland, F. P. Problems in homicide investigation IV: The relationship of alcohol to homicide. *Cincinnati Journal of Medicine,* 1955, *36,* 28–30.

Clinard, M. *Sociology of deviant behavior.* New York: Holt, Rinehart & Winston, 1963.

Clinard, M. B., & Quinney, R. *Criminal behavior systems* (2nd ed.). New York: Holt, Rinehart & Winston, 1973.

Cloward, R. A., & Ohlin, L. E. *Delinquency and opportunity: A theory of delinquent gangs.* Glencoe, Ill.: Free Press, 1960.

Cloward, R. A., & Ohlin, L. E. Differential opportunity structure. In M. E. Wolfgang, L. Savitz, & N. Johnson (Eds.), *The sociology of crime and delinquency.* New York: Wiley, 1970.

Cochrane, R. Crime and personality: Theory and evidence. *Bulletin of the British Psychological Society,* 1974, *27,* 19–22.

Cocozza, J. J., & Steadman, H. J. Some refinements in the measurement and prediction of dangerous behavior. *American Journal of Psychiatry,* 1974, *131,* 9.

Cohen, H., & Filipczak, J. *A new learning environment: A case for learning.* San Francisco: Jossey-Bass, 1971.

Cohen, M. L., Garafalo, R., Boucher, R., & Seghorn, T. The psychology of rapists. *Seminars in Psychiatry,* 1971, *3,* 307–327.

Cohen, M., Seghorn, T., & Calmas, W. Sociometric study of the sex offender. *Journal of Abnormal Psychology,* 1969, *74,* 249–255.

Cohen, S. The politics of vandalism. *New Society,* 1968a, *12,* 872–874.

Cohen, S. The nature of vandalism. *New Society,* 1968b, *12,* 875–878.

Cole, K. E., Fisher, G., & Cole, S. S. Women who kill. *Archives of General Psychiatry,* 1968, *19,* 1–8.

Coleman, J. C. *Abnormal psychology and modern life* (5th ed.). Glenview, Ill.: Scott, Foresman, 1976.

Commission on Obscenity and Pornography. *The report of the Commission on Obscenity and Pornography.* Washington, D.C.: U.S. Government Printing Office, 1970.

Conger, J. J. *Adolescence and youth: Psychological development in a changing world* (2nd ed.). New York: Harper & Row, 1977.

Conger, J. J., & Miller, W. C. *Personality, social class and delinquency.* New York: Wiley, 1966.

Conger, J. J., Miller, W. C., & Walsmith, C. R. Antecedents of delinquency, personality, social class and intelligence. In P. H. Mussen, J. J. Conger, & J. Kagan (Eds.), *Readings in child development and personality.* New York: Harper & Row, 1965.

Conklin, J. E. *Robbery and the criminal justice system.* Philadelphia: Lippincott, 1972.

Connell, P. H. Use and abuse of amphetamines. *General Practitioner,* 1968, *39,* 261–265.

Cortes, J. B., & Gatti, F. M. *Delinquency and crime: A biopsychosocial approach.* New York: Seminar Press, 1972.

Craft, M. The meanings of the term "psychopath." In M. Craft (Ed.), *Psychopathic disorders and their assessment.* Oxford: Pergamon Press, 1966.

Craft, M., Stephenson, G., & Granger, C. A controlled trial of authoritarian and self-governing regimes with adolescent psychopaths. *American Journal of Orthopsychiatry,* 1964, *34,* 543–554.

Critchley, M. *The trial of Neville George Clevely Heath.* London: William Hodge & Co., 1951.

Critchton, R. *The great imposter.* New York: Random House, 1959.

Crites, L. Women offenders: Myth vs. reality. In L. Crites (Ed.), *The female offender.* Lexington, Mass.: Lexington Books, 1976, 33–44.

Crowe, R. R. An adoptive study of antisocial personality. *Archives of General Psychiatry,* 1974, *31,* 785–791.

Dailey, J. T., & Pickrel, E. W. Federal Aviation Administration's behavioral research program for the defense against hijacking. *Aviation, Space and Environmental Medicine,* 1975, April, 423–427.

Dale, M. W. Barriers to the rehabilitation of ex-offenders. *Crime and Delinquency,* 1976, *22,* 322–337.

Dalgaard, O. S., & Kringlen, E. A Norwegian twin study of criminality. *British Journal of Criminology,* 1976, *16,* 213–233.

Dalton, K. Menstruation and crime. *British Medical Journal,* 1961, *2,* 1752–1753.

Dalton, K. *The premenstrual syndrome.* Springfield, Ill.: Charles C Thomas, 1964.

Daniels, D. N., & Gilula, M. F. Violence and the struggle for existence. In D. Daniels, M. Gilula, & F. Ochberg (Eds.), *Violence and the struggle for existence.* Boston: Little, Brown, 1970.

Darley, J., & Latané, B. Bystander intervention in emergencies: Diffusion of responsibility. *Journal of Personality and Social Psychology,* 1968, *8,* 377–383.

David, P. R. *The world of the burglar.* Albuquerque: Univ. of New Mexico Press, 1974.

Dengerink, H. A., O'Leary, M. R., & Kasner, K. H. Individual differences in aggressive responses to attack: Internal-external locus of control and field dependence-independence. *Journal of Research in Personality,* 1975, *9,* 191–199.

Derville, P., L'epee, P., Lazarin, H. J., & Derville, E. Statistical indications of a possible relationship between alcoholism and criminality: An inquiry in the Bordeaux region. *Revue Alcoholisme,* 1961, *7,* 20–21.

Diener, E., Fraser, S. C., Beaman, A. L., & Kelem, R. T. Effects of deindividuation variables on stealing among Halloween trick-or-treaters. *Journal of Personality and Social Psychology*, 1976, 33, 178–183.

Diener, E., Westford, K. L., Dineen, J., & Fraser, S. C. Beat the pacifist: The individuation effects of anonymity and group presence. *Proceedings of the American Psychological Association*, 1973, 8, 221–222.

Dion, K. Physical attractiveness and evaluations of children's transgressions. *Journal of Personality and Social Psychology*, 1972, 24, 207–213.

Dion, K., Berscheid, E., & Walster, E. What is beautiful is good. *Journal of Personality and Social Psychology*, 1972, 24, 285–290.

Dollard, J., Doob, L. W., Miller, N. E., Mowrer, O. H., & Sears, R. R. *Frustration and aggression.* New Haven, Conn.: Yale Univ. Press, 1939.

Donnerstein, E., & Donnerstein, M. Research in the control of interracial aggression. In R. G. Geen & E. C. O'Neal (Eds.), *Perspectives on Aggression.* New York: Academic Press, 1976.

Driver, E. D. Interaction and criminal homicide in India. *Social Forces*, 1961, 40, 153–158.

DSM-II. *Diagnostic and statistical manual of mental disorders* (2nd ed.). Washington, D.C.: American Psychiatric Association, 1968.

Dunn, C. S. The patterns and distribution of assault incident characteristics among social areas. Albany, N.Y.: Criminal Justice Research Center, Analytic Report 14, 1976.

Easterbrook, J. A. *The determinants of free will.* New York: Academic Press, 1978.

Eaton, J., & Polk, K. *Measuring delinquency.* Pittsburgh: Univ. of Pittsburgh Press, 1961.

Ebbesen, E. B., Duncan, B., & Konecni, V. G. Effects of content of verbal aggression on future verbal aggression: A field experiment. *Journal of Experimental Social Psychology*, 1975, 11, 192–204.

Eckerman, W. C., Bates, J. D., Rachal, J. V., & Poole, W. K. *Drug usage and arrest charges.* Washington, D.C.: U.S. Government Printing Office, 1971.

Efran, M. G., & Cheyne, J. A. Affective concomitants of the invasion of shared space: Behavioral, physiological, and verbal indicators. *Journal of Personality and Social Psychology*, 1974, 29, 219–226.

Ehrlich, S. K., & Keogh, R. P. The psychopath in a mental institution. *Archives of Neurology and Psychiatry*, 1956, 76, 286–295.

Eiseley, L. *The unexpected universe.* New York: Harcourt Brace Jovanovich, 1969.

Eiseley, L. *The night country.* New York: Scribner's Sons, p. 85, Copyright © 1971 by Loren Eiseley. Courtesy of Charles Scribner's Sons, 1971.

Eisenhower, M. S. (Chairman). *Commission statement on violence in television entertainment programs.* Washington, D.C.: U.S. Government Printing Office, 1969.

Ellinwood, E. H. Assault and homicide associated with amphetamine abuse. *American Journal of Psychiatry*, 1971, 127, 90–95.

Epstein, S., & Taylor, S. P. Instigation to aggression as a function of degree of defeat and perceived aggressive intent of the opponent. *Journal of Personality*, 1967, 35, 265–289.

Eron, L. D. Relationship of TV violence habits and aggressive behavior in children. *Journal of Abnormal and Social Psychology*, 1963, 67, 193–196.

Erskine, H. *Alcohol and the criminal justice system: Challenge and response* (LEAA). Washington, D.C.: U.S. Government Printing Office, 1972.

Ervin, F. R., & Lion, J. R. Clinical evaluation of the violent patient. In National Commission on the Causes and Prevention of Violence, *Crimes of violence. Vol. 13.* Washington, D.C.: U.S. Government Printing Office, 1969.

Evans, D. Exhibitionism. In C. G. Costello (Ed.), *Symptoms of psychopathology: A handbook.* New York: John Wiley, 1970. 560–573.

Eysenck, H. J. *Crime and personality.* London: Routledge & Kegan Paul, 1964.

Eysenck, H. J. *The biological basis of personality.* Springfield, Ill.: Charles C Thomas, 1967.

Eysenck, H. J. *Readings in extraversion-introversion. Volume 2. Fields of application.* New York: Wiley-Interscience, 1971.

Eysenck, H. J. Obscenity—officially speaking. *Penthouse*, 1972, November, 95–102.

Eysenck, H. J. *The inequality of man.* San Diego, Calif.: Edits Publishers, 1973.

Eysenck, H. J. The biology of morality. in T. Lickona (Ed.), *Moral development and behavior.* New York: Holt, Rinehart & Winston, 1976, 108–123.

Eysenck, H. J. *Crime and personality.* London: Routledge & Kegan Paul, 1977.

Eysenck, H. J., & Eysenck, S. B. G. A comparative study of criminals and matched controls on three dimensions of personality. *British Journal of Social and Clinical Psychology*, 1971, 10, 362–366.

Eysenck, H. J., & Rachman, S. *The causes and cures of neurosis.* San Diego, Calif.: Robert R. Knapp, Publishers, 1965.

Eysenck, S. B. G., & Eysenck, H. J. Crime and personality: An empirical study of the three-factor theory. *British Journal of Criminology*, 1970, 10, 225–239.

Eysenck, S. B. G., & Eysenck, H. J. Crime and personality: Item analysis of questionnaire responses. *British Journal of Criminology*, 1971, 11, 44–62.

Eysenck, S. B. G., & Eysenck, H. J. The personality of female prisoners. *British Journal of Psychiatry*, 1973, 122, 693–698.

Feingold, B. *Why your child is hyperactive.* New York: Random House, 1974.

Feldman, M. P. *Criminal behavior: A psychological analysis.* London: John Wiley, 1977.

Fenichel, O. *The psychoanalytic theory of neurosis.* New York: W.W. Norton, 1945.

Fisher, R. S. Symposium on the compulsory use of chemical tests for alcoholic intoxication. *Maryland Medical Journal*, 1951, 3, 291–292.

Fisher, G., & Howell, L. M. Psychological needs of homosexual pedophiliacs. *Diseases of the Nervous System*, 1970, 31, 623–625.

Fiske, D. E., & Maddi, S. R. *Functions of varied experience.* Homewood, Ill.: Dorsey, 1961.

Fitch, J. H. Two personality variables and their distribution in a criminal population: An empirical study. *British Journal of Social and Clinical Psychology*, 1962, 1, 161–167.

Fodor, E. M. Moral development and parent behavior antecedents in adolescent psychopaths. *The Journal of Genetic Psychology*, 1973, 122, 37–43.

Fois, A. The electroencephalogram of the normal child. Springfield, Ill.: Charles C Thomas, 1961.

Fossier, H. E. The marihuana menace. New Orleans Medical and Surgical Journal, 1931, 44, 247–252.

Foster, R. M. Intrapsychic and environmental factors in running away from homes. American Journal of Orthopsychiatry, 1962, 32, 486–491.

Fox, R. G. The XYY offender: A modern myth? Journal of Criminal Law, Criminology, and Police Science, 1971, 62, 59–73.

Franke, D. The torture doctor. New York: Avon, 1975.

Freedman, J. L. Crowding and behavior. San Francisco: W. H. Freeman, 1925.

Freedman, J. L., Levy, A., Buchanan, R. W., & Price, J. Crowding and human aggressiveness. Journal of Experimental Social Psychology, 1972, 8, 528–548.

Freedman, J. L., Sears, D. O., & Carlsmith, J. J. Social Psychology. (3rd ed.). Englewood Cliffs, N.J.: Prentice-Hall, 1978.

French, J. D. The reticular formation. Scientific American, 1957, 196, 54–60.

Frisbie, L. V. Treated sex offenders who reverted to sexually deviant behavior. Federal Probation, 1965, 29, 52–57.

Frodi, A., Macaulay, J., & Thome, P. Are women always less aggressive than men? A review of the experimental literature. Psychological Bulletin, 1977, 84, 634–660.

Garofalo, J. Public opinion about crime: The attitudes of victims and nonvictims in selected cities. Washington, D.C.: U.S. Government Printing Office, 1977.

Gebhard, P. H., Gagnon, J. H., Pomeroy, W. B., & Christenson, C. V. Sex offenders. New York: Harper & Row, 1965.

Gibbens, T. Female offenders. British Journal of Delinquency, 1957, 8, 23–25.

Gibbens, T. C., Pond, D. A., & Stafford-Clark, D. A follow-up study of criminal psychopaths. British Journal of Delinquency, 1955, 5, 126–136.

Gibbons, D. Society, crime and criminal careers (3rd ed.). Englewood Cliffs, N.J.: Prentice-Hall, 1977.

Gibson, E., & Klein, S. Murder. London: H.M. Stationary Office, 1961.

Gillies, H. Murder in West Scotland. British Journal of Psychiatry, 1965, 111, 1087–1094.

Gillin, J. C., & Ochberg, F. M. Firearms control and violence. In D. N. Daniels, M. F. Gilula, & F. M. Ochberg (Eds.), Violence and the struggle for existence. Boston: Little, Brown and Co., 1970.

Glaser, D. The effectiveness of a prison and parole system. Indianapolis, Ind.: Bobbs-Merrill, 1964.

Glaser, D. Crime in our changing society. New York: Holt, Rinehart & Winston, 1978.

Glass, D. C. Behavior patterns, stress, and coronary disease. Hillsdale, N.J.: Erlbaum, 1977.

Glueck, S., & Glueck, E. Unraveling juvenile delinquency. New York: Harper & Row, 1950.

Glueck, S., & Glueck, E. Physique and delinquency. New York: Harper & Row, 1956.

Gold, L. H. Psychiatric profile of the firesetter. Journal of Forensic Sciences, 1962, 7, 404–417.

Gold, M. *Delinquent behavior in an American city.* Monterey, Calif.: Brooks/ Cole, 1970.

Goldemeier, J., & Dean, R. D. The runaway: Person, problem or situation. *Crime and Delinquency,* 1973, *19,* 539–544.

Goldman, H. The limits of clockwork: The neurobiology of violent behavior. In J. P. Conrad & S. Dinitz (Eds.), *In fear of each other.* Lexington, Mass.: Lexington Books, 1977.

Goldstein, J. H. *Aggression and crimes of violence.* New York: Oxford Univ. Press.

Goldstein, M. J. A behavioral scientist looks at obscenity. In B. D. Sales (Ed.), *The criminal justice system. Vol. I.* New York: Plenum Press, 1977.

Goring, C. *The English convict: A statistical study.* Montclair, N.J.: Patterson Smith, 1972.

Gossop, M. R., & Kristjansson, I. Crime and personality. *British Journal of Criminology,* 1977, *17,* 264–273.

Gray, K. G., & Hutchison, H. C. The psychopathic personality: A survey of Canadian psychiatrists' opinions. *Canadian Psychiatric Association Journal,* 1964, *9,* 452–461.

Greenwald, H. *The call girl.* New York: Ballantine Books, 1958.

Greer, S. Study of parental loss in neurotics and sociopaths. *Archives of General Psychiatry,* 1964, *11,* 177–180.

Griffith, W., & Veitch, R. Hot and crowded: Influences of population density and temperature on interpersonal affective behavior. *Journal of Personality and Social Psychology,* 1971, *17,* 92–98.

Groth, A. N., & Burgess, A. W. Motivational intent in the sexual assault of children. *Criminal Justice and Behavior,* 1977, *4,* 253–271.

Group for the Advancement of Psychiatry. *Psychopathological disorders in children.* New York: Author, 1966.

Gulevich, C. D., & Bourne, P. G. Mental Illness and violence. In D. N. Daniels, M. G. Gilula, & F. M. Ochberg (Eds.), *Violence and the struggle for existence.* Boston: Little, Brown, 1970.

Guttmacher, S. *The mind of the murderer.* New York: Farras, Straus and Cudahy, 1960.

Guze, S. B. *Criminality and psychiatric disorders.* New York: Oxford Univ. Press, 1976.

Häfner, H., & Böker, W. Mentally disordered violent offenders. *Social Psychiatry,* 1973, *8,* 220–229.

Haft, M. G. Hustling for rights. In L. Crites (Ed.), *The female offender.* Lexington, Mass.: Lexington Books, 1976.

Hall, C. S., & Lindzey, G. *Theories of personality* (2nd ed.). New York: John Wiley, 1970.

Halleck, S. L. *Psychiatry and the dilemmas of crime.* New York: Harper & Row, 1967.

Halleck, S. L., & Witte, A. D. Is rehabilitation dead? *Crime and Delinquency,* 1977, *23,* 372–382.

Halloran, J. D., Brown, R. L., & Chaney, D. *Mass media and crime.* Leicester, England: Leicester Univ. Press. 1969.

Hamburg, D. A., Moos, R. H., & Yalom, I. D. Studies of distress in the menstrual cycle and the postpartum period. In R.P. Michael (Ed.), *Endocrinology and human behavior*. London: Oxford Univ. Press, 1968.

Harder, T. The psychopathology of infanticide. *Acta Psychiatrica Scandinavica*, 1967, 42, 196–245.

Hare, R. D. A conflict and learning theory analysis of psychopathic behavior. *Journal of Research in Crime and Delinquency*, 1965a, 2, 12–19.

Hare, R. D. Acquisition and generalization of a conditioned-fear response in psychopathic and nonpsychopathic criminals. *Journal of Psychology*, 1965b, 59, 367–370.

Hare, R. D. *Psychopathy: Theory and research*. New York: John Wiley, 1970.

Hare, R. D. Psychopathy and physiological responses to adrenaline. *Journal of Abnormal Psychology*, 1972, 79, 138–147.

Hare, R. D. Anxiety, stress and psychopathy. In G. Shean (Ed.), *Dimensions in abnormal psychology*. Chicago: Rand McNally, 1976.

Hare, R. D. Psychopathy, autonomic functioning and the orienting response. *Journal of Abnormal Psychology Monograph Supplement*, June, 1978, 73.

Hare, R. D., & Craigen, D. Psychopathy and physiological activity in a mixed-motive game. *Psychophysiology*, 1974, 11, 197–206.

Hare, R. D., & Quinn, M. Psychopathy and autonomic conditioning. *Journal of Abnormal Psychology*, 1971, 77, 223–239.

Hartshorne, H., & May, M. A. *Studies in deceit*. New York: Macmillan, 1928–1930.

Harvey, J. H., & Smith, W. P. *Social psychology: An attributional approach*. St. Louis: C.V. Mosby, 1977.

Hawke, C. C. Castration and sex crimes. *American Journal of Mental Deficiency*. 1950, 55, 220–226.

Hebb, D. O. Drives and the C.N.S. (Conceptual Nervous System). *Psychological Review*, 1955, 62, 243–254.

Hellman, D. S., & Blackman, N. Enuresis, firesetting, and cruelty to animals: A triad predictive of adult crime. *American Journal of Psychiatry*, 1966, 122, 1431–1435.

Hendrick, C., & Taylor, S. P. The effects of belief similarity and aggression on attraction and counter aggression. *Journal of Personality and Social Psychology*, 1971, 17, 342–349.

Henn, F. A., Herjanic, M., & Vanderpearl, R. H. Forensic psychiatry: Profiles of two types of sex offenders. *American Journal of Psychiatry*, 1976a, 133, 694–696.

Henn, F. A., Herjanic, M., & Vanderpearl, R. H. Forensic psychiatry: Diagnosis of criminal responsibility. *The Journal of Nervous and Mental Disease*, 1976b, 162, 423–429.

Henry, A. F., & Short, J. F. *Suicide and homicide*. Glencoe, Ill.: Free Press, 1954.

Hepburn, J., & Voss, H. L. Patterns of criminal homicide: A comparison of Chicago and Philadelphia. *Criminology*, 1970, 8, 19–45.

Herbert, M. *Emotional problems of development in children*. London: Academic Press, 1974.

Hersh, S. M. My Lai 4: A report on the massacre and its aftermath. *Harper's Magazine*, 1970, May, 53–84.

Hetherington, E. M., & Parke, R. D. *Child psychology: A contemporary viewpoint.* New York: McGraw-Hill, 1975.

Hildebrand, J. A. Why runaways leave home. *Journal of Criminal Law, Criminology, and Police Science,* 1963, *54,* 211–216.

Hill, D. EEG in episodic psychotic and psychopathic behavior: A classification of data. *EEG and Clinical Neurophysiology,* 1952, *4,* 419–442.

Hill, D., & Watterson, D. Electroencephalographic studies of the psychopathic personality. *Journal of Neurology and Psychiatry,* 1942, *5,* 47–64.

Hill, P. *Portrait of a sadist.* New York: Avon, 1960.

Hindelang, M. J. Decisions of shoplifting victims to invoke the criminal justice process. *Social Process,* 1974, *21,* 580–593.

Hindelang, M. J., Dunn, C. S., Sutton, L. P., & Aumick, A. *Sourcebook of criminal justice statistics, 1975.* Washington, D.C.: U.S. Government Printing Office, 1976.

Hirschi, T., & Hindelang, M. J. Intelligence and delinquency. *American Sociological Review,* 1977, *42,* 571–587.

Hochman, J. S., & Brill, N. O. "Chronic marihuana use and psychosocial adaptation." *American Journal of Psychiatry,* 1973, *130,* 132–139.

Hoffman, M. Sex differences in empathy and related behaviors. *Psychological Bulletin,* 1977, *84,* 712–722.

Hoffman-Bustamante, D. The nature of female criminality. *Issues in Criminology,* 1973, *8,* 117–136.

Hofmann, F. G. *A handbook on drug and alcohol abuse: The biomedical aspects.* New York: Oxford Univ. Press, 1975.

Hoghughi, M. S., & Forrest, A. R. Eysenck's theory of criminality: An examination with approved school boys. *British Journal of Criminology,* 1970, *10,* 240–254.

Homer, L. E. The anatomy of a runaway. *Human Behavior,* 1974, *3,* 37.

Hood, R., & Sparks, R. *Key issues in criminology.* New York: McGraw-Hill, 1970.

Horoszowski, P. Homicide of passion and its motives. In I. Drapkin & E. Viano (Eds.), *Victimology: A new focus. Vol. IV.* Lexington, Mass.: Lexington Books, 1975.

Hudson, J., & Mack, P. *The serious juvenile offender* (LEAA). Washington, D.C.: U.S. Government Printing Office, 1978.

Hughes, R., Crawford, G., Barker, N., Schumann, S., & Jaffe, J. The social structure of a heroin copping community. *American Journal of Psychiatry,* 1971, *128,* 554.

Hutchings, B., & Mednick, S. A. Registered criminality in the adoptive and biological parents of registered male criminal adoptees. In R. R. Fieve, D. Rosenthal, & H. Brill (Eds.), *Genetic research in psychiatry.* Baltimore: John Hopkins Univ. Press, 1975.

Hutchings, B., & Mednick, S. A. Criminality in adoptees and their adoptive and biological parents: A pilot study. In S. A. Mednick & K. A. Christiansen (Eds.), *Biological bases of criminal behavior.* New York: Gardner Press, 1977, 127–142.

Inciardi, J. A. The adult firesetter, a typology. *Criminology,* 1970, *3,* 145–155.

Jacobs, P. A., Brunton, M., Melville, H. M., Brittain, R. P., & McClemont, W. F. Aggressive behavior, mental subnormality and the XYY male. *Nature,* 1965, *208,* 1351–1352.

James, J. Motivations for entrance into prostitution. In. L. Crites (Ed.), *The female offender.* Lexington, Mass.: Lexington Books, 1976.

Janowsky, E. S., Gorney, R., & Mandell, A. J. The menstrual cycle: Psychiatric and ovarian adrenocortical hormone correlates. *Archives of General Psychiatry,* 1967, *17,* 459–469.

Jarvik, L. F., Klodin, V., & Matsuyama, S. S. Human aggression and the extra Y chromosome. *American Psychologist,* 1973, *28,* 674–682.

Jayewardene, C., & Ranasinghe, H. *Criminal homicide in the southern province.* Colombo: The Colombo Apothecaries Co., 1963.

Jenkins, C. D., Rosenman, R. H., & Zyzanski, S. J. Prediction of clinical coronary heart disease by a test for the coronary-prone behavior pattern. *New England Journal of Medicine,* 1974, *290,* 1271–1275.

Jenkins, W. O., & Barton, M. C. *Longitudinal follow-up investigation of the postrelease behavior of paroled or released offenders.* Elmore, Ala.: Rehabilitation Research Foundation, 1973.

Johns, J. H., & Quay, H. C. The effect of social reward on verbal conditioning in psychopathic military offenders. *Journal of Consulting Psychology,* 1962, *26,* 217–220.

Johnson, R. N. *Aggression in man and animals.* Philadelphia: W.B. Saunders, 1972.

Johnson, V. S. Behavior modification in the correctional setting. *Criminal Justice and Behavior,* 1977, *4,* 397–428.

Jones, C., & Aronson, E. Attribution of fault to a rape victim as a function of respectability of the victim. *Journal of Personality and Social Psychology,* 1973, *26,* 415–419.

Julien, R. M. *A primer of drug action.* San Francisco: Freeman, 1975.

Justice, B., Justice, R., & Kraft, I. A. Early warning signs of violence: Is a triad enough? *American Journal of Psychiatry,* 1974, *131,* 457–459.

Kahn, E. *Psychopathic personalities.* New Haven, Conn.: Yale Univ. Press, 1931.

Kassebaum, G., Ward, D., & Wilner, D. *Prison treatment and parole survival: An empirical assessment.* New York: John Wiley, 1971.

Kastl, A. Changes in ego-functioning under alcohol. *Quarterly Journal of Studies on Alcohol,* 1969, *30,* 371–382.

Katkin, D., Hyman, D., & Kramer, J. *Juvenile delinquency and the juvenile justice system.* North Scituate, Mass.: Duxbury Press, 1976.

Kelley, C. *Crime in the United States 1973: Uniform crime reports.* Washington, D.C.: U.S. Government Printing Office, 1974.

Kelley, C. *Crime in the United States 1976: Uniform crime reports.* Washington, D.C.: U.S. Government Printing Office, 1977.

Kendler, H. H. *Basic psychology* (3rd ed.). Menlo Park, Calif.: W. A. Benjamin, 1974.

Kennedy, R. E. Behavior modification in prisons. In W. Craighead, A. Kasdin, & M. Mahoney (Eds.), *Behavior modification: Principles, issues, and applications.* Boston: Houghton-Mifflin, 1976.

Kimble, G. A. *Hilgard and Marquis' conditioning and learning.* Englewood Cliffs, N.J.: Prentice-Hall, 2nd edition. 1961.

King, H. E. Psychological effects of excitation in the limbic system. In D. E. Sheer (Ed.), *Electrical stimulation of the brain.* Austin: Univ. of Texas Press, 1961.

Klein, D. The etiology of female crime: A review of the literature. *Issues in Criminology*, 1973, *8*, 3–30.

Knott, J. R., Platt, E. B., Ashby, M. C., & Gottlieb, J. S. A familial evaluation of the electroencephalogram of patients with primary behavior disorder and psychopathic personality. *EEG and Clinical Neurophysiology*, 1953, *5*, 363–370.

Kohlberg, L. Development of moral character and moral ideology. In M. L. Hoffmann and L. W. Hoffmann (Eds.), *Review of child development research, Vol. I*. New York: Russell Sage, 1964.

Kohlberg, L. Stage and sequence: The cognitive developmental approach of socialization. In D. A. Goslin (Ed.), *Handbook of socialization theory and research*. Chicago: Rand-McNally, 1969.

Kohlberg, L. Moral stages and moralization: The cognitive-developmental approach. In T. Lickona (Ed.), *Moral development and behavior*. New York: Holt, Rinehart & Winston, 1976.

Kohlberg, L. The child as a moral philosopher. In CRM. *Readings in developmental psychology today*. New York: Random House, 1977.

Kopp, S. B. The character structure of sex offenders. *American Journal of Psychotherapy*, 1962, *16*, 64–70.

Korman, A. *The psychology of motivation*. Englewood Cliffs, N.J.: Prentice-Hall, 1974.

Kornhaber, A. Marihuana in an adolescent psychiatric out-patient population. *Journal of the American Medical Association*, 1971, *215*, 1988.

Kozol, H. L., Boucher, R. L., & Garofalo, P. F. The diagnosis and treatment of dangerousness. *Crime and Delinquency*, 1972, *8*, 371–392.

Kranz, H. *Lebensschicksale kriminellen Zwillinge*. Berlin: Julius Springer, 1936.

Krasner, L. The future and the past in the behaviorism-humanism dialogue. *American Psychologist*, 1978, *33*, 799–804.

Krech, D., Crutchfield, R. S., & Livson, N. *Elements of psychology* (3rd ed.). New York: Knopf, 1974.

Kretschmer, E. *Physique and character*. New York: Harcourt Brace Jovanovich, 1925.

Kupperman, R. H. *Facing tomorrow's terrorist incident today* (LEAA). Washington, D.C.: U.S. Government Printing Office, 1977.

Kurland, H. D., Yeager, C. T., & Arthur, R. J. Psychophysiologic aspects of severe behavior disorders. *Archives of General Psychiatry*, 1963, *8*, 599–604.

Kurtines, W., & Greif, E. B. The development of moral thought: Review and evaluation of Kohlberg's approach. *Psychological Bulletin*, 1974, *81*, 453–470.

Kurtzberg, R. L., Mandell, W., Lewin, M., Lipton, D. S., & Shuster, M. Plastic surgery on offenders. In N. Johnson & L. Savitz (Eds.), *Justice and corrections*. New York: John Wiley, 1978.

Kutschinsky, B. The effect of easy availability of pornography on the incidence of sex crimes: The Danish experience. *Journal of Social Issues*, 1973, *29*, 163–181.

Landau, S. F., Drapkin, E., & Arad, S. Homicide victims and offenders: An Israeli study. *The Journal of Criminal Law and Criminology*, 1974, *65*, 390–396.

Landy, D., & Aronson, E. The influence of the character of the criminal and his victim on the decisions of simulated jurors. *Journal of Experimental Social Psychology*, 1969, 5, 141–152.

Lang, A. R., Goeckner, D. J., Adesso, V. G., & Marlatt, G. A. Effects of alcohol on aggression in male social drinkers. *Journal of Abnormal Psychology*, 1975, 84, 508–518.

Lange, J. *Vebrechen als Sochicksal.* Leipzig: Georg Thieme Verlag, 1929.

Lascari, A. D. The abused child. *Journal of the Iowa Medical Society*, 1972, 62, 229–232.

Law Enforcement Assistance Administration. *Survey of inmates of state correctional facilities, 1974: Advance report.* Washington, D.C.: U.S. Government Printing Office, 1976.

Law Reform Commission of Canada. *Fear of punishment: Deterrence.* Ottawa: Supply and Services Canada, 1976.

Leach, E. Don't say "boo" to a goose. In A. Montagu (Ed.), *Man and aggression* (2nd ed.). London: Oxford Univ. Press, 1973.

LeBon, G. *The Crowd.* London: Ernest Benn, 1896.

Lee, M., Zimbardo, P.G., & Bertholf, M. Shy murderers. *Psychology Today*, 1977, November, 68–70, 148.

Lefkowitz, M., Eron, L., Walder, L., & Huesmann, L. *Growing up to be violent: A longitudinal study of the development of aggression.* New York: Pergamon Press, 1977.

Legras, A. M. *Psychese en Criminaliteit bij Twellingen.* Utrecht: Keminken ZOON N.V., 1932.

Le Maire, L. Danish experiences regarding the castration of sexual offenders. *Journal of Criminal Law and Criminology*, 1956, 47, 294–310.

Lerman, P. Individual values, peer values, and subcultural delinquency. *American Sociological Review*, 1968, 33, 219–229.

Lerner, M. J. Evaluation of performance as a function of performer's reward and attractiveness. *Journal of Personality and Social Psychology*, 1965, 1, 355–360.

Lerner, M. J. The desire for justice and reactions to victims. In J. Macaulay & L. Berkowitz (Eds.), *Altruism and helping behavior.* New York: Academic Press, 1970.

Letkemann, P. *Crime as work.* Englewood Cliffs, N.J.: Prentice-Hall, 1973.

Leventhal, T. Control problems in runaway children. *Archives of General Psychiatry*, 1963, 9, 122–126.

Leventhal, T. Inner control deficiencies in runaway children. *Archives of General Psychiatry*, 1964, 11, 170–176.

Levin, B. Psychological characteristics of firesetters. *Fire Journal*, 1976, 70, 36–41.

Levine, S. Runaways and research in the training school. *Crime and Delinquency*, 1962, 8, 40–45.

Levitt, R. A. Recreational drugs and abuse. In D. C. Rimm & J. W. Somervill (Eds.), *Abnormal psychology.* New York: Academic Press, 1977.

Lickona, T. (Ed.). *Moral development and behavior.* New York: Holt, Rinehart & Winston, 1976.

Lipton, D., Martinson, R. M., & Wilks, J. The effectiveness of correctional treatment. New York: Praeger, 1975.

Little, A. Professor Eysenck's theory of crime: An empirical test on adolescent offenders. British Journal of Criminology, 1963, 4, 152–163.

Lombroso, C. Crime, its causes and remedies. Montclair, N.J.: Patterson Smith, 1968. (originally published, 1911).

Lombroso, C. Introduction. In Lombroso-Ferrero, G. Criminal man. Montclair, N.J.: Patterson Smith, 1972.

Lombroso, C., & Ferrero, W. The female offender. London: Fisher Unwin, 1895.

Lombrosco-Ferrero, G. Criminal man. Montclair, N.J.: Smith, 1972.

Lorenz, K. On aggression. New York: Harcourt Brace Jovanovich, 1966.

Lunde, D. T. Murder and madness. San Francisco: San Francisco Book Co., 1976.

Lykken, D. T. A study of anxiety in the sociopathic personality (Doctoral dissertation, University of Minnesota). Ann Arbor, Mich.: Univ. Microfilms, 1955. No. 55-944.

Lykken, D. T. A study of anxiety in the sociopathic personality. Journal of Abnormal and Social Psychology, 1957, 55, 6–10.

Lykken, D. The psychopath and the lie detector, Psychophysiology, 1978, 15, 137–142.

Lykken, D. T., & Venables, P. H. Direct measurement of skin conductance: A proposal for standardization. Psychophysiology, 1971, 8, 856–872.

MacDonald, J. M. The murderer and his victim. Springfield, Ill.: Charles C Thomas, 1961.

MacDonald, J. M. Homicidal threats. Springfield, Ill.: Charles C Thomas, 1968.

MacDonald, J. M. Rape: Offenders and their victims. Springfield, Ill.: Charles C Thomas, 1971.

MacDonald, J. M. Armed robbery: Offenders and their victims. Springfield, Ill.: Charles C Thomas, 1975.

MacDonald, J. M. Psychiatry and the criminal (3rd ed.), Springfield, Ill.: Charles C Thomas, 1976.

MacDonald, J. M. Bombers and firesetters. Springfield, Ill.: Charles C Thomas, 1977.

Maher, B. A. Principles of psychopathology. New York: McGraw-Hill, 1966.

Maier, G. J. Therapy in prisons. In D. J. Madden & J. R. Lion (Eds.), Rage • hate • assault and other forms of violence. New York: Spectrum, 1976.

Maier, N. R. F. Frustration: The study of behavior without a goal. New York: McGraw-Hill, 1949.

Maier, N. R. F., & Ellen, P. The integrative value of concepts in frustration theory. Journal of Consulting Psychology, 1959, 23, 195–206.

Maloney, M. P., & Ward, M. P. Psychological assessment: A conceptual approach. New York: Oxford Univ. Press, 1976.

Mark, V. H., & Ervin, F. R. Violence and the brain. Hagerstown, Md.: Harper & Row, 1970.

Marlatt, G. A. Alcohol, stress, and cognitive control. In I. G. Sarason and C. D. Spielberger (Eds.), Stress and anxiety, Vol. 3. Washington, D.C.: Hemisphere Publishing, 1976.

Martinson, R. M. What works—questions and answers about prison reform. *Public Interest*, 1974, *35*, 22–54.

Mayfield, D. Alcoholism, alcohol, intoxication and assaultive behavior. *Diseases of the Nervous System*, 1976, *37*, 288–291.

Mayor's Committee on Marihuana Report. *The marihuana problem in the city of New York.* New York: Cattell Press, 1944.

McCaghy, C. H. Child molesters: A study of their careers as deviants. In M. Clinard & R. Quinney (Eds.), *Criminal behavior systems: A typology.* New York: Holt, Rinehart & Winston, 1967.

McCaghy, C. H., Girodano, P. C., & Henson, T. K. Auto theft: Offender and offense characteristics. *Criminology*, 1977, *15*, 367–385.

McCaldon, R. J. Rape. *Canadian Journal of Corrections*, 1967, *9*, 37–46.

McClearn, G. E., & DeFries, J. C. *Introduction to behavioral genetics.* San Francisco: W.H. Freeman, 1973.

McClelland, D. C., Davis, W., Kalin, R., & Wanner, E. *The drinking man.* New York: Free Press, 1972.

McCombs, D., Filipczak, J., Friedman, R., & Wodarski, J. S. Long-term follow-up of behavior modification with high-risk adolescents. *Criminal Justice and Behavior*, 1978, *5*, 21–34.

McCord, W., & McCord, J. *The psychopath: An essay on the criminal mind.* Princeton, N.J.: Van Nostrand, 1964.

McCord, W., McCord, J., & Zola, I. K. *Origins of crime: A new evaluation of the Cambridge-Somerville Youth Study.* New York: Columbia Univ. Press, 1959.

McGlothlin, W. H., & West L. J. The marihuana problem: An overview. *American Journal of Psychiatry*, 1968, *125*, 126–134.

Mechoulam, R. Marihuana chemistry. *Science*, 1970, *168*, 1159–1166.

Mednick, S. A. A biosocial theory of the learning of law-abiding behavior. In S. A. Mednick & K. O. Christiansen (Eds.), *Biosocial bases of criminal behavior.* New York: Gardner Press, 1977.

Megargee, E. I. Undercontrolled and overcontrolled personality types in extreme antisocial aggression. *Psychological Monographs*, 1966, *80*, No. 3.

Megargee, E. I. The prediction of violence with psychological tests. In C. Spielberger (Ed.), *Current topics in clinical and community psychology.* New York: Academic Press, 1970.

Mendelson, W., Johnson, N., & Steward, M. A. Hyperactive children as teenagers: A follow-up study. *Journal of Nervous and Mental Disease*, 1971, *153*, 273–279.

Merton, R. K. *Social theory and social structure.* Glencoe, Ill.: The Free Press, 1957.

Middlebrook, P. M. *Social psychology and modern life.* New York: Knopf, 1974.

Milgram, S. Behavioral study of obedience. *Journal of Abnormal Social Psychology*, 1963, *67*, 371–378.

Milgram, S. *The individual in a social world.* Reading, Mass.: Addison-Wesley, 1977.

Millett, K. "J," The life. In E. Goode & R. Troiden (Eds.), *Sexual deviance and sexual deviants.* New York: William Morrow, 1974.

Millon, T., & Millon, R. *Abnormal behavior and personality.* Philadelphia: W. B. Saunders, 1974.

Miron, M. S., & Goldstein, A. P. *Hostage*. Kalamazoo, Mich.: Behaviordelia, 1978.

Mischel, W. Preference for delayed reinforcement and social responsibility. *Journal of Abnormal and Social Psychology*, 1961, *62*, 1–7.

Mischel, W. *Personality and assessment*. New York: Wiley, 1968.

Mischel, W. Toward a cognitive social learning reconceptualization of personality. *Psychological Review*, 1973, *80*, 252–283.

Mischel, W. *Introduction to personality* (2nd ed.). New York: Holt, Rinehart & Winston, 1976.

Mischel, W., & Mischel, H. N. A cognitive social-learning approach to morality and self-regulation. In T. Lickona (Ed.), *Moral development and behavior*. New York: Holt, Rinehart & Winston, 1976.

Mohr, J. W., Turner, R. E., & Jerry, N. B. *Pedophilia and exhibitionism*. Toronto: Univ. of Toronto Press, 1964.

Moll, K. D. *Arson, vandalism and violence: Law enforcement problems affecting fire departments* (LEAA). Washington, D.C.: U.S. Government Printing Office, 1974.

Monahan, J. Dangerous offenders: A critique of Kozol *et al*. *Crime and Delinquency*, 1973, *19*, 418–420.

Monahan, J. The prevention of crime. In J. Monahan (Ed.), *Community mental health and the criminal justice system*. New York: Pergamon Press, 1976.

Monahan, J. Social accountability: Preface to an integrated theory of criminal and mental health sanctions. In B. D. Sales (Ed.), *The criminal justice system*, Vol. 1. New York: Plenum Press, 1977.

Monahan, T. P. Family status and the delinquent child: A reappraisal and some new findings. *Social Forces*, 1957, *35*, 250–258.

Montagu, Ashley, *Man and aggression* (2nd ed.). London: Oxford Univ. Press, 1973.

Morris, D. *The naked ape*. New York: McGraw-Hill, 1967.

Morris, N. Who should go to prison? In B. D. Sales (Ed.), *The Criminal justice system*, Vol. I. New York: Plenum Press, 1977.

Morton, J., Addison, H., Addison, R., Hunt, L., & Sullivan, J. A clinical study of premenstrual tension. *American Journal of Obstetrics and Gynecology*, 1953, *65*, 1182–1191.

Mowrer, O. H. An experimental analogue of 'regression' with incidental observation on 'reaction formation.' *Journal of Abnormal Social Psychology*, 1940, *35*, 56–87.

Mowrer, O. H. Sin: The lesser of two evils. *American Psychologist*, 1960, *15*, 301–304.

Moyer, K. E. The physiology of aggression and the implication for aggression control. In J. L. Singer (Ed.), *The control of aggression and violence*. New York: Academic Press, 1971.

Moyer, K. E. The physiological inhibition of hostile behavior. In J. F. Knutson (Ed.), *The control of aggression*. Chicago: Aldine, 1973.

Mulvihill, D. J., Tumen, M. M., & Curtis, L. *Crimes of violence*. Washington, D.C.: U.S. Government Printing Office, 1969.

Nash, J. R. *Bloodletters and badmen: Book 3*. New York: Warner Books, 1975.

National Commission on Marihuana and Drug Abuse. *Marihuana: A signal of misunderstanding.* Appendix, Vol. 1. Washington, D.C.: U.S. Government Printing Office, 1972.

National Commission on Marihuana and Drug Abuse. *Drug use in America: Problem in perspective.* 2nd report. Washington, D.C.: U.S. Government Printing Office, 1973.

National Institute for Juvenile Justice and Delinquency Prevention. *The link between learning disabilities and juvenile delinquency: Current theory and knowledge* (LEAA). Washington, D.C.: U.S. Government Printing Office, 1976.

National Institute on Drug Abuse. Drug use and crime. In L. D. Savitz & N. Johnston (Eds.), *Crime in society.* New York: John Wiley, 1978.

Nebylitsyn, V. D., & Gray, J.A. *Biological bases of individual behavior.* New York: Academic Press, 1972.

Niedermeyer, A. A. *Der Nervenarzt.* 1963, *34,* 168.

Normandeau, A. Patterns in robbery. *Criminologica,* 1968, *1,* 2–13.

O'Leary, K. D., & Wilson, G. T. *Behavior therapy: Applications and outcome.* Englewood Cliffs, N.J.: Prentice-Hall, 1975.

O'Leary, M. R., and Dengerink, H. A. Aggression as a function of the intensity and pattern of attack. *Journal of Experimental Research in Personality,* 1973, *7,* 61–70.

Oltman, J., & Friedman, S. Parental deprivation in psychiatric conditions. *Diseases of the Nervous System,* 1967, *28,* 298–303.

Orris, J. B. Visual monitoring performance in three subgroups of male delinquents. *Journal of Abnormal Psychology,* 1969, *74,* 227–229.

Page, J. D. *Psychopathology: The science of understanding deviance.* Chicago: Aldine Publishing Co., 1975.

Palmer, S. *Psychology of murder.* New York: Thomas Y. Crowell, 1960.

Palmer, T. Martinson revisited. *Journal of Research in Crime and Delinquency,* 1975, *12,* 3–14.

Parlee, M. B. The premenstrual syndrome. *Psychological Bulletin,* 1973, *80,* 454–465.

Passingham, R. E. Crime and personality: A review of Eysenck's theory. In V. D. Nebylitsyn & J. A. Gray (Eds.), *Biological bases of individual behavior.* New York: Academic Press, 1972.

Pennington, L. A. Psychopathic and criminal behavior. In L. A. Pennington & I. A. Berg (Eds.). *An introduction to clinical psychology.* New York: Ronald Press, 1966.

Petersen, E. *A reassessment of the concept of criminality.* New York: Halstead Press, 1977.

Pfeiffer, E., Eisenstein, R., & Bobbs, E. G. Mental competency evaluation for the federal courts. *Journal of Nervous and Mental Disease,* 1967, *144,* 320–328.

Phares, E. J. A social learning theory approach to psychopathology. In J. Rotter, J. Chana, & E.J. Phares (Eds.), *Applications of a social learning theory of personality.* New York: Holt, Rinehart & Winston, 1972.

Piaget, J. *The moral judgment of the child* (1st ed. 1932). New York: Free Press, 1948.

Pittman, D., & Handy, W. Patterns in criminal aggravated assault. *Journal of Criminal Law, Criminology, and Police Science,* 1964, *55,* 462–470.

Pokorny, A. D. A comparison of homicide in two cities. *Journal of Criminal Law, Criminology and Police Science,* 1965, *56,* 479–484.

Pollak, O. *The criminality of women.* New York: A.S. Barnes, 1950.

Pomeroy, W. Some aspects of prostitution. *Journal of Sex Research,* 1965, *5,* 177–187.

Pomeroy, W. A. *Police chiefs discuss drug abuse.* Washington, D.C.: The Drug Abuse Council, 1974.

Pope, C. E. *Crime-specific analysis: An empirical examination of burglary offender characteristics* (LEAA). Washington, D.C.: U.S. Government Printing Office, 1977a.

Pope, C. E. *Crime-specific analysis: The characteristics of burglary incidents* (LEAA). Washington, D.C.: U.S. Government Printing Office, 1977b.

Pope, C. E. *Crime-specific analysis: An empirical examination of burglary offense and offense characteristics* (LEAA). Washington, D.C.: U.S. Government Printing Office, 1977c.

President's Commission on Law Enforcement and Administration of Justice. *The challenge of crime in free society.* Washington, D.C.: U.S. Government Printing Office, 1967.

Price, J. B. Some results on the Maudsley Personality Inventory from a sample of girls in borstal. *British Journal of Criminology,* 1968, *8,* 383–401.

Price, W. H., & Whatmore, P. B. Behaviour disorders and patterns of crime among XYY males identified at a maximum security hospital. *British Medical Journal,* 1967, *1,* 533–536.

Quay, H. C. Dimensions of personality in delinquent boys as inferred from the factor analysis of case history data. *Child Development,* 1964, *35,* 479–484.

Quay, H. C. Psychopathic personality: Pathological stimulation-seeking. *American Journal of Psychiatry,* 1965, *122,* 180–183.

Quay, H. C. Patterns of aggression, withdrawal, and immaturity. In H. Quay & J. Werry (Eds.), *Psychopathological disorders of childhood.* New York: John Wiley, 1972.

Quay, H. C. The three faces of evaluation: What can be expected to work. *Criminal Justice and Behavior,* 1977, *4,* 341–354.

Queen's Bench Foundation. The rapist and his crime. In L. D. Savitz & N. Johnson (Eds.), *Crime in society.* New York: John Wiley, 1978.

Rabkin, J. G. Criminal behavior of discharged mental patients: A critical appraisal of the research. *Psychological Bulletin,* 1979, *86,* 1–27.

Rachman, S. J. Sexual fetishism: An experimental analogue. *Psychological Record,* 1966, *16,* 293–296.

Rachman, S. J. *The effects of psychotherapy.* Oxford, England: Pergamon, 1972.

Rada, R. T. Alcoholism and forcible rape. *American Journal of Psychiatry,* 1975, *132,* 444–446.

Rappeport, J., & Lassen, G. Dangerousness-arrest rate comparisons of discharged patients and the general population. *American Journal of Psychiatry,* 1965. *121,* 776–783.

Raskin, D. C., & Hare, R. D. Psychopathy and detection of deception in a prison population. *Psychophysiology,* 1978, *15,* 126–136.

Ray, D. S. *Drugs, society and human behavior.* St. Louis: C. V. Mosby, 1972.

Reckless, W., Dinitz, S., & Kay, B. The self-component in potential delinquency and potential nondelinquency. *American Sociological Review*, 1957, *22*, 566–570.

Reppucci, N. D. & Saunders, T. J. Social psychology of behavior modification. *American Psychologist*, 1974, *29*, 649–660.

Resnick, P. Murder of the newborn: A psychiatric review of neonaticide. *American Journal of Psychiatry*, 1970, *126*, 58–63.

Revitch, E., & Weiss, R. G. The pedophiliac offender. *Diseases of the Nervous System*, 1962, *23*, 73–78.

Rimm, D. C., & Somervill, J. W. *Abnormal psychology*. New York: Academic Press, 1977.

Robbins, E., & Robbins, L. Arson with special reference to pyromania. *New York State Journal of Medicine*, 1964, *2*, 795–798.

Robey, A., Rosenwald, R., Snell, J. E., & Lee, R. L. The runaway girl: A reaction to family stress. *American Journal of Orthopsychiatry*, 1964, *34*, 762–767.

Robins, L. N. *Deviant children grow up*. Baltimore: Williams & Wilkins, 1966.

Robins, L. N., & O'Neal, P. The adult prognosis for runaway children. *American Journal of Orthopsychiatry*, 1959, *29*, 752–761.

Rodman, H., & Grams, P. Juvenile delinquency and the family: A review and discussion. In *Task Force Report: Juvenile delinquency and youth crime*. Washington, D.C.: U.S. Government Printing Office, 1967.

Rogers, K. *For one sweet grape*. Chicago: Playboy Press, 1974.

Rooth, G. Exhibitionists around the world. *Human Behavior*, 1974, *3*, 61.

Rosanoff, A. J., Handy, L. M., & Plesset, I. The etiology of child behavior difficulties, juvenile delinquency and adult criminality with special reference to their occurrence in twins. *Psychiatric Monographs*, 1941, *1*, Sacramento Department of Institutions.

Rosanoff, A. J., Handy, L. M., & Rosanoff, F. A. Criminality and delinquency in twins. *Journal of Criminal Law and Criminology*, 1934, *24*, 923–934.

Rosenblatt, E., & Greenland, C. Female crimes of violence. *Canadian Journal of Criminology and Corrections*, 1974, *16*, 173–180.

Rosenquist, C. M., & Megargee, E. I. *Delinquency in three cultures*. Austin: Univ. of Texas Press, 1969.

Rosenthal, D. *Genetic theory and abnormal behavior*. New York: McGraw-Hill, 1970.

Rosenthal, D. *Genetics of psychopathology*. New York: McGraw-Hill, 1971.

Rosenthal, D. Heredity in criminality. *Criminal Justice and Behavior*, 1975, *2*, 3–21.

Ross, A. *Psychological disorders of children*. New York: McGraw-Hill, 1974.

Rotenberg, M., & Diamond, B. The biblical conception of psychopathy: The law of the stubborn and rebellious son. *Journal of the History of the Behavioral Sciences*, 1972, *12*, 29–38.

Rotter, J. B. *Social learning and clinical psychology*. Englewood Cliffs, N.J.: Prentice-Hall, 1954.

Rotter, J. B. Beliefs, social attitudes and behavior: A social learning analysis. In J. B. Rotter, J. E. Chana, & E. J. Phares (Eds.), *Applications of a social learning theory of personality*. New York: Holt, Rinehart & Winston, 1972.

Rubin, B. Predictions of dangerousness in mentally ill criminals. *Archives of General Psychiatry,* 1972, *27,* 397–407.

Rubin, V., & Comitas, L. *Ganja in Jamaica.* Garden City, N.J.: Anchor Press, 1976.

Russell, D. Emotional aspects of shoplifting. *Psychiatric Annals,* 1973, *3,* 77–86.

Russell, D. E. H. *The politics of rape: The victim's perspective.* New York: Stein & Day, 1975.

Rychlak, J. F. *Introduction to personality and psychotherapy.* Boston: Houghton-Mifflin, 1968.

Sadoff, R. L. *Forensic psychiatry.* Springfield, Ill.: Charles C Thomas, 1975.

Sanders, W. B. *Juvenile delinquency.* New York: Praeger, 1976.

Santa Clara Criminal Justice Pilot Program. *Burglary in San Jose.* Springfield, Va.: U.S. Department of Commerce, 1972.

Santamour, M., & West, B. *The mentally retarded offender and corrections* (LEAA). Washington, D.C.: U.S. Government Printing Office, 1977.

Sarbin, T. The dangerous individual: An outcome of social identity transformation. *British Journal of Criminology,* 1967, *7,* 285–295.

Satterfield, J. H. EEG issues in children with minimal brain dysfunction. *Seminars in Psychiatry,* 1973, *5,* 35–46.

Satterfield, J. H. Neurophysiologic studies with hyperactive children. In D. P. Cantwell (Ed.), *The hyperactive child.* New York: Spectrum Publications, 1975.

Satterfield, J. H., Atoian, G., Brashears, G. C., Burleigh, A. C., & Dawson, M. E. Electrodermal studies of minimal brain dysfunction in children. In *Clinical use of stimulant drugs in children.* The Hague, Excerpta Medica, 1974.

Satterfield, J. H., & Dawson, M. E. Electrodermal correlates of hyperactivity in children. *Psychophysiology,* 1971, *8,* 191.

Savitz, L. D. Introduction. In G. Lombroso-Ferrero, *Criminal man.* Montclair, N.J.: Patterson Smith, 1972.

Saxby, P., Morris, A., & Feldman, M. P. Questionnaire studied self-reported antisocial behavior and extraversion in adolescents. Unpublished manuscript, Department of Psychology, University of Birmingham, 1970.

Scarr, H. A. *Patterns of burglary* (2nd ed.). Washington, D.C.: U.S. Government Printing Office, 1973.

Schachter, S. *Emotion, obesity, and crime.* New York: Academic Press, 1971.

Schachter, S., & Latané, B. Crime, cognition and the autonomic nervous system. In M. R. Jones (Ed.), *Nebraska symposium on motivation.* Lincoln, Neb.: Univ. of Nebraska Press, 1964.

Schands, H. C. A report on an investigation of psychiatric problems on felons in the North Carolina prison system. Chapel Hill, N.C.: Department of Psychiatry, Univ. of North Carolina, 1958.

Scheidenmandel, D., & Kanno, C. *The mentally ill offender: A survey of treatment programs.* Washington, D.C.: The APA Joint Information Service, 1969.

Schmideberg, M. Pathological firesetters. *Journal of Criminal Law, Criminology and Police Science,* 1953, *44,* 30–39.

Schulsinger, F. Psychopathy: Heredity and environment. *International Journal of Mental Health,* 1972, *1,* 190–206.

Schultz, L. G. *Rape victimology.* Springfield, Ill.: Charles C Thomas, 1975.

Schwitzgebel, R. K. Professional accountability in the treatment and release of dangerous persons. In B. D. Sales (Ed.), *Perspectives in law and psychology: The criminal justice system, Vol. I.* New York: Plenum Press, 1977.

Scott, P. D. Fatal battered baby cases. *Medicine, Science and the Law,* 1973, *13,* 197–206.

Sears, R., Maccoby, E., & Levin, H. *Patterns of child rearing.* Evanston, Ill.: Row, Peterson, 1957.

Seligman, M. E. *Helplessness: On depression, development, and death.* San Francisco: W.H. Freeman, 1975.

Sellin, T. A sociological approach. In M. E. Wolfgang, L. Savitz, & N. Johnson (Eds.), *The sociology of crime and delinquency* (2nd ed.). New York: John Wiley, 1970.

Shafer, S. *Introduction to criminology.* Reston, Va.: Reston Publishing Co., 1976.

Shaffer, John B. P. *Humanistic Psychology.* Englewood Cliffs, N.J.: Prentice-Hall, 1978.

Shah, S. Dangerousness: Some definitional, conceptual, and public policy issues. In B. D. Sales (Ed.), *Perspectives in law and psychology: The criminal justice system, Vol. I.* New York: Plenum Press, 1977.

Sheldon, W. H. *Varieties of delinquent youth: An introduction to constitutional psychiatry.* New York: Harper & Row, 1949.

Shellow, R., Schamp, J., Liebow, E., & Unger, E. Suburban runaways of the 1960's. *Monographs of the Society for Research in Child Development,* 1967, *32.*

Shields, J. *Monozygotic twins brought up apart and together.* Oxford: Oxford Univ. Press, 1962.

Shover, N. Structures and careers in burglary. *Journal of Criminal Law, Criminology and Police Science,* 1972, *63,* 540–548.

Shuntich, R. J., & Taylor, S. P. The effects of alcohol on human physical aggressions. *Journal of Experimental Research in Personality,* 1972, *6,* 34–38.

Shupe, L. M. Alcohol and crime. *Journal of Criminal Law and Criminology,* 1954, *44,* 661–664.

Siegel, A., & Kohn, L. Permissiveness, permission, and aggression: The effect of adult presence or absence on aggression in children's play. *Child Development,* 1959, *30,* 131–141.

Sigall, H., & Ostrove, N. Physical attractiveness and jury decisions. In N. Johnson & L. Savitz (Eds.), *Justice and corrections.* New York: John Wiley, 1978.

Simon, R. *Women and crime.* Lexington, Mass.: Lexington Books, 1975.

Singer, J. *The inner world of daydreaming.* New York: Harper & Row, 1975.

Skinner, B. F. *Beyond freedom and dignity.* New York: Knopf, 1971.

Skogan, W. G. Dimensions of the dark figure of unreported crime. *Crime and delinquency,* 1977, *23,* 41–50.

Skrzpek, G. J. The effects of perceptual isolation and arousal on anxiety, complexity preference and novelty preference in psychopathic and neurotic delinquents. *Journal of Abnormal Psychology,* 1969, *74,* 321–329.

Sleffel, L. *The law and the dangerous criminal.* Lexington, Mass.: Lexington Books, 1977.

Smart, C. Women, crime and criminology: A feminist critique. London: Routledge & Kegan Paul, 1976.

Smith, D. E., & Smith, D. D. Eysenck's psychoticism scale and reconviction. British Journal of Criminology, 1977, 17, 387–388.

Smith, R. L. Strange tales of medical imposters. Today's Health, 1968, 46, 44–47.

Smukler, A. J., & Schiebel, D. Personality characteristics of exhibitionists. Diseases of the Nervous System, 1975, 36, 600–603.

Snyder, S. H. Uses of marijuana. New York: Oxford Univ. Press, 1971.

Sobell, M. B., & Sobell, L. C. Individualized behavior for alcoholics. Behavior Therapy, 1973, 4, 49–72.

Solursh, L. P., & Clement, W. R. Abuse of methylamphetamine. Lancet, 1968, December, 1397–1398.

Spain, D. M., Bradess, F. A., & Eggston, A. A. Alcohol and violent death. Journal of the American Medical Association, 1951, 146, 334–335.

Spencer, C. A typology of violent offenders. Administrative abstract No. 23, California Department of Corrections, September, 1966.

Spinetta, J. J., & Rigler, D. The child abusing parent: A psychological review. Psychological Bulletin, 1972, 77, 296–304.

Staffieri, J. R. A study of social stereotypes of body image in children. Journal of Personality and Social Psychology, 1967, 1, 101–104.

Steadman, H. The psychiatrist as a conservative agent of social control. Social Problems, 1972, 20, 263–271.

Steadman, H. J. Predicting dangerousness. In D. J. Madden & J. R. Lion (Eds.), Rage • hate • assault and other forms of violence. New York: Spectrum Publishers, 1976.

Steadman, H. J., & Cocozza, J. J. Careers of the criminally insane. Lexington, Mass.: Lexington Books, 1974.

Steele, B., & Pollack, C. A psychiatric study of parents who abuse infants and small children. In R. Helfer & C. H. Kempe (Eds.), The battered child. Chicago: Univ. of Chicago Press, 1968.

Stonner, D. The study of aggression: Conclusions and prospects for the future. In R. Geen & E. O'Neal (Eds.), Perspectives on aggression. New York: Academic Press, 1976.

Stumpfl, F. Die Ursprunge des Verbrechens om Lebenshauf von Zwillingen. Leipzig: Georg Thieme Verlag, 1936.

Stumphauzer, J. Modification of delay choices in institutionalized youthful offenders through social reinforcement. In J. Stumphauzer (Ed.), Behavior therapy with delinquents. Springfield, Ill.: Charles C Thomas, 1973.

Sutherland, E. H., & Cressey, D. R. Criminology (9th ed.). Philadelphia: J. B. Lippincott Co., 1974.

Svalastoga, K. Homicide and social contact in Denmark. American Journal of Sociology, 1956, 62, 37–41.

Sylvester, S. F., Reed, J. H., & Nelson, D. Prison homicide. New York: Spectrum Publications, 1977.

Szasz, T. S. Ideology and insanity: Essays on the psychiatric dehumanization. Garden City, N.Y.: Doubleday-Anchor, 1970.

Szasz, T. S. The myth of mental illness. New York: Harper & Row, 1974.

Tamerin, J., & Mendelson, J. The psychodynamics of chronic inebriation: Observations of alcoholics during the process of drinking in an experimental setting. *American Journal of Psychiatry*, 1969, *125*, 886–889.

Tappan, P. W. Who is the criminal? *American Sociological Review*, 1947, *12*, 100–110.

Task Force Report. *Crime and its impact—An assessment.* The President's Commission on Law Enforcement and Administration of Justice. Washington, D.C.: U.S. Government Printing Office, 1967.

Task Force on Juvenile Delinquency. *Task Force Report: Juvenile delinquency and youth crime.* Washington, D.C.: U.S. Government Printing Office, 1967.

Tasto, D., & Insel, P. The premenstrual and menstrual syndromes. In S. Rachman (Ed.), *Contributions to medical psychology, Vol. I.* Oxford: Pergamon Press, 1977.

Taylor, S. P. Aggressive behavior and physiological arousal as a function of provocation and the tendency to inhibit aggression. *Journal of Personality*, 1967, *35*, 297–310.

Taylor, S. P., & Gammon, C. B. Effects of type and dose of alcohol on human physical aggression. *Journal of Personality and Social Psychology*, 1975, *32*, 169–175.

Taylor, S. P., Gammon, C. B., & Capasso, D. R. Aggression as a function of the interaction of alcohol and threat. *Journal of Personality and Social Psychology*, 1976a, *34*, 938–941.

Taylor, S. P., Vardaris, R. M., Rawitch, A. B., Gammon, C. B., Cranston, J. W., & Lubetkin, A. I. The effects of alcohol and delta-9-tetrahydrocannabinol on human physical aggression. *Aggressive Behavior*, 1976b, *2*, 153–161.

Teague, P. E. Arson: The growing problem. *Fire Journal*, 1976, *2*, 19.

Teger, A. I., Katkin, E. S., & Pruitt, D. G. Effects of alcoholic beverages and their congener content on level and style of risk taking. *Journal of Personality and Social Psychology*, 1969, *11*, 170–176.

Thornberry, T., & Jacoby, J. The uses of discretion in a maximum security mental hospital: The Dixon case. Unpublished manuscript, 1974.

Tinklenberg, J. R. Alcohol and violence. In P. G. Bourne (Ed.). *Alcoholism: Progress in research and treatment.* New York: Academic Press, 1973.

Tinklenberg, J. R., & Stillman, R. C. Drug use and violence. In D. Daniels, M. Gilula, & F. Ochberg (Eds.), *Violence and the struggle for existence.* Boston: Little-Brown, 1970.

Tinklenberg, J. R., & Woodrow, K. M. Drug use among youthful assaultive and sexual offenders. In S. H. Frazier (Ed.), *Aggression.* Baltimore: Williams & Wilkins, 1974.

Toch, H. *Violent men: An inquiry into the psychology of violence.* Chicago: Aldine Publishing Co., 1969.

Toch, H. *Police, prisons, and the problems of violence.* National Institute of Mental Health. Washington, D.C.: U.S. Government Printing Office, 1977.

Trojanowicz, R. C. *Juvenile delinquency: Concepts and control* (2nd ed.). Englewood Cliffs, N.J.: Prentice-Hall, 1978.

Trotter, R. J. Behavior modification: Here, there, and everywhere. *Science News*, 1973, *103*, 260–263.

Tupin, J. P., Mahar, D., & Smith, D. Two types of violent offenders with psychosocial descriptors. *Diseases of the Nervous System,* 1973, *34,* 356–363.

U.S. Department of Justice. *Bomb summary—1975.* Washington, D.C.: U.S. Government Printing Office, 1976.

U.S. Department of Justice. *Juvenile court statistics—1974.* Washington, D.C.: U.S. Government Printing Office, 1977.

U.S. Department of Justice. *Children in custody: A report on the juvenile detention and correctional facility census of 1973.* Washington, D.C.: U.S. Government Printing Office, 1978.

Valenstein, E. S. *Brain control.* New York: John Wiley, 1973.

Vann, C. R. Pre-trial determination and judicial decision-making: An analysis of the use of psychiatric information in the administration of criminal justice. *University of Detroit Law Journal,* 1965, *43,* 13–33.

Velarde, A. J. Become prostituted. *British Journal of Criminology,* 1975, *15,* 251–263.

Verkko, V. *Homicides and suicides in Finland and their dependence on national character.* Copenhagen: C.E.R. Gad, 1951.

Vetter, H. J., & Silverman, I. J. *The nature of crime.* Philadelphia: W. B. Saunders, 1978.

Virkkunen, M. Victim-precipitated pedophilia offenses. *British Journal of Criminology,* 1975, *15,* 175–180.

Vold, G. B. *Theoretical criminology.* New York: Oxford Univ. Press, 1958.

Voss, H. L., & Hepburn, J. Patterns in criminal homicide in Chicago. *Journal of Criminal Law, Criminology, and Police Science,* 1968, *59,* 499–506.

Wade, A. L. Social processes in the act of juvenile vandalism. In M. Clinard & R. Quinney (Eds.), *Criminal behavior systems: A typology.* New York: Holt, Rinehart & Winston, 1967.

Walker, D. K. *Runaway youth: An annotated bibliography and literature overview.* Office of Social Services and Human Development (HEW). Washington, D.C.: U.S. Government Printing Office, 1975.

Wallerstein, J. S., & Wyle, J. Our law-abiding law breakers. *Probation,* 1947, *25,* 107–112.

Walster, E. Assignment of responsibility for an accident. *Journal of Personality and Social Psychology,* 1966, *3,* 73–79.

Walters, G. C., & Grusec, J. E. *Punishment.* San Francisco: W. H. Freeman, 1977.

Walters, H. F., & Malamud, P. Drop that gun, Captain Video. *Newsweek,* 1975, March 10, 81–82.

Ward, D., Jackson, M., & Ward, R. Crimes of violence by women. In D. Mulvihill (Ed.), *Crimes of violence. Volume 13.* Washington, D.C.: U.S. Government Printing Office, 1969.

Warren, M. Q. Correctional treatment and coercion. *Criminal Justice and Behavior,* 1977, *4,* 355–376.

Watson, R. I. Investigation into deindividuation using a cross-cultural survey technique. *Journal of Personality and Social Psychology,* 1973, *25,* 342–345.

Weil, A. T. Adverse reactions to marihuana. *New England Journal of Medicine,* 1970, *282,* 997–1000.

Weiss, G., Minde, K., Werry, J., Douglas, V., & Nemeth, E. Studies on the hyperactive child: Five-year follow-up. *Archives of General Psychiatry*, 1971, *24*, 409–414.

Weiss, J., Lamberti, J., & Blackburn, N. The sudden murderers. *Archives of General Psychiatry*, 1960, *2*, 670–678.

Wenk, E. A., Robison, J. O., & Smith, G. W. Can violence be predicted? *Crime and Delinquency*, 1972, *18*, 393–402.

Wexler, D. B. Criminal commitment contingency structures. In R. D. Sales (Ed.), *The criminal justice system. Vol. I.* New York: Plenum Press, 1977.

Whitehill, M., DeMyer-Gapin, S., & Scott, T. G. Stimulation seeking in antisocial preadolescent children. *Journal of Abnormal Psychology*, 1976, *85*, 101–104.

Widom, C. S. An empirical classification of female offenders. *Criminal Justice and Behavior*, 1978, *5*, 35–52.

Wiesen, A. E. Differential reinforcing effects of onset and offset of stimulation on the operant behavior of normals, neurotics and psychopaths. (Doctoral dissertation, University of Florida). Ann Arbor, Mich.: University Microfilms, 1965, No. 65-9625.

Wilentz, W. C. The alcohol factor in violent deaths. *American Practitioner: Digest of Treatment*, 1953, *4*, 21–24.

Wincze, J. P. Sexual deviance and dysfunction. In D. Rimm & J. Somervill (Eds.), *Abnormal psychology.* New York: Academic Press, 1977.

Winfrey, C. Why 900 died in Guyana. *The New York Times Magazine*, February 25, 1979, Pp. 39–46; 50.

Winick, C., & Kinsie, P. *The lively commerce.* Chicago: Quadrangle Books, 1971.

Wolfgang, M. E. *Patterns in criminal homicide.* Philadelphia: Univ. of Pennsylvania Press, 1958.

Wolfgang, M. E. A sociological analysis of criminal homicide. *Federal Probation*, 1961, *25*, 48–55.

Wolfgang, M. E. Cesare Lombroso (1835–1909). In H. Mannheim (Ed.), *Pioneers in criminality.* Montclair, N.J.: Patterson Smith, 1972.

Wolfgang, M. E., & Ferracuti, F. *The subculture of violence.* London: Tavistock, 1967.

Wolford, M. R. Some attitudinal, psychological and sociological characteristics of incarcerated arsonists. *Fire and Arson Investigator*, 1972, *16*, 8–13.

Wolpe, J. *The practice of behavior therapy* (2nd ed.). New York: Pergamon, 1973.

Wong, M., & Singer, K. Abnormal homicide in Hong Kong. *British Journal of Psychiatry*, 1973, *123*, 37–46.

Worchel, S. The effects of three types of arbitrary thwarting on the instigation to aggression. *Journal of Personality*, 1974, *42*, 301–318.

Yoshimasu, S. The criminological significance of the family in the light of the studies of criminal twins. *Acta Criminologiae et Medicinae Legalis Japonica*, 1961, *27*, 117–141.

Yoshimasu, S. Criminal life curves of monozygotic twin-pairs. *Acta Criminologiae et Medicinae Legalis Japonica*, 1965, *31*, 9–20.

Zillman, D., & Cantor, J. R. Effect of timing of information about mitigating circumstances on emotional responses to provocation and retaliatory behavior. *Journal of Experimental Social Psychology*, 1976, *12*, 38–55.

Zimbardo, P. The human choice. Individuation, reason, and order versus deindividuation, impulse, and chaos. In W. J. Arnold & D. Levine (Eds.), *Nebraska symposium on motivation 1969.* Lincoln: Univ. of Nebraska Press, 1970.

Zimbardo, P. G. The psychological power and pathology of imprisonment. In E. Aronson and R. Helmreich (Eds.), *Social psychology.* New York: Van Nostrand, 1973.

Zimring, F. G. The serious juvenile offender: Notes on an unknown quantity. In U.S. Department of Justice, *The serious juvenile offender.* Washington, D.C.: U.S. Government Printing Office, 1978.

Zitrin, A., Hardesty, A., Burdock, E., & Drossman, A. Crime and violence among mental patients. *Scientific Proceedings of the 128th Annual Meeting of the American Psychiatric Association, Abstracts,* 1975, 142, 140–141.

Zubin, J., Eron, L. D., and Schumer, F. *An experimental approach to projective techniques.* New York: John Wiley, 1965.

AUTHOR INDEX

Hellman, D., 165
Hemmel, J., 45
Hendrick, C., 196
Henn, F., 157, 251, 260, 261
Henry, A., 225
Hepburn, J., 213, 214, 215
Herbert, M., 165
Hersh, S., 104
Hetherington, E., 27
Hildebrand, J., 139
Hill, D., 65
Hill, P. 54
Hindelang, M., 125, 126, 213, 247, 293
Hirschi, T., 125, 126
Hochman, J., 333
Hoffman, M., 282
Hoffman-Bustamante, D., 286
Hofmann, F., 329, 330, 331, 332, 336, 337, 338, 339, 340, 341, 342
Hofhughi, M., 45
Holanchock, H., 46, 230
Homer, L., 139
Hood, R., 122
Horoszowski, P., 286
Howard, L., 25
Howell, L., 261
Hudson, J., 117
Hughes, R., 79, 344
Huston, A., 93
Hutchings, B., 30, 31
Hutchison, H., 77

Inciardi, J., 309, 310, 312, 313
Insel, P., 285

Jacobs, P., 285
Jacoby, J., 170
James, J., 289, 290, 291, 292
Janowsky, E., 196
Jarvik, L., 203
Jenkins, C., 226
Jenkins, W., 378
Johns, J., 59
Johnson, R., 197, 284
Julien, R., 329, 341
Justice, B., 165
Justice, R., 165

Kahn, E., 52
Kanno, C., 160
Kasner, K., 226
Kassebaum, G., 367

Kastl, A., 347
Katkin, D., 100
Kelley, C., 116, 136, 197, 208, 211, 212, 214, 215, 216, 247, 250, 251, 276, 316, 319, 320
Kendler, H., 90
Kennedy, R., 369, 373, 374, 378
Keogh, R., 65
Kilmann, P., 70
Kimble, G., 87
King, H., 199
Kinsey, A., 242
Kinsie, P., 288
Klein, D., 213, 274
Klodin, V., 203
Knott, J., 65
Koch, J., 52
Koepfer, E., 347
Kohlberg, L., 128–132
Kohn, L., 191
Kopp, S., 252
Korman, A., 70
Kornhaber, A., 333
Kozol, H., 145, 169
Kraepelin, E., 52
Kraft, I., 165
Kranz, H., 28
Krech, D., 19, 28
Kretschmer, 22
Kringlen, E., 28, 29
Kristjansson, I., 45
Ku, N., 97
Kupperman, R., 305
Kurland, H., 66
Kurtzberg, R., 25
Kutchinsky, B., 258

Landau, S., 213
Lang, A., 349
Lange, J., 27, 28
Lascari, A., 287
Lassen, G., 157
Latane, B., 73, 110, 382
Lawton, S., 189
Leach, E., 184
LeBon, G., 234
Lee, M., 223, 224
Lefkowitz, M., 96, 194, 283
Legras, A., 27, 28
LeMaire, L., 197
LePage, A., 187
Lerman, P., 119

SUBJECT INDEX

431

Physique, 22–26, 284
Polygraph, 72, 75, 248
Population density, 184–186
Pornography, 231, 257, 258
Positive spikes, 66, 200
Prediction, 12, 13, 218, 164–171 (See also, Dangerousness)
Prejudice, 227
Premenstrual syndrome, 196, 284–285
President's Commission on Law Enforcement and Administration of Justice, 86
Prisoners:
behavior modification and, 372–374
brain surgery, 200
cortical arousal, 70, 72–73
castration of, 197
drugs and, 334
Eysenckian theory, 46
homicide among, 231–233
intelligence and, 127
lie detection, 75
mental illness and, 157–159
premenstrual syndrome and, 285
psychopathy, 59–60
punishment of, 360
violence triad and, 165–166
XYY syndrome and, 203
Prisonization, 378
Prostitution, 21, 60, 275, 287–292, 329, 339, 343, 344
Psychedelic drugs (See Hallucinogens)
Psychiatry, 5–7, 144–145, 217–220 (See also, Psychoanalytic theory)
Psychoanalytic theory:
aggression, 181–182, 193
arson, 311–312
bombing, 315
enuresis, 165
frustration, 97–98
murder, 220
prediction of dangerousness, 164–166
prostitution, 290
runaways, 138
Psychological tests, 126–127, 166, 218, 280

Psychopaths:
behavioral characteristics, 55–59
childhood, 29, 76–82
crimes of, 54, 224, 256, 263
females, 59–61, 280
history, 51–52
moral development of, 129, 132
physiological characteristics, 61–76, 200
sexual, 162–163
treatment, 70, 73, 381–383
types, 55
Psychosis, 40, 148–149
crime and, 157, 161, 252, 267
drugs and, 332, 337, 339, 340
in prisoners, 159
Psychotechnology (See Brain surgery)
Psychotherapy, 366, 368–369, 377 (See also, Behavior modification)
Psychoticism, 32–34, 40, 47, 53
Punishment, 44, 80–82, 87–89, 116, 121, 132, 191, 192, 355–363
Pyromania, 311

Race:
assault and, 216
auto theft and, 136
burglary, 316
female crime and, 277
homicide and, 212–213
IQ and, 126
looting and, 95
prison homicide and, 232
rape and, 250
robbery and, 322
Rape:
aggression and, 180, 212
alcohol and, 347
definitions, 245–247
drugs and, 343
offender characteristics, 250–252
other sex offenses and, 269
population density and, 186
prostitutes and, 289
situational characteristics, 248–250
statistics, 117, 247, 249
victims of, 247–248
(See also, Rapists)